Only the Most Able

Only the Most Able

Moving Beyond Politics in the Selection of National Security Leaders

Stephen M. Duncan

ROWMAN & LITTLEFIELD PUBLISHERS, INC.
Lanham • Boulder • New York • Toronto • Plymouth, UK

Published by Rowman & Littlefield Publishers, Inc.
A wholly owned subsidiary of The Rowman & Littlefield Publishing Group, Inc.
4501 Forbes Boulevard, Suite 200, Lanham, Maryland 20706
www.rowman.com

10 Thornbury Road, Plymouth PL6 7PP, United Kingdom

British Library Cataloguing in Publication Information Available

Library of Congress Cataloging-in-Publication Data

Duncan, Stephen M.
Only the most able : moving beyond politics in the selection of national security leaders / Stephen M. Duncan.
p. cm.
Includes bibliographical references and index.
ISBN 978-1-4422-2022-5 (alk. paper) — ISBN 978-1-4422-2023-2 (electronic)
1. United States—Officials and employees—Selection and appointment. I. Title.
JK731.D86 2013
352.6'5—dc23
2012029340

Printed in the United States of America

To Natalie, whose dedication to high-quality public service continues to inspire me,

To the many conscientious, talented, and often unknown public servants who successfully work the levers of government on behalf of us all,

and

To the men and women in uniform who provide the leadership that makes the American Armed Forces the best in the world.

Contents

Introduction

In an essay published eight years before the commencement of the conflict that became World War II, Winston Churchill contemplated the impact that modern science was having upon the lives of ordinary people and the increasing speed with which scientific change was taking place. Although the polio vaccine, personal computers, travel to the moon, heart transplants, the Internet, and many other developments made possible by advances in science were still years or even decades away, he was certain that the scientific revolution would continue at an increasing rate.

His certainty in scientific advances was not matched by his confidence in political institutions. In words that sound particularly relevant today, he noted that "the Parliaments of every country have shown themselves quite inadequate to deal with the economic problems which dominate the affairs of every nation and of the world."[1] He was especially concerned about the absence of competent leaders. "Great nations are no longer led by their ablest men," he said, "or by those who know most about their immediate affairs, or even by those who have a coherent doctrine. Democratic governments drift along the line of least resistance, taking short views, paying their way with sops and doles, and smoothing their path with pleasant-sounding platitudes. Never was there less continuity or design in their affairs."[2]

One can only imagine what Churchill would say today about the responsiveness of governments to the far more complex dangers of the twenty-first century. Some of the continuing evidence of the attitude of Americans on the subject was announced in the summer of 2011. On August 11, we opened our newspapers to find a headline that reflected a stunning lack of faith by our countrymen in democratic governance. Only a month before the tenth anniversary of the national nightmare that took place on September 11, 2001, a national poll by the *Washington Post* found that nearly eight in ten

1

Americans surveyed were dissatisfied with the way the country's political system was working.[3] In a Gallup poll conducted eighteen days later, the federal government was ranked at the absolute bottom of twenty-five business and industry sectors. Some 63 percent of Americans across the country expressed a negative view of the government. Even government employees in some departments expressed great dissatisfaction with their leaders. In a 2011 survey, only 37 percent of the employees of the Department of Homeland Security said they believed that they were motivated by their senior leaders and only 3 percent expressed satisfaction with their senior leaders' policies and practices.[4]

The developments were not a total surprise. For many years, the number of Americans who express a lack of faith in the ability of elected and appointed political leaders to effectively address the nation's problems has been increasing. At the same time, the level of trust and confidence in government generally has been dropping. Evidence that a large percentage of political appointees are simply incapable of effectively *executing* and *implementing* important public policies has been increasing. The sheer number of recent expressions of national dissatisfaction with the performance of political leaders has also been disturbingly high. The intensity of the feelings expressed, and the fact that the dissatisfaction cuts across political party lines, may be even more of a cause for concern.

Expressions of a lack of confidence in the performance of leaders are, of course, practical manifestations of core elements of democratic theory, capitalism, war fighting, and other forms of human endeavor. Such expressions are neither unique to the United States nor limited to criticism of political leaders. Business leaders who fail to achieve results are usually fired. Military leaders who fail to win battles are usually retired or moved to less critical positions. Pitchers who can't pitch and batters who can't hit don't make a successful career of baseball.

Upon becoming prime minister in the crisis-ridden month of May 1940, Churchill had his own reasons to express a lack of confidence. In that case, it was a lack of confidence in Britain's military leaders. The chiefs of the three military services, whom he had inherited from Neville Chamberlain, were simply not up to the urgent, difficult tasks at hand. He promptly replaced two of them, but he soon became unhappy with the performance of one of the replacements. A biographer has written that as the chiefs departed from a meeting late one night, Churchill disdainfully remarked to an associate, "I have to wage modern war with ancient weapons."[5]

It is the thesis of this book that since the attacks of 9/11, the nature of the threats that the United States now faces has drastically reduced the margin for error in senior political appointments in the departments and agencies of government that are responsible for our security; that it is now necessary for presidents and senators to reject the historical practice in the selection and confirmation of senior national and homeland security officials; that a totally new approach is required; and that we can no longer accept the risk of relying upon even just a few ancient weapons.

Many of the political appointees with whom I served in the government were of the highest professional caliber. Americans of almost any political persuasion would have been surprised and grateful to learn just how much of a personal and financial sacrifice so many highly qualified men and women were willing to make in order to enter public service for even a brief period. Unfortunately, it has also been true that for much of the nation's history, too many political appointees have been out of their depth in the responsibilities which they have been given.

Unlike Britain's parliamentary system, which permitted an overnight change in the civilian leadership of all ministries whose work was critical to the war effort in World War II, America's system of government is not so flexible. Short of impeachment, physical incapacity, or death, a Neville Chamberlain cannot be replaced by a Churchill until the next presidential election, no matter what national or homeland security crisis may be at hand. This fact makes it imperative that the cabinet and subcabinet officials who carry day-to-day responsibility for getting things done in their respective departments and agencies be of the highest caliber possible.

To illuminate the problem of unqualified political appointees, I have compared in this book the processes used by several presidents in the selection of appointees with the efforts by the Armed Forces to improve the professionalism of military leaders. Business leaders recognize the fact that the Armed Forces have been developing leaders much longer than the corporate world and that military officers are trained "in ways that build a culture of readiness and commitment."[6] The chapters that describe the growth of military professionalism pretend to be nothing more than a swift, brief summary of some of the major developments in different periods of our history. They are offered merely as part of an effort to illustrate the continued improvement in the quality of our military professionals as a class and to contrast that improvement with the amateurism that has too often characterized both the appointment *process* by which the most senior civilian leaders within the Department of Defense, Homeland Security, and other departments have been selected and the *quality* of the appointees. Failures in the process have permitted the rise of too many senior appointees who lack the competence of their military subordinates.

If one counts George Washington as a professional soldier, it is a somewhat astonishing fact that by 1957, fully one-fifth of all American presidents had been professional soldiers. During the four decades between the 1952 and 1992 elections, the position of commander in chief was filled by eight military veterans. They included a five-star general and at least two authentic war heroes. One of those presidents had graduated from West Point, and another from Annapolis. Churchill would undoubtedly have been an admirer of such a trend. Throughout his life he thought that military service was an essential ingredient of a political career. His chief political opponent, Labour leader Clement Atlee, observed that when Churchill came to a powerful station, "he never cared much—though he sometimes had to condone it—for putting ministers into his government or shadow cabinet who had not exposed themselves to the fire of the enemy in either of the two world wars."[7]

Only one of the three presidents since 1993 has served in the Armed Forces and his service was limited and controversial. Because conscription has not existed since 1974, presidents and leaders of Congress without military service are certain to be the future norm. It cannot, of course, be plausibly argued that personal military service is an absolute requirement for success as president, political appointee, or even chairman of a major congressional committee. Military service does not guarantee wisdom or judgment. But it usually says something about character. It shapes the way a person thinks, not only about security risks, but also about accountability, public service, and the price of freedom. It certainly lends credibility to statements and policy positions on national security issues, especially on matters relating to military personnel.

What, then, are the implications of a nation led by presidents and leaders of Congress who have no military experience and no experience leading and managing large, complex organizations? One is very clear. If the surgeon who is to perform critically important and complex heart surgery has little or no experience, then it is absolutely essential for the remainder of the surgical team to be made up of world-class experts with major experience. The patient is not interested in having enthusiastic or even well-read amateurs anywhere near the operating room. Still less is the patient interested in having a surgical team of people who are only present because they are close friends of the surgeon or members of the surgeon's family, because they contributed to the surgeon's tuition expenses in medical school, or because they have written several articles for editorial pages on the theoretical principles of heart surgery.

Historically, the Senate has generally accepted the notion that presidents are entitled to fill executive-branch positions with whomever they wish, so long as the nominees meet the minimum thresholds of qualification required by law. Adequacy is too often considered sufficient. When the White House and Senate are controlled by leaders from the same political party, the confirmation scrutiny by the Senate is often perfunctory at best. Even when the Senate is controlled by a different party, unqualified presidential nominees are too often approved, especially at the subcabinet or lower levels. Presumably, many senators conclude that little political reward is to be gained by a strenuous effort to block nominees for those positions. The principle of reciprocity is also undoubtedly at play. Why make a fuss over the other party's mediocre or even very poor nominees when we will have our own share of such nominees when we once again control the White House?

Notwithstanding the facts that American culture has long fostered populism and that it has become almost radically egalitarian in recent decades, we can no long afford to criticize elitism among our senior public officials if that elitism is based not just upon academic pedigree, perceived technical competence, or political credentials, but also upon a clear record of high competence and achievement in fields that involve our security and in positions in industry, the military, or elsewhere that are related to the official positions they currently hold, or that at least require the same skills and experience. It is imperative that in their examination of the qualifications of future applicants for senior positions in the departments and agencies that are responsible for our safety, presidents and senators now search for truth and reality regarding the expertise, experience, and quality of performance of each applicant. A meritocracy of government officials must be the objective, not political expediency.

In his legal argument in defense of British soldiers in the 1770 Boston Massacre trials, John Adams observed that "facts are stubborn things." He went on to say, "Whatever may be our wishes, our inclinations, or the dictates of our passion, they cannot alter the state of facts and evidence." In considering whether to place great (if only partial) responsibility for the nation's safety in the hands of a particular individual, it is now more important than ever that presidents and the Senate fully consider the hard evidence and true facts that define that individual's particular capabilities. However successful a nominee may have been in other fields, however much he or she may have contributed to a president's election, however qualified the nominee may appear to be on paper or to serve as a political appointee in another position, no person should be nominated or confirmed unless that person is unquestionably the best qualified candidate—by skills, experience, and demonstrated accomplishments—to perform the duties of the particular position for which he or she is being considered.

Since the tragic events of 9/11, Americans have come to understand what the newspapers tell us daily: The Cold War may be over and there may as yet be no single nation that presents a threat to us, but we live in what the Defense Science Board has called a "vastly changed world."[8] It is an increasingly dangerous world, one in which our leaders may be less concerned about a competitor nation's intercontinental ballistic missiles than the prospect of a single person carrying a weapon of mass destruction in a suitcase. As a consequence, we can no longer passively accept something less than the best in the quality and capabilities of those who are charged with the responsibility for our safety.

Previous generations could afford to permit their presidents the luxury of choosing political friends or even family members to serve in positions of major responsibility that involved or touched upon national security. Previously, political debts could be paid or political objectives achieved through the appointment of officials who were demonstrably unqualified, or barely qualified, for their jobs in the Department of Defense or other national security or foreign policy agencies. New presidents knew that criticism would soon pass and the people would turn to other matters. Such luxuries are no longer affordable. Our most potentially lethal adversaries are not guided by rationality as we understand that term. They cannot be prevented from doing us great harm by traditional policies of deterrence. We have much yet to learn about their objectives and motivation. The old, familiar "indications and warning systems"[9] are not very useful and we are still developing new ones. We can no longer afford to have an inexperienced commander in chief *and* inexperienced or incompetent members of his or her national security team. The enormously complex business of national security must no longer be learned on the job.

Having already placed its confidence in a newly elected president, the nation is entitled to insist that, henceforth, the highest standards will be applied by the president-elect to the selection of those political appointees who will carry the day-to-day and hourly burden of the nation's security. Whatever else may be said about the political desirability of rewarding average, run-of-the-mill political allies and paying political debts, those rewards and payments pale in comparison to the nation's safety. If rewards and political payments must be charged to the nation's account, it must be a collateral account that has no relationship to the protection of more than three hundred million American citizens.

Our recent experience suggests that this will not be easy in a political capital known more for political brinksmanship, self-interest, and the absence of independent thinking and political courage than for the embrace of hard truths. In responding to a question about the termination of General Stanley McChrystal in June 2010 for the comments McChrystal and his staff purportedly made to a reporter, a respected scholar referred to the incident as a classic Washington gaffe: "You don't get in trouble for saying things that are false; you get in trouble for saying things that are true, or largely true."[10] Nevertheless, it is time for informed and honest judgments to be made, and for hard truths to be said about the civilian leaders we place in charge of our Armed Forces and other public safety organizations—that is, the leaders who are the stewards of our security, the guardians of the gate.

Much greater public attention must also be given to the *performance* in office of the great majority of senior government officials. Scholars, journalists, and others write volumes about perceived problems in civilian-military relations, the inefficiency or lethargy of some career civil servants, and individual acts of corruption, sexual misconduct, and other failings by government officials. But they have troubled themselves little, or not at all, with either the actual previous *accomplishments* of nominees for political office or the day-to-day *performance* of officials after they are confirmed. Too often, it is assumed without question that if a senior appointee completes even a short term of office with no public awareness of any significant failure, he or she must have been successful. Too often, observers of an appointee's service in political office place a premium upon the ability to keep out of trouble, rather than upon the achievement of results. Apparently, critical analyses of the problem of the lack of sufficient political appointees who are truly capable of performing well in the positions to which they are appointed have been avoided because of a lack of confidence, "given past practice, that a remedy will [ever] be forthcoming."[11]

A contemporary historian has written that "nowadays, historians write mainly for other historians, with little expectation that their specialized tomes will reach a larger public or make any appreciable impact on burning questions of public policy."[12] It is certainly true that the many failings of the process through which people are nominated by a president and confirmed by the Senate for high public office have been recognized for many years and that few improvements have even been attempted. But I remain hopeful. The purpose of this book is to assert unabashedly the need to improve the quality of those senior political appointees who are charged even in part with the nation's security and to offer suggestions about how we should go about the business of doing that. It is my ambition that the book *will* have an appreciable impact. First, upon American voters, who alone are in a position to insist upon improvements in the political appointment process. Second, and through the voters, upon presidents who nominate individuals to serve in those senior positions, and upon members of the United States Senate who will decide whether or not to confirm the nominations.

Napoleon purportedly asserted that there are no bad regiments; there are only bad colonels. Not long after the death of Stonewall Jackson, whom he had referred to as his right arm, Robert E. Lee commented on the quality of the forces under his command in a letter to Confederate Major General John Bell Hood. "There were never such men in an army," Lee said. "They would go anywhere and do anything if properly led. But, there is the difficulty—proper commanders—where can they be obtained?"[13] It does not require great powers of insight to recognize the importance in war and peace of civilian leaders like Lincoln, Churchill, the two Roosevelts, and Reagan. But, just as Lee needed high-quality lieutenants, so do modern presidents. The question remains: Where, and how, can—and should—they be obtained?

Stephen M. Duncan
Alexandria, Virginia

Chapter One

The Power to Appoint Civilian Leaders

The President . . . by and with the Advice and Consent of the Senate, shall appoint Ambassadors, other public Ministers and Consuls, Judges of the supreme Court, and all other Officers of the United States.
                                   —United States Constitution, Article II, Sec. 2

I have done all I could, and I think I may say more than any other President has ever done, in the direction of getting rid of the system of appointing and removing men for political considerations.
                                   —President Theodore Roosevelt, May 13, 1905

He was a Rhodes Scholar. He had received a PhD in economics from MIT a quarter of a century earlier. He had served in Congress for two decades and as chairman of the House Armed Services Committee for seven years. He had even served in the army for two years.

A previous occupant of the office had declared that "the list of secretarial responsibilities is so imposing that no single individual can totally fulfill them all."[1] But when he was nominated to be secretary of defense by the newly elected President Bill Clinton in January 1993, few of the political elites in the nation's capital were surprised. Although he had opposed U.S. participation in the war in Vietnam and had been elected to Congress in 1970 after campaigning as a peace candidate, most political observers shrugged off those facts. After all, the new president had been a military draft dodger during the Vietnam era, had made many antimilitary comments, and had even organized and led antiwar demonstrations while he was a student in London.

Because of his long involvement in Washington politics and in congressional defense policy matters and the fact that the U.S. Senate was controlled by friendly Democrats, the nominee was quickly confirmed. Politics being what they are in Washington, it had not mattered that he had never managed an agency of government or served in any kind of executive capacity; that he had never been held accountable to shareholders or to a corporate boss for his performance of a job or mission where the stakes were high; that he had no experience in leading large, complex organizations; that the organization he would lead had an annual budget of approximately $270 billion, one million civilian employees and more than three and a half million active and National Guard/reserve military personnel; that he had never engaged in diplomatic or other delicate negotiations with foreign leaders; that, aside from a two-year stint as a young university instructor and his two years in the army, he had no experience in any professional endeavor outside of politics; that he was notoriously disorganized; that it was well known that he was inclined to indulge in rambling philosophical discussions more appropriate to a classroom instead of engaging in hard discussions in a conference room where trade-offs and difficult policy decisions had to be made; that he was in poor health; and that his dated, rumpled suits, wrinkled shirts, askew ties, "leg-over-the-arm-of-the-chair posture," and nonmilitary bearing projected an image that was "not likely to inspire confidence in our troops or allies."[2]

After Les Aspin assumed office, matters quickly deteriorated. General Colin Powell, then chairman of the Joint Chiefs of Staff, later wrote of Aspin's disorganization, undisciplined habits, and casual management style: "We never knew what time Les was coming to work in the morning. Staff meetings were sporadic. When meetings were held, they turned into marathon gabfests, while attendees for subsequent meetings stacked up in the hallways."[3] Aspin ruminated and engaged in wandering discussions while his subordinates waited for decisions and orders. He explored options rather than offering recommendations. According to one observer, Clinton once described Aspin to an associate as "a man with one thousand brilliant questions, but few answers and no plan of action."[4] A senior National Security Council official said that "Aspin's inability to distinguish between discussion and decision" and his "inability to make choices drove the uniformed guys crazy."[5] His schmoozy, arm-around-the-shoulder style clashed with the formal culture of senior officers. Even Powell regarded him as a publicity hound, an unusual indictment from one who many considered a professional in the business of self-promotion.

He also tried to manage what is clearly one of the largest and most complex organizations in the world with a small cadre of unqualified advisors. He wanted to be surrounded by "wonk practitioners" who could dominate policy matters within the interagency process—thus he worked to appoint as assistant secretaries of defense an unusual group of academics and personal friends and former members of his congressional staff who acted as a palace guard. Most had no management experience whatsoever, and their only experience in the specific policy areas for which they were now responsible was as congressional staffers. Many of the new assistant secretaries "disagreed and competed with each other, and few were truly plugged into the bureaucracies beneath them. They were so dysfunctional they often could not produce even the briefing memos needed for high level meetings."[6]

Despite his intelligence, Aspin was inarticulate in public. He lacked the sense of command expected of a cabinet member and was unable to serve as an effective advocate of administration policy. He also resisted meetings with foreign leaders who came to Washington. "When he did see them, Les would hunch over the table and say, 'So how's it going in your country?' The burden of conversation fell on his guests, and after forty-five minutes, they would leave, having learned little about the new administration's foreign and defense intentions. In one meeting with King Hussein of Jordan, [Colin Powell] watched as his majesty had to carry on a monologue while Les polished off 13 hors d'oeuvres from a tray placed between them."[7]

In February, only a month after he assumed office, a serious heart ailment put Aspin in the hospital for several days. Bad management, poor leadership, a series of gaffes, and even poor health might have been insufficient to cause Aspin's removal from office if another factor had not intervened. In early December 1992, six weeks before the Clinton administration assumed office, a mercy mission to Somalia had been authorized by the outgoing Bush administration to provide relief to starving Somalians caught up in a civil war between several clans. Some 25,400 troops had ultimately gone ashore at Somalia's capital, Mogadishu.

As summer approached, plans called for bringing most of the troops home, leaving about four thousand to support a continuing UN mission there. In June, however, a shoot-out between followers of a prominent warlord resulted in the deaths of two dozen Pakistani soldiers assigned to the UN mission. After the United Nations passed a resolution authorizing a hunt for the perpetrators, American casualties began to climb. When the senior American commander requested tanks and armored vehicles to protect his supply convoys from attack by warlords, Aspin responded with the words "It ain't gonna happen."[8] Shortly thereafter, in a disastrous battle in Mogadishu, the forces of a prominent warlord killed eighteen U.S. soldiers and wounded more than seventy-five. Three helicopters were also shot down, and one pilot was captured.

Aspin's defenders would later say that he had sound political reasons for denying the request to send armor reinforcements to Somalia. But several members of Congress immediately called for his resignation and Clinton distanced himself from the issue. On December 15, less than eleven months after he entered office, Aspin resigned under pressure. A distinguished historian would later observe that Aspin's appointment had been "in many ways . . . a disaster, unacceptable for the country and the administration."[9] Certainly, the appointment was a classic example of a president placing a patriotic, well-intentioned person in a position totally inappropriate to his skills and experience. A veteran defense official summed up Aspin's tenure at the Department of Defense more succinctly: "Les was just in over his head."[10]

The Federal Emergency Management Agency (FEMA) was established in April 1979 as part of an effort to consolidate federal policies relating to the management of emergencies, including preparedness, mitigation, disaster response, and recovery.[11] As recently as 2009, FEMA had over thirty positions to be filled by political appointees. Some were senior positions that were reserved for political appointees nominated by the president and subject to Senate confirmation. Most were lower-ranking, but still senior political positions that could be filled by appointees who did not have to be confirmed and were not required to compete for their positions through the use of regular civil service procedures.

For several years, critics of the agency had viewed it as a dumping ground for political appointees who had little or no emergency management experience and who could not be placed elsewhere. Too often, the positions had been filled by junior political operatives, such as local or regional political organizers, event planners, political party leaders from a state important in the incumbent president's election or reelection, campaign advance men, and so on. As a result, FEMA's poor response to hurricanes Hugo (1989) and Andrew (1992) had led Senator Ernest Hollings (D-SC) to call FEMA's leadership "the sorriest bunch of bureaucratic jackasses I've ever known."[12]

When President George W. Bush was elected in 2000, he appointed Joe M. Allbaugh as the director of FEMA. Allbaugh was a career political operative who had managed Bush's 1994 campaign for governor in Texas. After serving as gubernatorial chief of staff, he helped manage Bush's 2000 presidential election campaign. When he resigned on March 1, 2003, the day on which FEMA was reorganized as an agency within the newly created Department of Homeland Security, he was succeeded by Michael Brown.

Brown was an old friend of Allbaugh's from the days of their work in Republican state politics. They had also been neighbors. Brown had been hired by Allbaugh as FEMA's legal counsel before serving briefly as the agency's deputy director. Before coming to FEMA, Brown had practiced law in the small city of Edmond, Oklahoma, for a few years. His most significant prior work experience had been as the judges and stewards commissioner for the International Arabian Horse Association. He had no military or law enforcement experience. That fact, as well as the exact nature and scope of his work in emergency management, was disputed,[13] but it is clear that this work was limited to work for the city of Edmond, Oklahoma, while he was in college. Thus, a year and a half after the 9/11 terrorist attacks, a person very inexperienced in emergency management, who had never previously managed a single federal agency, was appointed as the leader of the agency that had responsibility for building and supporting the emergency management system for the entire nation.

On February 15, 2005, in a development that had overtones of a perfect storm, a new secretary of Homeland Security assumed office. Michael Chertoff had given up a seat and life tenure on the U.S. Court of Appeals to accept the position. Chertoff was a highly regarded career lawyer who had served as a federal prosecutor and as an assistant attorney general in the U.S. Department of Justice. He had been quickly selected to replace Tom Ridge, the first secretary of HLS, after the controversial Bernard Kerik had been announced as the replacement, only to withdraw a few days later.[14] The new Department of Homeland Security over which Chertoff would preside was a consolidation of twenty-two federal agencies, including FEMA. Each agency had its own culture. The new department had almost 170,000 employees. It was charged with protecting a "gloriously unrestricted nation of more than 2,800 power plants, 190,000 miles of natural gas pipelines, nearly 600,000 bridges, 463 skyscrapers, 20,000 miles of border, and 285,000,00 people,"[15] all of which were subject to easy terrorist attack. Tom Ridge had compared the new effort to provide homeland security to three historic national endeavors: the victory in World War II, the step of an American on the moon, and the construction of the transcontinental railroad.[16] Unfortunately, Chertoff's entire professional life had been in the law. He had no emergency management experience. He had never led a large, complex organization or served in the Armed Forces or any other organization with operational responsibilities. To make matters worse, when he moved to the new department he surrounded himself with more lawyers. He was also Michael Brown's boss. It was evident to most informed observers, not including the Bush White House, that Chertoff's qualifications for the particular job he had just accepted were not equal to his courage and self-sacrifice in accepting it.

In late August 2005, it became apparent that Hurricane Katrina was likely to hit the Gulf Coast. On August 27, two days before the hurricane made landfall, President Bush declared a state of emergency in selected areas of Louisiana, Mississippi, and Alabama. When the hurricane hit southeastern Louisiana on the morning of August 29, it soon became a catastrophe. It ultimately caused such destruction that it was rated as one of the five deadliest hurricanes in the history of the United States. At least 1,836 people lost their lives in the hurricane and the subsequent floods. Hundreds of thousands were forced from their homes. Property damage was estimated at $81 billion.

On August 31, after the hurricane was declared to be an "incident of national significance," Brown was designated as the principal federal official and placed in charge of the federal government's response. On September 2, at Regional Airport in Mobile, Alabama, Bush praised Brown's efforts, saying, "Brownie, you're doing a heck of a job." Nevertheless, only a week later, Chertoff relieved Brown of all on-site relief duties along the Gulf Coast and replaced him with Coast Guard commandant Admiral Thad Allen. Three days later, Brown announced his resignation. Over the subsequent weeks and months, Brown became a symbol of all that went wrong with the federal government's response to Katrina. There were several reasons why.

After conducting an extensive investigation of the response to the hurricane, a committee of the U.S. House of Representatives published a lengthy report of its findings. The committee noted that the hurricane had been "forecast with startling accuracy for five days." The committee report then disclosed several specific findings regarding Brown, Chertoff, FEMA, and DHS. Among other failures, the report included findings that DHS and FEMA lacked adequately trained and experienced staff for the Katrina response;[17] that there had been no preplanning;[18] that Chertoff should have designated the hurricane as an "incident of national significance" earlier;[19] that he should have designated the principal federal officer earlier;[20] that he should have done more to switch DHS from a reactive to a proactive mode of operations;[21] that he generally activated the government's emergency response systems "late, ineffectively, or not at all";[22] that, overall, DHS was not prepared to respond to the catastrophic effects of Katrina; that the readiness of FEMA's national emergency response teams was inadequate;[23] that FEMA's management lacked situational awareness of existing requirements and of resources in the supply chain;[24] and that long-standing weaknesses prevented FEMA from providing adequate emergency shelter and temporary housing.[25] Concluding that the response to the hurricane had been a "failure of leadership," the committee declared that "if this is what happens when we have advance warning, we shudder to imagine the consequences when we do not."[26]

How did it happen? Why did it happen? How is it that one president could appoint to the senior defense leadership position in the government, a position so critical to the safety and security of the American people, a man who lacked so many of the personal attributes, skills, and experience in the areas that were essential to success? How is it that another president, less than eighteen months after the terrorist attacks of 9/11, could appoint as the leader of FEMA, the agency charged with ensuring that the nation is prepared for future catastrophic emergencies, a man so obviously unqualified for the position? Why was the person selected to lead DHS, one of the most complex government organizations ever created, so lacking in the leadership and management experience that was necessary for success in the response to an event like Hurricane Katrina?

In requiring that the Senate vote to confirm the most senior executive-branch appointments, the drafters of the Constitution were seeking competence in the appointments. They were also aware that democratic governments are very vulnerable to corruption. Thus, in Federalist No. 51, James Madison famously wrote:

> If men were angels, no government would be necessary. If angels were to govern men, neither external nor internal controls on government would be necessary. In framing a government which is to be administered by men over men, the great difficulty lies in this: you must first enable the government to control the governed; and in the next place to control itself.

While examples of incompetence and conflicts of interest in presidential appointees can be found as early as the first administration of President George Washington,[27] until the election of President Andrew Jackson, the transfer of political power from one presidential administration to another had generally been characterized by moderation. Jackson's inauguration in 1829 marked a sharp departure from that practice. Many of the leaders of his campaign had been lavish in their promises of positions in the new administration in exchange for political support. To an astonishing degree these promises were honored after Jackson assumed power. Some 919 officials, in almost 10 percent of all government positions, were removed. It soon became apparent that the primary criterion for the selection of replacements was political loyalty to Andrew Jackson. The practice became known as the "spoils system," a term derived from a comment by New York Senator William L. Marcy. Defending Jackson's nomination of Martin Van Buren as minister to the United Kingdom in 1832, Marcy had declared that "to the victor belong the spoils of the enemy."[28]

Later presidents continued the use of the spoils system to entice others to vote for them and to control the executive branch. Certainly the concept of friendship was never far from President Lincoln's feelings about patronage. The demands on him were, of course, great. According to one historian, after Lincoln's election "every Republican in Congress wished to strengthen his political organization; every editor coveted a post-office connection to swell his subscription list; every jobless politician wanted a salary."[29] Lincoln started out with a "determination to make no improper appointments," but he found, to his surprise, that even members of his cabinet "had been recommending parties to be appointed to responsible positions who were . . . physically, morally, and intellectually unfit for the place."[30]

His notions of patronage also changed with time. As a Whig, he had opposed Andrew Jackson's embrace of the spoils system and had referred to it as "the culture of party favoritism and official incompetence at the expense of the people."[31] But he slowly came to the conclusion that "parties were built on patronage as well as principles."[32] Biographer Carl Sandburg wrote that "during four years and one month of presidential appointive powers, Lincoln, according to a later estimate rather carefully based, removed 1,457 out of a possible 1,639 officials. In this period some offices were vacated two or three times. Naturally, to begin with, hundreds of open secessionists, or sympathizers with secession, had to go. In many responsible wartime positions the strictest of loyalty was a requirement; all under doubt had to go. Also, there was the young growing Republican Party organization with a genuine minimum of demands beyond denial."[33]

When the Civil War began, the Union had more than 3.5 times as many white men of military age as the Confederacy, but its troop strength was low. After initially appealing for 75,000 state militia volunteers for ninety days of federal service, Lincoln realized that the war was likely to last more than three months and to require far greater numbers of troops. He soon expanded the regular army by 23,000 men and called for 42,000 three-year volunteers, but it would take some time before the volunteer units could be molded into effective fighting forces.

The greatest problem for the Union, however, was an acute shortage of seasoned officers. A large number of West Pointers had resigned their commissions and returned to their Southern homes to fight for the Confederacy. Other experienced officers like Grant and Sherman had left the army to pursue private ventures. This problem was exacerbated by the insistence of the volunteer citizen-soldiers that they elect many of their officers. Coming from a highly politicized society, they saw little difference in voting for governors and congressmen on the one hand and colonels and captains on the other. They had enlisted to preserve a democracy and "it was the democratic way, they felt, for them alone to decide whom they would obey and when. They considered an officer equivalent to an elected official, and obedience to his orders discretionary and conditional."[34]

Political criteria thus played a very prominent role in the appointment of what became known as "political generals." Lincoln did not hesitate to appoint senior officers who had no military experience and were very unlikely to become competent field commanders, but who could bolster his political support in Congress and in the statehouses. In doing so, he sought to secure broad support for the war effort and to stimulate recruiting efforts. For similar reasons, he also rewarded with appointments leaders of important ethnic groups like the German American and Irish American communities. According to a biographer, prominent Democrats were commissioned "in what was a successful effort to mobilize their constituencies for what some perceived as a Republican war."[35] The appointments were valued highly: "Many politicians coveted a brigadier's star for themselves or their friends."[36] In John

Ford's 1959 Civil War movie *The Horse Soldiers*, Colonel Phil Secord expresses a popular perception of the role of politics in the selection of military and civilian leaders: "Let me lead this charge. Why, with a success like this, governor be damned, I could land in the White House!"

As inept as many of the political generals proved to be, scholarly opinion is divided on the extent to which the political generals benefited the Union cause.[37] One view is that the mass mobilization which brought 637,000 men into the Union Army in less than a year "could not have taken place without an enormous effort" by politicians and ethnic leaders like those who received commissions as senior officers.[38] While the appointments made political sense and on occasion produced a competent military leader, they sometimes produced military calamity. The West Point professional and army chief of staff Henry W. Halleck hated the political appointments of amateur generals. "It seems little better than murder," he wrote to General William Tecumseh Sherman, "to give important commands to such men . . . but it seems impossible to prevent it."[39] The term "political general" became almost a synonym for incompetency in the North.[40]

By the late 1860s, reformers began demanding a civil service system. Those efforts went nowhere during the presidency of Ulysses S. Grant. Grant had no sense of statecraft and spent an inordinate amount of time on "capricious and fitfully personal" political appointments "in an endless attempt to balance state representation and placate party factions."[41] The general air of corruption and the sorry business of what became known as the "Whiskey Ring Frauds"[42] during the Grant administration reenergized the interest in reform. After the assassination of James A. Garfield by a rejected office-seeker in 1881, public outrage and a fear of further political violence resulted in even more intense calls for civil service reform.

Passage of the Pendleton Act in 1883 brought an end to the spoils system at the federal level, at least in the way it had previously been practiced. The new statute created the concept of job classification for certain jobs and removed them from patronage. The classified list was expanded over time so that by 1897, eighty-six thousand—almost half of all federal employees—were in classified positions.[43] A bipartisan Civil Service Commission was also created. Henceforth, candidates for positions in the government would be evaluated on a nonpartisan merit basis. The reach of the new law was expanded over the next twelve years as the two main political parties alternated control of the White House at each of the three elections during that period.

In April 1889, newly elected President Benjamin Harrison appointed a young civil service reformer named Theodore Roosevelt to the U.S. Civil

Service Commission. Roosevelt, who declared that the spoils system "[had] been for seventy years the most potent of all forces tending to bring about the degradation of our politics,"[44] turned what was previously an office of minor importance into one with national prominence. Injecting his unique spirit and energy into the work, he took on the Congress for greater appropriations for the work he believed to be essential and absolutely necessary "to raise the tone of public life." During his six years in office as a commissioner, more than twenty thousand positions for government employees were changed from political appointment positions and added to the classified service to be obtained and retained for merit only. By 1900, most federal jobs were handled through the civil service system. Political appointees were limited to very senior positions.

While the abuses of the spoils system were largely eliminated, problems associated with patronage were not. In a letter to an English statesman in 1905, ten years after he had completed his work as a civil service commissioner, now president Theodore Roosevelt complained of those problems.

> I was much struck by your congratulations upon my being free from "the wearing, distracting, and sometimes most ignoble details of parliamentary warfare." They must be wearing and distracting, and often ignoble, but upon my word I can hardly believe they are worse than what comes to any American President in the matter of patronage. I have done all I could, and I think I may say more than any other President has ever done, in the direction of getting rid of the system of appointing and removing men for political considerations. But enough remains to cause me many hours of sordid and disagreeable work, which yet must be done under penalty of losing the good-will of men with whom it is necessary that I should work.[45]

Today, there are three types of political appointees, not including those who serve as personal assistants to the president, such as the national security advisor, or who serve on advisory commissions. The most visible, most senior, and often the most controversial positions are those presidential appointments (PAS) that require nomination by the president and the "advice and consent" of the U.S. Senate. Article II, Section 2 of the U.S. Constitution requires that all "Ambassadors, other public Ministers and Consuls, Judges of the supreme Court, and all other Officers of the United States" be appointed in this manner. In 2004, there were 1,137 PAS positions in the executive branch. Within seven years, the total would increase to 1,416. Congress actively defines the general functional responsibilities of several PAS positions—for example, those of the assistant secretary of defense for reserve affairs. The secretary of defense does, however, have authority to assign some PAS positions to functional areas of his or her own choosing. Roughly 450 of the positions were important policy-making positions, such as the secretary, deputy secretary, undersecretaries, and assistant secretaries of defense. These presidential appointees have the authority of, and a proto-col rank equivalent to, four-star general and flag officers of the Armed Forces.

In addressing the issue of competence in the appointment of people to serve in such positions in the federal government, Alexander Hamilton stated the obvious in observing "that the true test of a good government is its aptitude and tendency to produce a good administration."[46] He assumed that because a president has the constitutional obligation to see that the laws are faithfully executed and has an "exact regard" to his own reputation, he will be "more interested to investigate with care the qualities requisite to the stations to be filled, and to prefer with impartiality the persons who may have the fairest pretensions to them."[47] He recognized the dangers that a president may be misled in making appointments "by the sentiments of friendship and of affection," that during political negotiations one political leader or faction is likely to say to another, "Give us the man we wish for this office, and you shall have the one you wish for that," and that in such circumstances, "it will rarely happen that the advancement of the public service will be the primary object."[48] Thus, he placed the primary responsibility for high-quality politi-cal appointments in the hands of the president. "As the President nominates his ministers and may displace them when he pleases," he said in 1800, "it must be his own fault if he be not surrounded by men, who for ability and integrity, deserve his confidence."

But the Founding Fathers also viewed the confirmation role of the Senate as critically important. They believed that "the possibility of rejection [of a president's nominee by the Senate] would be a strong motive to [the presi-dent's] care in proposing," and "tend greatly to prevent the appointment of unfit characters." They desired to place "an excellent check upon a spirit of favoritism in the President," and to make him "ashamed and afraid to bring forward, for the most distinguished . . . stations, candidates who [have] no other merit than that of . . . being in some way or other personally allied to him, or of possessing the necessary insignificance and pliancy to render them the obsequious instruments of his pleasure."[49] The Founders ascribed to the Senate a disinterested concern for the public welfare in the confirmation process. "Having no agency in the nomination, nothing but simply consent or refusal," one early constitutional scholar wrote, "the spirit of personal in-trigue and personal attachment must be pretty much extinguished, from a want of means to gratify it."[50]

Unfortunately, and despite the efforts of the Founders, a spirit of intrigue has been present during most of the country's history. President Washington encountered it in connection with one of his first political appointments. Only three months after his inauguration in 1789, his first formal clash with Congress arose when the Senate rejected his nominee for the position of tax collector of the port of Savannah. Though ailing from a serious abscess on his thigh, he traveled to the second-floor Senate chamber in New York's Federal Hall to upbraid the twenty-two members of the Senate. He demanded to know why his nominee had not been confirmed. After what has been described as a "long, awkward silence," a senator from Georgia arose and, out of personal respect for Washington, explained his opposition to the nominee. The senator then apparently said that he wanted it understood that the Senate felt no obligation to explain its reasoning to the president. According to a recent biography of Washington, the episode "marked the start of 'senatorial courtesy,' whereby Senators reserve the right to block nominations [of individuals from] their home states."[51]

Presidential appointees are not, of course, the only political appointees. The Civil Service Reform Act of 1978 created a cadre of approximately seven thousand senior management officials as part of a new Senior Executive Service (SES). The SES includes both political appointees who are designated as noncareer members of the Service, and career employees. Political members of the SES are usually appointed by the head of the department or agency in which they serve and do not require Senate confirmation. They usually leave office at the conclusion of the term of the president who appointed the department or agency head. The law currently prohibits the number of political appointees in the SES from exceeding 10 percent of the entire Senior Executive Service or 25 percent of the SES positions allocated to a particular department or agency. In 2004, there were 6,811 people serving in SES positions, including 674 political appointees. Members of the SES are organized in a three-tier structure that groups positions according to the level of complexity, the span of control, and other factors. Depending upon which tier group they fall within, they have a protocol rank equivalent to that of a brigadier general, major general, or lieutenant general. They typically serve as deputy assistant secretary, deputy general counsel, and similar positions.

A third type of political appointee is a Schedule C appointee. These government employees serve in positions of a confidential or policy-determining *nature*, and they may even have project management responsibilities. But they usually do not have policy-making *authority*. They typically serve as special or confidential assistants to presidential appointees, within legislative liaison offices, as directors of public affairs offices, and on special projects. In 2004, some 1,596 people were serving in Schedule C positions. The most senior of the Schedule C employees—that is, those who serve in a GS-15 pay grade—have a protocol rank equivalent to that of a full colonel in the army or a navy captain.

Recent scholarship has determined that presidents "persistently prefer more appointees than most perfectly informed voters would want and a significantly higher percentage than other well-functioning developed nations."[52] In the century and a quarter since the Pendleton Act was passed, the size of the government generally, and the number of political appointees, have increased at an astounding rate. The report of a recent study on government performance noted that in our nation's history "there have never been more layers in government or more leaders per layer."[53] When John Kennedy assumed office in 1961, for example, he had 286 positions to fill requiring Senate confirmation. By the end of the Clinton administration, there were 914 such positions. Since Kennedy's administration, the number of cabinet secretaries has increased from 10 to 15, the number of deputy secretaries from 6 to 24, the number of undersecretaries from 15 to 53, and the number of assistant secretaries from 87 to 257.[54] Many of the additional positions have been mandated by Congress for the oversight of new programs or to improve management.[55] When Barack Obama was elected in 2008, he had more than 4,000 political appointments to make, including those for 1,409 positions requiring the advice and consent of the Senate. Within the Department of Defense, PAS appointments occupy the forty-eight most senior positions. Twelve new positions have been added in recent years. Indeed, the entire Pentagon bureaucracy is much larger than it was at the height of the Cold War. In 1960, there were seventy-eight deputy assistant secretaries of defense. By 2010, more than two decades after the Berlin Wall came down, there were 530.[56] Fortunately, a small measure of common sense encroached upon the appointments process in 2011, when the Senate voted to curb its own power by dropping the confirmation requirement for 169 federal positions filled by appointees.

The most senior appointees have traditionally been selected during the two-and-a-half-month transitional period between the election of a president and the inauguration, but the increases in the layers of leadership over the last several decades and the resulting large numbers of political appointees have contributed to increased delays in both the nominating and the confirmation processes—"from 2.4 months under Kennedy to 3.4 under Nixon, 4.6 under Carter, 5.3 under Reagan, 8.1 under Bush, and 8.5 under Clinton."[57] The appointment records of presidents Clinton, George W. Bush, and Obama indicates that "about 50 percent of what most would consider to be the seventy-five most time-sensitive national security positions"—that is, the "senior officials dealing with agency leadership, homeland defense, preparedness, intelligence, terrorism, response and/or border patrol"—were still vacant by the one hundredth day (May 1) of each administration's first year.[58] Several of the most senior appointees had not been selected and confirmed until several months after the election. Bill Clinton's choice for secretary of the army, for example, was not confirmed until eleven months after his inauguration as president.

The problem does not lie entirely with the Senate. In the George W. Bush administration, it took months for the president's nominees to receive the necessary security clearances. According to Donald Rumsfeld, Bush's first secretary of defense, the White House Office of Presidential Personnel was also "painfully slow in vetting candidates." At the time of the 9/11 terrorist attacks, Bush had barely half of his political appointees in place, and by the end of his first year in office, some two hundred positions requiring Senate confirmation were still open. The cumulative effect was that "on average [DoD] operated with 25.5 percent of the key senior civilian positions vacant over the [first] six years" of the Bush presidency.[59]

The record of the Obama administration was even worse. It took four months to get all fifteen of President Obama's cabinet officers confirmed. In his first one hundred days, Obama managed to get only 76 of the top 516 Senate-confirmed positions filled, or about 15 percent.[60] After one year in office, the Obama administration lagged behind all four previous administrations in the percentage of appointees confirmed by the Senate. Only 59.2 percent of the Senate-confirmed executive positions had been filled, compared to 86 percent for the Reagan administration.[61] The administration ranked last or next to last in filling important positions in ten of sixteen major federal agencies.[62] "By all measures," the leaders of a bipartisan commission declared in April 2011, "the Federal appointments process is broken and urgently needs substantial reform."[63]

This situation contrasts sharply with the situation in other major democratic countries, such as Britain, France, and Germany. In those countries, the number of appointees is between one hundred and two hundred. In Britain, a change in prime ministers is virtually instantaneous. Within hours of an election result, the outgoing prime minister leaves 10 Downing Street. Shortly thereafter, and after receiving a request from the queen to form a government, the new prime minister enters No. 10 and the twenty-two new members of the cabinet assume responsibility for their respective ministries.

Fortunately, since the election of 2008 a new effort has been made by Congress to improve the transition from one administration to another—at least during the preelection period. The Pre-Election Presidential Transition Act, which became law on October 16, 2010, implicitly recognizes that, in the words of the Partnership for Public Service, "A new President must be ready to govern with his senior leadership team on the job on or shortly after Inauguration Day."[64] Pursuant to the new statute, the U.S. General Services Administration will now provide "transition support, including fully equipped office space, communication services, briefings and other assistance, to the major party candidates to enable them to prepare to govern."[65] The law further permits the candidates to raise money for transition planning.

Major problems remain. There are "too few resources available for vetting candidates, too much red tape for the nominees to wade through, and too little sense of urgency when a sense of urgency is exactly what we need."[66] Moreover, the Senate confirmation process is still too slow and, despite action taken in 2011 to reduce the number of positions requiring Senate confirmation, the number remains unreasonably formidable.

The reasons for particular political appointments do, of course, vary widely. All presidents face pressure to reward campaign supporters who contributed to their election. They also have obligations to their political party to fill positions with party loyalists who may have previously contributed much more to the party than to the candidacy of the new president. Political debts have to be repaid. The recommendations of friendly members of Congress also have to be considered. Even the recommendations of members who belong to the other major party cannot be ignored, especially if that party controls even one of the two houses of Congress. Sometimes, even the recommendations of political enemies in Congress have to be considered in an effort to neutralize a potential future obstacle to a president's legislative agenda.

Having said that, it is undeniable that many political party job seekers are not qualified for the jobs they desire. From his years as a civil service commissioner, Theodore Roosevelt accepted that fact instinctively. Only days after becoming president as a result of President McKinley's death at the hands of an assassin, he commented in a conversation with a senator from Illinois that political connections would not trump merit in his appointments. "I want to stand with the [party] organization, and all that," he said, "but I wish it distinctly understood that I will appoint no man to office, even if recommended by the organization, unless he is wholly qualified for the position he seeks and is a man of integrity."[67]

Franklin D. Roosevelt's biographer noted that the thirty-second president "was not above back-alley horse trades" in political appointments. The story is told of a senator from South Carolina who, in the spring of 1934, blocked Roosevelt's nomination of Rexford G. Tugwell, a young professor at Columbia University, to serve as undersecretary of agriculture. The senator was trying to get Roosevelt's attention because he badly wanted the president to appoint one of the senator's supporters as a United States marshal. The supporter apparently had a good reputation, "except for a slight case of homicide." Roosevelt made the deal, and "greeted an astonished Tugwell with the cheery remark: 'You will never know anymore about it, I hope; but today I traded you for a couple of murderers'!"[68]

President Eisenhower's approach to appointments could hardly have been more different. Having never been engaged in politics prior to his election, he was very wary of recommended appointments that were not based upon careful investigation of the potential nominee. Even political supporters were often frustrated. His senior White House aide later wrote that "more than once, when a Republican leader sought a favor for somebody who had been helpful to the Eisenhower cause during the 1952 campaign, the president said with vehemence, 'I owe no one anything for putting me into this position. I didn't seek this honor, and those who sought it for me did so, not for me, but because they believed it was for the best interests of their country.'"[69]

Several presidents have had little to say about their appointments beyond their selection of the members of their cabinet. Eisenhower, for example, "gave each Cabinet member and agency director complete responsibility for his department and almost never intervened in the selection of their assistants and other key personnel."[70] Because the methods of selection of political appointees follow no set lines and are essentially limited only by the discretion of the incumbent president, it is surprisingly easy for the wrong person to be selected for the wrong position for the wrong reasons, even within departments and agencies that are responsible for the nation's security, organizations in which the margin for acceptable error in the selection of its leadership should be close to zero. Elliot L. Richardson, a combat veteran of the Normandy Invasion, a secretary of defense, and the only person to hold four cabinet-level positions in the U.S. government,[71] referred to this problem in these words:

> [A] White House personnel assistant sees the position of Deputy Assistant Secretary as a fourth-echelon slot. In his eyes that makes it an ideal reward for a fourth-echelon political type—a campaign advance man, or a regional political organizer. For a senior civil servant, it's irksome to see a position one has spent 20 or 30 years preparing for preempted by an outsider who doesn't know the difference between an audit exception and an authorizing bill.[72]

Richardson could also have mentioned the reaction of senior military officers who have spent twenty to thirty years in their profession only to find that in their current assignment, they report to a new deputy assistant secretary who doesn't know the difference between the fire control system of a field gun and the Uniform Code of Military Justice.

In recent years, other reasons for political appointments have become public. In a book published in early 2010,[73] it was reported that President Obama tried to push his disgruntled White House counsel out of the White House by offering him an appointment to the U.S. Court of Appeals for the District of Columbia Circuit. A September 2009 article in the *Denver Post* described another Obama offer of a job to a Democratic candidate for the U.S. Senate in Colorado if he would step aside and agree not to challenge a White House–backed incumbent in the primary election. The White House denied that an offer of a specific job had been made, but it admitted that possible administration jobs had been discussed with the candidate in the hope that he would drop out of the race. In May 2010, three months after the matter had been disclosed by Congressman Joe Sestak of Pennsylvania, the White House finally admitted that former president Bill Clinton had been asked to act on behalf of the Obama administration for the purpose of offering Sestak a position on an executive branch senior advisory board if he would end his candidacy for the U.S. Senate seat in favor of the incumbent, who was backed by the White House.

The rigorous selection process through which candidates for appointment in DoD and all other departments and agencies must travel would appear, at least superficially, to be sufficiently stringent to prevent the nomination of unqualified people. Extensive background information must first be provided to the White House. Current and former employers, professional contacts, and many other people are interviewed by the FBI in a full-field investigation. Considerable financial information must be provided by the tentative nominee to the Internal Revenue Service. Detailed checks for possible conflicts of interest are made. After a nomination is finally forwarded to the Senate, considerable additional information must be provided to Senate investigators. The overall confirmation process for nominees for PAS positions lasts an average of eight and a half months.[74]

The total SES population within DoD (including career and noncareer combined) is approximately 1,230. Some sixty-eight serve in noncareer SES positions at the deputy assistant secretary of defense level. Of those, forty-five serve in the Office of the Secretary of Defense, nine in the Office of the Secretary of the Army, eight in the Office of the Secretary of the Air Force, and six in the Office of the Secretary of the Navy.[75]

Although it varies from administration to administration, political appointments are usually centralized in the White House Office of Presidential Personnel from the start. During the vetting process, members of the White House staff and DoD officials ask each candidate for information on a wide range of subjects ranging from all sources of earned income since the age of twenty-one and whether or not the candidate has ever been late in making child support payments, to information about the candidate or any member of the candidate's family that could be "a possible source of embarrassment to [the candidate, his or her family], or the President."

Several aspects of the appointment process act as deterrents for many qualified individuals who might otherwise be willing to bring their skills and experience to government service. One notable deterrent is the pay of public employees. Many capable potential appointees balk at the reduction in salary that is required in order to join the government for what is, in effect, a noncareer position. One student of the issue believes that it is because of the salary obstacle that so many political appointees are both very young and very inexperienced. "Political appointees across the Executive Branch," he asserts, "represent a U-shaped curve. That is, the majorities of political appointees are old enough to afford to leave lucrative positions or are young enough to see such positions as career-building appointments."[76]

Other potential appointees, who may be willing to make significant financial sacrifices in order to serve as a presidential appointee, are simply unwilling to undergo the burden of collecting and organizing the voluminous personal background information that is required by the White House and, separately, by the Senate. The onerous White House process requires the completion of at least three lengthy questionnaires, the reporting of detailed financial and tax information, and an FBI background check. The Senate requires the completion of additional questionnaires and imposes additional disclosure requirements. The co-chairs of the bipartisan commission referred to previously have declared that the burden on nominees to gather such background data "could not be more unnecessarily burdensome if designed to be so."[77]

Other potential nominees, who also have nothing to hide, are simply unwilling to undergo what has been called a "political colonoscopy"[78] —that is, the intense scrutiny of almost every aspect of their professional and personal lives. Nominees are interviewed numerous times. They are "asked about small financial transactions, travel and personal and business contacts going back decades. They also are routinely fingerprinted and required to provide detailed medical records, reveal if they have employed domestic help, provide information on their families and job history, and disclose any information going back years that might prove embarrassing."[79]

The financial holdings of some potential appointees can present particular problems. All holdings and sources of income must be disclosed and they are closely reviewed for possible conflicts of interest. If any such conflict is perceived, the stocks, bonds, or other investments that are the source of the concern must be divested or placed in a special trust, or the conflict must be otherwise remedied. If a potential appointee is an executive of a company in an industry that does business with the Pentagon, the chances are great that a significant portion of his investments are in his own company. Depending upon the nature of the investments and the timing, the remedies to the perceived conflict can be very costly to the owner.[80]

Another deterrent for some potential nominees is the people who conduct the vetting process. More often than not, a presidential candidate gives very little thought to personnel matters until he has been elected. Even then, he often fails to give the matter sufficient attention. Sometimes, it is because the president-elect has never before run a large organization and he has no experience in what many CEOs believe to be the most important executive responsibility—selection of senior leaders. At other times, he may focus only on the selection of his cabinet and leave to individual cabinet members the selection of the senior leadership of their respective departments or agencies. That course of action has many risks, as we shall see in chapter 3. Even when a president-elect retains overall control of the appointment process, major mistakes are often made. Having given little or no thought to the importance of senior leaders and other key personnel in the process of *governing*, as opposed to *campaigning*, he is likely to delegate the vetting process to political operatives who proved their loyalty during the recently completed campaign.

But who are these political operatives? Often, they are bright, ambitious, young people who have never previously been so close to such political power. They often have substantially less experience in the areas of responsibility for which they are vetting candidates than the serious, accomplished, older potential nominees whom they are vetting. Aside from their exaggerated sense of self-importance and the absence of any experience in executive search work, the vetters may share the ideological agenda of the president-elect. That is good—except when ideological issues are inserted inappropriately into the vetting. In recent years, for example, a highly qualified candidate for the position of secretary of energy withdrew after the vetters asked for his position on the question of abortion. It turned out that his position was generally consistent with that of the president-elect, but he was offended by the question.

The lack of substantive experience in the vetters often leads to another problem. There is an old adage in government that "A's hire A's, and B's hire B's and C's." If the vetters are not accomplished and seasoned in the work for which they are evaluating candidates, or in a related field, or at least in the business of selecting senior executives, it is almost certain that the person they select for a particular position will be a C at best, and perhaps only a D or F.

Even when the vetting questions are reasonable upon their face, the hubris of the vetters themselves can be off-putting. Experienced lawyers who are at the top of their profession, for example, are often unwilling to be grilled in an interview by arrogant young lawyer-vetters in connection with a vacancy in a federal judgeship. Many times, the young vetters have little or no courtroom experience themselves and don't even ask intelligent questions. More than a few would be unable to obtain a job in the firm of the lawyer they are vetting. Seasoned business executives usually find it very difficult to be examined on their qualifications by people who have never managed an organization of any consequence or had to meet a payroll, or create a job, or terminate employees.

Yet another deterrent for some otherwise interested and qualified candidates is the employment restrictions imposed by law upon appointees after they have completed their government service. These are also intended to prevent conflicts of interest. The nature of the restrictions depends on the level of the position held while working for the government. Upon leaving office, all government employees must refrain from communicating with the office in which they served in connection with a matter in which they "participated personally and substantially." A two-year restriction is placed on a former appointee's communication with his former office "concerning particular matters under [his previous] official responsibility."

The Senate's very partisan behavior in many confirmation hearings since 1987 has also attracted considerable criticism. Perhaps the leading case in point involved Judge Robert H. Bork. Bork was a legal scholar who had served with distinction as U.S. solicitor general and acting attorney general. In 1982, he was unanimously confirmed by the Senate as a judge on the U.S. Court of Appeals for the District of Columbia Circuit. In 1987, he was nominated by President Reagan to the U.S. Supreme Court. After a highly partisan debate in the Senate, the nomination was defeated in a vote of 58–42. One critic has described the Senate's behavior in this fashion:

> Until the 1980s, the Senate seldom blocked a nomination, believing that the President had a right to choose his team, so long as its members were not corrupt or under-qualified. Since the defeat of Robert Bork's nomination to the Supreme Court in 1987, this has changed. Now a nominee's views, and the minute details of his life, can turn the Senate against him. Sometimes a nomination is blocked for reasons that have nothing to do with the nominee, and everything to do with some unrelated dispute between President and Senate. . . . The Senate's willingness to block nominees on ideology grounds reflects a larger shift in American politics. It used to be that, having won election, the President was presumed to have a mandate to rule, so the Senate felt obliged to defer to his appointments. Now, in an era of constant polling and the permanent campaign, elections no longer confer such authority on the victor. Administration and congressmen alike immediately launch themselves on the next election, and fights over nominations become one of the battlefields.[81]

I had a front-row seat for the change in the nature of Senate confirmations. On August 7, 1987, I was nominated by President Reagan to serve as an assistant secretary of defense. In September, the Senate Judiciary Committee conducted a lengthy confirmation hearing on the nomination of Judge Robert Bork to the Supreme Court. By any reasonable standard, that hearing was intensely partisan, contentious, and unfair. The Democrats, who controlled both the Judiciary Committee and the Senate, were determined to prevent the confirmation of Bork at all costs. They saw the confirmation fight as an important battle in the nation's cultural wars. Despite his long and distinguished career as a judge and lawyer, and the fact that the Senate had previously confirmed his nomination to the U.S. Court of Appeals by a unanimous vote, Bork was demonized. Even his video rental list was leaked to the press.

On October 16, my own confirmation hearing was held. Fortunately, the Senate Armed Services Committee panel was chaired by Senator John Glenn (D-OH). I was asked several challenging questions over a period of two to three hours, but none were out of bounds. During a meeting with then secretary of defense Caspar Weinberger early in the following week, the secretary's legislative assistant informed us that she had good news and bad news regarding my nomination. Weinberger asked for the good news first. "The Senate is going to vote on Steve's nomination on Friday afternoon," she replied. The secretary responded with delight and then asked, "What could the bad news possibly be?" "The vote on Steve," she replied, "is going to take place immediately after the vote on Judge Bork."

At 2:00 PM on Friday afternoon, the Senate began to vote on the Bork nomination. At approximately 4:15 PM, it was announced that the nomination had been defeated. The normally soft-spoken Senator John Danforth (R-MO), his voice rising, declared, "What has happened to Robert Bork is wrong. The man's been trashed in our house. Some of us helped generate the trashing, others yielded to it, but all of us are accomplices." As soon as the votes on the Bork nomination were announced, the Senate floor emptied like air from a balloon. Within a few minutes, only the majority leader and minority leader remained. Within only a couple of additional minutes, the Senate had consented unanimously to my nomination.

Despite the obstacles, the rewards of public service at senior levels of the government are more than sufficient to attract the kinds of leaders and managers the nation needs. The fundamental question addressed in this book is whether presidents, cabinet secretaries, and members of the United States Senate, will—especially in the Departments of Defense, Homeland Security, and Justice—change the historical pattern of behavior and place the nation's security interests above their own political, ideological, and personal preferences by nominating and confirming only those candidates for particular positions in those departments who are demonstrably the best qualified of the available candidates. The question is not an academic one. There is huge interest in the answer, especially among military, law enforcement, and emergency response professionals whose lives may literally depend upon the capabilities of their civilian leaders.

Chapter Two

The Professionalism of Military Leaders Prior to 1972

Your mission remains fixed, determined, inviolable—it is to win our wars.
—General of the Army Douglas MacArthur, West Point, May 12, 1962

Our political leaders had led us into a war for the one-size-fits all rationale of anticommunism, that was only a partial fit in Vietnam. . . . Our senior officers knew the war was going badly. Yet they bowed to groupthink pressure. . . . As a corporate entity, the military failed to talk straight to its political superiors or to itself.
—General Colin Powell, former chairman, Joint Chiefs of Staff

In considering the reasons why it is so important that senior civilian national security officials be capable of performing at a high level, it is useful to understand the sometimes tortuous, sometimes humorous journey that has been taken by America's military leaders over the course of our history to improve their own professionalism.

The first bearing of arms among men for the purpose of fighting other men is lost in ancient history. But service under arms has been considered by many, at various times and places, as almost a sacred calling, with many of the characteristics of the priesthood, at least in the dedication and sacrifice required.[1] Referring to West Point, General John J. "Black Jack" Pershing once wrote, "Cadets who enter it with the purpose of following a military career yield the hope of wealth and consecrate themselves to the service of country as completely as young men studying to take Holy Orders consecrate their lives to the service of the Church."[2]

Members of the U.S. Armed Forces are warriors in the profession of arms, a skilled profession. Their core task is to win the nation's battles, campaigns, and wars, and to sustain the peace. Perhaps the best statement of this principle was made by General Douglas MacArthur in an address to the Corps of Cadets at West Point in May 1962. "[T]hrough all this welter of change and development," he said, "your mission remains fixed, determined, inviolable—it is to win our wars. Everything else in your professional career is but a corollary to this vital dedication. All other public purposes, all other public projects, all other public needs . . . will find others for their accomplishment; but you are the ones who are trained to fight."

Men and women who wear the military uniform of the United States serve at "frequent cost to their convenience, their comfort, the stability of their families, and often their limbs and lives."[3] Service to the nation in the Armed Forces is neither a beautiful abstraction nor a box to be checked en route to a career in industry, politics, or some other profession. It is real. It is the "sternly concrete and unremitting obligation of service to the regiment, the squadron, or the ship's company."[4] The leaders of the Armed Forces must be much more than merely technically competent, for it remains their unique responsibility "to ask other people's children to do very dangerous things."[5]

The belief that leaders of fighting men should prepare for their service by undergoing specialized training and education beyond practical experience, is of comparatively recent origin. For centuries, the tradition was for young military officers to learn the rudiments of their work "at the cannon's mouth."[6] This was most certainly the case for much of American history. When the representatives of the Second Continental Congress elected George Washington as the commander in chief of the yet-to-be-formed American army in the late spring of 1775, they were literally writing on a blank page. It had been sixteen years since Washington had retired as the commander of the Virginia Regiment,[7] a militia unit. His early military career had been marked by ambition, courage, a capacity for hard work and detail, and a talent for careful observation. But he had necessarily had to learn his military skills on the job, his experience was very limited, and his battlefield performance had been uneven.

The new army consisted primarily, at least in the short term, of the militias of the individual states. Americans were fearful of large standing armies, a fear that was rooted in English history and the belief that a potential contemporary dictator could use such an army as a tool of oppression. They equated military service in the militias with citizenship. The military training of the militias varied widely, but most of it was very elementary in nature. Washington knew that for the core of the new army he would need regular troops, Continentals, who he hoped would be better disciplined and better trained and who would not owe their primary allegiance to the colonial governors of their respective states.

The Second Congress initially appointed four major generals and eight brigadier generals for the new Continental Army that would be made up of recruits from all of the states. Those officers were subsequently supplemented by a limited number of foreign officers, such as Baron Friedrich Wilhelm von Steuben and the Marquis de Lafayette, who would prove to be invaluable. By the war's end, twenty-nine major generals had been appointed.[8] Beyond that, the Congress engaged in very little effort to work out the details of rank and seniority. It also failed to establish a central strategic authority, to organize the army, or to create a bureaucracy to manage the army's logistical and other needs.

Very few of the general officers knew anything about war or the military, but because they each had their constituencies in the Congress, Washington had to tread carefully. He often deferred to the advice of his officers during the war. It is unclear whether he did so because of doubts about his own military ability or because of Congress's 1775 injunction that he act only after "advising with your council of war."[9] Whatever the reason, it is clear that the Armed Forces of colonial America were essentially antiprofessional in nature.

It has been asserted that "the idea that war consisted of more than the practical art of throat cutting—in other words, that it rested on a substantial body of theoretical knowledge that had to be mastered—is largely a product of modern technology."[10] The impact of the idea was first felt in such fields as artillery, navigation, and engineering. Formal academies for military training were probably first established in the seventeenth century when French, Spanish, and Dutch military commanders set up private academies to train the boys who applied for positions at their headquarters. In 1741, King George II of Britain signed a royal warrant establishing what became the Royal Military Academy, the first of several antecedents of today's Royal Military Academy, Sandhurst.

In America, there was a brief flurry of interest in military academies at the close of the Revolutionary War. Benjamin Lincoln, the secretary of war for the Continental Congress, submitted a plan in 1783 that proposed the establishment of military academies at each of five magazines or arsenals to be located throughout the states. The plan further proposed that "officers of ability and information" should "superintend the instruction of the scholars in the mathematics and such other branches of education" that would be required "to form a perfect engineer—artillerist—dragoon and Infantry officer."[11] In the same year that Lincoln presented his plan, John Paul Jones proposed the organization of an academy at every American navy yard to teach young officers "the principles of mathematics and mechanics" and a "fleet of evolution." Each navy vessel would have "a little academy onboard" to conduct practical exercises. But nothing came of the Lincoln and Jones proposals in the short term. Once independence from England was gained, Congress even abolished the Continental Navy, believing it to be an unnecessary expense. The United States Navy was not permanently established until 1794.

In its early days, the navy believed that officers were born, not made. To the extent that education was considered necessary to foster specific attributes in young midshipmen, it was the common wisdom that the only place for it was at sea. The preference was for larger ships, where midshipmen could learn navigation, seamanship, gunnery, tactics, command presence, and the professional culture of the service.[12] Large ships also offered several role models in the captain and his lieutenants. Objections to the idea of a permanent educational institution ashore for prospective naval officers, free from the demands of sea duty, were strong in the first quarter of the nineteenth century despite the increasingly obvious advantages of the idea. Jeffersonian Republicans believed that "besides being a waste of public monies and a dangerous extension of federal power, there was something inherently aristocratic and hence un-American in such an institution."[13] That kind of objection continued through the Age of (Andrew) Jackson, an era "known for its emphasis upon egalitarianism and amateurism."[14]

The Continental Army was not entirely abolished, however,[15] and the idea of a military academy to be established at West Point was finally approved by Congress in 1802. Forty-three years later, six years after the technology revolution had touched the navy and it had placed orders for three steam-driven ships, an industrious secretary of the navy named George Bancroft found the means to disarm the political opposition and to establish a new United States Naval Academy on the site of the army's old Fort Severn. In October 1845, the academy's first superintendent, Commander Frank Buchanan, and seven new faculty members received the first class of entering midshipmen.

For several decades after the birth of the nation, the new American government raised one army after another to respond to various types of emergencies. Very few officers or enlisted men, however, served for more than a short period of time. Indeed, for the thirty years following the Revolution, the most important characteristic of the army's officer corps was the high attrition level. The officer corps consisted only of "a mass of individuals from different backgrounds, whose generally brief military careers were simply interruptions of their civilian lives."[16] There was no community of trained soldiers who felt a continuing obligation to the nation or any sense of belonging to a profession.

An element of American military tradition had, in fact, evolved that retarded the development of a professional ethic. A preeminent American political scientist called this element "technicism." The element stressed the "general capability of all Americans, irrespective of knowledge or training, to excel in the military art."[17] An officer's training was not in general military skills that he shared with all other officers, skills that distinguished them from the rest of society and made them part of a profession. Rather, the officer was expected to be expert in only one of several technical specialties, "competence in which separated him from other officers trained in different specialties and at the same time fostered close bonds with civilians practicing his specialty outside the military forces."[18]

The War of 1812 convinced many civilian and military leaders that the nation could no longer afford to rely for its defense upon state militias of uneven quality and hastily formed regulars. Reformers started work on plans for a permanent officer corps. Regulations were codified. Tactical manuals were prepared. Professional journals in which views on various subjects could be exchanged began to be published.

One of the greatest influences on the professionalization of the army between the War of 1812 and the Civil War was a six-feet-five-inches-tall Virginian named Winfield Scott. His imposing physical presence was matched by his intellect, his energy, and his ambition. After practicing law for little more than a year, the twenty-two-year-old Scott sought and received a commission as a captain of artillery in 1808 when Congress increased the authorized strength of the army due to rising tensions with Britain. He immediately began to read widely on military matters.[19] He advanced rapidly, due in part to political influence. By March 1814, he had been promoted to brigadier general and had achieved a reputation for the training of troops. After being severely wounded and gaining national fame for his heroism during the battles of Chippewa and Lundy's Lane in the War of 1812, Scott was subsequently assigned to a board that reconstructed the army's officer corps. Not sufficiently challenged, he received permission to create a badly needed system of general regulations for the administration of the army,[20] which he called *Military Institutes*.

By 1845, Scott had reached the pinnacle of his military career. He was a veteran of the Seminole War and difficult peacetime operations, as well as the War of 1812. He had been involved in one way or another with several reductions and reorganizations of the army. He had continued to read widely, studying subjects from the common law to military law. Since he could read French well, he had also translated French military works. He was now general in chief of the army and had been a general officer for thirty-two years. He had made the army's artillery branch the best in the world. His triumphant expedition to Veracruz in 1847 during the war with Mexico, and the subsequent Battle of Chapultepec in which American forces occupied Mexico City, enshrined his name forever in the nation's military annals. When Scott finally retired in 1861, he had served for over fifty-three years under fourteen presidents. The son of another famous general, who subsequently served as president, has called Scott "the first truly professional soldier in the American military establishment."[21]

In the years following the Civil War, a distinctive American professional military ethic began to emerge. American officers began to regard themselves as members of a fighting profession that was not open to just anyone who wished to join. Certain standards of qualification began to take hold. "By the beginning of the 20th century," a military historian has written,

> the Army, Navy and Marines were . . . on a professional par, with general staffs controlling expertise at the strategic and operational levels; separate and distinct professional jurisdictions over land power and sea power expertise; a system of hierarchical education, including war colleges, to instruct officers in those esoteric skills; strict standards of entry and promotion based upon both seniority and merit; service ethics that valued military subordination to civilian authority; and clearly defined occupational cultures comprising uniforms, language, behavior, and traditions that delineated their cultures from each other and the rest of society.[22]

Simultaneously, a worldwide change in attitude toward military professionalism began to take place. A well-known student and practitioner of the profession of arms described the change in these terms: "Before 1800 there was virtually no such thing as a professional officer corps anywhere [in the world]. After 1900 no sovereign power of any significance, either in the old world or the new, was without one."[23]

Historically, a profession was distinguished from an occupation on the ground that the former involved a service to society, while the latter was merely a means for earning money. Traditionally, the professions included doctors, priests, lawyers, and educators. Since its publication in 1957, soldiers have relied primarily upon Samuel P. Huntington's classic work *The Soldier and the State: The Theory and Politics of Civil-Military Relations*[24] as a point of departure for discussions of military professionalism. Huntington believed that officers are members of a profession that he defined as "a peculiar type of functional group with highly specialized characteristics." The characteristics, he said, include such traits as expertise, responsibility, and corporateness.[25]

Expertise, he asserted, is obtained both by prolonged education and experience. Professional education consists of two phases: "the first imparting a broad, liberal, cultural background, and the second imparting the specialized skills and knowledge of the profession."[26] A military officer's expertise, he said, is the employment and management of force and violence to achieve a political objective. Other scholars have noted that since the military is the only profession that does not get to practice its profession on a regular basis,[27] the study of past military campaigns and of military history generally are essential to gaining expertise.[28] The element of responsibility meant a responsibility to perform functions beneficial to society. The responsibility of a military officer is to aide in the protection of the nation. Corporateness referred to a collective self-consciousness that sets professionals apart from the rest of society. It flows from the educational process, the customs, and the traditions that develop within the profession, as well as the unique expertise and responsibility shared by group members.[29]

In recent years, various trades, occupations, and other groupings have claimed professional status. Even within the army a vigorous debate is under way on the questions of whether enlisted personnel, career civilians, and so forth are professionals in the profession of arms in the same sense as officers serving in the army's combat arms branches. Advocates who want to incorporate additional occupations into what are considered to be professions argue that the historic definition should be expanded. Perhaps the best definition is one that was suggested more than three decades ago by a military historian who is also a military veteran. An occupation is a profession, he said, if it "is a full-time and stable job, serving continuing societal needs; is regarded as a lifelong calling by the practitioners, who identify themselves personally with their job subculture; is organized to control performance standards and recruitment; requires formal theoretical education; has a service orientation in which loyalty to *standards of competence* and to clients' needs is paramount; [and] is granted a great deal of collective autonomy by the society it serves, presumably because the practitioners have proven their high ethical standards and trustworthiness."[30]

While these concepts of professionalism would eventually become associated with career military officers in America, many military and even political leaders were slow to accept it. As early as the eighteenth century, the emphasis on enlightenment in all fields of endeavor had resulted in an unprecedented production of military books on theoretical matters and history, but for much of the nineteenth and twentieth centuries, the leadership of the American Armed Forces continued to evidence a disdain for overtly intellectual activities. To many, if not most officers, "such interests fell short in reflecting the manliness expected of those in uniform. Hard fighting, hard riding, and hard drinking elicited far more appreciation from an officer's peers than the perusal of books."[31]

Perhaps the most vivid and popular example of this attitude is that of Teddy Roosevelt in his references to the Rough Riders in the Spanish-American War. Formally known as the First United States Volunteer Cavalry Regiment, the Rough Riders were commanded by Leonard Wood, a doctor who had won the Medal of Honor fighting Apaches in the 1880s. He was made the colonel of the regiment, initially at the suggestion of Roosevelt, who, though he had served as assistant secretary of the navy, had no personal military experience whatsoever. Roosevelt was, however, confidently of the opinion that it would take no more than a month for him to "learn to command the Regiment." He was appointed a lieutenant colonel.

He would later describe Wood in terms that emphasized manliness, but that said nothing about professional education and leading troops in combat.[32] The Rough Riders regiment eventually consisted of something over 1,250 men, who were recruited from all over the United States. They included cowboys, Indians, Ivy League athletes, and aristocratic sportsmen from the East. Roosevelt's description of them was equally long on his characterization of their manly attributes, their athletic ability, their thirst for adventure, their desire to "see hard and dangerous service," and the fact that they were men "in whose veins the blood stirred with the same impulse that once sent the Vikings over the sea."[33] Nothing was said about their previous military training or experience. They could ride and shoot and they were in shape. It was presumed that they could be made ready for war in a very short period of time.

Similar attitudes prevailed in the army of Great Britain during the Victorian-Edwardian era. A brief study of that army is amusing and useful for a couple of reasons: first, because the professional standards required of its officers remind one of the kinds of standards that are used far too often today in the selection of senior political appointees; and second, because it helps us remember the wisdom of the observation made by Thucydides: "We must remember that one man is much the same as another, and that he is best who is trained in the severest school."

The British army was one of the world's most peculiar fighting forces. Its peculiarities were undoubtedly due to a great extent to the fact that, after Waterloo, British political leaders did not see a need to be prepared to use land forces on the European continent. The island had a strong insular position and the operating principle of the day was to place the nation's security in the hands of the powerful Royal Navy. It was British policy to keep the navy—330 warships, manned by 92,000 tars—larger than the combined navies of any other two continental powers. At its core, the very essence of the British army was the regimental system. There were no corps or divisions, or even brigades. The army was, in fact, a collection of regiments with their very distinct and individual traditions, degrees of prestige, uniforms, personalities, and mementos of war. The individual regiments usually served in the far-flung corners of the empire. The total British army was always small, so much so that Bismarck reportedly remarked in the 1860s that if it ever landed on the Prussian coast, he would send a policeman to arrest it.

Not having the advantage of a written constitution, important questions about the relationship of British civilian and military leaders were only vaguely resolved. "Throughout the Victorian era," one keen student of that period has written, "[t]here was a continuing debate as to whether the army belonged to the Crown or Parliament. The soldiers loved their Queen, but Prime Ministers and other members of the Government were frequently damned. The politicians won in the end," he has concluded, "but the arguments over the degree of civilian interference or influence on army affairs continued."[34] In fact, it would be more accurate to say that until 1871, when the government of the day decided to buy it back by abolishing the purchase system,[35] the army was owned by its officers.

British troops were led by patricians, but there was no standardized commissioning system. The prestige of a man's family and the size of his income mattered if he wished to become and to remain an officer. In the cavalry and infantry, commissions and even promotions were purchased. The highest rank that could be purchased was lieutenant colonel, but a person of limited ability who could afford such a purchase need not fear being passed over for promotion. After a certain number of years in grade, promotion to the rank of colonel was automatic. Most regiments required that an officer have a certain level of income, which was necessarily a level far above the regular army pay. Officers who were without independent means had no choice but to marry a woman with a fortune or to supplement their army career with other employment.

Until the middle of the Victorian era, not much education was required of an officer. "Discipline and steadiness were the qualities considered vital; initiative and intelligence were looked upon as civilian qualities, and therefore suspect."[36] It was considered necessary and even sufficient to be a gentleman, as that term was vaguely defined at the time. Social position was important. It was no accident that officers came almost exclusively from the aristocracy. Their snobbery was often insufferable. If one was a product of a "good family," and was "of the right sort"—that is, was "sound"—he was well on his way to a commission. Even after commissioning, social position mattered. It was long "considered more important to come from an aristocratic family than to have passed through Staff College, to possess social graces rather than military abilities."[37]

Despite the eccentricities of the British regimental system, its defenders argued that it created "that spirit in its combatant services which won wars."[38] One of the reasons it won wars was what an American author and combat veteran called the "sublime, unfathomable" courage of its officers. "Braver officers never led men into battle," he wrote.[39] But they did so at great cost. Before the Boers turned to commando guerrilla warfare in what was referred to as the Second South African War, British "infantry officers with swords and buttons shining brightly [still] led their men in line attacks . . . presenting an excellent target and suffering heavy casualties."[40] There is little doubt that the absence of standardized commissioning, professional education, and promotion systems enabled rich or socially connected incompetents to climb the military ladder and be given responsibilities for which they were clearly unqualified.

Long before the Victorian-Edwardian era, the Royal Navy had established a more straightforward approach to the commissioning of officers. A potential officer might start out in the enlisted ranks aboard merchant ships or serve an apprenticeship aboard ship as a young midshipman. Whatever the initial source of entry, however, one could not obtain commissioned rank as a lieutenant until a rigorous oral examination for that rank was passed. This was considered one of the greatest ordeals of the officer's career. Nevertheless, the naval profession was attractive to all classes as a way in which to serve king and country. Even though officers were expected to pay from their private funds many things that today's officers automatically assume is a government expense, a commission offered the prospect of making great sums of money, since officers received a share of the value of enemy ships and cargo captured.

The gaining of theoretical professional knowledge through formal education was not necessary for Royal Navy officers for most of the eighteenth and much of the nineteenth centuries. Starting in 1738, the navy was engaged in major war for fifty of the next seventy-five years. The quality of that empirical education was unprecedented: "Two and a half generations of naval officers tested the limits of their ships, their weapons, and their methods."[41] They progressively reinterpreted the rigid tactical doctrine written by the Admiralty "until sheer professional competence drove them more than theory."[42] The endless on-the-job training permitted the setting aside of books and written procedures and reliance on a new unwritten doctrine of informed initiative.

The growing recognition of the need to improve the professionalism of the U.S. Armed Forces in the last years of the nineteenth century and the first years of the twentieth was accompanied by an effort to reform the promotion of officers. Heretofore, promotion had been based almost exclusively on seniority. Officers could be trapped at one rank for long periods of time merely because those senior to them failed to retire. Reformers demanded promotion on ability and recommended rigorous examinations and annual fitness reports or personnel evaluations. In 1890, the army required examinations for officers below the rank of major, and within five years it instituted efficiency reports for all officers. In 1899, the navy took a small step in the same direction when it established a system for the "selecting out" of ineffective officers who reached the rank of captain.

During the same period of time, the navy took a large step toward greater professionalism that was soon emulated by the army. In 1885, a Naval War

College was established in Newport, Rhode Island. Its stated mission was simple: research on war, on statesmanship connected to war, and on the prevention of war. The college focused on war-gaming as early as 1887. Almost instantly, it gained fame. One of its first four faculty members was Captain Alfred Thayer Mahan. In 1890, Mahan published his *The Influence of Sea Power upon History, 1660–1783*. The work had an immediate, powerful, international influence on military and naval theorists.

The Spanish-American War had revealed several major deficiencies in American war planning, military organization, and logistical support. After decades of tactical employment in small units to administer post–Civil War Reconstruction in the South and to fight the Indian wars in the Western territories as a frontier constabulary, the army had "performed abysmally at the strategic and operational levels when it deployed to Cuba."[43] Army leaders knew that something had to be done. Fortunately, the timing was good. Theodore Roosevelt was now president and the brilliant and energetic Elihu Root was serving as secretary of war. Root had no interest in piecemeal reforms: he wanted the army to reflect the nation's ascendancy as a world power. He seized the moment to call for several initiatives, including remaining current with technological developments and emphasizing merit in the officer corps, improvement and better coordination of the army's educational training programs, and a more coherent relationship between the regular army and the National Guard.[44] He energized a feeble system of professional postgraduate education for army officers with the establishment of a new Army War College in 1903. The first classes were conducted in 1904. He established a new General Service and Staff College at Fort Leavenworth in 1902.

When Henry L. Stimson, Root's law partner and protégé, became secretary of war in 1911, he found that while the army was "slowly awakening," much remained to be done. The older officers who dominated the army were holding fast to old ideas of organization and training.[45] Recalcitrant bureau chiefs in the War Department were resistant to the creation of a new general staff. The various regiments, battalions, and smaller units of the army were still organized in administrative type units.

Slowly, matters began to change. By executive degree, Stimson ordered a new organization of the army on a tactical basis. Generals were shifted from being primarily administrators, to commanders. The standards required of a military professional, including educational requirements, began to rise. It was no longer sufficient to keep a military post "in good order with proper supply accounts and the garrison appropriately drilled and disciplined."[46] After the passage of the Dick Act in 1903, the quality of National Guard units also began to improve. Upon the request of state governors, the federal government provided weapons and equipment in return for a commitment by the states to conform to federal standards and to permit their National Guard units to participate in maneuvers with the regular army. When millions of American doughboys entered World War I a decade later, they "mobilized and deployed on the orders of a General Staff that was much smaller than those of the major European countries, but composed of Leavenworth and War College graduates who were speaking and writing a common professional lexicon."[47]

Despite these developments, America was unprepared for the Great War. At the beginning of 1917, four months before the United States entered that conflict, the army, in contrast to our large and modern navy, ranked seventeenth in size in the world, with only 107,641 men. A respected military historian has written that the army had "no experience of large-scale operations since the armistice at Appomattox fifty-one years earlier, and possessed no modern equipment heavier than its medium machine guns."[48] In fact, the army had been using field artillery to a limited extent. By March 1918, 318,000 Americans had reached France, the vanguard of 1,300,000 that would be deployed by March.

Fortunately, in General John J. "Black Jack" Pershing, the commander of the new American Expeditionary Force, and Secretary of War Newton D. Baker, America was blessed with military and civilian leaders who worked very well with each other. Prior to his appointment by President Wilson, Baker had had no military experience. But he was clearly competent. At their first meeting, he impressed Pershing as being "frank, fair, and businesslike," having a "broad and comprehensive" conception of the problems the unready nation faced, and not hesitating "to make definite decisions on the momentous questions involved."[49] He believed that in war, civilian leaders should select the military leaders, give them what they asked for, hold them accountable for producing results, and give them the authority and discretion needed to succeed. He told Pershing, "I shall give you two orders. One to go and one to return."[50] By the date of the armistice, names like Chateau-Thierry, Cantigny, Belleau Wood, Sainte-Mihiel, and Argonne had been added to the nation's battle streamers, but the war to make the world safe for democracy had been costly. More than 116,500 men never came home.

The experience of the Great War informed American military leaders of just how much more had to be learned. It was obvious that technology increasingly affected how well military forces performed in combat. In addition, the war experience raised many new tactical and operational questions. A scholarly student of the history of the United States Army wrote that "America in the 1920s was dedicated not only to the dream that [with the termination of World War I] wars had ended forever, but even more strongly to the more prosaic fetish of economy in government."[51] Another student of army history has asserted that during the 1920s and 1930s, the public desire to cut government expenditures "and traditional antimilitary attitudes combined with the dominant isolationist mood to reduce the Army to the point that it was negligible as a world power."[52] In referring to that period of time, General Douglas MacArthur was recorded as saying, "In many cases, there is but one officer on duty with an entire battalion; this lack of officers has brought Regular Army training in the continental United States to a virtual standstill."[53]

Fortunately, the Armed Forces in general, and the army in particular, had other resources of strength. During the interwar period, the army paid much more attention to the several complex elements of the mobilization of a "citizen" or nonprofessional army. The War and Navy Departments created an interservice industrial planning agency, the Army and Navy Munitions Board. The most important innovation, however, lay in the continued gains in the quality of officer education.

Pershing had been so impressed with the performance of Leavenworth graduates during the Great War that when he later served as army chief of staff, he placed great emphasis on professional education. The number of graduates of what had become known as the Command and General Staff School began to increase dramatically. Academic standards were raised. Graduation from Fort Leavenworth became a prerequisite for attendance at the Army War College. Since the army did not have sufficient troops to engage much in maneuver warfare training, the schools helped officers "visualize the command of the large units."[54] The effectiveness of this method was validated in World War II. Of the thirty-four corps commanders in that conflict, twenty-five had spent ten or more years in army schools as students or instructors.[55] When asked to identify the greatest difference in the army before and after World War I, General Omar Bradley responded that it was the army's school system.[56]

Similar developments were taking place within the navy. A series of large-scale landing exercises were conducted to test the Marine Corps's developing amphibious doctrine. Using various war gaming scenarios, the Naval War College became a world-class laboratory for the development of war plans. After World War II ended, Fleet Admiral Chester Nimitz was quoted as saying that "the war with Japan had been [enacted] in the game rooms at the Naval War College by so many people in so many different ways, that nothing that happened during the war was a surprise . . . absolutely nothing except the kamikaze tactics toward the end of the war."[57]

In an address delivered eight months after the war, even Winston Churchill saluted America's system of professional education for officers:

> The rate at which the small American Army of only a few hundred thousand men, not long before the war, created the mighty force of millions of soldiers is a wonder of history. . . . Professional attainment, based upon prolonged study and collective study at colleges, rank by rank, age by age—those are the title deeds of commanders of future armies and the secret of future victories.[58]

When Harry Truman assumed the presidency in the waning days of World War II, one of his strongest convictions was that "the antiquated defense setup of the United States had to be reorganized quickly as a step toward insuring [the country's] future safety and preserving world peace."[59] In his view, there was unnecessary duplication of effort by the army and navy and the tragedy of the attack in Pearl Harbor was due as much to "the inadequate military system that provided for no unified command" as to any personal failures of army or navy commanders.[60] He had definite ideas about the most appropriate remedy. A new national defense program should involve "not just reorganization of the Armed Forces, but actual coordination of the entire military, economic, and political aspects of security and defense."[61]

In July 1947, Congress passed the National Security Act of 1947. The act merged the Department of War and the Department of the Navy into a National Military Establishment under the general control of a secretary of defense. It also created a new Department of the Air Force from the existing Army Air Forces and a Joint Chiefs of Staff.[62] James Forrestal, the first secretary of defense, reported in December 1948 that the National Security Act had aided in the formulation of strategic plans, the development of an integrated budget, the coordination of service procurement efforts, and the establishment of additional overseas unified commands. But he recommended several amendments.

One of the remaining problems was the disagreement between the military services over their respective roles and missions. President Truman later sarcastically observed that the "the Navy, had its own 'little army that talks Navy' and is known as the Marine Corps. It also had an air force of its own, and the Army, in turn, had its own little navy, both fresh water and salt."[63] That problem was complicated by Truman's desire to balance the budget by limiting defense expenditures. A meeting between Forrestal and the Joint Chiefs at Key West, Florida, in 1948 temporarily resolved several of the differences of the services.

The amendments to the National Security Act that became law in 1949 removed the service secretaries from the National Security Council and made them the heads of *military* departments under the authority of the secretary of defense. A new executive department, the Department of Defense, replaced the National Military Establishment. The amendments also established the offices of deputy secretary of defense, three assistant secretaries of defense, and a nonvoting chairman position for the Joint Chiefs of Staff.

As soon as World War II concluded in 1945, a pell-mell demobilization of the Armed Forces took place. Within two years, American military strength shrank from about twelve million to one and a half million. The secretary of war and the secretary of the navy warned President Truman in October 1945 that the demobilization jeopardized the American strategic position in the world, but Truman did not want to resist public opinion and the strong outcry to bring the troops home.[64] As we have seen, he also wanted to reduce defense expenditures to fund his domestic priorities. Thus, less than five years after the Japanese surrender, despite the glowing tributes to the professionalism of American military forces during the war, and despite the far-reaching reorganization and unification of the defense establishment immediately following the war, the country was totally unprepared for the next major armed conflict.

On the night of June 25, 1950, ten divisions of elite North Korean troops launched a full-scale invasion of South Korea with the intention of conquering the South in three weeks. After the UN Security Council voted to send military forces to prevent the total collapse of South Korea, Truman ordered American ground troops into the country. The closest forces were in Japan. Because time was of the essence, a single undermanned battalion of approximately four hundred men (Task Force Smith) was sent into the breach. Most of the unit's soldiers were teenagers who had been on peacetime garrison duty in Japan and had no combat experience. Only a third of the officers had combat experience. The pathetic state of U.S. forces in general on the date of the invasion has been described by one distinguished historian in the following terms: "Under-manned, poorly trained American units, with faulty, often outmoded equipment and surprisingly poor high-level command leadership, were an embarrassment. The drop-off between the strength the Army [veterans] had known at the height of World War II, its sheer professionalism and muscularity, and the shabbiness of American forces as they existed at the beginning of the Korean War was nothing less than shocking."[65] For three years the Cold War turned hot. The price for what President Truman called a "police action" was high. An estimated 33,000 Americans died in it. Another 105,000 were wounded.

Over the next decade and a half, senior military leaders spent considerable effort attempting to prepare the Armed Forces for implementation of radically different military doctrines established by civilian leaders of different administrations. A good doctrine "describes how a nation intends to fight in war and, by so doing, guides how it organizes, trains and equips its military forces."[66] The first doctrine was announced early in the Eisenhower administration. In a speech on January 12, 1954, Secretary of State John

Foster Dulles declared that, in the future, the U.S. would respond to military provocation "at places and with means of our own choosing." He further declared that "local defense must be reinforced by the further deterrent of massive retaliatory power." To help implement this doctrine, the chief of naval operations, World War II hero Admiral Arleigh "31 Knot" Burke, successfully promoted the development of a Polaris missile with a nuclear warhead that could be launched from a submerged submarine. Burke would again demonstrate thoughtful leadership after his retirement from the navy when he helped establish and then led a new think tank, the Georgetown University Center for Strategic and International Studies (CSIS).

This concept of "massive retaliation" or "massive deterrence" was rooted in two factors. First, there was the imbalance of conventional fighting power between American forces and those of the Soviet Union. The Soviets maintained "something in the neighborhood of 175 divisions active in Europe at all times. The United States had twenty divisions, only five of which were in Europe."[67] The second factor was Eisenhower's desire for "an adequate but not extravagant defense establishment" because "long-term security required a sound economy."[68] Missiles were cheaper than troops and their equipment. It was thus administration policy that, should the Communists "be guilty of major aggression, we would strike with means of our own choosing at the head of the Communist power."[69] In short, the United States would respond to any serious threat with a retaliatory attack using nuclear weapons on a massive scale. The doctrine was, of course, designed to deter aggression. But it had several weaknesses, including the extent of its deterrent effect.[70] It was also difficult to make it credible since a nuclear response would be so devastating and possibly out of all proportion to the aggression that triggered it. Moreover, it was an inherently inflexible tool with which to deal with foreign crises marked by ambiguity, misunderstanding, and the use of conventional forces alone.

One of the outspoken opponents of the massive retaliation doctrine was General Maxwell Taylor, who served as army chief of staff from 1955 to 1959. A few months after he retired, his book *The Uncertain Trumpet* was published. In it he criticized Eisenhower's defense strategy and advocated the building of more effective and flexible conventional ground forces that could respond to a variety of contingencies. During the presidential campaign of 1960, Kennedy, the Democrat nominee, adopted Taylor's views, calling for a muscular "flexible response" doctrine.[71]

When Kennedy assumed office in 1961, the administration began the task of rebuilding the nation's conventional forces. It also reformed the management practices of the Pentagon and reassessed America's global security interests. Kennedy's choice for secretary of defense was Robert McNamara, president of Ford Motor Company. McNamara had no experience in national security leadership or strategic matters. However, he did have a background in applying statistical analysis to management problems. As a condition of accepting the proposed political appointment, he demanded that he be given total authority over political appointments in the Department of Defense. Kennedy agreed. It did not take long for a relationship of mutual distrust to arise between senior military leaders and the new civilian officials in DoD. Kennedy placed a premium on academic qualifications and self-assurance. In McNamara and McNamara's "Whiz Kids," he got both.

McNamara symbolized a new kind of defense executive, a well-educated technician who could take complicated problems that were almost mathematical in their complexity, and break them down. He was a statistician, a systems analyst. He craved data and facts. He soon installed an entirely new system of management within DoD.[72] But, while he was a brilliant manager of systemization, he was not a leader. He was not wise. He did not understand that computers and slide rules cannot solve all military or international problems involving human beings. And, after first losing his credibility, he would be forever reviled by military leaders for continuing to send young men to die in a war that he believed was militarily unwinnable.[73]

McNamara's young assistants were arrogant, full of certitude, autocratic, and condescending, just like their boss. Compared to their predecessors, they were more difficult to deal with, a circumstance that one student of the period believes "permeated all else that transpired."[74] Many of them had served in think tanks and research institutions and they were eager to apply their quantitative analysis techniques to national security issues. The Whiz Kids disparaged military advice based on experience because they were certain that their own intelligence and analytical methods could compensate for their lack of military experience.[75] It was widely perceived that they considered military leaders to be intellectually inferior. A distinguished army general who served as NATO's supreme allied commander, Europe, would later recall the senior DoD civilians in the administrations of Kennedy and Lyndon Johnson with these words: "You had . . . on the civilian side, a group of very intelligent people who were completely unaware of the limits of their competence. Those limits in terms of understanding the military art were quite severe."[76]

This problem was compounded by the young president's style of decision-making. Kennedy was very informal, preferring discussions with a small group of close political advisors rather than the more systematic and established procedures of the National Security Council, the Pentagon, and other institutions of government. By the time of Kennedy's assassination in November 1963, the U.S. position in the conflict in Vietnam was deteriorating. Lyndon Johnson, the new president, inherited an inner circle group of political advisors that treated officers, "particularly the Joint Chiefs of Staff, more like a source of potential opposition than of useful advice."[77] Johnson was widely quoted as saying that "the generals know only two words—spend and bomb."[78] Insecure in foreign policy matters, Johnson nevertheless wanted advisors who would tell him what he wanted to hear.

McNamara and his senior assistants rejected military recommendations for a demonstration of force and a show of determination in Vietnam. Instead, they directed a policy of graduated pressure on North Vietnam, believing that such a policy would limit the possibility of China or the Soviet Union entering the conflict. Whatever the merits of the policy, it was conceived and ordered in a way that did great injury to civilian-military relations. General Maxwell Taylor, the chairman of the Joint Chiefs of Staff, assisted McNamara in suppressing JCS objections to the policy of graduated pressure and in severing communications between the military chiefs and the president. The chiefs watched with increasing frustration as civilians in the Pentagon, believing that they could control events, assumed ever greater control of the conduct of the war. Army Chief of Staff Harold Johnson complained in a letter to a friend that "we now not only have civilian control, but we have civilian command, and there is a very real difference."[79]

One of the best descriptions of the breakdown in the 1960s of an effective relationship between military and civilian leaders was made by Henry Kissinger. "Misuse of systems analysis apart," he wrote, "there was a truth that senior military officers had learned in a lifetime of service that did not lend itself to formal articulation: that power has a psychological and not only a technical component. In the final analysis," he continued, "the military profession is the art of prevailing, and while in our time this required more careful calculations than in the past, it also depends on elemental psychological factors that are difficult to quantify. The military found themselves designing weapons on the basis of abstract criteria, carrying out strategies in which they did not really believe, and ultimately conducting a war that they did not understand."[80]

The breakdown continued throughout the 1960s, a decade in which "the military were torn between the commitment to civilian supremacy inculcated through generations of service and their premonition of disaster, between trying to make the new system work and rebelling against it. They were demoralized by the order to procure weapons in which they did not believe and by the necessity of fighting a war whose purpose proved increasingly elusive. A new breed of military officer emerged: men who had learned the new jargon, who could present the systems analysis arguments so much in vogue, more articulate than the older generation and more skillful in bureaucratic maneuvering. On some levels it eased civilian-military relationships; on a deeper level it deprived the policy process of the simpler, cruder, but perhaps more relevant assessments that in the final analysis are needed when issues are reduced to a test of arms."[81]

Meanwhile, other developments were causing fractures in the institution of the Armed Forces. In order to meet personnel requirements, recruiting standards were lowered. The individual rotation system in Vietnam was disrupting unit cohesion. Discipline and drug problems were becoming severe. Too many officers were enmeshed in "careerism," more concerned with their own advancement and avoiding hard decisions for which they might be criticized than taking care of the people they were privileged to lead. Training was suffering. As a result of a shortage of junior officers, many NCOs were being given direct commissions, requiring "younger or not so good older people" to be made into staff NCOs. [82]

The rapidly declining professionalism and morale at all levels of the Armed Forces was obviously a serious matter. Even more dangerous was the worsening relationship between civilian and military leaders in the Pentagon. That relationship reached its nadir when President Johnson refused the recommendation of the Chiefs to mobilize reservists for the war despite a strong warning that the continuing buildup of U.S. forces in Vietnam after July 1965 would greatly erode the quality of the ground forces unless reservists were called up. Johnson's political advisors argued that a mobilization of reservists would be tantamount to a declaration of war and would likely result in a full-scale conflict in Southeast Asia. [83] It might also act as an anchor on Johnson's reelection prospects.

By August 1967, civilian and military leaders were in open conflict. The strategy of attrition employed by General William Westmoreland, the American commander in Vietnam, was not working. Johnson and his aides now were perceived to be more worried about the implications of decreasing public support of the war effort on his chances of reelection in 1968 than doing whatever was necessary to achieve military success. Military leaders were convinced that their professional views were neither being heard nor welcomed by the president, and that the administration was deceiving both Congress and the American people as to the true nature and costs of the war.

According to one account of the incident, on August 25, 1967, General Earl Wheeler, then chairman of the Joints Chief of Staff, convened an unofficial meeting of the Chiefs in his office. After receiving a pledge from each that the ensuing conversation would be kept secret as long as any of them remained alive, Wheeler proposed that they resign en masse. At the end of a lengthy discussion, they all agreed. Apparently, the most outspoken proponent of resignation was the army chief, General Harold Johnson, who believed that the Armed Forces were being blamed by the public for the conduct of a conflict over which they had no control. After reflecting upon the matter overnight, Wheeler is alleged to have changed his mind and to have convinced the Chiefs to change theirs. [84]

Years later, General Johnson described his earlier thinking about resignation during the Vietnam conflict.

> I remember the day I was ready to go over to the Oval Office and give my four stars to the President and tell him, "You have refused to tell the country they cannot fight a war without mobilization; you have required me to send men into battle with little hope of their ultimate victory; and you have forced us in the military to violate almost every one of the principles of war in Vietnam. Therefore I resign and will hold a press conference after I walk out of your door."[85]

According to his biographer, Johnson then added with a look of anguish, "I made the typical mistake of believing I could do more for the country and the Army if I stayed in than if I got out. I am now going to my grave with that lapse in moral courage on my back."[86]

In his memoirs, a future chairman of the Joint Chiefs of Staff, General Colin Powell, reflected on his own experience as a junior officer in Vietnam.

> Our political leaders had led us into a war for the one-size-fits-all rationale of anticommunism, that was only a partial fit in Vietnam. . . . Our senior officers knew the war was going badly. Yet they bowed to groupthink pressure. . . . As a corporate entity, the military failed to talk straight to its political superiors or to itself.[87]

Perhaps the harshest, but most accurate, conclusion about the effect of both incompetent political leaders and the decline of professionalism among military leaders during the war in Vietnam is that of an author who has, even today, been personally involved in other armed conflicts and in the army's efforts to maintain the professional standards it achieved after Vietnam. In his view, the war in Vietnam was "lost in Washington, D.C." It was not the result of impersonal forces, he has concluded, but "a uniquely human failure, the responsibility for that was shared by President Johnson and his principal military and civilian advisors. The failings were many and reinforcing; arrogance, weakness, lying in the pursuit of self-interest, and, above all, the abdication of responsibility to the American people."[88]

Four years after the completion of the Johnson administration, a new institution was created that would have a profound effect upon the leadership and professionalism of all of the Armed Forces: the all-volunteer force. That development will be discussed in chapter 5. Now we turn our attention to the types of processes that have been used by recent presidents to select civilian leaders.

Chapter Three

Personnel Is Policy

There is nothing I am so anxious about as good nominations, conscious that the merit as well as reputation of an administration depends as much on that as on its measures.

—Thomas Jefferson to Archibald Stuart, 1801

Of legal knowledge I acquired such a grip
That they took me into the partnership.
And that junior partnership, I ween,
Was the only ship that I had ever seen,
But that kind of ship so suited me,
That now I am the ruler of the Queen's Navee!
Now landsmen all, whoever you may be,
If you want to rise to the top of the tree,
If your soul isn't fettered to an office stool,
Be careful to be guided by this golden rule.
Stick close to your desks and never go to sea,
And you all may be rulers of the Queen's Navee!

—Gilbert and Sullivan, *HMS Pinafore*

There are few propositions more widely accepted, or written about, than the proposition that the performance of an organization depends to a very great extent, sometimes almost exclusively, on its leadership. Bookstores have entire sections devoted to such titles as the *Leadership Secrets of Attila the Hun*. Norman Augustine, who served as chairman and CEO of Lockheed Martin Corporation, as well as undersecretary of the army, asserts, "In any organization—whether the English army of the fifteenth century or the global corporation of the twenty-first—strong and wise leadership makes all the difference. Superb leadership . . . can compensate for shocking shortcomings elsewhere. Likewise, weak leadership . . . can just as readily undermine

extensive strengths."[1] Jack Welch, the highly successful former chairman
and CEO of General Electric, set what has been described in his book *Winning* as the gold standard in business leadership, involving an "optimistic, no
excuses, get-it-done mind-set," and a "be-the-best" style.[2] Dr. W. Edwards
Deming, who was known as the father of the Japanese postwar industrial
revolution, believed that doing one's best was not sufficient. "It is first necessary," he said, "that people know what to do," and then they should do their
best.[3] He also believed that it is the responsibility of leaders not only to
improve performance but also to "improve the system" and to accomplish
"ever greater and greater consistency of performance."[4] Larry Bossidy, the
former chairman and CEO of Honeywell International, asserts that in order to
put the kind of execution culture in place that is essential to success, a leader
must make the appraisal and selection of people his most important job.
Why? "With the right people in the right jobs, there's a leadership gene pool
that conceives and selects strategies that can be executed."[5]

Referring to the rapidity with which change is occurring in the marketplace, one leadership guru has declared, "The future has no shelf life."[6] It is
increasingly recognized in developed countries that most work now is
"knowledge work in which people manage information, deal in abstract concepts, and are valued for their ability to think, analyze, and problem solve."[7]
Modern leaders must know everything from how to use and apply new technologies to understanding the new questioning mentality that modern employees bring to the workplace.

When it comes to leading there is no magic formula. Or, as two executive-search experts have put it, "As executives who have embraced everything from total quality management to reengineering have learned the hard
way, today, when it comes to leading, one size does not fit all."[8] Still,
leadership means leading people. It means holding people accountable for
performance. There is no getting around the fact that successful leaders must
be very capable performers themselves. President Harry Truman and former
New York mayor Rudy Giulian both embraced this concept. Truman's desk
had a sign that read, "The buck stops here." Giuliani's had one that read,
"I'm responsible."[9] John Paul Jones (1747–1792), the legendary Revolutionary War captain of the *Bonhomme Richard* during its battle with H.M.S.
Serapis, may well have proclaimed—as his first lieutenant later recollected—that "I have not yet begun to fight," but that confidence was due to
his declared belief that with proper leadership, "men mean more than guns in
the rating of a ship." Philip II of Macedon (382–336 BCE), the father of
Alexander the Great, stated the principle in simpler terms: "An army of deer
led by a lion is more to be feared than an army of lions led by a deer."

The first clue as to the future performance of a new presidential administration is the manner in which it selects its leaders. Bob Brudno, one of the nation's top executive recruiters, has worked in presidential campaigns. He says that the critical question is "to whom do they delegate authority for selecting the leaders."[10] In his view, a sure sign of indifference to the selection process is the delegation of authority to campaign functionaries. "Young campaign workers," he says, "believe they have found the honey pot when their candidate wins the election and they are asked to help select the leaders of the new administration. They are often young sycophants and self-promoters who don't know what they don't know. Too often, they have never been held accountable for achieving results and have spent much of their time working in a world of politics where appearances, not actual results, are what matters. Nevertheless," he concluded during an interview, "despite their lack of experience and the fact that they are supposed to be helping the president-elect select his most senior leaders, they often feel themselves entitled to high office in the new government."[11]

Another group of people who are often ambitious self-promoters are those people who are asked to work on the transition teams in the various departments and agencies. They may have worked in the campaign, but they are usually more experienced than the typical young campaign worker. Having decided that they would like to receive a senior appointment in a particular department, they set up offices in the building in which the department is housed and presume to speak for the president-elect or his senior advisors on a range of subjects while they await the arrival of the new cabinet official who will lead the department. Their primary objective is often less to ensure a smooth transition from one administration to another than to camp near the center of power in order to influence the selection of the department's other new leaders—all with the hope, of course, that they will soon be one of those leaders.

Cap Weinberger, the secretary of defense who had recommended to President Reagan that I be nominated as an assistant secretary, described with some humor his own experience when he arrived at the Pentagon to prepare to take over the Department of Defense in December 1980. "A minor problem . . . arose," he later wrote, "when it became apparent that the so-called 'Defense Transition Team' . . . had taken on a life of its own. In December, after receiving numerous complaints from military personnel that the Transition Team seemed more interested in [certain classified war plans] than on helping to plan the transition, I asked the head of the Team . . . when he anticipated the Team would complete its work. 'Oh, possibly by next June,' he replied. Having seen a part of its product to date and not finding it helpful, and having in mind that Inauguration Day was January 20, I thanked him and told him that the Team's services would no longer be needed."[12]

Over the last half century, the process followed and the criteria used by new administrations for the selection of federal government political leaders generally, and national security leaders in particular, has varied widely. The selections have often been made with surprisingly little thought, especially about the many factors that could determine a potential nominee's success or failure—that is, whether he or she is fully capable of handling all of the important aspects of the particular position under consideration.

A few weeks after he was elected, President-elect John F. Kennedy invited a distinguished former political appointee to his home in Georgetown for a chat. "He had spent the last five years," he said to his guest, "running for office, and he did not know any real public officials, people to run a government, serious men. The only ones he knew, he admitted, were politicians."[13] He asked for advice about who he should appoint to serve as secretaries of defense and state.

The guest was Robert A. Lovett, a World War I veteran who had served as both secretary of defense and undersecretary of state. With respect to Defense, Lovett was blunt. "An empire too great for any emperor," he said. When Kennedy asked what makes a good secretary of defense, Lovett answered, "A healthy skepticism, a sense of values, and a sense of priorities. That and a good President," he continued, "and he can't do much damage. Not that he can do much good, but he can't do that much damage."[14] A short time later, and after making sure that he had voted for the president-elect, Kennedy's brother-in-law arranged for Robert McNamara to travel to Washington. When he met Kennedy for the first time, he was immediately offered the position of secretary of defense.

The search for a man to fill the senior and arguably most important cabinet post of secretary of state was made with a remarkable criterion. For a job "requiring infinite qualities of intelligence, wisdom and sophistication, a knowledge of both this country and the world," the Kennedys were looking "not for the most talent, the greatest brilliance," but instead for someone who had the "fewest black marks," who had "offended the fewest people."[15] The ultimate choice was thus determined to a considerable degree by mediocrity. After Dean Rusk was appointed, it soon became apparent that he was working for a president with whom he could not communicate. They were simply not on the same wavelength. Rusk's inability to adjust to the "freewheeling, deliberately disorganized Kennedy system" of governing was also a serious problem.[16]

Because so much of the relationship between a president and his senior political appointees "depends on personalities—the energy level of the Cabinet officer and President,"[17] Kennedy's selection of McNamara and Rusk can only be described as remarkable. These two personnel decisions would soon have historic consequences for the country and for a president whose first year in office would be described as "the most incompetent first year of any presidency."[18]

One of the more surprising of the processes used by presidents was that by which the senior lieutenants of Richard Nixon were selected. Nixon's knowledge of foreign affairs was deep, as was his understanding of the mechanics of American politics. But there were great and surprising gaps in his knowledge of the federal government, despite his eight years of service as vice president, two years in the Senate, and four years in the House of Representatives. "From the gaps," said two of his biographers, "came the appalling vacuum of advance planning on how to organize and operate one of the biggest and most intricate governments in the world."[19]

Lacking any clear purpose for doing so other than a desire to appoint a high-level Democrat to his cabinet, Nixon offered the position of secretary of defense to Senator Henry M. "Scoop" Jackson of Washington. Jackson was very knowledgeable about defense matters, having served for several years on the Armed Services Committee, but he declined the offer. When Jackson gave him the bad news, Nixon reportedly acted by instinct and without much thought offered the job to Congressman Melvin Laird, a senior Republican in the House of Representatives who had advised Nixon during the election campaign and who was a known critic of the Johnson administration's defense policies and the management practices of Robert McNamara, Johnson's first secretary of defense. Laird had served in the navy for three years at the end of World War II, but he had never worked in any executive capacity, and his career had been devoted exclusively to politics since he was elected to the Wisconsin legislature at age twenty-three.

A person who was involved in the selection of other political appointees has described the process used by the Nixon administration as a BOGSAT system—"a bunch of guys sitting around the table"[20] selecting people for the administration's team. From the first hours of his administration, Nixon's personal interest was in foreign policy. When he finally did focus on patronage at one of his early cabinet meetings, he was not prepared. He impulsively delegated primary responsibility for filling the (then) 2,500 noncareer political positions to the individual cabinet officers. He then informed the cabinet that the political jobs should be filled on the basis of ability first and loyalty second. But as he left the cabinet room, he reportedly turned to an aide and said, "I just made a big mistake."[21]

Future developments confirmed his fear. When the young, inexperienced politician who was technically in charge of patronage would demand that a cabinet officer name a politically reliable Republican to a particular appointive position, "the Cabinet member would invariably reply: The President told me when I signed on that I could run my own shop."[22] This would not have been particularly bad but for another factor—the inexperience of the cabinet officers. "In department after department," it was later written, "holdover partisan Democrats were running things. Baffled by the intricacies of government, the cabinet officer would turn day-to-day operations over to the administrators inherited from the Johnson Administration."[23] The perceived core of the Nixon patronage failure was thus "his failure to pay it enough heed . . . a lack of hard attention."[24]

President Jimmy Carter ran as an outsider against the Washington establishment. During the 1976 campaign he looked for ways to set himself apart. His inauguration was described as "a day more for the symbolic than the concrete."[25] He chose to be inaugurated in a business suit instead of the traditional formal wear, presumably to demonstrate that he was just a common man. His low-key and forgettable inaugural address was followed by a well-received rendition of "The Battle Hymn of the Republic" by the all-black members of the Atlanta University Center Chorus. Commentators were quick to note that Carter was the first president to be elected from the Deep South in 127 years. More symbolism followed in the inaugural parade. It had barely started down Pennsylvania Avenue when the new president and First Lady and their daughter Amy stepped out of the presidential limousine and proceeded to walk the entire distance to the White House.

During the campaign, Carter had invested skillfully in such symbols. He had worked hard to establish himself in the eyes of the public "as a common man, just another American hired to do a particular job."[26] Upon assuming office, he followed the recommendations of his pollster and began to build an administration that "emphasized style over substance."[27] He terminated the playing of "Hail to the Chief" when he entered speaking venues. He sold the presidential yacht *Sequoia*. For his first televised address to the nation, he wore a cardigan sweater and an open-necked shirt. He declared that the energy crisis was the moral equivalent of war. To help win that "war," he announced that the White House thermostat would be turned down.

In a lead article the month Carter was inaugurated, *Time* described his search for cabinet appointees. He seemed at times, the magazine said, "hesitant and frustrated—disconcertingly out of character. His lack of ties to Washington and the party establishment—qualities that helped raise him to the White House—carry potential dangers. He does not know the Federal Government or the pressures it creates. He does not really know the politicians whom he will need to run the country, and it is far from clear how his temper and his ego will stand up under probable battles with Congress, the clamorous interest groups, and the press."[28] An observer who was in a position to know would later write that Carter's "amateurish inexperience was most immediately evident in the appointments process, and this in turn complicated and aggravated all of his subsequent problems."[29] The *New York Times* suggested that one factor in his 1978 selection of a new chairman of the Joint Chiefs of Staff was his pleasure in being able to discuss religion with the officer.[30]

Carter's nominee for the office of secretary of defense, however, was well received. Dr. Harold Brown, a trained physicist, was the first scientist to be selected for the position. He had substantial experience in DoD, having served in the Kennedy and Johnson administrations as director of defense research and engineering and secretary of the air force. He was in his eighth year as president of the California Institute of Technology when he was selected by Carter. Brown's academic background and DoD experience were apparently not the only reasons for his selection. According to one account, Carter was very concerned about the power of the Joint Chiefs of Staff and the possibility that the Chiefs could derail Carter's plans for a treaty that would return the Panama Canal to Panama or interfere with his plans for the SALT II Treaty with the Soviet Union or other defense objectives. Carter reportedly wanted a secretary of defense who possessed recognized expertise in national security affairs, but who had no political base, either within the Carter camp or the Democratic Party: "Lack of a political base [would] make it much easier for the White House to persuade the Secretary to support its policies and to use his expertise to oppose that of the JCS [if the uniformed officers should oppose administration policy], and [would] make it easier to threaten to fire the secretary if that should become necessary."[31]

Many of the other key political appointments were given to Georgians who had a close connection to Carter.[32] Charles Duncan Jr., who was appointed deputy secretary of defense, had lived in Atlanta off and on since 1964 and knew Carter when he was governor of Georgia, and Duncan was president of the Atlanta-based Coca-Cola Company. Loyalty and inexperience were common profiles of many of the other appointees. Carter gave free rein to Hamilton Jordan, his long-time political advisor from Georgia who would later serve as White House chief of staff, to fill top White House positions "with token appointees to please different interest groups," and in selecting those appointees to place "loyalty and submissiveness above competence."[33] The September 1977 issue of the *Washington Monthly* magazine reported that there were fifty-one Georgians on the White House staff and eighteen more at the Office of Management and Budget.

One of the "unequivocal objectives" that Carter brought with him to the White House was an intention to "increase dramatically the percentage of senior positions in the federal government filled by minorities and

women."[34] Except for this mandate, he gave his cabinet officers great freedom in selecting senior political appointees in their departments, including
PAS appointees. Harold Brown rejected at least two people whose appointments to senior defense positions had already been announced in the press.
As a result, the quality of appointees was uneven, and their loyalty was often
directed more to the cabinet officer who selected them than to Carter. One
observer reportedly declared, "In his goodness he would ask someone to be
in his cabinet, then give away the candy store."[35]

A sympathetic biographer, who served as special assistant to Carter in the
White House, would later write, "By filling jobs with people who had no
federal government experience, or who were weak, ineffectual, or there solely through loyalty to Jordan, Carter was denied the range of talent and expertise he desperately needed in dealing with Washington. Such appointments
occur in every White House, but are less consequential to a President who is
already a Washington insider."[36] The Carter administration's down-home
style and youth culture also did not sell well. "There was an innocence, and
an arrogance, about the idea that you could run the country with your Atlanta
statehouse team," one historian concluded.[37] "Every President brings his
people, but most Presidents bring people who are seasoned."[38] Two respected defense writers later summarized the performance of Carter's administration in more pithy language: "notable for its vacillation and moralistic
amateurism."[39]

When George Herbert Walker Bush was elected in 1988, it was the early
conventional wisdom that the transition from the Reagan administration
would be very smooth. After all, Bush had just completed eight years in the
White House as vice president and, except for the Johnson administration,
which followed the Kennedy assassination, the election marked the first time
since FDR that an administration was followed by another from the same
party. Moreover, the new head of the White House Office of Presidential
Personnel had served as assistant secretary of the navy in the Reagan administration.

Soon after the election it became apparent that Bush's promise to select a
"brand-new team" could not be dismissed as mere postelection rhetoric. Reagan appointees were requested to submit their resignations and to be out of
their offices by the day of the inauguration. A small group chaired by Bush's
eldest son, George W., was formed and given responsibility for "scrubbing"
all potential new appointments to make sure that their loyalties were to Bush
and not to Reagan. James Baker, a Texan who was a longtime personal friend
of Bush, who would serve as the new secretary of state, and who had served

Reagan as White House chief of staff and secretary of the treasury, declared to his staff, "Remember, this is not a friendly takeover."[40]

It was nowhere less friendly than at the Department of Defense. Even though he had served for only a year and hoped to be reappointed, Secretary of Defense Frank Carlucci did not even receive the courtesy of a telephone call from Bush, much less a request to continue his work. In an interview much later, Carlucci noted that he barely received advance notice of his replacement: "I got no word whatsoever other than one hour prior. Craig Fuller [Bush's vice presidential chief of staff] called me [on December 16, 1988] and said, 'In one hour, the President-Elect is going to announce John Tower as your replacement.'"[41] Tower had been elected to the Senate in 1961 as the first Republican U.S. senator from Texas since Reconstruction. A World War II veteran, he had remained in the Naval Reserve and was a master chief petty officer at the time of his selection. He had served as a member of the Armed Services Committee for twenty-three years. On March 9, however, the Senate rejected the Tower nomination by a vote of 53–47. The next afternoon, Bush announced his intent to nominate Congressman Dick Cheney of Wyoming as secretary of defense.

Cheney had never served in the Armed Forces and a biographer would later write that he "plainly did everything he could to avoid service."[42] His entire career had also been devoted to politics. Except for his service for a little more than a year as the White House chief of staff in the Ford administration, he had never managed any organization, much less a large one. He did, however, have the kind of credentials that matter in Washington—personal contacts. In the Ford administration he had become close to Ford's national security advisor, Brent Scowcroft, now serving in the same capacity for Bush. With the defeat of Tower, Bush was anxious to announce a new nominee as soon as possible. Given his own naval combat service in World War II and his broad and distinguished service in a series of senior national security positions in the government, he was almost certainly willing to accept more unknowns in his secretary of defense than he might have otherwise been. The Senate was likely to have few reservations about an elected member of the House. Scowcroft was anxious for a known commodity to be running the Pentagon.[43] Jim Baker, who had worked closely with Cheney during Ford's 1976 campaign, also supported him.

I had a unique perch from which to watch the selection process. In 1987, President Reagan had appointed me to the position of assistant secretary of defense. I had started the new year of 1989 with the assumption that my family and I would be returning to our home in Colorado sometime soon after the inauguration. To my surprise, I was asked by the new administration to continue my service as assistant secretary and to assume a new dual role as the Pentagon's drug czar,[44] with responsibility for all strategies, policies, and actions involving the use of the Armed Forces to carry out counterdrug missions assigned by Congress and the implementation of a National Drug Control Strategy to be developed by the new president. Overall, the selection process for other senior appointees in the new administration proceeded very slowly, due in part to the FBI background investigations and the need to obtain appropriate security clearances for the people appointed to defense or other sensitive positions. Another reason related to Bush's instructions to "go beyond white males." Eventually, some 19 percent of his appointees were women, and 17 percent identified with a racial minority.[45] A third reason was Bush's instruction to place greater emphasis on technical competency than on ideology.[46] The Reagan-to-Bush turnover was close to 80 percent, a figure that those who worried about the fate of the "Reagan Revolution" found unsettling.[47]

Perhaps the most undisciplined process for the initial selection of appointees was that used by Bill Clinton. Although work on the selection of a Cabinet began the morning after the 1992 election, it was unstructured. A small group consisting of the president-elect and certain Clinton friends sat around a table in the family room of the governor's mansion in Little Rock to ruminate about possible candidates for particular offices. They were usually joined by Hillary Clinton. The process deficiencies, including unprecedented slowness, were exacerbated by Clinton's campaign pledge to place a premium on ethnic and gender factors. His promise to appoint an administration that "looks like America" spurred speculation that women and minority appointees were not chosen on their merits. *Time* called it a "strict quota policy."[48] The *New Republic* slammed the idea: "Rigging certain departments for a single gender or race, tracking down an individual not for her intrinsic talent but for her ethnic make-up, is an insult to minorities and a depressing sign of the cultural balkanization of our politics. It is the old Democratic Party speaking."[49] The "one and only legal affirmative action category that the Administration failed abysmally to honor in hiring for Schedule C appointments was that of Vietnam era veterans, who would have been three times as numerous among Clinton personnel if they had been appointed in proportion to their percentage of the American population."[50]

In retrospect, given Clinton's casual style of management, his distrust of the Armed Forces, and his total lack of experience and interest in national security matters, his nomination of Les Aspin to be secretary of defense was almost inevitable. A superficial glance—especially by someone with no experience—would suggest that Aspin had all the right credentials. He had a reputation as a defense intellectual. The Cold War was over and America did not yet have any peer competitor who was an adversary. The only national security objective on Clinton's agenda was to open up the Armed Forces to openly practicing homosexuals. Indeed, because of his lack of experience and interest in national security and foreign policy matters, his primary criterion for the selection of his secretary of defense and secretary of state was whether they could keep those matters off his desk so that he could focus on domestic policy.[51] Few selections, however, could have been more disastrous. Even the people who worked for Aspin in the Pentagon were distrusted by the uniformed services. One liberal journalist would later write that Aspin's lieutenants "were seen as militarily ignorant, culturally distant, and inadvertently condescending."[52]

Hillary Clinton took Bill's pledge to appoint more women and minorities than any previous president to the outer limits. She pressured him to fill half of the senior positions with women and to appoint a woman to one of the "big four" cabinet positions—that is, as secretary of defense, state, or treasury, or as attorney general.[53] By December 15, 1992, only ten days prior to Clinton's self-proclaimed deadline of appointing his entire cabinet, the only one of the "big four" positions yet to be filled was that of attorney general. On December 22, Clinton interviewed Zoë Baird, the chief lawyer for Aetna. Two days later, he announced her selection. A major problem soon arose: Baird and her husband had employed illegal immigrants and had not paid Social Security taxes on them. Over the next four weeks, congressional support for the Baird nomination deteriorated rapidly. Shortly after midnight on the day of the inauguration, Baird withdrew. Clinton issued a statement conceding that his review of her candidacy had been rushed. George Stephanopoulos, Clinton's new White House communications director, would later say that Baird "had neither the high-level government experience nor the close personal connection with the President that had always been the traditional requirements for Attorney General." He would add that "by turning [the choice of Baird] into a quota, we put ourselves in a box . . . scrambling to find the best female Attorney General rather than the best Attorney General."[54] He and others concluded that Baird didn't have the independent stature or breadth of experience to survive a confirmation battle and that "our systems failed us at every crucial step."[55]

Clinton was further handicapped by the limited pool of talent from which he drew. Democrats had been out of power for twelve years. Strong choices were often vetoed. Except for subcabinet positions, which he often permitted his cabinet officers to fill, he and Hillary chose a White House staff "almost exclusively from the campaign ranks and Little Rock buddies."[56] "There were," said one student of the process, "so many thirtysomethings that they earned the nickname 'The Brady Kids.'"[57] The nominations of Baird and Aspin for positions as important as attorney general and secretary of defense were a devastating indictment of Clinton's selection process, as was the speed with which selections were made. Three weeks before the inauguration, only one hundred out of three thousand PAS positions were filled. At the end of June 1993, six months after the inauguration, only ten of the twenty-four positions in the Department of Defense requiring Senate confirmation were filled.[58] A senior White House official would later say that part of the problem was the headiness, if not arrogance that resulted from the election victory. He would also admit, "We just weren't ready—emotionally, intellectually, organizationally, or substantively."[59]

Not quite seven months after he assumed the powers of the presidency from George H. W. Bush, Clinton received a letter from a fellow Democrat, New York Senator Daniel Patrick Moynihan. The senator wrote to complain about the quality of some of Clinton's national security appointments. "The system that altogether failed to foresee the collapse of communism and the end of the Cold War and the onset of ethnic violence is still in place and untouched," he said. "You have not sent to us for confirmation a single person who had any inkling . . . none. The standard conservatives have been replaced by the standard liberals. Shouldn't that bother you?"[60]

By the time that George W. Bush became president, the presidential appointments process had become—in the words of one student of the problem—"a monster that quickly overwhelms any new administration's capacity to tame it."[61] The *number* of political appointments had grown steadily over the recent decades so that Bush had nearly thirty-three hundred positions to fill from a pool of eighty thousand applicants.[62] He created additional political appointment positions during his presidency. As we saw in chapter 1, the length of *time* between inauguration and confirmation for the average presidential appointee had also increased. Bush also faced a historically unprecedented problem. Because the legal battle over the disputed ballots in Florida lasted until the Supreme Court's 5–4 decision on December 12, 2000, he had only five and a half weeks to select some of the most senior and most important officials for the new administration. Fortunately, almost all of the most senior national security and foreign policy figures upon whom he would come to rely had played prominent roles in the recently completed campaign.

Ever since he had announced his candidacy, Bush had been sensitive to criticism that he had no interest or experience in international affairs. He had countered the criticism that he was a novice with comments like the one he made on NBC's *Meet the Press*: "One of the things about a President Bush is that I'll be surrounded by good, strong, capable, smart people who understand the mission of the United States is to lead the world to peace."[63] He had also surrounded himself during the campaign with seasoned national security and foreign policy veterans, including Dick Cheney, Condoleezza Rice, Richard Armitage, Paul Wolfowitz, Steve Hadley, and others. In selecting the most senior members of his national security team, the president-elect met in a series of meetings with only three people: Vice President–elect Dick Cheney; Andy Card, the designated new White House chief of staff; and Clay Johnson, Bush's Phillips Academy prep school friend and Yale room-mate, who had served as chief of staff in the Texas governor's office and who would soon become the director of the White House Personnel Office.[64]

Colin Powell had strongly indicated his interest in serving as secretary of state. There was no strong competing interest for that office, so he became the choice. Having served not only as chairman of the Joint Chiefs of Staff during the administration of Bush's father but also as President Reagan's national security advisor, Powell's credentials could not be challenged. But because many of the conservatives who constituted Bush's base of political support did not trust him, an effort soon arose to limit Powell's authority. Eventually, that effort resulted in the selection of Donald Rumsfeld as the new secretary of defense. Rumsfeld had previously served as secretary of defense and White House chief of staff during the Ford administration, as well as in several other senior positions in government and industry. He was crafty and tough in bureaucratic in-fighting,[65] but his aggressive and often arrogant temperament would make his stewardship of the DoD much rougher than it should have been. Because of both his personal conflicts with Rums-feld and his close friendship with Powell, Rich Armitage (who, like Powell, was a Vietnam veteran) was selected as Powell's deputy secretary at the State Department. Despite a career limited to academia and government and his notable lack of skill and experience in business or as a leader/manager of huge bureaucracies, Paul Wolfowitz became the choice for deputy secretary of defense, the person normally responsible for running the Pentagon and managing its $400 billion budget.

Thus, the senior ranks of Bush's new foreign policy team included two former secretaries of defense (Cheney, Rumsfeld), a former chairman of the Joint Chiefs of Staff (Powell), a former undersecretary of defense (Wolfo-witz), a former assistant secretary of defense (Armitage), and a former senior member of the National Security Council staff (Rice). Bush would later be quoted as saying, "If I have any genius or smarts, it's the ability to recognize talent, ask them to serve and work with them as a team."[66] Despite the fact that foreign policy decision-making in his administration would soon be dominated by an informal network of neoconservative political appointees, there is every reason to believe that Bush selected Cheney, Rumsfeld, Wolfo-witz, Armitage, and the other senior members of his national security team not to satisfy any particular ideological grouping, but because he genuinely believed that he was choosing the strongest possible performers.

That was not the case with many other senior appointees, who would serve in subcabinet positions. To a great extent, he delegated the selection authority for those positions to his cabinet officers. A perception soon arose within the Pentagon that the position of undersecretary within each of the three military departments, the number two position, was reserved for women. It was also believed that because of the great importance that Karl Rove, Bush's senior political advisor, placed on the future Latino vote, preference was being given to Hispanic candidates,[67] irrespective of their credentials relative to other applicants.

In the second Bush administration, the Office of Presidential Personnel was placed in the hands of a thirty-one-year-old woman, the youngest person ever to head that office. Her own professional experience had been limited to work on the staff of Republican congressman Dick Armey and a stint on the staff of the Republican National Committee, where she coordinated congressional affairs and helped the lobbying offices that wanted to recruit Republicans. After only a few months in Presidential Personnel, she was succeeded by one of her deputies, who also had very modest credentials and even less experience in government.

As Bush entered into the second term, great concern began to be expressed about the priority he was now giving to individual loyalty in political appointments rather than to competence, fresh ideas, or novel perspectives.[68] One respected observer wrote that the most baffling thing about the Bush presidency was this: "If you had worked for so long to be President, wouldn't you want to staff your administration with the very best people you could find?"[69] U.S. Comptroller General David Walker, then head of the Government Accountability Office, Congress's investigative arm, was compelled to declare that "there needs to be more emphasis on the qualifications of individuals that have key positions."[70]

Several of the appointments in Defense and Homeland Security were highly questionable, if not disturbing. When it became apparent that she could not win early Senate confirmation because of her lack of relevant experience, Bush gave a recess appointment[71] to a thirty-six-year-old woman as assistant secretary of Homeland Security for Immigration and Customs Enforcement (ICE), a law enforcement agency responsible for identifying and eliminating security vulnerabilities at all U.S. borders and in a wide range of other areas.[72] She replaced a twenty-five-year veteran. The woman had no experience in Homeland Security matters, but she was the niece of the chairman of the Joint Chiefs of Staff and married to the chief of staff for Secretary of Homeland Security Michael Chertoff, to whom she reported after finally assuming office.

In the Pentagon, Rumsfeld was given discretion over political appointments, even for senior positions. His hold on Bush was difficult for outsiders to fathom. He had not been Bush's first choice to lead the Defense Department.[73] Rumsfeld's method for selecting senior officials was also strange. His preference for people with significant business experience was understandable, but at a time when the nation was engaged in wars in Iraq and

Afghanistan and struggling to find ways to effectively turn from conventional war fighting to counterinsurgency, he seemed to go out of his way to select
people who had no personal military experience. It became clear that he
would not select a secretary of the army who had served in the army, a
secretary of the navy who had naval experience, or a secretary of the air force
who had served in that service.[74] Thus, he refused to select as secretary of the
army the then current undersecretary, a highly decorated army combat veteran who had been serving very capably as acting secretary for a year and a
half, and who had worked for eighteen years as a professional staff member
of the Senate Armed Services Committee and aide to Senator John Warner of
Virginia. Instead, he selected a man who had never served in either the
Armed Forces or the government, and who was himself fired by Rumsfeld's
successor. Future historians will undoubtedly be puzzled by the absurdity
and arrogance of a selection process in which personal experience was a
disqualifying factor.

Eventually, even Bush tired of Rumsfeld. He had first considered replac-
ing the secretary of defense as early as 2004. By 2006 he had decided to do
so. Had he taken the action early in the year, it would likely have benefited
the Republicans in the mid-term election in the fall. But he felt compelled to
wait until after the election in order to avoid an appearance that he was
making "military decisions"—in the middle of two armed conflicts—"with
politics in mind."[75] Another factor that influenced his decision to wait was
the criticism of Rumsfeld by six retired generals who publicly called for his
resignation. No president could afford to even appear to be vulnerable to that
kind of pressure.[76]

Barack Obama's informal, preelection personnel operation was very well
organized and well financed. As early as the spring of the 2008 election year,
he had a transition budget of roughly $400,000 from privately raised funds.
Over the ensuing months, he was helped by "a complete inventory and description of all the appointed jobs in government," which had been prepared
by the outgoing staff of the George W. Bush White House and given to both
Obama and his Republican opponent, Senator John McCain.[77] By the time
the formal postelection transition commenced, Obama's staff had determined
the order in which they hoped to fill the three hundred top jobs.

On the date of his election, Obama had run no state or local government,
he had chaired no Senate committees, he had never run a large organization
or served in the Armed Forces, and he had no close friends with major
business experience upon whom he could rely. He had made "few high-level
connections beyond his campaign supporters, his Harvard Law and Chicago
circles, and the group of former . . . aides [to Democratic Senator Tom

Daschle] who helped him when he first arrived in Washington" four years earlier.[78]

In these circumstances, he asked John Podesta, a political friend from Chicago and Bill Clinton's White House chief of staff, to be the point man for his transition team. Other members included Valerie Jarrett, another close friend from his Chicago days; Sonal Shah, a University of Chicago graduate who was heading Google's philanthropic arm; Pete Rouse, Obama's chief of staff in his Senate office; and, eventually, Rahm Emanuel, the controversial congressman from Chicago who would serve as the White House chief of staff.

The early political appointees reflected Obama's preference for academics, especially those from elite universities. He surrounded himself with policy theorists, "even if almost none of them knew anything about what it was like to work in small business . . . or other parts of the real economy."[79] At one point, one in four of his appointees either graduated or taught at Harvard. This reminded those old enough to remember of the famous remark by Sam Rayburn, the late Speaker of the House. When Vice President Lyndon Johnson told Rayburn about the well-educated, Ivy League aides that President Kennedy had appointed, Rayburn said, "I'd feel a lot better if some of them had run for sheriff just once."

Carter-esque symbolism was also important. A transgender appointee was named as a senior technical advisor in the Commerce Department. Democratic officials said that she might be the first transgender presidential appointee. An openly gay man became the director of the Office of Personnel Management, thus becoming the highest-ranking openly gay official to serve in the executive branch in any administration. Within twenty-five months of assuming office, Obama would appoint more openly gay officials than any president in history, including the first open homosexual to serve in the highly visible position of White House social secretary.

It soon became apparent, however, that despite the fast start that Obama's transition team had made, his nomination process for political appointees was badly flawed. He quickly formed a list of two or three names for each cabinet position, but "[h]is short lists . . . were [only] wish lists of acquaintances he had met briefly or heard good things about."[80] He had few, if any, ideas regarding who should be appointed to subcabinet positions, where much of the real work of the government gets done. "Incompetence, inattention to detail, and apathy were [also] common threads—running stitches"[81] in the vetting scheme used. Damaging issues that should have been detected were not.

No small part of the problem was due to the work of the person selected as the first director of the White House Office of Presidential Personnel. Donald H. Gips, a vice president of a Colorado-based telecom company, had delivered more than $500,000 in contributions to the Obama campaign. Two other senior company executives had collected at least an additional $150,000. In the short time that he was there, Gips was a powerful White House force in "helping to place loyalists and fundraisers in many key positions."[82] But he did little to deal with the many other applicants for positions. Eight years earlier, the Bush transition team had received about forty thousand resumes. Obama's office stopped counting when they got to five hundred thousand.[83] After only six months of handling appointments, Gips was rewarded again when he was named as the American ambassador to South Africa. Although he would later say that he was unaware of the fact, he apparently did not deny a report that in a little more than two years after Obama assumed office, Gips's former company, in which he retained stock, was awarded some $13.8 million in federal stimulus contracts.[84]

On December 3, 2008, only a month after the election, Obama announced his nomination of New Mexico governor Bill Richardson to be secretary of commerce. On January 4, 2009, Richardson announced his withdrawal after news of a grand jury investigation and unrelated ethical issues surfaced. Great fanfare surrounded Obama's nomination of Tom Daschle, the former Democratic leader in the Senate, to be secretary of health and human services. On February 3, 2009, and after allegations of tax evasion became public, Daschle withdrew. The following day, CBS News reported that, in a series of interviews, the president "repeatedly said that the appointment scandal was his responsibility and apologized over (and over) again." On NBC, he declared, "I'm frustrated with myself, with our team, and I'm here on television saying I screwed up." When ABC's Charles Gibson asked Obama what type of message he thought investigations into three of his appointee's taxes sent, he responded, "Well, I think it sends the wrong one. And that's you know, something I take responsibility for."[85]

But the problem didn't stop there. After retired four-star marine general Anthony Zinni was told by Vice President Biden, Secretary of State Hillary Clinton, and National Security Advisor James Jones that he was going to be nominated as the U.S. ambassador to Iraq, the appointment was withdrawn without explanation. Other withdrawals involved the woman who had been tapped to be the chief performance officer and deputy director of OMB, the man nominated to be deputy administrator of EPA, and even the man nominated to serve as director of the National Intelligence Council. By mid-March 2009, only one of the fifteen key Treasury Department positions requiring Senate confirmation had been filled. At the end of his first one hundred days in office, Obama "had set a turnover record for an incoming cabinet with four major withdrawals . . . and a spate of lower posts."[86] According to the *National Journal*, President Clinton had six major nominee withdrawals over the course of his eight-year presidency, George W. Bush had only two over his eight years in office, and presidents George H. W. Bush, Ronald Reagan, and Jimmy Carter had only one each.[87]

The appointment of ambassadors also created a political problem. In July 2009, it was reported that "an old college roommate, the head of an entertainment production company, and a lawyer whose family made its money selling vacuum cleaners [were] among more than a dozen people who [had] been given ambassadorships after raising a total of at least $4 million for Mr. Obama's campaign."[88] Less than two years later, and despite the 1980 Foreign Service Act, which declares that political contributions "should not be a factor" in the selection of ambassadors, one-third of Obama's ambassadors were political appointments given primarily to people who had been involved in Obama's fundraising efforts. The president of the American Foreign Service Association was quoted as saying that the rejection of career diplomats in favor of very large donors amounts to "selling ambassadorships." Her position was strongly supported by a distinguished former ambassador and the then chair of the American Academy of Diplomacy.[89]

Like other presidents, Obama has tended to politicize departments and agencies that have policy views dissimilar to his own by increasing, or at least failing to reduce, the number of senior political appointees in them. Another recent example of this approach was that followed by the Clinton administration, an administration characterized by a suspicion and even a fear of all things military. When Clinton assumed office, there were only two undersecretary of defense positions[90] for a department that had only recently been dealing with the challenges of the Cold War and the 1990–1991 Persian Gulf War. As recently as the previous year, the Armed Forces had numbered approximately 1,943,937 active personnel and 1,806,092 members of the National Guard and other reserve components.[91] By the time Clinton left office, there were four undersecretary of defense positions and a large number of other PAS positions within DoD, even though the authorized end strength of the active forces had been reduced to 1,382,242 and the National Guard and other reserve components had also been reduced.[92]

Obama has also tended to select more competent appointees for those departments and agencies that do not generally share his views—that is, departments perceived to be more moderate or conservative than he is (for example, Defense and Homeland Security). Politically connected but less qualified candidates have been selected for departments that are generally liberal in their orientation, such as Education and Housing and Urban Development. Less qualified appointees have also been appointed to departments not responsible for key administration priorities. The author of a study at Vanderbilt University attempted to explain this trend. "One theory for this pattern," he said, "is that Democratic patronage appointees prefer jobs in agencies that will advance their career prospects within the party or the constellation of groups around the party. For Democrats, these would be jobs in areas such as labor, the environment and housing. This coincides with the

President's interests since a President needs many of the best qualified appointees to run agencies that do not share his or her views."[93]

The reasons behind Obama's selections of secretary of state and secretary of defense are particularly interesting. Hillary Clinton, his strongest competitor in the 2008 election campaign, was a "must" appointment for political reasons—namely, for the purpose of eliminating a potential opponent for the Democratic nomination in 2012. It was assumed that she would accept nothing less than a major position. Despite the facts that she had no foreign policy experience, that she had no executive experience, that the nation was involved in two major armed conflicts, and that the current foreign policy problems involving Iran, North Korea, the Middle East, Sudan, China/Taiwan, and Russia were complex and resistant to quick or easy solution, she quickly became the leading candidate. Obama was apparently impressed by her "resilience" during the Monica Lewinsky scandal during her husband's administration.[94] Podesta liked her "visibility."[95]

When Clinton expressed doubts that the position of secretary of state would be "right for her," Podesta reportedly assured her that she would be "a big deal," that she could "pick her own deputies and staff," that her acceptance of the proposed appointment would "show she was a good sport" who didn't carry grudges, that she "would be in the public eye all of the time," and that "Obama's favorable press could spill over to her."[96] Most important, in view of "a weakness that had become evident" in the recently completed presidential campaign, "being secretary of state would give her absolute bona fides in foreign policy and national security."[97] Seldom, if ever, have more indefensible reasons been given as justification for the selection of an unqualified appointee for a critically important position. And seldom, if ever, has a president with no experience in either foreign policy or national security matters selected someone for on-the-job training as secretary of state in the middle of two wars. Clinton was presumably not bothered by the prospect. She had already publicly embraced the old saying, "Fake it till you make it."[98]

To balance the Clinton appointment, Obama asked Secretary of Defense Robert Gates, a respected Bush appointee, to continue in office. Even though his military service was limited, and he was known to have a healthy ego and a streak of self-righteousness, Gates had good credentials.[99] He was the ultimate Washington man, an effective but cautious pragmatist, a consensus-oriented and savvy political survivor who, as a career technocrat, had never been active in Republican Party politics or expressed strong views on policy matters that might endanger his career progression. He knew about accountability. He had fired several military leaders for failures of performance.

Gates's performance to date, however, was not the primary reason for his selection. There was no qualified Democrat available who had national stature and "visibility." Continuity in DoD during the wars in Iraq and Afghanistan would be important, particularly in view of Obama's and Clinton's inexperience. By the selection of Gates, Obama would also be seen as giving a serious nod to bipartisanship. And, not least important, it made sense to retain Gates at the Pentagon to provide political cover for Obama. Retired general Jim Jones, the new national security advisor, was the only new senior White House aide to come out of the Armed Forces. Perhaps he and Gates could quell, or at least reduce, the expected Republican opposition in Congress to any future plans by the White House to remove U.S. combat troops from Iraq and Afghanistan by dates certain rather than upon the completion of planned missions, and to repeal the "Don't ask, don't tell" statute that barred open homosexuals from military service.

A very unusual approach to management became apparent over the administration's first months in office. A series of White House issue specialists, policy "czars," and commissions were appointed to perform work that had traditionally been performed by cabinet members or other government officials with executive responsibilities. Special assistants to the president or special representatives were appointed for policy areas as diverse as green jobs and domestic violence. Some counts listed as many as forty high-level executive "czar" positions.

The "czar" appointments did not come without political cost. They were criticized in the Senate by Democrats like Senator Robert Byrd (D-WV) and Republicans such as Senator Lamar Alexander (R-TN). By early 2011, even members of Obama's own administration were expressing criticism and frustration with the "czars."[100] Political opponents were particularly harsh. After the British Petroleum oil spill in the Gulf of Mexico, one pundit objected to the practice with these words:

> Here is the Obama Management Theory: In times of crisis, you can never have enough unelected, unvetted political appointees hanging around.
>
> [T]his White House has bypassed the Senate advise-and-consent role and unilaterally created a two-tiered government. It's fronted by cabinet secretaries able to withstand public scrutiny (some of them just barely) and then managed behind the scenes by shadow secretaries with broad powers beyond congressional reach. Bureaucratic chaos serves as a useful smoke-screen to obscure the true source of policy decision-making.
>
> It's government by proxy and government by press release all rolled into one.
>
> Executive leadership doesn't need to be outsourced when the executive in office knows how to lead.[101]

The appointment by presidents of commissions to do the kind of work that incumbent government leaders are supposed to do is of long-standing precedent. Commissions are often appointed because, in the absence of courage, government leaders seek political cover for difficult policy decisions that need to be made. In early 2010, for example, President Obama appointed such a commission, and he was candid about his reason for doing so. The critically important issue involved too much political risk. After acknowledging the government's major budget problems, including a historically unprecedented deficit, he declined to offer a plan for fiscal solvency. "[T]he politics of dealing with chronic deficits," he said, "is fraught with hard choices, and therefore, it's treacherous to officeholders here in Washington. As a consequence," he continued, "nobody has been too eager to deal with it."[102] On February 18, he announced the creation by executive order of a new Debt Commission to address the problem. The commission was charged to submit its report on the highly contentious subject of the ways to reduce the federal deficit in December, the month after the midterm congressional election. One year later, Obama submitted to Congress his proposed budget for FY 2012. None of the most important of his Debt Commission's recommendations were included. The Democratic co-chair of the commission said that the proposed budget was "nowhere near where they have to go to resolve our fiscal nightmare."[103] Even editorials in administration-friendly newspapers called the proposed budget "remarkably weak and timid."[104]

As if he did not have enough problems with his political appointments, Obama ran into more with an announcement on March 27, 2010, that he was making fifteen recess appointments, including a controversial appointment to the National Labor Relations Board. Critics were quick to point out that when President Bush made a recess appointment of John Bolton as the U.S. ambassador to the United Nations in 2005, then senator Obama had referred to the absence of Senate confirmation and called Bolton "damaged goods." Four years later, the Obama administration had come into office promising to do away with recess appointments.

The most systematic, and probably the best, political appointee selection process at the beginning of an administration was that used by the Reagan administration. A full year before the 1980 election, Pendleton James, a leading professional in the executive search business, approached Ed Meese, one of Reagan's senior aides, to ask how he could help in the coming election campaign. In addition to his work as a corporate headhunter, James had also served previously as a staff member in Nixon's Presidential Personnel Office. Meese immediately asked him to prepare a plan for a Reagan presidential personnel operation that would be ready to implement if Reagan was elected. By April of the election year, work on a staffing plan was under way. The participants included people who had previous experience in other administrations. By September, the small staff had compiled data on the three thousand appointments that would have to be made. They had also developed a system for recruiting qualified candidates and handling the thousands of applications they expected from candidates already interested in serving.

One of the interesting factors at play was the nature of Reagan's own political experience. When he was elected president, he was sixty-nine years old. He had not entered public life as governor of California until he was fifty-five. As a consequence, "he didn't have the usual long list of commitments and political associations picked up through years of wheeling and dealing in the party system,"[105] or, as his biographer put it, he "lacked the network of alliances and friendships normally forged by politicians as they scramble up the career ladder."[106] For these reasons, one of the first and most important actions taken by James and his staff was to compile a "talent bank of experts." He explained his reasoning as follows:

> We needed to develop a nationwide talent bank. And when you look at that talent bank, the men and women that came into the administration, they're not all Washington lawyers; they're not all Washington lobbyists.
>
> Now, let me say we do not talk to people, we do not interview people, we do not ask people to apply; but I'm a headhunter in real life, and I do this for a living. So we put together who are the leaders in the field in agriculture, who are the leaders in defense, foreign policy, economic trade, and things like that, and came together with a long list of names.
>
> None of these were political; none of them came out of the campaign. You get plenty of that feedback. You don't have to search for those.[107]

The Reagan team applied specific criteria to each candidate in order to determine who should be recommended for appointment. They included philosophical commitment to Reagan's intended programs and policy objectives; the highest personal qualifications, competence, and integrity; experience and skills that would fit the task at issue; the toughness considered essential to withstand the pressures and inducements of the Washington establishment; and the willingness to be a "team player"—that is, the absence of any desire to use a position in the administration as a vehicle to seek another post-administration job or to pursue another personal agenda.[108]

For the positions of secretary of defense and secretary of state, Reagan accepted the advice of former president Nixon. In an eleven-page memorandum written seven days after the 1980 election, Nixon had told Reagan, "You cannot afford on-the-job training for your secretaries of state and defense." In a letter reply of November 22, Reagan thanked Nixon "for the guidelines you gave me on personnel," and added, "This will be done."[109] He did select individuals with impeccable credentials and experience. For Defense, he nominated Caspar Weinberger, who had impressed Reagan with his extensive grasp of fiscal matters when he served as director of finance in Sacramento while Reagan was governor. A graduate of Harvard and its law school, he had served in the Pacific during World War II with the army's

Forty-First Infantry Division and as an intelligence aide to General Douglas MacArthur. In the Nixon administration, he had served as chairman of the Federal Trade Commission, director of the White House Office of Management and Budget, and secretary of health, education and welfare. While at OMB, he had earned the nickname "Cap the Knife" for his cost-cutting ability. He had later served as vice president of the huge Bechtel Corporation.

For the State Department, Reagan selected Al Haig. A West Point graduate, Haig had received graduate degrees from Columbia and Georgetown Universities in business and international relations respectively. As a four-star general in the army, he had served as vice chief of staff of the army and as supreme allied commander in Europe. A veteran of both the Korean and Vietnam Wars, Haig had also served as White House chief of staff in the administrations of presidents Nixon and Ford.

Reagan constantly reminded Pendleton James and the other senior aides involved in the selection of senior officials for the government that he only wanted "the best people" in the administration. To that end, he refused to follow the Carter example of permitting cabinet members to select their own senior staff personnel. Control of PAS appointees would remain within the White House. A senior official in several Republican administrations and the author of a book on presidential leadership has applauded Reagan's decision. "[T]he appointments power is a major tool of Presidential control," he has written, "that I do not believe should be traded away. The dictum 'personnel is policy' has too much truth in it. . . . Using this tool was one of Reagan's strengths."[110]

After Reagan's inauguration, a formal selection process was established. Pendleton James described it this way:

> The process was controlled by [White House Chief of Staff Jim] Baker, [Deputy Chief of Staff Mike] Deaver, [Presidential Counselor Ed] Meese, and James. Every day at 5:00 weekdays we met in Jim Baker's office. . . . [There] were only the four of us.
>
> At that time, books would have been prepared by my staff over in the Old Executive Office Building saying, "Today we are looking at the Assistant Secretary for whatever." First page of the book was what is the job, what is the job description, what is his authority? The second page was the candidate, his or her background, capabilities. . . . The third page was political support, who's been lobbying to get this appointment, who was for him, who was against him. And the fourth page, what they always looked at first, was who else was considered. . . . It would be at that 5:00 staff meeting that the President's senior team would make a judgment as to whom they would recommend to the President.[111]

For cabinet-level appointments and the selection of senior members of the White House staff, another factor was at play—the First Lady. Nancy Reagan knew that her husband was so loyal to his staff that he couldn't fire anyone and was blind to faults that she could see. She worked with great effectiveness behind the scenes to protect him from people who were not serving him well, establishing unusual direct lines of communication with senior officials. The evidence strongly suggests that she orchestrated the resignations of both William Clark, one of Reagan's national security advisors, and Donald Regan, a former Treasury secretary who was serving as White House chief of staff.

Whatever the merits of the system used by a newly elected president for the selection of people to serve in PAS positions, there is reason to believe that a less rigorous process will be used to select replacements for senior appointees who leave office after only a brief period of time. This sometimes occurs as a result of personnel turnover in the White House Office of Presidential Personnel. At other times it occurs because of a rush to announce a replacement for a departing official. At yet other times it occurs because a White House staffer, or someone else in the administration, has expressed interest in a vacancy and established a personal relationship with someone who will have great influence in the selection of the new appointee.

In such circumstances, there is high risk that the best possible person for the position will not be selected. Personal loyalty to the president or to a key person who will influence the president's decision too often plays a disproportionate role. The Office of Presidential Personnel may not have given serious thought to a vacancy or identified a group of potential candidates who are clearly qualified for the position. People in the nation's capital are very likely to learn of a vacancy or potential vacancy long before a potential candidate who lives and works in the heartland, giving the former group an immense advantage in mobilizing letters and calls of recommendation.

On some occasions, speed of appointment is incorrectly considered to be more important than selecting the best qualified person for a particular job. In 1983, for example, Bill Clark, President Reagan's national security advisor and close personal friend, was almost nominated as secretary of the interior when James Watt resigned. Clark had no particular credentials for interior, but he was "worn down" by the responsibilities of his current position and he had the president's ear. Similarly, when President Clinton decided to replace Les Aspin as secretary of defense in 1993, he was advised that it was essential to have a replacement ready when Aspin's departure was announced or "the press will kill us."[112] With minimal discussion and even less vetting, Admiral Bobby Ray Inman, a former deputy director of the CIA, was selected. Aspin's "resignation" was announced at the White House on December 15. The next day the nomination of Inman was announced. In his acceptance remarks, Inman angered Clinton by describing the turmoil he had gone through in deciding whether to take the job. He said he had had to reach "a level of comfort that we could work together, that I would be very comfortable in your role as Commander-in-Chief." There were also other problems. On January 18, Inman held a news conference to announce his withdrawal.

The factors described above may not be of critical importance when a vacancy occurs in a noncabinet PAS position for which a large supporting staff exists or a position involved in the execution of minor policies and programs. But it must be recognized that the tendency to quickly appoint a loyal face who is nearby rather than engage in a vigorous new search for the best executive talent available for the specific position under consideration is almost certain to result in the selection of someone who meets an "acceptable" standard, rather than a "best available" one. The federal departments and agencies, as well as the American people in general, deserve better.

Whatever process is used by an incoming presidential administration for the selection of its civilian leadership, the result matters greatly, especially for the departments and agencies that are responsible for the nation's security. No matter what may be said about political loyalty to the new president—and that is not entirely inconsequential—an administration's success or failure will depend in very great part upon the quality of its senior political appointees.

Chapter Four

Politics and Unqualified Civilian Leaders

When it comes to selecting the top leadership of the executive departments and agencies in our national government . . . we abandon essentially all professional standards. We accept the rather mindless notion that any bright and public-spirited citizen can run a government agency, bureau, or office.
—David M. Cohen, former senior civil servant, 1996

Many of those who want to rush the country into war and think it would be so quick and easy, don't know anything about war. They come at it from an intellectual perspective versus having sat in jungles or foxholes and watch their friends get their heads blown off.
—Senator Chuck Hagel (R-NE), September 2002

Andrew Oliver (1706–1774), was a merchant and public official in colonial Massachusetts. He was one of the founders of the American Academy of Arts and Sciences. Upon his graduation from Harvard College, he decided to enter politics. He enjoyed considerable success, and when he died he was serving as lieutenant governor of the colony. In 1765, he accepted a commission to do what appeared to involve no more than a proper enforcement of the law. Unfortunately, the law was the unpopular Stamp Act. He was personally against the act, but felt it was his duty to administer it. After being hanged in effigy from Boston's Liberty Tree, his home was ransacked by an angry crowd and he was compelled to resign his commission. Despite his anxieties about his chosen work, Oliver said this in an address delivered in Boston in 1774:

Politics is the most hazardous of all professions. There is no other in which a man can hope to do so much good to his fellow creatures—and neither is there any in which, by a mere loss of nerve, he may do as widespread harm. There is not another in which he may so easily lose his own soul, nor is there another in which a positive and strict veracity is so difficult. But danger is the inseparable companion of honor. With all the temptations and degradations that beset it, politics is still the noblest career any man can choose. [1]

The biographer of the legendary U.S. Court of Appeals judge Learned Hand has written that during America's Gilded Age, the fashionable attitude about politics in many circles was one of distance and aloof contempt: "Politicians were a distant world of crude climbers . . . scrambling for petty spoils; principles seemed remote from party divisions, where the issues apparently did not go much beyond battles between the ins and outs." [2] Winston Churchill, who made his first foray into politics just as the Gilded Age was coming to a close, had a realistic view of the bruising aspects of it, but he also recognized how much better it was as a method of governance than the systems of the past.

> There are . . . some who will be inclined to think that no element of the heroic enters into [political] conflicts, and that political triumphs are necessarily tarnished by vulgar methods. The noise and confusion of the election crowds; the cant phrases and formula; the burrowings of rival caucuses, fell with weariness and even terror persons of . . . exquisite sensibility. It is easy for those who take no part in the public duties of citizenship to sniff disdainfully at the methods of modern politics. But, it is a poor part to play. Amid the dust and brawling with rude weapons and often an unworthy champion, a real battle for a real and precious object is swaying to and fro. Better for the clamor of popular disputation with all of its most blatant accessories hammering from month to month and year to year the labored progress of the common people in a work-a-day world, than the poetic tragedies and violence of the chivalric ages. [3]

A former member of the U.S. Senate has asserted—I believe correctly—that politics is a noble endeavor, but "only if it is about public service." [4] In the case of political appointees, the motivation of the appointee is very important. Did he accept the appointment in order to make a positive, demonstrable impact upon the work of the department or agency to which he was appointed, or was he primarily interested in the perks of office, in being addressed as "Mr. Secretary," in padding his resume, or in making new contacts before a quick return to private pursuits? Recent evidence suggests that the political appointment process may attract people who are motivated more by personal rewards than by the intrinsic value of public service. [5] Even if a potential appointee's motives for seeking a particular appointment are pure, he should not be nominated unless he is demonstrably the best qualified by both skill and experience for the position he seeks. Thus, the foundation question for all appointing officials must always be this: Have I selected the right person for the right position for the right reason? In other words, fit matters—a great deal!

In the best sense of the word, the contributions to the public good of political appointees are often incalculable. Some, like General of the Army George C. Marshall, have already established international reputations in military uniform and continue their service to the nation with great distinction. After being called the "true organizer of victory" in World War II by Winston Churchill, Marshall went on to serve as secretary of state and secretary of defense. He is the only general to be awarded the Nobel Peace Prize. Many other appointees enter office from the pinnacles of executive careers outside of government. They often bring great skills and experience to their office and make great professional and personal sacrifices in order to serve. One of the best examples of this type of public servant was David Packard. Before he was appointed deputy secretary of defense in 1969, he had founded and served as chairman of the board and chief executive officer of Hewlett-Packard Company, then the world's largest producer of electronic testing and measurement devices, and a major producer of computers, calculators, and other electronic equipment. Long after he left office, Packard continued to serve as an advisor to the White House on defense procurement. He also chaired the president's Blue Ribbon Commission on Defense Management (the "Packard Commission") in the 1980s. Whatever their previous experiences, many political appointees bring great leadership and performance-enhancing skills and influence to their new public office. It has been correctly observed that they can "improve agency performance by counteracting inertia, bringing energy and vision, and introducing new and useful information into a stale and insular decision-making environment."[6]

In theory, presidents should seek to appoint cabinet members, especially those responsible for the nation's security (such as the secretaries of defense, state, and homeland security, and the attorney general), who are of high quality, who have experience in the work of the department or agency that they will lead, who have successfully led a large, complex organization, and who have independent national stature. Senior subcabinet officials should also be of high quality and possess substantial experience in the kind of work that their more narrowly focused responsibilities will entail. In theory, and in order to take advantage of the talent located all over the nation, new senior political appointees should not be part of the revolving door in Washington, D.C., between governing and lobbying; they should serve for a period of time sufficient to make significant contributions to the work of the government, and then return to the private sector in their home states. In theory, the professional credentials of these senior appointees should be so obvious (and perhaps so unique) and they should have been so thoroughly vetted that the only real purpose of their confirmation hearings is the solicitation of their views on policy issues.

In practice, the results are usually much different. In a public lecture in 1963, President Kennedy's special counsel pointed out what we have always known—namely, that a typical cabinet member is "not necessarily selected for the President's confidence in his judgment alone—considerations of politics, geography, public esteem, and interest group pressures" also play a role.[7] Our history has many examples of political appointees who have been selected without proper vetting, without important relevant experience, or for indefensible reasons. Three will suffice for illustrative purposes. In selecting his even younger and inexperienced brother to be United States attorney general, a young, flippant, new American president might jokingly say, "I can't see that it's wrong to give him a little legal experience before he goes out to practice law," but the attempt at humor could not erase the fact that the nominee had very few professional credentials and would have never been confirmed had he not been the president's brother or had the Senate been controlled by the opposition party.[8] President George W. Bush's announcement on December 3, 2004, of his nomination of Bernard Kerik as secretary of homeland security was even less defensible. A week after the announcement, Kerik's nomination was withdrawn. A thorough vetting of the nominee would have disclosed several confirmation-defeating incidents and major reasons not to make the nomination.[9]

President Obama's choice for the Pentagon's second-highest executive office involved a different kind of problem. During the almost two years of the 2008 presidential campaign, Obama repeatedly promised that, if elected, he would clean up the way Washington works and stop the way in which "our leaders have thrown open the doors of Congress and the White House to an army of Washington lobbyists who have turned our government into a game only they can afford to play." He vowed to "close the revolving door" that permits lobbyists to go to work for the federal government and oversee contracts that could help—or harm—their former employer.[10] One of the first things he did after his inauguration was to sign an executive order barring former lobbyists from joining his administration to work at the departments or agencies they recently lobbied.

And yet, only a few days after signing the executive order, and at the request of Secretary of Defense Gates, Obama issued a waiver that permitted William Lynn, the top lobbyist for Raytheon, a multibillion-dollar-a-year defense contractor, to be nominated as the deputy secretary of defense.[11] The nominee was known in some circles as "the Granddaddy of lobbyists," but with a straight face the administration made the bogus argument that he was "uniquely qualified," overlooking the obvious fact that almost any business executive of a large company has more management experience than a lobbyist. In testimony before the Senate Armed Services Committee, Gates argued indirectly for the nomination saying that the federal ethics rules have "created a situation in which it is harder and harder for people who have served in industry, who understand the acquisition business, who understand systems management to come into the public service."[12] In addition to illustrating his ignorance of industry generally, Gates's suggestion that Lynn was somehow indispensable looked silly only two and a half years later. In July 2011, only a week after Gates left the Pentagon, Lynn announced his own resignation. It was reported that he had "seemed to struggle to find his place in the Pentagon under . . . Gates," that "Gates tended to turn to his chief of staff . . . to lead the most important initiatives, like finding efficiencies in the defense budget," and that "Lynn got cut out of a lot of the action."[13]

More often than not, presidents have been less interested in the quality and effectiveness of their senior appointees within a department or agency than in whether or not they are responsive to his control and political needs. This is not to say that presidents do not care about policy outcomes. They usually do, "either because they inherently prefer a specific public policy or because their policy choices influence how voters and historians perceive them."[14] Presidents are also politically risk averse and are anxious to ensure that mistakes, particularly extreme mistakes by their senior appointees, are minimized.[15] But since they need to ensure bureaucratic responsiveness and generate support for their programs, policies, and reelection through the distribution of patronage, presidents are usually willing to trade competence in their senior appointments in order to have appointees who can control their agencies and get them to do the president's bidding.[16]

There is, of course, considerable truth in allegations that the modern bureaucratic state poses problems of inertia and resistance to some policy initiatives by political leaders. Henry Kissinger has written of these problems. "[A] large bureaucracy," he believes, "however organized, tends to stifle creativity. It confuses wise policy with smooth administration. . . . A complex bureaucracy has an incentive to exaggerate technical complexity and minimize the scope or importance of political judgment; it favors the status quo, however arrived at, because short of an unambiguous catastrophe the status quo has the advantage of familiarity and it is never possible to prove that another course would yield superior results."[17] Nevertheless, loyalty to the president is not the same thing as competence in leadership and management. All are vital to a successful implementation of administration policy.

The subject of the quality of political appointees has been receiving increased attention in recent years. A pointed reminder of its importance was made in a think tank paper prepared in 1996 by a former career senior executive in the federal government. "We are a society obsessed with credentials," the author of the paper wrote. "We demand board certifications for our professionals and licenses for just about everything, from plumbers to day care providers. In addition to formal training and degrees, we also expect demonstrated experience and the testimonials of satisfied clients and customers. Yet," the author added, "when it comes to selecting the top leadership of the executive departments and agencies in our national government—including not only cabinet secretaries and agency administrators but also the many hundreds who head the next two or three organizational echelons—we abandon essentially all professional standards. We accept the rather mindless notion that any bright and public-spirited citizen can run a government agency, bureau, or office."[18]

The federal government employs more than four million people, purchases more than half a trillion dollars each year in goods and services, and occupies more than one billion square feet of office space.[19] Successful leaders of such an organization must necessarily possess unusual leadership, management, and administrative experience. Some political appointees have technical or program policy expertise, but no experience in *executing* policy, in designing and effectively carrying out new programs, in implementing key legislation, or in delivering services. "Most appointees are rank amateurs in administering large organizations and budgets, supervising people, and *executing* (as contrasted with developing or promoting) policy."[20] Too many lack the management and operational experience, intellectual skills, substantive technical or other relevant experience, working networks, and political and interpersonal skills that facilitate public management and that the positions to which they have been appointed require. Too many are nothing more than politically connected neophytes—that is, young congressional staffers, lobbyists, academics, presidential campaign workers, and aides to more senior appointees—as opposed to leaders and managers with demonstrated competence in getting things done.

In asserting that good management skills are essential for government jobs, a former director of research and engineering in the Department of Defense has argued the obvious, saying that presidential appointees should be accomplished in something more "than working the Washington political system." He has suggested that candidates for senior defense positions should think about the following questions: "Have you managed a budget? Have you run an organization, been a university president, run a company? Can you fire somebody? Can you do the things that a manager has to do?"[21]

In February 2000, the Committee on Government Affairs of the U.S. House of Representatives expressed concern that too many political appointees in the executive branch lacked "the requisite leadership and management skills and background to successfully address the challenges facing federal agencies."[22] In an effort to address the problem, the Government Accountability Office prepared a list of questions on selected leadership and management issues, and it suggested that "if the Senate asks these questions as part of the confirmation process, then future Presidents may place added importance on ensuring that nominees have the requisite leadership and management experience for their positions before submitting their names to the Senate for confirmation."[23] It is not clear that the questions have ever been asked, much less on a regular basis.

Three years later, these concerns were the subject of the Final Report of the National Commission on the Public Service. In the January 7, 2003, report, the commission declared, "Something . . . alarming has . . . happened over the last 50 years. Trust in Government has eroded. Government's responsiveness, its efficiency, and too often its honesty, are broadly challenged as we enter the new century. The bonds between our citizens and our public servants, essential to democratic government, are frayed even as the responsibilities of government at home and abroad have increased."[24] In general, the government was "not performing nearly as well as it can or should."[25] Recent opinion polling had found "strong relationships between negative perceptions of the performance of government and distrust of government."[26] One of the commission's main recommendations was that executive departments should be run by managers chosen for their operational skills. "Of particular importance," it said, "is that managers . . . have the appropriate experience, training, and skills to manage effectively."[27]

The administration of President George W. Bush initiated what has been described as the most ambitious attempt in history to measure the quality of the management of federal programs. The Office of Management and Budget designed and publicly vetted a series of measures with which program management was assessed: "They settled on a definition of the components of good management and they adjusted the measures . . . to be applicable across programs."[28] Two scholars subsequently used the resulting grades to compare the quality of management of federal programs by political appointees with that of career managers from the Senior Executive Service. They found that programs managed by political appointees performed significantly worse in all but one category of management grades, and in that one, there was no significant difference.[29]

More recent studies have confirmed both a lack of confidence in government and some of the main reasons for it. In late 2007 and early 2008, a survey was taken of the fellows of the National Academy of Public Administration (NAPA). NAPA is a nonprofit coalition of distinguished leaders and public management experts who provide independent and qualified counsel to government. The issue in the survey was the federal government's ability to execute programs and policies. Approximately 68 percent of those surveyed perceived the government as less likely to successfully execute projects today than at any time in the past. According to the respondents, one of the primary reasons is the lack of effective political leadership.[30]

A separate survey was taken in March and April 2008 of the membership of the government's own Senior Executive Service. The same issue was addressed. Some 76 percent of the respondents said that the federal government's image has deteriorated in the past three decades. Approximately half of them deemed the government to be less capable at the time of the survey than ten years earlier. Once again, the lack of effective political leadership was identified as a primary factor.[31] Three years later, nothing had improved. On March 15, 2011, the results of a new *Washington Post*–ABC News poll were announced. Only 26 percent of Americans said that they were optimistic about "our system of government and how well it works," a low point in the polls dating back to 1974.

It is useful at this point to consider the broad differences between the necessary *leadership* abilities of senior political appointees, and their *management* abilities. There is no better place to start than a lecture delivered to the Adelaide Division of the Australian Institute of Management in 1957. The speaker was the governor-general of Australia, the former British field marshal Sir William Slim, the famous victor in the Burma campaign in World War II. He introduced his subject by observing, "The problems met at the top of any great organization, whether military or civilian, are basically the same—questions of organization, transportation, equipment, resources, *the selection of men for jobs*, the use of experts, and above all and through all, human relations."

Slim conceded that military units prefer to speak of leadership, rather than management, and he saw a distinct difference in the two activities. "The leader and the men who follow him," he said, "represent one of the oldest, most natural and most effective of all human relationships. The manager and those he manages are a later product, with neither so romantic nor so inspiring a history. Leadership is of the spirit, compounded of personality and vision; its practice is an art. Management is of the mind, more a matter of accurate calculation, of statistics, of methods, timetables and routine; its practice is a science. Managers are necessary; leaders are essential. A good system will produce efficient managers, but more than that is needed. We must find managers who are not only skilled organizers, but inspired and inspiring leaders." More recently, U.S. Army leaders have declared, "Management has to do with an organization's *processes*—performing them correctly and efficiently; leadership has to do with our organization's *purposes*."[32]

Successful civilian leaders often exercise leadership traits that are different from those exercised by military leaders, but the objective remains to get things done. An excellent example is the conduct of Winston Churchill after he became prime minister on May 10, 1940. His biographer has described the effect of that conduct. "The British civil service," he wrote, "has a long tradition of being imperious and of outmaneuvering, ignoring, and sometimes sabotaging appointed ministers. Everything changed starting on May 11, 1940. The Whitehall bureaucrats had never encountered a man quite like Churchill, and the shock was sudden and intense. The days of peacetime nine-to-five work hours evaporated almost overnight. . . . They were replaced by a virtual frenzy of intensity, electricity that shot through the entire spectrum of a government bureaucracy used to doing business in a slow-paced manner."[33]

As we shall see in chapter 7, the armed conflicts in Iraq and Afghanistan have stimulated fresh thinking among military leaders about the kind of leadership traits that are required for success in the Armed Forces. Such personal factors as discipline and team building skills will always be required, but in a security environment in which leaders must regularly navigate in ambiguous, high-risk situations, such traits as adaptability, agility, integrity, communication skills, mental toughness, resilience, and what General David Petraeus has called "sheer professional expertise"[34] are now more important than ever. In an era in which military forces will be involved in homeland security efforts and are likely to be engaged in a series of protracted foreign conflicts that include many of the elements of nation building and humanitarian efforts, as well as war fighting, old leadership styles and traditional competencies will not be sufficient. The complexity of the security challenges will necessarily require leaders to follow the advice of former Coast Guard commandant, Admiral Thad Allen, to "lead from everywhere."[35]

Americans have long recognized that military leaders have skills that are of great value outside the strict confines of the Armed Forces. A study by the executive search firm Korn/Ferry in 2005 found that while former military officers constitute only 3 percent of the U.S. adult male population, they make up about three times that of the CEOs of S&P 500 firms.[36] In recent years, business leaders have increasingly recognized that in several ways, military leaders even provide a model for business leaders. The editor in chief of the *Harvard Business Review*, for example, has noted that "leaders in both spheres must deal with a world of 24/7 information and public scrutiny, cope with perpetual ambiguity, and adjust to ever-changing goals."[37]

Even junior military officers command respect. Competition for them among business recruiters has become fierce in recent years. General Petraeus has explained their appeal. "Tell me anywhere in the business world where a 22- or 23-year-old is responsible for 35 or 40 other individuals on missions that involve life or death," he said to *Fortune* magazine. "Their tactical actions can have strategic implications for the overall mission. And they're under enormous scrutiny, on top of everything else. These are pretty formative experiences. It's a bit of a crucible-like experience that they go through."[38] That kind of under-fire judgment experience, the ability to make fast and effective decisions after working long hours in difficult conditions and intense circumstances, has caused several companies to create elite management programs specifically designed to attract young lieutenants and captains. According to a senior recruiting manager at Walmart, "The thinking was that we could bring in world-class leadership talent that was already trained and ready to go. And then we could teach them retail."[39]

The director of the Center for Leadership and Change Management at the University of Pennsylvania's Wharton School has observed that the Armed Forces have been developing leaders much longer than the corporate world and that military officers are trained "in ways that build a culture of readiness and commitment."[40] For that reason, he and his colleagues incorporate military leadership principles into Wharton's MBA and Executive MBA programs. One of the most important leadership precepts to be taught is that of mission focus: "Mission must come first, self-interest last."[41] This idea is, of course, directly contrary to the motivational impulses of those political appointees who seek public office solely, or even primarily, for personal rewards.

Clearly, there are many differences between the kind of leadership that must be exercised by those in military uniform and that which must be exercised by political appointees. But there are also many similarities. In an era in which military forces are likely to be engaged in a series of protracted conflicts that include many of the elements of nation building and humanitarian efforts, as well as war fighting, the similarities will almost certainly increase. The first activity—uniquely civilian in nature—involves creating or strengthening government institutions and the commercial and other infrastructure of countries. Like humanitarian activities, it may include everything from providing electricity and building hospitals to keeping banks solvent. One need only think of Afghanistan and the January 2010 earthquake in Haiti to understand.

It is also civilian leaders who will provide counsel in the future and/or ultimately decide in which armed conflicts or other crises America will shed its blood and spend its treasure. It is civilian leaders who have to educate and persuade their countrymen on the question of why such sacrifices are necessary. It is civilians who must lead the execution and implementation of the complex, expensive, and very important policies and programs mandated by Congress or directed by the president. It is civilians who must demonstrate the kind of wisdom that comes only from relevant experience and who must command the respect of military leaders and other uniformed personnel upon whom the success of any defense policy, program, or operational mission ultimately depends.

In performing their duties, civilian leaders work continuously with military professionals who have spent a career preparing for their current and future responsibilities. These professionals are products of the best leadership development program in the world. They are highly educated. They have years of operational experience. They have worked under intense conditions. They understand that no plan survives the first contact with the enemy and that matters of national security are, more often than not, messy and uncertain.

Members of the uniformed services do not expect senior civilian leaders to be masters of the details of all activities for which they are technically responsible. Indeed, as we shall see below, some civilian leaders have few leadership or management responsibilities and are almost exclusively in the policy formulation business. Nevertheless, the civilian and military personnel who must implement policies and execute operational activities expect their civilian leaders to be very knowledgeable and realistic about their work. They also expect—and have a right to expect—that civilian leaders have moral courage, the judgment to make hard but correct decisions, integrity, and a desire to place mission first and self-interest last.

A civilian leader's method of operation or his failure to act may be as important as his actions. Donald Rumsfeld's brusque and sometimes abrasive management style often alienated senior military leaders and even other cabinet members and White House staffers. But it was his treatment of retiring Army Chief of Staff General Eric Shinseki that burned the last of his communication bridges among military leaders. Several reasons have been offered as to why Rumsfeld disliked Shinseki.[42] General Hugh Shelton, then chairman of the Joint Chiefs of Staff, would later accuse Rumsfeld of a general "antimilitary bias."[43] But there is little doubt that a primary reason was Shinseki's answer in late February 2003 to a question at a congressional hearing. When asked by a member of the Senate Armed Services Committee to give "some idea as to the magnitude of the army's force requirement for an occupation of Iraq following a successful completion of the war," Shinseki replied that "something on the order of several hundred thousand soldiers" would be about right.[44] That estimate was considerably higher than the one supported by Rumsfeld, and Paul Wolfowitz, his deputy, immediately rejected it. After being effectively ignored for the remaining three months of his tenure as chief of staff, Shinseki retired in a large ceremony at Fort Myer on June 11. Neither Rumsfeld nor Wolfowitz were in attendance. It was later described as "an extraordinary situation: While the nation was at war and American soldiers were dying, the Pentagon's top civilians were estranged from the Army's leadership."[45]

The causes of the estrangement were less important to tens of thousands of people in military uniform than was the obvious insult. Whatever may have been said of the policy dispute, the facts were that Shinseki had completed a very distinguished career of thirty-eight years; that he had been wounded three times in combat, the last time losing half of his right foot to a land mine; and that while Rumsfeld was pursuing a career in politics and earning millions in his business career, Shinseki and his family were being uprooted every few years to move from one military posting to another and making other sacrifices. Rumsfeld's failure to appear at the retirement ceremony would be compared very unfavorably to the conduct of his successor as secretary at the retirement ceremony for General Stanley McChrystal.[46] Even President Bush would later call Rumsfeld's absence from Shinseki's retirement ceremony "a mistake."[47]

Sometimes, people who appear to have good qualifications on paper for service as a senior political appointee, turn out to be major disappointments. In July 2011, a senior Obama appointee was the subject of an investigation by the inspector general of the Department of Labor. The assistant secretary of labor who was responsible for that department's Veterans' Employment and Training Service had come under scrutiny at the request of Senator Claire McCaskill (D-MO) and as a result of allegations of misconduct by whistleblowers within the program. After an internal investigation found that he had steered federal contracts to friends and former colleagues and used his position to coerce or intimidate employees to make the awards without open competition, all in violation of federal procurement rules and ethics principles, he resigned. Senator McCaskill was quoted as saying, "I would challenge anybody to look at his resume and not be impressed."[48] It may be wondered whether, at the time of his confirmation hearing, it ever occurred to her or any other member of the Senate to look beyond the resume.

The too often poor quality of appointed political leaders is not limited to those who are appointed to positions that require strong management skills and leadership experience. Many senior appointees are placed in positions that are almost exclusively policy making and planning in nature. Unfortunately, in the same way that the British aristocracy of the Victorian era was unable to provide uniformly able military leaders, the American political appointee "aristocracy" has been unable to provide uniformly able national security and homeland security policy makers. This has been especially true when appointed policy makers have had no practical operational experience in military uniform or otherwise. Too often, strategic or even operational theories of senior civilian officials have not been informed, much less tempered, by personal experience. Having no idea what an operation looks or feels like, they adopt unrealistic expectations for the scope of a mission and the human beings who must carry it out. Having never personally experienced the difficulty of executing a plan with many variables, they don't fully appreciate the wisdom of Prussian Field Marshal von Moltke's observation: "No plan of operations extends with certainty beyond the first encounter with the enemy's main strength." The problem is exacerbated considerably when a civilian official's arrogance prevents him from open-minded reconsideration of his theories. In this context, it is informative to reflect upon our recent experience in the war in Iraq.

One does not have to be a student of the history of civilian-military relations to recognize that in democracies, it is the role of military leaders to advise on operational matters, on how wars should be waged, and to evaluate the nature and severity of the risks associated with a proposed course of action. In addition to the management of large, complex defense programs, it is the role of civilian leaders to decide what risks to accept and whether to proceed with a recommended action. In most cases, although most certainly less so now than in previous decades, civilian leaders are likely to have a better understanding of the political context and stakes involved in decisions of whether or not to engage in an armed conflict.

In the run-up to the war in Iraq, a public debate arose between those who were skeptical about the wisdom of a military intervention there, or actually opposed to the idea, and those who were aggressively promoting it. The former group included several combat veterans, some retired military leaders, and many of President Bush's political opponents. The latter group consisted of several administration officials or policy advisors, almost all of whom were members of the "neoconservative" movement,[49] many of whom had never served in military uniform. For their lack of military service, they were sometimes disparagingly referred to as "Chickenhawks."[50] They included Paul Wolfowitz, the deputy secretary of defense; Douglas Feith, the undersecretary for policy; Richard Perle, a former assistant secretary of defense in the Reagan administration and chairman of the Defense Policy Board in the Bush administration; and several others.

Republican senator Chuck Hagel, a combat veteran of the war in Vietnam, gave voice to the doubts and frustration of the skeptics. Declaring, "You can take the country into war pretty fast, but you can't get out as quickly—and the public needs to know what the risks are," he added, "Maybe Mr. Perle would like to be in the first wave of those who go into Baghdad."[51] He was subsequently more pointed in his criticism of the policymaking officials who had no military experience. "Many of those who want to rush the country into war and think it would be so quick and easy," he said, "don't know anything about war. They come at it from an intellectual perspective versus having sat in jungles or foxholes and watch their friends get their heads blown off."[52]

Predictably, the Chickenhawks and their policy allies struck back. Conceding that "there is a large moral difference between those who served and those who deliberately evaded the draft," a respected scholar argued nevertheless that this "does not translate into a difference in strategic insight," that "in matters of war and peace veterans should receive no special consideration for their views," and that being a veteran "is no guarantee of strategic wisdom."[53] This argument, however, creates an unnecessary straw man and misses the point. There are few guarantees of any kind of wisdom, especially in politics. And it is usually easy to find historical exceptions to principles described as inviolate. Moreover, it cannot be reasonably argued that a former sergeant in the army's Signal Corps or a former navy quartermaster will not necessarily have greater strategic wisdom than former academics or corporate executives who never served.

But these are extreme examples. In making senior political appointments, presidents should deal with real-world probabilities, not extreme exceptions to general rules. One does not have to be a Fitzroy Maclean[54] to recognize that it is more probable than not that a political appointee who has had personal experience in the planning or execution of complex operational matters, whether in military uniform or not, will be better qualified to make judgments on other complex operational matters than someone who has merely thought about them conceptually or written about them. Someone who knows firsthand the inevitability of changed circumstances, who understands from experience that any plan is only as good as each of the underlying assumptions upon which it is based, who knows the humility of having to deal with plans gone awry—that person is better qualified to engage in the formulation of policies and the planning of complex operations than is someone who has not had such experience. It is more probable than not that an appointee who has personally experienced military service and the important and unique cultural elements of such service is better qualified to deal with important manpower and personnel issues in the Armed Forces than someone who has not. Whether academics recognize these facts is immaterial. The people in uniform who will be affected by a civilian leader's actions do. A recent example is illustrative.

When President George W. Bush appointed Douglas Feith as the undersecretary of defense for policy, the third-most-senior position within DoD, he appointed someone who had good credentials of a sort, but not the right ones for the position to which he had been appointed. A Harvard graduate with a law degree from Georgetown University, Feith had spent his entire career in law or political appointments in Washington, D.C., and was part of the political appointee aristocracy. But he had no operational, management, or leadership experience whatsoever. He had never served in the Armed Forces, he had never led any kind of large organization, and he had never served in any kind of significant executive capacity.

Within months of his appointment, Feith's own staff found it necessary to confront him on his management flaws. One aide said it was the worst policy office she had ever seen. Another said that the decision-making process in

Feith's office was the worst he had seen in twenty years of government work.[55] Feith would later be described as a "management disaster who served as a bottleneck on decision-making and as a theorist whose ideas were often impractical."[56] Nevertheless, in the months following 9/11, when defense leaders started planning for a war in Iraq, Feith was placed in charge of policy for the post-combat period. It was his job to plan for and oversee almost all aspects of the postwar reconstruction of a nation on the other side of the world, whose history, culture, politics, traditions, and anticipated needs are as different from America's as night is from day.

From the beginning, Feith was not popular with military leaders. One who has written about that period has said that he appeared "to equate policy with paper."[57] While he was hardly an impartial observer, Army General Tommy Franks, the commander of U.S. Central Command who was responsible for the combat operations, told his staff that Feith had a reputation as the "dumbest f— guy on the planet."[58] Retired lieutenant general Jay Gardner, who later reported to Feith for five months as the Bush administration's first head of the postwar mission in Iraq, would say that Feith was incredibly dangerous. "He's a very smart guy whose electrons aren't connected, so he arc lights all the time. He can't organize anything."[59] The then chairman of the Joint Chiefs of Staff later referred to him as a "henchman" of Rumsfeld.[60] The selection of Feith for the responsibilities he was given had almost incalculable consequences. Autobiographies are not known for their objectivity, but in admitting to a "major error," even Feith has summarized in a single sentence the failures in planning that led to the high cost in blood and treasure in Iraq over several subsequent years: "The crippling disorder we call the insurgency was *not* anticipated."[61]

In August 2010, after seven years of war in Iraq and more than forty-four hundred American combat fatalities and almost thirty-two thousand wounded casualties, the final U.S. combat brigade left the country. Some fifty thousand troops remained to train Iraqi security forces and to support Iraqi counterterrorism efforts.

A personal trait that is essential for all senior officials is one that too rarely makes its presence felt in political circles within the federal government: accountability. Blatant corruption by political appointees is not the issue here. Rather, I refer to the common tendency to avoid individual responsibility when things go wrong. Far too often, appointees deny responsibility or attempt to shift blame to their political opponents, to another individual, or to circumstances beyond their control, such as a once-in-a-hundred-years flood. When bureaucratic delays in outpatient care and the moldy, cockroach-infested facilities for housing the wounded at Walter Reed

Hospital became public in early 2007, for example, the secretary of the army appeared to be much more interested in attacking the perceived unfairness of the news coverage of the deficiencies than the problem itself. He was promptly fired, but his termination was a rarity. Disciplinary measures against political appointees are almost unheard of unless they cause embarrassment to the appointing administration and a scapegoat must be found. Perhaps the lack of accountability among his political masters is what motivated French Marshal Joffre's response to a questioner long after the victory through which he had saved France in 1914 had been fought. "I don't know who won the Battle of the Marne," he said. "But had it been lost, I know who they would say lost it."

It has not escaped the attention of men and women in uniform that the most senior civilian leaders of the government, whether in the executive branch or the legislative branch, almost always escape accountability for their conduct. When, for example, then commander in chief Bill Clinton engaged in sexual misconduct with a White House intern, his wife Hillary vaguely blamed initial reports of the incidents on some "vast right-wing conspiracy" that was purportedly trying to destroy Clinton. Although Clinton later admitted that his actions were "damaging to the presidency and the American people,"[62] he continued his effort to escape accountability by placing blame on what he called the "power lust" of his accusers. And who can forget Democratic senator Robert Byrd of West Virginia declaring on the floor of the Senate that, in connection with the Monica Lewinsky affair, Clinton had "plainly lied to the American people" and that he had "also lied under oath in judicial proceedings," but that those offenses did not constitute an abuse or violation of some public trust?[63] In Clinton's impeachment trial, Byrd voted not to convict.

The conduct of former senator Joe Biden provides another example. On the third day of the 1987 confirmation hearing by the Senate Judiciary Committee on the nomination of Judge Robert Bork to the U.S. Supreme Court, Biden, then chairman of the committee, admitted that he had plagiarized a law review article for a paper he had written in law school.[64] Further investigation revealed that Biden had also "borrowed" words from a speech that had been given by British Labour Party leader Neil Kinnock, who had run unsuccessfully against Prime Minister Margaret Thatcher. It would later be reported that Biden had not just "borrowed" boilerplate political phrases. A *New York Times* reporter wrote that Biden had "lifted Mr. Kinnock's . . . speech with phrases, gestures, and typical Welch syntax intact."[65] He also has a history of what his biographer has soothingly called "shaded or stretched facts."[66] Others have not been so charitable. One journalist has written that "the sheer number and extent of Biden's fibs, distortions, and plagiarisms struck many observers at the time as worrisome."[67] His reputation for stretched facts remained an issue as recently as the 2008 presidential election. When then Senator Obama was considering Biden as his running mate, a factor in the decision-making process was the fact that Biden had, in the words of Obama's campaign manager, "a history of coloring outside the lines a bit."[68] This proved to be no deterrent to his selection. On January 20, 2009, he became the vice president of the United States.

A more recent example is the story of the former chairman of the powerful House Ways and Means Committee, New York Democratic Representative Charlie Rangel. In late 2010, the House Ethics Committee, chaired by a fellow Democrat, concluded that Rangel, an expert in tax law and spending procedures, had not paid taxes for seventeen years on property he owned in the Dominican Republic. The committee further concluded that he had accumulated more than $500,000 in unreported financial assets and that he had raised "millions" of dollars for the Rangel Center at City College of New York "from corporations that did business before his Ways and Means Committee."[69] Some 333 members of the House voted to formally censure Rangel. Only 79 opposed the move. Nevertheless, Rangel blamed a conservative ethics group and his former chief of staff.

It is one thing when strict standards of accountability are not applied to the private lives of civilian leaders. It is quite another thing when civilian officials escape accountability for major failures in the performance of their public duties. On December 21, 2010, and while the U.S. was struggling to fully emerge from the devastating global recession of 2008 and 2009 and fight wars in Afghanistan and Iraq, the U.S. Government Accountability Office (GAO) announced that for the fourteenth consecutive year it could not render an opinion on the consolidated financial statements of the federal government. Once again, one of the primary obstacles to a GAO opinion were the "serious financial management problems at the Department of Defense that made its financial statements unauditable." In a report of its examination of DoD, the GAO described the Pentagon's financial management problems as "pervasive and long standing." Among the "widespread material internal control" failures cited, the GAO said, "As in past years, DoD did not maintain adequate systems or have sufficient records to provide reliable information" on either the existence or the condition of assets.

In mid-2011, another financial problem made the news—again. The 2008 Defense Authorization Act had directed the Pentagon to find out how many private contractors it employs by creating an annual inventory of the number of people working for DoD under service contracts. Three years later, DoD had not complied with the law. The Pentagon comptroller only said that the matter was very complicated.

If the auditors of a publicly held U.S. corporation issued statements like those issued by the GAO regarding the Department of Defense, regulators from the Securities and Exchange Commission would immediately check to see what corrective action was being taken by the company and what information about the problems was being given to shareholders. Shareholders would be outraged by the almost inevitable decline in the value of their investments. It would not take long for the heads of senior company officers to roll. If a private company failed to comply with the law, lawyers from the Justice Department would be all over the matter in an effort to determine what civil or criminal sanctions were appropriate.

Unfortunately, despite the fact that the Defense Department was then receiving well over $500 billion per year from American taxpayers, or some 15 percent of all U.S. expenditures; despite the fact that when the current deputy secretary of defense was selected after the 2008 election, a well-connected Democrat in defense circles had described the position as one "for someone who understands the budget and can manage the bureaucracy";[70] and despite the fact that the deputy secretary of defense had previously served for several years as the DoD comptroller, one looked in vain for any announcement that the deputy secretary and/or the current undersecretary of defense (comptroller) had resigned or been terminated.

A much less egregious example of a situation in which civilian accountability was not as present as it should have been was one that I personally observed. On the hot afternoon of Sunday, July 3, 1988, I drove to the Pentagon after church to prepare for matters with which I would have to deal during the next week. When I parked my car just outside the river entrance to the building, I noticed an unusual number of other cars in the lot. As soon as I entered the building, I learned that a few hours earlier, the navy's guided missile cruiser USS *Vincennes* had accidentally shot down an Iranian civilian airliner over the Strait of Hormuz, mistaking it for an attacking military aircraft. At the time of the incident, the aircraft was within Iranian airspace. All 290 passengers and crew members, including 66 children, had been killed.

To their collective credit, Secretary of Defense Frank Carlucci and Admiral Bill Crowe, the chairman of the Joint Chiefs of Staff, urged immediate public disclosure of the incident. When President Reagan agreed, an announcement was promptly scheduled for the Pentagon News Room. It had been assumed that, as the senior defense official, Carlucci would face the media with the grim news. But the senior DoD public affairs official believed that the secretary should not be the one to announce it. It fell to Crowe to endure the painful grilling of the press. To his credit, the public affairs official (a colleague of mine) later told Crowe that of all the things he had done in the Pentagon, "the decision not to let Carlucci make the announcement was his most serious mistake."[71]

A good and very rare example of a civilian leader accepting responsibility for failures not directly attributable to his personal conduct comes quickly to my mind. The leader was an English politician. Throughout the first months of 1982, tensions were increasing between Argentina and Great Britain in the ongoing dispute over the sovereignty of the Falkland Islands, an archipelago in the South Atlantic Ocean located approximately 250 nautical miles from the coast of mainland South America. Britain had ruled the islands since 1833 and the islanders had consistently rejected Argentina's claims. On August 2, Argentine military forces invaded the islands. Three days later, Lord Peter Carrington, the British foreign secretary, resigned. He later wrote that "it was not a sense of culpability" that led him to resign. Rather, with the nation feeling that it had been disgraced, "someone must have been to blame. The disgrace [had to] be purged. The person to purge it should be the minister in charge. That was me."[72] An appointee with that kind of honor was properly recognized as invaluable. He subsequently served with distinction as the secretary-general of NATO.

Normally, the circumstances that call for individual accountability are less dramatic than these examples. Perhaps the issue is who should testify before a hostile committee of Congress on a matter involving an operational failure. Even if a bad policy made the failure almost inevitable, senior political appointees are too often inclined to send a military officer or a civil servant to explain the mishap rather than face the committee's wrath themselves.

It is, of course, very difficult for an appointing official, whether the president or a cabinet member, to know much about the sense of personal responsibility felt by a person seeking a political appointment. Nevertheless, the subject should be discussed with the job seeker. To ignore the issue is to court embarrassment, or worse, in the event that the person is appointed and subsequently attempts to evade personal responsibility on a matter where bad public policy or harmful political fallout could have been avoided simply through a sense of accountability.

Military experience may not be necessary and it is obviously not sufficient to guarantee that a particular official is qualified to recommend policies involving the conduct of war or to manage a department, agency, or one of their subdivisions in peace. But perhaps it or some other significant law enforcement or other leadership or operational experience is necessary, at least for those departments and agencies that are charged with the nation's security. Previous service in the Navy Department, even as a civilian, does not guarantee future success as assistant secretary of the navy for manpower and reserve affairs, but a person nominated for that position should at least know the culture of the navy *before* assuming office, including the difference between a petty officer first class who is a cryptologic technician and a second-class petty officer who is a boatswain's mate. Previous military or other operational experience does not guarantee future success as a senior leader in FEMA, but it is hardly asking too much to demand that nominees for such positions have significant emergency management/response experience. A thirty-something political appointee is not necessarily unqualified to serve in a senior position, but any such person who is nominated should be required to meet a strict burden of proof in demonstrating why they have sufficient relevant experience and are otherwise fully qualified to serve in that particular position.

Neither Congress nor recent administrations have done anything significant to ensure consistently high-quality senior appointees. The gap between the demands of increasingly vast and complex government policies and programs and the ability of government leaders to deliver them is widening. Major national and homeland security failures in recent years have been wide-ranging, involving the intelligence community, the response to Hurricane Katrina, the navy's shipbuilding program, the air force's lack of effective oversight over nuclear weapons,[73] the unacceptable facilities at the army's Walter Reed Medical Center, and many others.

An April 2010 national poll indicated that nearly 80 percent of Americans say that they do not trust the federal government.[74] A more recent study concluded that the primary reason for this distrust is that the government "is trying to cope with an increasingly complex world while hobbled with an inflexible, outdated management structure. It is run," according to the authors of the study, "by a revolving door of political appointees, many with limited management skills and little interest in long-term efficiency. In short," they continued, "the federal government is an anachronism in a world where technology enables new and versatile ways of working. It is increasingly unsuited to deliver complex services."[75]

Additional evidence in support of these conclusions was regrettably obvious in the results of a survey conducted in April 2011 by *Government Executive*'s research division, the Government Business Council. The respondents were all senior career federal executives and managers. They rated Obama political appointees even lower than those in previous administrations. More than 30 percent gave Obama appointees a "D" or "F" for overall job performance.[76] Admiral James Loy, a former deputy secretary of homeland security and a former commandant of the Coast Guard, has summarized the problem. "We are in a post 9/11 security environment," he says. "We need skills and competencies that never before were part [of government service]. . . . Now there's a need for agility, adaptability and speed of service. If government is going to gain the capacity to do what needs to be done, we must have these capabilities."[77]

To obtain these capabilities, presidents and cabinet secretaries are going to have to reject strong tendencies to appoint people to senior positions in the departments and agencies responsible for the nation's security merely because they have good political credentials or because they are women or because they fall in a particular ethnic grouping. If the repayment of political debts and the promotion of diversity are goals, extra care will necessarily need to be taken to ensure that the nominees who are the beneficiaries of those goals are demonstrably highly qualified—because of their past experience—in the areas for which they will be responsible. The nation can no longer afford to have well-intentioned but inexperienced theorists serving as guardians of the gate. Good political appointees can't solve all government problems, but they can at least be helpful in preventing them from becoming worse. Even if it is temporarily impossible to find a high-quality appointee for a particular position, presidents and the Senate will do well to remember one of the principal precepts of medical ethics: *Primum non nocere* ("First, do no harm").

Another major problem is the limited amount of time for which far too many appointees agree to serve. This problem is particularly acute in the departments responsible for the nation's security. In the Department of Defense, for example, the most senior political appointees—the secretary of defense, deputy secretary of defense, and military department secretaries—only serve an average of between eleven and twenty months.[78] The average tenure of other political appointees is not much greater, if it is greater at all. Far too often, senior political appointees are more interested in their personal careers, in adding a title to their resumes, and in feeling the respect and prestige accorded to senior government officials than in engaging in the drudgery and the often contentious, unpleasant, difficult, risky, sometimes behind-the-scenes hard work and sacrifices that characterize many senior positions and that are usually essential for the execution and implementation of complex policies and programs. Too many appointees, having contributed little or nothing to the government's major objectives, are anxious to sell the institutional knowledge they have obtained and their personal contacts to companies that do business with their department or agency.

Ironically, the political culture of the nation's capital often encourages short tenures and mediocre or poor performance in government. The *quality* of an appointee's service in public office is rarely examined, even if he is subsequently nominated for another position. Appointees whose tenure is very brief and those who accomplish nothing whatsoever their length of service are usually accorded the same postservice recognition and respect as those who record major successes in very difficult circumstances. Success in keeping out of trouble is accorded the same weight as a record of significant accomplishments.

This should not be acceptable. Constant shuffling of appointees can have numerous detrimental effects, many of which I have observed personally.

Frequent turnover creates leadership vacuums, confusion in reporting chains, and "uncertainty or even paralysis as civil servants wait for signals from the top." Turnover "disrupts working relationships among functionally related agencies and programs achieved through interagency and intra-agency working groups."[79] Presidents cannot ensure accountability, much less provide inspiration, "when their appointees start packing for their next jobs only 18 to 24 months after arriving."[80] This is particularly true in the Department of Defense, which has more than 2.9 million active and reserve personnel, a civilian work force of more than 700,000, and a FY 2012 budget of $691 billion, and also in the new Department of Homeland Security, a consolidation of twenty-two federal agencies, which has more than 200,000 employees and an annual budget of almost $50 billion. The nation may not be seriously injured if a deputy secretary of labor or an assistant secretary of education only serves for a year and a half. But we can no longer afford to be changing leaders who have significant responsibilities within national and homeland security departments and agencies at that rate. Jack Welch could not have made the impact he did at General Electric in an eighteen-month period. Neither can senior political appointees.

Noting that the U.S. Marines teach responsibility to duty and to others before self, that any chain is only as strong as its weakest individual link, and that the marine officer does not eat until after the subordinates for whom he is responsible—the corporals and privates—have been fed, a well-known liberal political columnist and commentator has asked a question well worth considering in the context of the loyalty of senior appointees to the implementation of the vision and programs of the administration in which they serve: "Would not our country be a more just and human place if the brass of Wall Street and Washington and executive suites believed that 'officers eat last?'"[81] One thing is certain: our government would be more effective.

Chapter Five

The Professionalism of Military Leaders from 1972 to September 11, 2001

This victory belongs . . . to the Regulars, to the Reserves, to the National Guard. This victory belongs to the finest fighting force this nation has ever known in its history.
—President George Bush, Address to the Congress and the nation after the Persian Gulf War, March 6, 1991

The detection and countering of the production, trafficking and use of illegal drugs is a high priority national security mission of the Department of Defense.
—Secretary of Defense Dick Cheney, September 18, 1989

During the 1950s and 1960s, no incumbent presidential administration, Democratic or Republican, made a move to end the draft system that had been in place in some form since World War I. By 1968, however, presidential candidate Richard Nixon had concluded that it should be ended. Conceding that for many years since World War II he had believed that "even in peacetime, only through the draft could we get enough servicemen to defend our nation," he now asserted that "once our involvement in the Vietnam War is behind us, we will move toward an all-volunteer force."[1]

The need for at least a reform of the nationwide system of conscription had been apparent for some time. By the early 1960s, the Selective Service had become "a draft agency that did more deferring than drafting."[2] In 1962, only 76,000 young men were drafted. But more than 430,000 draft-eligible men were given educational or occupational deferments. Over 1,300,000 were deferred because of paternity.[3] President Kennedy was even known to have extended deferments to married men who were not fathers.

There were other reasons, some demographic, some social and economic, and some political. A practical demographic fact was that the baby boom generation would mature during the 1970s. A volunteer force could be recruited from the expected large pool of young people. The socioeconomic factor related to the inequities associated with the way the draft system was being implemented. A random lottery had replaced draft-board decisions, but the disproportionate number of exemptions and a perceived economic burden on those drafted made the system appear to be unfair.

The political reasons cut across partisan lines. Some conservatives and liberals, being more concerned with the rights than the duties of citizenship, opposed the draft on the grounds that it was inconsistent with a free society. Young liberals were increasingly opposed to the war in Vietnam. Between 1965 and 1968, more than one thousand antiwar demonstrations had taken place in the country.[4] Many involved widely publicized burnings of draft cards. In 1966, *Newsweek* reported that, for the first time since the Civil War, avoidance of military service in times of armed conflict had become socially acceptable.[5]

By 1971, matters were worse in the field. Disturbing reports continued to reach the Pentagon of poor morale, racial incidents, and drug use among American troops in Vietnam. Available data suggested that at least 25 percent of all U.S. soldiers had used drugs. There were other reports of failed discipline and the disintegration of unit cohesion. Some soldiers in the combat theater were refusing to fight, deserting, and even rebelling against their officers. It is believed that in the three years following the 1968 Tet Offensive in Vietnam, more than 350 officers were assaulted by their own troops, a figure that purportedly far exceeded that of similar incidents during World War II.[6] In only two years, army investigators recorded eight hundred instances of hand grenade attacks by American soldiers in Vietnam against unpopular leaders. The practice of "fragging" had left forty-five officers and noncommissioned officers dead.[7]

In March 1969, two months after Nixon assumed office, the Gates Commission, chaired by former secretary of defense Thomas S. Gates Jr., was appointed to study the costs and practicality of an all-volunteer military force. The commission was not asked to address the philosophical question of duty. In February 1970, it unanimously reported that compensation could successfully replace compulsion as the vehicle for the manning of the Armed Forces. "We believe," the commission said, "that the nation's interest will be better served by an all-volunteer force, supported by an effective standby draft, than by a mixed force of volunteers and conscripts." The decision to implement the commission's recommendation was a tactical decision based upon short-term—primarily political—considerations. It was considered by many to be a risky idea. Even though voluntarism is a highly prized military virtue, many military leaders believed that the concept of an all-volunteer force could not work, and that whatever incentives were put in place, insufficient numbers of high-quality volunteers would step forward to serve. Nevertheless, in September 1971, President Nixon signed into law a bill that laid the foundation for professional American Armed Forces consisting entirely of volunteers.

Ten years later, another legislative act that would affect the quality of military leaders went into effect. The Defense Officer Personnel Management Act (DOPMA) unified in a single act several reforms that had been initiated after World War II and the thirty-five years of officer management experience during the Cold War. It established a common officer management system upon the basis of a uniform approach to the way officers should be appointed, trained, promoted, separated, and retired. It required advanced education as a prerequisite for appointment as a commissioned officer. Among other things, Congress specified in the statute the number of officers it would allow in the mid-level and senior ranks. It required that all officers on active duty, whether regular (career) or reserve officers, become regular officers by the time they reached their eleventh year of service. In the mid-1990s, Congress also passed the Reserve Officer Personnel Management Act (ROPMA) to govern the management of reserve officers.

The heart of DOPMA for all of the military services is the uniform "up-or-out" promotion system and common separation and retirement rules that, in the judgment of Congress, provide "in peacetime, a useful, vigorous, full combat-ready officer corps."[8] The "up" portion of the up-or-out system generally provides that officers will move through their careers in groups ("cohorts") determined by the year in which they were commissioned. They will compete for promotion to the next higher grade against other members of the group at set *years-of-service* points. The "out" portion of the system provides that "officers twice passed over for promotion, after a certain number of years, depending upon their particular grade, are to be separated from active service and, if eligible, retired." There are exceptions to the mandatory separation rules and the president can waive the provisions of DOPMA during a mobilization.

The secretary of each military service now convenes annual promotion boards for each competitive category to select officers for promotion. Each board is composed of officers who have demonstrated outstanding performance of duty, maturity, judgment, and experience. Each member of a promotion board takes an oath to consider all eligible officers without partiality and to recommend for promotion only those officers who are "best qualified." The proceedings of each board are confidential. Board recommendations are reviewed by the senior uniformed leadership of the respective service, the secretary of the service, and the secretary of defense. Inevitably, the up-or-out provisions of DOPMA prevent the promotion of several qualified officers, and the statute has been criticized as too rigid. Nevertheless, since it came into effect, the quality of our military leadership has continued to improve.

The creation of an all-volunteer force of professionals was accompanied by an important related development. On August 21, 1970, six months after the Gates Commission made its recommendation, Secretary of Defense Melvin Laird issued a memorandum to each of the military services that articulated in express terms a "Total Force" approach to the design and management of military forces:

> Within the Department of Defense . . . economies will require reductions in over-all strengths and capabilities of the [active] forces, and increased reliance on the combat and combat support units of the Guard and Reserves. Emphasis will be given to the concurrent consideration of the Total Forces, active and reserve, to determine the most advantageous mix to support national strategy and meet the threat. A total force concept will be applied in all aspects in planning, programming, manning, equipping and employing Guard and Reserve forces.[9]

The fiscal concerns that lay behind the new approach to force planning were obvious. A few months later Laird observed that "lower sustaining costs of non-active duty [i.e., reserve] forces . . . allows more force units to be provided for the same costs as an all-active force structure, or the same number of force units to be maintained at lesser costs."[10] On August 23, 1973, James R. Schlesinger, Laird's successor as secretary of defense, issued new directions that formalized the Total Force idea. Schlesinger's memorandum declared, "Total Force is no longer a 'concept.' It is now the Total Force Policy which integrates the Active, Guard and Reserve forces into a homogeneous whole."[11]

By 1973, the transition to an all-volunteer force was well under way. The implementation of the new Total Force Policy, however, was running into obstacles. While the active forces had been reduced to 2,252,000 from the 1968 figure of 3,547,000,[12] the planned increased reliance on reserve forces, accompanied by increases in reserve manpower, was not taking place. Reserve strength had, in fact, begun to decline. Other serious problems also existed. On August 18, 1970, two days before Laird had signed his Total Force memorandum, the chief of naval operations had expressed the judgment that the United States had only a 55 percent probability of prevailing in a conventional war at sea with the Soviet Union.[13] Matters did not improve over the subsequent nine years. In a meeting with President Carter in November 1979, and again in testimony to Congress in the spring of 1980, the army chief of staff declared that the nation had a "hollow Army." At the same time, the chief of naval operations referred to a "hemorrhage of talent" and a shortfall of navy petty officers in excess of twenty thousand.[14] The shortage of personnel was causing longer deployments of navy ships, which in turn was adversely affecting retention rates.

Fortunately, by the late 1980s, a series of new manpower policies and certain external factors were causing a dramatic change in the active/reserve "mix" of the Armed Forces.[15] By the time the Bush administration assumed office in 1989, the number of active component personnel had increased from 2,040,000 to 2,133,000 during the previous decade. But the number of selected reservists[16] had increased from 869,000 to 1,171,000.

More important than the numbers was the evidence of dramatic improvement in the quality of the Armed Forces, including military leaders. By 1988, experienced military personnel who had completed their active service obligation were seeking positions in the reserve components. Some 92 percent of naval reserve officers, for example, had active-duty experience. They were capable and desirous of continuing their military careers even while they pursued their civilian careers. Almost 59 percent of the reserve enlistees had prior military service. The scores of the active and the reserve components on standardized IQ tests were soon well above those of the general civilian population.

The enlisted personnel in the Armed Forces were also better educated. More than 92 percent of the non-prior-service enlistees had a high school education or the equivalent thereof. More than 95 percent of them tested in the three highest categories of the Armed Forces Qualification Test.[17] Within a few years, some 95 percent of active-force officers had baccalaureate degrees and 38 percent had graduate degrees. The accumulation of greater intelligence and more education had consequences. Training required fewer resources and less time. The quality of the leadership of officers and noncommissioned officers improved. Retention improved. The readiness condition of military units improved.

Another reason why the quality of the Armed Forces improved in the decade of the 1980s was the new approach taken by military leaders to the problem of drug abuse. In the 1970s, drug use among young Americans was of epidemic proportions. Recruits coming into the new all-volunteer force had come of age as the drug culture was expanding. The number of drug offenses within the Armed Forces was therefore rising. A 1971 DoD study found that 50 percent of American troops in Vietnam were drug users. While marijuana was most commonly used, hard narcotics like heroin, cocaine, opium, and amphetamines were dirt cheap on the black market, and they could be easily obtained.

In May 1981, the USS *Nimitz* (CVN-68) was conducting sea trials off the coast of Florida when an EA-6B Prowler aircraft crashed on her flight deck during a routine night landing. Fourteen crewmen were killed. Forty-eight others were injured. Seven aircraft were destroyed and eleven more were damaged. An investigation of the crash could not conclusively establish a cause, but it did reveal that at least some of the flight deck crewmen had tested positive for drug use. Not long after the crash, a DoD self-reporting survey indicated that 47 percent of the navy's junior enlisted personnel had used marijuana during the previous month.

Many people doubted that much could be done about the problem. "After all," the argument went, "sailors are merely a reflection of the broad values and experiences of society at large and there is a nationwide drug epidemic." Civilian leaders within DoD worried that any crackdown would result in class action lawsuits and have a devastating impact upon recruiting and retention on what was now an all-volunteer force.

Admiral Thomas P. Hayward, then serving as chief of naval operations, refused to accept the status quo. In a courageous act initiated in December 1981, he instituted a new policy that he referred to as "zero tolerance." In a no-nonsense videotape presentation that was sent to all navy commands and was required viewing by all hands, Hayward was blunt: "We're out to help you or hammer you—take your choice." Henceforth, he continued, there would be "one simple set of standards: 'Not here—Not on my watch—Not on my ship—Not in my Navy.'" To enforce the new policy, random urinalysis testing was instituted and searches were conducted using dog teams. The testing and searches were accompanied by new prevention efforts, education, and rehabilitation activities, but continued drug use resulted in separation from the navy.

Originally, the new policy was intended only for officers and noncommissioned officers. Junior enlisted personnel were to be given a second chance. To their great credit, however, chief petty officers in the fleet asked that no exceptions be made for enlisted personnel. They wanted to use the new "zero-tolerance" policy as a weapon against the peer pressure felt by young sailors to use drugs.[18] Early positive results of the new navy policy caused it to be adopted by the entire Department of Defense. Within only a few years, dramatic results were achieved. By March 1990, eleven months after I assumed responsibility as the new DoD drug czar,[19] I was able to report to Congress that DoD had achieved an 82 percent reduction in reported drug use since 1980. It soon became navy policy to separate all first-time drug offenders. The Marine Corps required separation for first-time offenders in the rank of E-4 or above and for all second-time offenders regardless of rank. Separation was mandatory within the army for first-time offenders who had three or more years of service. [20]

The drug-testing program was soon extended to the DoD civilian workforce of over one million people. In April 1989, the month that I became the DoD drug czar, it was extended to all political appointees and other senior officials in the offices of the secretary of defense and the chairman of the Joint Chiefs of Staff. I remember vividly an occasion when Secretary Cheney heard me grumbling at a meeting that I had been "randomly" selected for testing two times within a single month. He laughed and told me that he had been tested the previous day. It was a story I told often to military audiences to illustrate that no one was exempted from the testing program. The deterrent effect of those policies caused the trend in the rate of drug use to continue downward. It was soon substantially less than the rate among the general civilian population and no longer a problem in the Armed Forces.

Much has been written about the revolutionary changes that took place in the Armed Forces after the end of the conflict in Vietnam. The move to an all-volunteer force; the appearance of precision-guided munitions; the application of advances in information technology to command and control and many other processes; the gutty responses to drug use, racial tensions, and lack of discipline in all of the services; and the effort to more effectively integrate the reserve components were some of the more visible of the changes. Less conspicuous, perhaps, but equally important changes were also made by military leaders in the battle doctrines of the individual services.

Throughout our history each of the military services has searched for the right balance between preserving the hard lessons learned in previous armed conflicts and those things that are unique and valuable in their individual traditions, while at the same time making whatever changes in strategy, doctrine, force structure, and weapons systems may be necessary to win the most likely conflicts of the future. As was noted in chapter 2, the development of an intellectual war-fighting rationale, or doctrine, became the subject of increased concern and attention after World War II, due in part to interservice competition over roles, missions, and funding. Most organizations develop an institutional philosophy, but in contrast to most civilian groups, the doctrines of the military services tend to be more "formal, self-conscious, and explicit." [21] A leading scholar on civil-military relations explained the importance of service doctrine a half century ago. Its importance stems, he said, "from the extent to which the military groups are perceived to be and perceive themselves to be simply the instruments of a higher national policy.

The Armed Services explicitly rationalize their existence in terms of a higher national end, and each activity and unit is justified only by its contribution to the realization of the prescribed hierarch of values and purposes."[22]

The first moves to develop a new doctrine after 1972 were made by army leaders. The Yom Kippur War in October 1973 provided a laboratory for fresh thinking. The Arabs had used Soviet-supplied weapons and Soviet tactics. The numerically inferior but triumphant Israelis had primarily used Western arms, especially weapons supplied by the United States. The lethality of the weapons, particularly the accuracy and range of the modern tanks, was substantially greater than that of weapons used in previous wars. In less than two weeks, the Arabs and Israelis had together lost more tanks than the United States then had in all of Europe to defend against an attack by the Warsaw Pact. This was especially troubling in view of the fact that, at the time, the number of Warsaw Pact tanks was more than twice that of NATO forces.

But the outcome of the conflict suggested that if field commanders could seize the initiative and deceive and outmaneuver their foes by rapidly exploiting tactical opportunities, a war against Warsaw Pact forces in Europe was winnable with conventional weapons. Fortunately, and despite the fact that the fortunes of the army were at a very low ebb, it was blessed by having two brilliant leaders in General William E. DePuy, the commander of the army's new Training and Doctrine Command (TRADOC), and General Donn Starry, DePuy's successor at TRADOC. Together, they began work on the development of a radically new battle doctrine.

A critical lesson from the Yom Kippur War was the need to establish battlefield superiority early. Israel was too small to assume that it would have a second chance, so it had vigorously trained its forces, most of which were reservists, to a high state of readiness. A slow, World War II–style mobilization of U.S. industry and personnel would ensure defeat in the next war. Somehow, the U.S. Army would also have to find a way to fight and win the first battle, even if outnumbered.

Over the next few years, the army recognized and then established a new operational level in its doctrine. Previously, it had recognized only two levels of war—tactical and strategic. Its then current "active fefense" doctrine was based on a concept of small but high-tech and agile forces that could stop the first wave of a massive conventional attack by the Soviet Union, presumably through Germany's Fulda Gap. Nowhere in the army's training and later development processes did it address the perspective of commanders and staffs at levels from corps to theater. "Yet," a future army chief of staff would write, "the 'battle' perspective of these operational-level commanders differs markedly in terms of time, space, and resources from that of both tactical-level commanders and national-level authorities. In fact," he continued, "virtually every doctrinal consideration—technology, organization, command and control, training, leader development, military-political inter-action—differs substantially from the tactical to the operational level and, again, from the operational to strategic level."[23]

Critical new analyses were made by army leaders of combat training, Soviet doctrine, and the weapons in development that would enter the arsenal within a few years. A decision was made to shift army combat training "from an emphasis on static firing ranges, to free-form, force-on-force tactical en-gagements."[24] By 1981, the 650,000 acres of land in the Mojave Desert designated as the National Training Center had been turned into a training battlefield for maneuvering, brigade-sized forces.

Meanwhile, the air force was taking its own first steps to prepare for war in Europe. To a great extent, the air force's doctrinal beliefs had remained unchanged since World War II. During Vietnam, air forces were generally considered delivery vehicles for tactical nuclear and conventional weapons, as well as air defense or tactical attack platforms. In the mid-1970s, the service began to consider how new smart weapons might permit NATO air forces to attack Warsaw Pact vulnerabilities, such as lengthy logistical lines.

By now, Donn Starry had relieved DePuy as the head of TRADOC and was exploring the concept of the extended battlefield, an idea that involved attacking the expected enemy's rear with helicopters and "smart" precision weapons to delay the movement of its rear echelon forces to the "front," or "main battle area," thereby giving NATO forces a temporary tactical advan-tage.[25] Army and air force planners began the development of an integrated attack plan that would use mobile ground forces to conduct a series of limited offensives, while air forces, artillery, and special operations forces blocked the movement of enemy reserves toward the main battle area. The objective would be to stretch out the advance of the numerically superior Warsaw Pact forces in order to allow NATO forces to gradually wear down the strength of the enemy all along the battlefield while reinforcements arrived in piecemeal fashion.[26] This AirLand Battle concept of 1981 became the official doctrine of the army and the de facto doctrine of the air force, and was adopted by NATO in 1984 as its primary battle plan.

A new post-Vietnam battle doctrine for the navy evolved in a different way. It was not, in fact, a tactical doctrine at all, but rather a vehicle for shaping and disseminating "a professional consensus" on war fighting.[27] In the 1970s, the navy faced a major force structure problem. The fleet was too small and almost every category of ship was undergoing bloc obsolescence. At the same time, the Soviet fleet was growing in numbers as well as in design. In 1980, the chief of naval operations reported to Congress that American naval forces were seriously overextended and that, for the first time in memory, the navy was unable to meet all of its peacetime commit-ments.[28]

The following year, the new Reagan administration declared that the United States had lost the margin of superiority that a maritime power required, noting that the navy was only half the size it had been ten years earlier and that its operating tempo was 20 percent greater than it had been in Vietnam. The administration's new budget proposal included a shipbuilding program that would produce approximately thirty ships a year as part of a longer-term effort to achieve a six-hundred-ship navy, including fifteen carrier battle groups, by the end of the decade.

Predictably, Congress was skeptical. Questions were raised about the rationale for a fleet of that size and about the reasoning behind the administration's requested mix of specific ship types. General answers were provided in early 1983. In a posture statement presented to the House Armed Services Committee, the navy secretary declared, "Unlike land warfare . . . conflict . . . between the navies of the United States and the Soviet Union . . . will be instantaneously a global conflict. We must, therefore, recognize that the choice is to maintain security of the sea lanes in each [ocean area] or write them off and suffer the consequences."[29] Security would require a forward strategy.

The elements of the forward strategy were described by CNO Admiral James D. Watkins. The peacetime element of the new Maritime Strategy would involve forward deployments of U.S. naval forces all over the world. In the event of a war with the Soviet Union, the U.S. Navy would seize the initiative as far forward as possible, contributing to the land battle on the central front by attacking the Soviets on their maritime flanks. Attack submarines, aircraft, and mines would be used to "establish barriers at key world chokepoints . . . to prevent leakage of enemy [naval] forces to the open ocean where the Western Alliance's resupply lines [could] be threatened."[30] An aggressive campaign would also be conducted against all Soviet submarines, including ballistic missile submarines. The objective would be to destroy all Soviet fleets—in fact, to "defeat Soviet maritime strength in all its dimensions, including base support," even if that should require conducting operations "close to the Soviet motherland."[31]

During World War I, the marines had organized an expeditionary brigade, which was cobbled together from several ships and naval installations. In the 1918 Battle of Belleau Wood, those "Devil Dogs" established a record of toughness and valor that merits a special chapter in the annals of the nation's martial history. For the next twenty years, they were involved in guerrilla warfare in Central America. The lessons from those conflicts were formally published in the *Small Wars Manual*, "a guide to irregular conflict that is still in print (and in demand) today."[32] During World War II, the Marine Corps developed what had previously been a skeletal amphibious doctrine and served as the point of the nation's spear in the island-hopping battles of the Pacific. After the war, they developed the concept of "vertical envelopment," an idea for the use of helicopters to support maneuver and logistical requirements over great distances. After the end of the conflict in Vietnam, they created a new Marine Air Ground Task Force (MAGTF) doctrine to give combatant commanders "scalable, versatile expeditionary forces [that are] able to respond to a broad range of crisis and conflict situations."[33]

In June 1985, the Marine Corps announced a new Amphibious Warfare Strategy, which was developed as a subset of the navy's Maritime Strategy. In the event of war with the Soviets, mass amphibious task forces, together with supporting battleship surface action groups, would undertake landings to retake territory conquered by the enemy and to seize key objectives in the Soviet rear.[34] Landings would take place "on the North Cape, the eastern Baltic or the Black Sea coasts, in the Kuriles, or on Sakhalin Island."[35] After the first Persian Gulf War (Operation Desert Storm, 1990–1991), the Marine Corps anticipated the later irregular warfare and stability operations in Iraq and Afghanistan with their concepts of the "Three Block War" and "Strategic Corporal."[36]

It has been rightly noted that "massive organizations on the scale of the Armed Services [need] a common direction to focus the efforts of their many disparate commands."[37] While there were obvious differences, the AirLand Battle doctrine, the Maritime Strategy, and the innovative concepts developed by Marine Corps leaders all served the same purpose. In addition to establishing a credible war-fighting rationale for the budgets and programs recommended by the professional leaders of each of the services, the concepts provided a valuable unity of purpose.

By 1990, whether they were members of the active forces, the National Guard, or the federal reserve components, America's soldiers, sailors, airmen, and marines had been serving in uniform because they wanted to for almost two decades. They were professionals. They were not joining to avoid the draft or because they were unqualified for other employment. They were joining because they were motivated, whether by a thirst for travel and adventure, for the educational and other economic benefits, or for patriotic reasons. One test, however, had not yet been passed. How would the all-volunteer Total Force, including National Guard and reserve troops who had never been mobilized, perform in a major armed conflict? American forces had performed well in Operation Just Cause, the December 1989 attack on Panamanian Defense Forces led by Manuel Noriega, but that operation had taken place close to home and had involved only about twenty-six thousand American troops, few of whom were in the reserve components. The question remained. How would the all-volunteer Total Force perform in a major conflict? In 1990–1991, the world found out. This conflict was called Desert Shield/Desert Storm.

When combat operations in the Persian Gulf War ceased on February 28, 1991, 202,337 selected reservists and 20,277 members of the Individual Ready Reserve had been activated. Some 106,000 National Guardsmen and reservists had served in the Kuwait theater of operations. They had participated in all phases of the Gulf conflict, from the initial response through the redeployment of forces. Twenty-eight army reservists had been killed. Five days after the cease-fire was begun, I received a handwritten note from General Colin Powell, the chairman of the Joint Chiefs of Staff, which referred to the performance of the guardsmen and reservists. It said simply, "It was a great team effort." He would later refer to that performance in similar fashion: "We could not have gone to war without them, and they were to perform superbly."[38]

It is useful to consider how the results were perceived by independent observers. In a statement that was undoubtedly out of proportion to the achievement, two military analysts wrote that the victory in the Gulf was a "defining moment in military history, a campaign as momentous in operational terms as Cannae, Agincourt, Waterloo, the Somme, or Normandy."[39] John Keegan, described by Colin Powell as "the world's foremost contemporary military historian," has written that "the Gulf War . . . was a triumph of incisive planning and almost faultless execution."[40] A Pulitzer Prize–winning author and journalist said, "In terms of military objectives conquered, allied casualties minimized and popular support on the home front sustained, the war was that rarest of prizes in the age of relativity: an absolute victory."[41] One of the architects of the army's AirLand Battle doctrine, now retired, wrote to Powell to say, "There is emerging a distinctive American style of war, a style that is essentially joint, drawing on the unique capabilities of each service via centralized planning and decentralized execution. This jointness, plus an amalgam of surprise, discriminate use of overwhelming force, high op tempo, and exploitation of advanced technology, has led to a whole new order of military effectiveness."[42]

Two thoughtful and respected authors wrote that the Gulf War confirmed the nation's reliance on a well-trained volunteer force of regulars and reserves. "Never in the history of the republic," they said, "has a more competent and proficient military been fielded. The high quality displayed by all the services is a function of four things: high-caliber personnel, professional education, realistic and continuous training, and leadership."[43]

That leadership included many veterans of the war in Vietnam who had not given up during the several depressing years following that conflict. Despite the drug problems in the Armed Forces and the general antimilitary attitude that prevailed among large segments of the American population, they had soldiered on. Noting that "[l]eadership, both in senior Pentagon management and in small field units, remains the intangible key to holding together a quality institution and saving lives in precarious situations," a student of the rebuilding of the Armed Forces since 1972 has written that while only around 3 percent of the Desert Shield/Desert Storm active-duty forces were Vietnam veterans, "they played the premier role in planning the operations and leading the forces into battle in the air, on land, and at sea."[44]

In a televised address to a joint session of Congress and the nation only days after the cease-fire brought an end to forty-three days of sustained combat, President Bush was very succinct in his characterization of the performance of America's Armed Forces: "This victory belongs to the finest fighting force this nation has ever known in its history."

Even while the Armed Forces were engaged in Desert Shield/Desert Storm, they were also engaged in another international conflict that tested their professionalism in other ways. This conflict was called the "drug war." After almost two decades of unsuccessful assaults by several administrations on the national drug problem, public pressure on Congress to do something about the problem during the election year of 1988 was intense in all parts of the country. Americans had reason to be worried. The National Institute on Drug Abuse estimated that 37 percent of the population over twelve years old had used illegal drugs. Trafficking in illegal drugs was a major source of crime and corruption. Drug abuse was degrading both the health and the morality of society. The economic cost of drug abuse through lost work time and diminished productivity had been estimated as $59.7 billion in 1983 alone. The increasing power of international drug traffickers was undermining the stability of governments friendly or important to U.S. interests. Efforts to interdict illegal drugs entering the country were being thwarted by various realities. In 1988, 355 million people entered or reentered the country, along with more than a hundred million vehicles, two hundred twenty thousand seagoing vessels, six hundred thirty-five thousand aircraft, and eight million containers. Any of the people or conveyances could have been carrying illegal drugs.

A belief was rapidly gaining traction within Congress that the Armed Forces could succeed where civilian law enforcement agencies had failed, especially in interdiction efforts over international waters and in countries overseas. Military and civilian leaders in the Pentagon, however, were almost universally opposed to the idea. Some pointed out that military forces are trained to seek out and destroy an enemy in wartime (or, as some in the Armed Forces colorfully put it, to "kill people and break things"), and that they are not trained in the nuances of civilian law enforcement or the subtleties of constitutional law. Several military leaders were concerned that law enforcement–related and other such "Operations Other Than War" would dilute the warrior ethos of the Armed Forces. They also worried about the murkiness of the drug war and the possibility that soldiers and sailors would be drawn into the corruption of the drug trade.

Opposition to the idea soon became moot. Shortly before the 1988 election, Congress passed legislation that gave unprecedented new counterdrug authority and responsibility to the Department of Defense. DoD was now directed to "serve as the single lead agency of the federal government for the detection and monitoring of aerial and maritime transit of illegal drugs into the United States."[45] The new statute also gave DoD planning responsibility for a communications network that would support the integration of U.S. command, control, communications, and technical intelligence assets dedicated to drug interdiction. Finally, the new law provided for an enhanced role for the National Guard, under the direction of state governors, to support state drug interdiction and related law enforcement operations. It authorized additional funding for the National Guard, but in order to receive the funds, the governor of each state was required to submit to the secretary of defense a proposed plan for the use of the Guard (in its "state" or Title 32 status)[46] in drug enforcement and interdiction operations.

The new president, George H. W. Bush, had made the drug problem a major issue in his 1988 campaign. Soon after he was inaugurated, work began on the preparation of the first National Drug Control Strategy, which had to be submitted to Congress. In addition to the new counterdrug missions mandated by Congress, the Armed Forces would be required to carry out additional missions as part of the new strategy. Immediately after the new strategy was announced, Secretary of Defense Dick Cheney issued policy guidance to all elements of DoD. He declared that the supply of illicit drugs to the United States from abroad, the associated violence and international instability, and the use of illegal drugs within the country all posed a direct threat to the sovereignty and security of the country. As a consequence, the new counterdrug mission would henceforth be a "high priority national security mission" of the Department of Defense.[47]

In April 1989, I was appointed as the DoD coordinator of drug enforcement policy and support. The new assignment as the Pentagon "drug czar" was in addition to my continuing work as the assistant secretary of defense for reserve affairs. Fortunately, I was given the authority to build an entirely new counterdrug staff to help me with my broad and very complex new responsibilities. The new counterdrug mission was fraught with political, institutional, federal interagency, federal-state, operational, legal, and policy obstacles. The Armed Forces would also be operating in a fishbowl of public scrutiny.

I knew that one of my greatest challenges would be to obtain the energetic support, not just grudging acquiescence, of military leaders for DoD's new counterdrug missions. To that end, I took advantage of a meeting one day attended only by Cheney, the Joint Chiefs of Staff, and myself. The declared purpose of the meeting was for me to brief my proposed Drug Policy and Action Plan. I did so, but I quickly turned to my real purpose. "I am fully aware," I said, "that in the last [Reagan] administration—of which I was a member—civilian leaders didn't even want to talk about the counterdrug missions proposed for the Armed Forces and too many senior political appointees were content to let you take the heat from Congress and the media for that administration's reluctance." I then proposed a new modus operandi. I would be the lead, and usually the exclusive, DoD witness in all future congressional hearings on the subject of illegal drugs. I would personally respond to all written congressional inquiries. I would handle all difficult media questions relating to the new missions and deal with all legal issues. I asked the Joint Chiefs to ensure that military commanders focused exclusively on what they could do best—the planning and execution of the operational aspects of the several new missions.

The Chiefs agreed and were true to their commitment. The hundreds of operational matters that were conducted over the subsequent four years were essentially flawless. A mission that military leaders did not want, and for which they had almost no experience, was performed with admirable professionalism. At a May 1988 hearing during the last year of the Reagan administration, an important committee of the U.S. House of Representatives had caustically criticized the counterdrug work of the Armed Forces. In May 1991, the same committee issued a report in which it declared, "The Committee is pleased with the continuing progress of the Department of Defense in carrying out the priority drug interdiction missions mandated by Congress in 1989. . . . Indeed, the success of the Department is evident."[48]

On November 9, 1989, I flew to Boston to address the Annual Conference of the International Security Studies Program of Tufts University's Fletcher School of Law and Diplomacy. The conference was co-sponsored by the Army War College. My subject was the role of the Armed Forces under the new National Drug Control Strategy. As I got off the elevator at the hotel where the conference was being held, one of my hosts approached me and in an excited tone informed me that only moments earlier a news bulletin had announced that the Berlin Wall had just been opened.

When I entered the large ballroom where the conference was being held, the army general who was scheduled to speak before me was in the middle of his remarks. As I took a seat at the back of the room, an aide approached the podium and whispered something to the speaker, Lieutenant General Gordon Sullivan, then serving as the army's deputy chief of staff for operations and plans. Sullivan, a Boston native who would later serve as the army's thirty-second chief of staff, has a dry wit. He turned to his audience and, after pausing for a moment, slowly said, "Ladies and gentlemen, you have asked me to speak to you on the subject of the future of the United States Army. I've just been informed that the Berlin Wall has been opened. I can't begin to tell you what I do not know about the future of the United States Army!"

The opening of the Berlin Wall, the collapse of the Iron Curtain, the demise of the Warsaw Pact and the Soviet Union, and the end of the Cold War involved changes in the strategic environment that were so profound that civilian and military leaders found them difficult to understand. The complexity of the immediate tasks were evident to all. First, it was necessary to rethink the nature of the security threats that were likely to be the reality of the future. Uncertainty surrounded that issue. Some academics were predicting the end of war, or at least its diminution in the affairs of the world.[49] One veteran observer of wars and political upheaval, however, expressed a view shared with many others: "[I]n a world in which democracy and technology are developing faster than the institutions needed to sustain them—even as states themselves are eroding and being transformed beyond recognition by urbanization and the information age—[the U.S. foreign policy of the future] will be the art . . . of permanent crises management."[50] But what kind of crises, and where?

Second, it was necessary to reshape and refocus the Armed Forces to meet the future threats. Both tasks had to be performed in the context of a shrinking defense budget. The political pressure for a "peace dividend" from the end of the Cold War was intense. The uncertainty and the challenges that faced each of the military services can, perhaps, be best understood by focusing on one—the army.

It has been said that the history of the ground forces of America prior to 1991 can be divided into two distinct periods. According to one former army leader, the first period was bounded by the Revolution and World War II, which "saw America secure itself with a small force of regulars, backed by a large, mobilizeable, yet relatively untrained militia and emergency conscripts."[51] Subsequent to World War II, "intercontinental flight and the division of the world into two armed camps forced America to a second system of ground force preparedness and security. For the first time, a large standing force, well trained and equipped with the latest technology, was reinforced by a large reserve component—the Army Reserve and the Army National Guard. Both components were organized, equipped and trained, and manned for a mobilization war on the plains of central Europe and a potential global conflict that never came."[52]

After the Cold War and the conclusion of Desert Storm, army leaders were candid about the magnitude of the changes that had to be made, for American strategy still relied "on a Cold War–derived understanding of military power."[53] To a very great extent, the Armed Forces were still organized the way they were at the height of the Cold War. Much of the new challenge that army leaders faced related to the sheer size of the organization that had to be changed. "Think of it this way," two of the senior leaders wrote later. "If the Army were a private enterprise, it would be a U.S. based multinational corporation with nearly 1.5 million employees, annual revenues of $63 billion, branch offices in more than one hundred countries, and strategic alliances in virtually all the major nations of the world, under intense pressure to perform more effectively every day."[54] The Armed Forces in general, and the army in particular, have demonstrated over many decades that they are good at adapting to gradual change, but they were "poorly prepared to handle the avalanche of change thrust upon [them] as the Cold War came to a close."[55] A significant part of that change would require the army to reduce its size by more than one-third—that is, by more than six hundred thousand—while maintaining its combat readiness.

Despite these obstacles, change was well under way by 1996. The progress of the change, particularly the way in which army leaders were transforming the army into a learning organization, was significant enough to attract the attention of business leaders. "Much of the way American management works," the dean of the Boston University School of Management wrote, "was learned from the World War II practices of the U.S. military. That 'command and control' model of management is structurally hierarchical, top-down driven, and precise in its statistical controls. I think," he continued, "that the American organization that has arguably reinvented both its management system and its leadership culture most dramatically is the United States Army, the very organization from which industry learned the original management approach it is now trying to change. In fact, the Army is once again leading industry in the creation of new approaches to management challenges."[56]

Even while the Armed Forces were working through the mountain of change brought about by the end of the Cold War and simultaneously dealing with the armed conflict in the Balkans, which required the employment of American air power in Kosovo and Serbia in the first national security test of the post–Desert Storm era, they were struggling to implement additional change mandated by Congress. Passed by Congress over the strong objection of the then secretary of defense, Caspar Weinberger, and most of the chiefs of the individual military services, the Goldwater-Nichols Defense Reorganization Act of 1986 centralized the authority of the Joint Chiefs of Staff in the person of its chairman, who was designated as the principal military advisor to the secretary of defense and the president.

The legislation illustrated the recognition by Congress that, in addition to service-competent officers, the Armed Forces needed high-quality officers competent in joint matters. The intent of the drafters of the legislation was to mold the unique characteristics and strengths of the individual services so that they complemented one another and their collective efforts as a whole became more than the sum of their individual efforts, all as part of a broader effort to foster better war-fighting expertise. Both the attempt to rescue Americans held hostage in Iran during the Carter administration and the rescue of medical students in Grenada during the Reagan administration had been flawed operations. The perceived advantage of military leaders experienced in jointness rested on certain realities—for example, the facts that "new global threats require the continuous development, testing and implementation of new joint doctrine and tactics"; that new reconnaissance, weapons and other systems require continuous leadership and oversight to ensure joint interoperability; and that the "natural turnover of military personnel requires a continuous joint training program."[57] The Goldwater-Nichols legislation was designed to establish "clearer lines of command and control and [to improve] the ability of the services to work with each other in truly joint, rather than simply multi-service operations."[58]

Joint matters were defined in the statute as "matters relating to the achievement of unified action by multiple military forces in operations conducted across domains such as land, sea, or air, in space, or in the information environment, including matters relating to (A) national military strategy; (B) strategic planning and contingency planning; (C) command and control of operations under unified command; (D) national security planning with other departments and agencies of the United States; and (E) combined operations with military forces of allied nations." "Multiple military forces" were defined to include other departments and agencies, the military forces or agencies of other countries, and nongovernmental persons or organizations.[59]

As part of the move to both improve the effectiveness of the chain of command and to improve the quality of joint combat operations, the Goldwater-Nichols legislation also increased the power of the regional military commanders in chief (CINCs),[60] all at the expense of the service chiefs. The latter were left with the task of providing trained manpower and resources to the CINCs. The legislation did nothing to dispel what one former CINC has called the "natural tension between service chiefs, who are responsible for a longer-term view, and the regional commanders responsible for the immediate response to crises."[61]

Nor did the new law do much to mitigate the inevitable strains in high-level command relationships between senior civilian leaders and senior military leaders. Those strains became the subject of focused study by military leaders after the publication in 1997 of a new book about the absence of competence and honest civilian and military leadership during the war in

Vietnam. H. R. McMaster's *Dereliction of Duty*[62] became required reading for senior officers. In 2005, the author, then a colonel in the army, was recalled from Iraq to debrief the Joint Chiefs of Staff on his five years of research for the book, his findings, and his conclusions. As we saw in chapter 2, the dustjacket of the book declared that the disaster that followed President Lyndon Johnson's decision to intensify the American military commitment in Southeast Asia "was not caused by impersonal forces but by uniquely human failures at the highest levels of the U.S. government: arrogance, weakness, lying in the pursuit of self-interest, and above all, the abdication of responsibility to the American people." The recurring theme of the book had been succinctly expressed by Carl von Clausewitz, the nineteenth-century Prussian soldier and military theorist, in words that echo the theme of this book and the need for competent civilian leaders in matters of national security: "The first duty . . . is to keep policy from demanding things that go against the nature of war, to prevent the possibility that out of ignorance of the way the instrument works, policy might misuse it."[63]

Whatever its deficiencies, the Goldwater-Nichols legislation had slowed the historic tendency toward ad hoc improvisation by the individual military services in the planning and execution of operations. In Desert Storm, General Colin Powell had aggressively used the new power given to the chairman of the Joint Chiefs to shape the way the war was fought—that is, jointly and along the lines of the doctrine that had been declared in the 1980s by then Secretary of Defense Weinberger and subsequently amended by Powell.[64] As a result, the authors of the official post-conflict DoD report to Congress on the conduct of the war concluded that "Operation Desert Storm was a clear demonstration of the overwhelming effectiveness of joint and combined operations synchronized by sound doctrine and experienced leaders."[65]

The effect of the Goldwater-Nichols legislation was felt very strongly in the 1990s. Critics continued to complain that Congress was inappropriately micromanaging the military services, and there was merit to the assertion. As part of the effort to reduce service parochialism, Congress had initiated a series of sweeping new policies on joint education and joint duty. Officers were already spending as much as a third of their careers in classrooms. As junior officers, they learned the operational skills and other rudiments of their profession at various service schools and through practical experience. As field-grade officers at mid-career, they attended command-and-staff colleges and other service schools. They could expect to attend the war college of their service or another senior institution of professional military education as they approached flag (admiral or general) officer rank.

Now joint professional military education would be used to prepare officers for joint duty assignments. The length of the joint duty assignments would be calibrated to leverage an officer's joint professional education and other joint operational experience. In order to strengthen interoperability and a commitment to joint operations, Congress directed that positions on joint staffs and in joint commands be generally filled by officers who were already certified or were on track to become certified as "joint specialty officers." Promotion standards would be revised to ensure that only high-quality officers were assigned to joint duty. Joint duty assignments would be required as a prerequisite for promotion to flag officer rank unless a waiver was granted by the secretary of defense. Finally, reports to Congress would be required of the military services to ensure that the legislative objectives were being met.

As America approached the end of the century and the presidential election of 2000, it had an uncertain view of its international security interests. A decade of strategic drift had not resulted in a new consensus about the size, shape, and use of the Armed Forces. The Clinton administration had reduced the force structure by more than a third from the level set after the Cold War by the administration of President George H. W. Bush, but the op tempo— that is, the pace of peacetime operations and deployments—had increased by 300 percent. The danger of an unexpected armed conflict remained. In their 1968 book, *The Lessons of History*, Will and Ariel Durant asserted that in the 3,421 years of recorded history, only 268 had been free of war. Military historians knew that since 1783, the United States had sent military forces into harm's way every twenty years. [66]

But there were grounds for hope. The Soviet Union and the Warsaw Pact were gone. The Cold War was over and America was the only remaining superpower. No nation in the world could match our war-fighting capabilities. One of the world's most highly respected military historians had just written that while man is a volatile and risk-taking species, he is also a *rational* one, and that "the worst of war is now behind us and . . . mankind, with vigilance and resolution, will henceforth be able to conduct the affairs of the world in a way that allows war a diminishing part." [67]

Informed leaders, both civilian and military, weren't so sure. A nagging feeling persisted that not all future disputes would be resolved in courts of law or other civilized institutions in which rationality and logic prevailed. A few were aware of Winston Churchill's words in similar circumstances some eight decades earlier. Writing about the miscalculations and ineptness that had led to the horrific tragedy of World War I, he reflected upon the danger signals that had failed to prevent that conflagration: "It is nothing. It is less than nothing. It is too foolish, too fantastic to be thought of in the twentieth century. . . . No one would do such things. Civilization has climbed above such perils. The interdependence of nations in trade and traffic, the sense of public law, the Hague Convention, Liberal principles, the Labour Party, high finance, Christian character, common sense have rendered such nightmares impossible. Are you quite sure? It would be a pity to be wrong. Such a mistake could only be made once—once for all."[68]

Despite the recent NATO victory in Kosovo, the war in the Balkans had, in many ways, been unsatisfactory and incomplete. One student of America's armed conflicts wrote that it had nevertheless been a valuable lesson for what he called "teacup wars" (small, manageable conflicts in which casualties were low).[69] Others did not know what the future would hold, but they sensed that civilian and military leaders needed to assume that future threats to our security would be much different from those of the past. In a September 23, 1999, speech at the Citadel in Charleston, Republican presidential candidate George W. Bush promised that, if elected, he would "renew" the bond of trust between the American president and the Armed Forces. He then called vaguely for defense leaders to envision "a new architecture of American defense for decades to come." A few months later, an academic who would subsequently become Bush's national security advisor and later secretary of state identified four key priorities that needed to be addressed by the next administration. One of the four was the need "to deal decisively with the threat of rogue regimes and hostile powers, which is increasingly taking the forms of the potential for terrorism and the development of weapons of mass destruction."[70]

Whatever the nature of future conflicts, the professionalism of America's guardians of the gate in the year 2000 was much different from that of earlier times. The quality of the Armed Forces and of the nation's military leadership had improved dramatically in the almost three decades since the transition to an all-volunteer force. However, cause for concern remained. The margin for error in dealing with future threats was smaller. The number of active military forces had been reduced significantly from those that existed at the time of the 1991 Persian Gulf War, and the recent intense use of reservists had become the subject of national attention. Reservists were now being considered routinely for a wide range of peacetime operations, including disaster relief, humanitarian assistance, security and advisory assistance, support of domestic civil authorities, counterdrug operations, and so forth.

Since America's potential adversaries had also read the history of Desert Storm and studied the strategies, doctrines, methods, and equipment that the United States had used there, it was likely that the national security challenges of the first decade of the twenty-first century would be more complex and perhaps more difficult to deal with than those in previous decades, which, in retrospect, now seemed a much simpler time. Planners were already characterizing the most likely future threats as "asymmetric" in nature. But, for now, the sword was sharp. The leaders of America's Armed Forces were highly capable professional warriors. The only remaining question related to tensions in the relationship between the sword and those civilian leaders who would wield it.

Chapter Six

Civilian Leaders Who Can Get Things Done

Being able to execute . . . means a person knows how to put decisions into action and push them forward to completion, through resistance, chaos, or unexpected obstacles. People who can execute know that [success] is about results.

> —Jack Welch, former chairman and CEO of General Electric

Let my deeds be witness of my worth.

> —Aaron, in Shakespeare's *Titus Andronicus*

While it is true that a talented and experienced member of a president's cabinet can be an important contributor to the effectuation of administration policy, it is equally true that most cabinet members are selected for political reasons unrelated to executive experience. More often than not, they do not assume the role of chief executive of their departments in all respects, so much as that of chairman of the board. They mainly act as spokespersons for the administration in which they serve on matters within their department's area of responsibility. By making speeches and meeting with important constituent groups, they carry important administration themes to the country. In their appearances before Congress, they serve as advocates for the administration's priorities.

Sometimes, even that function is curtailed by the White House or intentionally self-limited by a particular cabinet member. In March 2011, for example, the "badly frayed relations" between President Obama's White House and his cabinet became the subject of front-page news. A "pervasive sense of exclusion" reportedly existed among several members of the cabinet.[1] Obama's White House aides admitted that there were "mediocre players

and outright disappointments" in the cabinet and that the aides were sometimes "disappointed not to be able to rely more heavily on the relevant
cabinet members to help fix . . . problems."[2]

Too often, cabinet officials do not serve for the full term of the president
who appointed them. In those circumstances, it is very difficult for them to
leave any lasting footprint. The bureaucracies simply wait them out, dragging
their collective feet on the implementation of new administration policies.
One small example involved Obama's secretary of defense. As we have seen,
Robert Gates came to power at the end of President George W. Bush's
second term. Almost everyone was surprised when Obama asked Gates to
remain in office. Speculation soon arose, however, as to how long he would
remain. Gates himself had made no secret of his desire to leave the government at an early date. As a result, he described his efforts to push senior air
force leaders—many of whom were former fighter pilots—to move quickly
on the purchase and use of unmanned aerial vehicles for intelligence, surveil-
lance, reconnaissance, and combat missions as comparable to "pulling
teeth."[3] He faced similar challenges in his efforts to dampen the enthusiasm
of the leaders of the other services for costly weapons systems more appropriate for possible future conflicts than for the current conflicts in Iraq and
Afghanistan.

These kinds of factors make critically important the selection of the senior political appointees who serve as subcabinet officials, for they are the
ones upon whose shoulders responsibility primarily falls for the *implementation* of major administration policy and programs. This is especially true
within the Department of Defense. Historically, secretaries of defense have
concentrated on the formulation of major strategy and defense policies and
have left the day-to-day business and management of DoD to their deputies.
The deputy secretaries, undersecretaries, and assistant secretaries of defense,
and their counterparts within the military departments of the army, navy, and
air force, must each serve as chief operating officers, or at least as political
battlefield commanders, within their defined areas of responsibility. They are
the ones who must bridge the gaps between political/strategic concepts and
theories, and operational, tactical, and programmatic realities. They are the
ones who must constantly audit military judgment and prevent differences in
civilian and military culture from impeding the performance of important
missions and the accomplishment of policy and program objectives. Their
performance as effective leaders and managers must be demonstrated on an
almost daily basis.

Churchill understood that "the formulation of strategy in war did not
consist merely in the drawing of state documents sketching out a comprehensive view of how [a] war would be won, but in a host of detailed activities
that together amounted to a comprehensive picture."[4] He understood that
undergirding high-level strategic decisions are other, less visible, but no less

important, activities that "involve decision-making about matters of detail—important detail, but detail none the less."[5] In summarizing Churchill's views on the point, one respected scholar has written that "any observer of government or business knows [that] conception or vision makes up at best a small percentage of what a leader does. It is the *implementation* of that vision that requires unremitting attention and effort."[6] Churchill applied that principle in the selection not only of his generals but also of civilian leaders, several of whom proved critical to Britain's war effort.[7]

William Blake, the eighteenth-century English artist, lyric poet, and etcher, once wrote that "execution is the chariot of genius." Whatever the abstract merit of an administration's policy idea, its actual effectiveness will only be as good as the ability of its political leaders to execute it. Business and military leaders know that until a strategy or plan is *executed*, it remains only a strategy or plan; that until it is executed, no strategy or plan is flawed and no preparation is inadequate; and that execution is required to close the gap between the results promised or desired and the results delivered. On the basis of many years of combat experience, one of the most decorated American general officers in the last century described this principle in more pithy fashion: "Any damned fool can write a plan," he would say, but "it's the execution that gets you all screwed up."[8]

Two successful business leaders have defined *execution* as "a systematic process of rigorously discussing hows and whats, questioning, tenaciously following through, and ensuring accountability. It includes," they argue, "making assumptions about . . . the environment [in which an organization operates], assessing the organization's capabilities, linking strategy to operations and the people who are going to *implement* the strategy, synchronizing those people and their various disciplines, and linking rewards to *outcomes*."[9] Simply stated, "execution is a systematic way of exposing reality and acting on it."[10] Jack Welch, the legendary former chairman and CEO of General Electric, is typically more blunt in his own definition. "Being able to execute," he has said, "means a person knows how to put decisions into action and push them forward to completion, through resistance, chaos, or unexpected obstacles. People who can execute know that [success] is about *results*."[11]

It has been asserted that three questions go to the heart of what business is all about—that is, they are the fundamentals of business thinking. First, "what's the nature of the game we're in?" Second, "Where is it going?" Finally, "How do we make money in it?[12] Execution in government, of course, means something different, but it is still about *results*. John Whitehead, who served as deputy secretary of state and as a leader of several nonprofit organizations, has observed that "the essential issue for a nonprofit is the degree to which it is fulfilling its mission. And so the most important task [of the leadership of a nonprofit] is to identify the mission . . . and to establish measurements for determining how well the nonprofit is accomplishing it."[13] It is the same with government. The civilian leader of every organization within a department or agency must understand fully the unique mission of the organization and establish criteria for the measurement of determining whether the mission is being fulfilled.

Unfortunately, many senior political appointees think of themselves as merely administration representatives, as political overseers, or as vision experts who are exempt from the details of actually running the organization that they were appointed to lead. Sometimes they regard execution as detail work that is beneath their dignity. At other times, they don't have the necessary skills and experience to deal with details. Most successful leaders, however, believe that execution and the achievement of results is their *major* job.

Regrettably, the achievement of tangible results is absent from the performance of far too many political appointees. That absence does not go unnoticed. A recent report of research on government performance noted that "Americans pay close attention to the news of the day—the sluggish jobless recovery, terrorist plots, poorly supported soldiers, poisoned food, vacancies in the top jobs of government, waste and improper payments to undeserving citizens and corporations—all of which seemingly reinforce the Federal Government's persistent inability to assure the highest performance possible." The public perception that government "is both ineffective and inefficient," the report continued, "fosters mistrust in government's willingness to do its job well."[14]

A primary cause of the lack of government effectiveness is, of course, poor leadership. In addition to a well-trained workforce and sufficient resources, "[t]he government's ability to prevent a crisis, respond to a disaster," and conduct routine business "depends on the strength of its leaders."[15] Unfortunately, as this report noted, "Leadership at the federal level has been inconsistent at best, negligent at worst. Leaders of agencies typically are often too focused on 'policy' instead of management; and in the worst cases, they are unqualified and serve solely a political purpose."[16]

The execution or implementation of public policy, it has been correctly observed, is a "complex process with numerous potential failures along the way from articulation of goals to the delivery of a product."[17] Slippage between what senior political leaders want and what is actually delivered can be caused by "a variety of factors, including resource constraints, political disagreements, difficulty observing outcomes, task size, and the complexity of joint action."[18] Leadership in government, therefore, must necessarily involve much more than thinking big, or imposing ideology on the "worker bees," or schmoozing with members of Congress or important constituent groups. Cool, glib, detached, and even cerebral appointees can often get by in positions of authority for a while. But when the pressure is on; when a vitally important program, mission, or project must absolutely be executed successfully; or when an unexpected crisis occurs, people ease away from a figurehead and look to those whom they can trust, those who they know can get the job done.

Effective political appointee-leaders are actively involved in the day-to-day work of their organization. They immerse themselves in the substance of execution and the details. They create a culture and processes for execution. They clearly state priorities, assign the most important tasks to people who get things done, and work to ensure that the right people, individually and collectively, are focused on the right details at the right time. They use their comprehensive knowledge of the work of the organization to constantly probe and question. They are not satisfied to merely approve a course of action recommended by their staffs. They refuse to serve as mere political figureheads.

In order to even have credibility, much less to have any chance of success, subcabinet-level political appointees must bring to their work well-structured experience and demonstrated performance. Studying the history of national security strategy formulation may give a person insight into the mistakes and successes of earlier conflicts, but it does not teach how to *implement* a strategy in today's circumstances. Reading texts and receiving briefings on complex weapons-acquisition programs, mobilization procedures, or the standards by which the combat readiness of military units are measured is helpful to the untutored, but that kind of preparation is no substitute for actual experience in executing acquisition programs and mobilizations or in improving the readiness of particular units. Tangible achievements by a political nominee in the specific field of activity for which he will be responsible if confirmed, or at least in a closely related field, is absolutely essential.

Two insightful veterans of government service have observed that "charisma and effort alone won't get the job done."[19] Nor will technocratic expertise. Writing in August 2011 about the major financial problems in Europe and the United States, a respected scholar and student of the classics and military history noted that "[k]indred media elites in Europe and the United States lauded supposed technocratic expertise [by public officials] without much calibration of *achievement*. . . . [A] small group of self-assured professors, politicians, and well-compensated lobbyists hawked unproven theories as fact—as if they were clerics from the Dark Ages who felt their robes exempted them from needing to read or think about their religious texts."[20] All nominees for political office should be willing to be judged by the standard set by Aaron in Shakespeare's *Titus Andronicus*: "Let my deeds be witness of my worth."

It is not sufficient to have succeeded as a leader and manager in a different setting. In the 1960s, a popular management philosophy had it that a good executive can manage anything. That idea has largely been discredited.[21]

One reason is that, more often than not, "the sets of skills and aptitudes that [lead] to success in one walk of life either do not carry over or are downright dysfunctional in another."[22] Because it is so difficult to attract the very best talent to government service, it will, of course, always be a challenge to find potential political appointees who have experience in the exact field of activity in which they would like to serve. This fact makes it even more important to select candidates who have at least demonstrated leadership and managerial competence in a related or very similar field.

When I entered the Pentagon in 1987 as the new assistant secretary of defense for reserve affairs, my duties were very clear. By law,[23] I was now responsible for the manpower; readiness and sustainability; weapons systems, equipment, and material; personnel and compensation; operations, training, and force structure; mobilization, demobilization, and reconstitution; (active/reserve) force mix; installations and facilities; and other functional areas for all 462,000 members of the Army National Guard, the 601,000 members of the Army Reserve, the 238,000 members of the Naval Reserve, the 115,000 members of the Air National Guard, the 153,000 members of the Air Force Reserve, and the 88,000 members of the Marine Corps Reserve. Overall, the reserve components totaled over 1.67 million uniformed personnel, or 43 percent of the Armed Forces. I reported directly to the secretary of defense. There was no intervening undersecretary or other official who could assume part of the responsibility that was mine or share any blame if I failed to perform to the standards previously set.

A few weeks prior to my confirmation hearing, then Secretary of Defense Cap Weinberger had only half-jokingly asked at a senior staff meeting whether national guardsmen and federal reservists would show up if they were called to active duty. The fact was that since the nation had adopted the all-volunteer force in 1973, none of the reserve components had ever been called to active duty—not once. As a result, many reservists and their civilian employers didn't believe that they would ever be called. Many senior military officers shared that view. After all, no mobilization plan had ever been tested. Remembering the poor quality of many reservists during the war in Vietnam, many senior officers in the active forces retained grave doubts that the current reserve forces could perform effectively if they were activated. The readiness indicators provided a basis for their concern, for many units did have readiness problems. None of that affected the law. I was still personally responsible for ensuring the combat readiness of all of the reserve components and their smooth mobilization if the war tocsin sounded.

Fortunately, I had the help of many people. I was also intimately familiar with the field of activity in which I was required to operate. I had completed twenty-eight years of military service, including more than ten years of active service and eighteen years of service in the reserve components. I was a combat veteran and had trained many sailors and junior officers for combat duty. I had commanded reserve units. I was familiar with military and international law. I had managed different kinds of organizations. From my law practice, I was experienced in complex financial, organizational, and management-related matters. I knew my business. So did most of my colleagues in the departments of the army, navy, and air force. So, by the time the unexpected happened in 1990, an effective mobilization plan was in place and the reserve components were ready. Almost a quarter of a million guardsmen and reservists were activated in connection with operations Desert Shield/Desert Storm (also known as the first Persian Gulf War) and, as we have seen, they performed their missions superbly.[24] They deserved and received the gratitude of the nation. The point is that this unexpected conflict might have ended with a very different result if the several political appointees who shared responsibility for the reserve components had not been well versed in the nuts and bolts of the reserve forces.

In considering the qualities that political appointee leaders in departments like Defense and Homeland Security need to possess, it is important to understand the kinds of unique challenges with which government officials routinely have to deal. One daunting challenge is that posed by networked organizations. DoD, for example, is almost exclusively a traditional hierarchal bureaucracy. When the department was created by the National Security Act of 1947, its organizational, management, and personnel systems were designed to operate within a hierarchal framework, not a networked model. Thus, problems can arise in command and control—for example, in the control of the Army and Air National Guard. A network that includes the governors of the several states is involved. Until and unless the president federalizes the Guard of a particular state pursuant to Title 10 of the U.S. Code, its commander in chief is the governor of the state. Tensions naturally exist when a president sends Guard units on extended foreign missions like the armed conflicts in Iraq and Afghanistan at the same time that the governor of the state from which the Guard units are taken needs the units in connection with forest fires, flooding, or some other emergency within the state.

Another recent study of leadership in the public sector has concluded that there are, in fact, several distinct ways in which the challenges for civilian leaders in the government are unique.[25] One is the dispersion of authorization to make decisions. At a minimum, the leaders of a department or agency must be sensitive to the views of the authorizing and appropriations committees of both the Senate and House of Representatives, for those committees have significant power over department/agency spending and policies. Since DoD includes the three military departments, the civilian and military leaders of each of those departments must regularly appear before the authorizing and appropriation committees in connection with the budget and programs of the U.S. Army, Navy, Marine Corps, and Air Force. The committees closely scrutinize all existing and proposed programs. The most extreme example of this kind of dispersed authority involves the Department of Homeland Security. Senior officials of that department must report to more than seventy committees of Congress, each of which asserts jurisdiction over some aspect of that large department's work.

Another unique challenge identified by the study leaders is that of compulsory performance requirements. Industry leaders can sell or terminate an unprofitable line of business. They can reinvest the savings or pass them along to shareholders. Government leaders (for example, officials in the Department of Veterans Affairs) do not select the constituencies they serve. They are rarely able to use operating efficiency or some form of financial results to demonstrate success. This is not bad *per se*, but managing to performance can be very difficult when Congress legislates performance objectives and measures that are ambiguous, change, or focus on short-term political outcomes. I experienced this challenge in spades in connection with the drug war.

When I assumed responsibility for the complex new counterdrug program in April 1989, the secretary of defense delegated his counterdrug responsibilities to me. This included control—with the U.S. attorney general—of the entire counterdrug budget of the federal government. At that time, the budget was approximately $1.2 billion.

There were many problems. First, military leaders, most federal law enforcement agencies, some diplomats, and civil libertarians were opposed to the whole idea of assigning the counterdrug missions to the Armed Forces. Military leaders were certain that the Armed Forces could do nothing that would have an appreciable impact upon the trafficking in illegal drugs, and that even the effort to do so would reduce the readiness of military units to engage in conventional combat. The leaders of the law enforcement agencies were concerned that DoD was so large that its leadership would act with heavy hands, infringe upon their bureaucratic turf, and deprive them of resources. Diplomats forecast inevitable foreign policy problems, especially in Mexico and Central and South America. Civil libertarians feared that the use of military personnel for what was perceived as police work would cause permanent damage to long-established personal freedoms at home. Since I had been delegated authority to approve or reject the individual counterdrug plans submitted by the fifty governors, even my own new counterdrug staff was concerned about endless political problems that would interfere with our performance of the several new missions.

Second, it was necessary for me to work closely with the State Department's Bureau of International Narcotics Matters; the more than 150 agents of the Drug Enforcement Administration who were collecting intelligence and engaging in paramilitary activity in seventeen countries; the agents of the CIA, Customs Service, and FBI; the Coast Guard; the U.S. Information Agency and the National Security Agency; and a wide range of state, local, and foreign agencies. The missions necessarily took place in a fluid policy and operational environment. In order to make the interagency process work, operational agility and sensitivity to the cultural norms of the agencies was essential.

There was no doctrine or operational template to which I could turn for guidance. In order to successfully execute the new missions—that is, to get things done—it was necessary for me to stimulate commitment by all concerned and to foster a climate of trust. My personal credibility and competence had to be beyond question. My new responsibilities as the Pentagon's "drug czar" did not diminish my continuing responsibilities in the essentially unrelated position of assistant secretary for reserve affairs. I was personally responsible for executing the missions and programs associated with each position and for achieving results.

The primary measures of my performance in the reserve affairs job were relatively straightforward. I could, for example, demonstrate that the combat readiness of each of the reserve components, and the quality and numbers of people joining one of the reserve components, was improving. My work as the Pentagon "drug czar" was not so easily evaluated. Much of the work involved classified operations, behind-the-scenes interagency policy making, persuasion of foreign leaders to cooperate with our counterdrug efforts, motivation of military leaders who were still not enthusiastic about the new missions, and patient efforts to put into action new methodologies by which the experience and unique capabilities of the Armed Forces could effectively support law enforcement agencies. Congress had failed to provide the type of clear-cut goals that were needed to assess results and the adequacy of resources. Some measurements were simply impossible to make. It was impossible, for example, to measure the deterrent effects of some of our efforts (such as counting the number of planes or boats that *would have* carried illegal drugs across the Caribbean to the United States but for the new presence of military radar platforms and other detection equipment). Fortunately, I was eventually able to devise measures of performance that Congress found acceptable.

Another challenge for government leaders, especially in the departments of Defense and Homeland Security, is the lack of effective information systems. For the most part, industry executives are not limited in the sharing of information within their own companies. Government departments and agencies, on the other hand, must work together in preventing terrorist attacks, interdicting illegal drug shipments, and tracking down criminals, both at home and overseas. Much of the information needed by one department or agency is classified as secret by another and cannot be shared. Privacy and confidentiality laws further restrict the sharing of information.

It is also perhaps an inevitable fact that political leaders and the career civil service leaders with whom they work think very differently about how to get things done. Political leaders are particularly prone to what one of them has called "the culture of short-termism that dominates our society."[26] They too often favor short-term over more sound long-term results. They tend to think about performance in the context of short-term election cycles and to focus on quick successes and short-term crisis management. They are "frequently ill informed about the mechanics" of their department or agency.[27] Career civil service leaders have more of a long-term horizon. They "are more concerned about operational implications and service delivery on the ground—effects that often take many years to emerge."[28] They are also often slow to adapt to sudden changes in political direction and style.

The tension caused by these differences usually cannot be avoided. Among the leadership qualities that must be exhibited by political appointees if desired change is to become permanent is the patience to listen and the ability to obtain the support and expertise of the career professionals. Unfortunately, these qualities are often lacking. President Obama's political appointees provide a current example. In the April 2011 survey of senior career federal executives and managers referred to in chapter 4, one respondent declared that the appointees with whom he works have "unbelievably poor communication with career employees." Almost 40 percent of the executives and managers gave the appointees "Ds" or "Fs" on collaboration and communication with their staffs. Another respondent noted that the appointees "have a divide-and-conquer strategy." At another agency, a manager said that the result has been "politicization of normal agency functions."[29]

In addition to the various systemic challenges with which senior political appointees in the Pentagon routinely have to deal, different kinds of new challenges have arisen in recent years. One complex new managerial problem involves resources. In a speech at Notre Dame University on May 22, 2011, then secretary of defense Robert Gates warned against cuts to weapons programs and troop levels that would make the country vulnerable in "a complex and unpredictable security environment." He further declared, "[M]ake no mistake, the ultimate guarantee against the success of aggressors, dictators and terrorists in the 21st century, as in the 20th, is . . . the size, strength and global reach of the United States military." At the time of this speech, the U.S. defense budget, including the costs of the wars in Iraq and Afghanistan, accounted for only 4.5 percent of the nation's GDP and 19 percent of total federal spending. By comparison, fifty years ago, defense spending accounted for 47 percent of total federal spending, and throughout the more than four decades of the Cold War the United States spent, on average, 7.5 percent of the GDP on defense.[30]

Seventeen days later, the then deputy secretary of defense gave a speech in which he predicted that the wars of the future will be longer, deadlier, and waged against a more diverse variety of enemies than ever before.[31] Terrorists and insurgents can now strike civilian and military targets with improvised weapons and deadly effect, he said. "Rogue states seek nuclear weapons. [And] some criminal organizations even possess world-class cybercapabilities."[32] This means, he continued, that "we cannot prepare exclusively for either a high-end conflict with a potential near-peer [nation-state] competitor or a lower-end conflict with a counterinsurgency focus." Instead, the Armed Forces "must be able to confront both high-end and low-end threats."[33]

At the time that these speeches were made, the nation was laboring under a $1.4 trillion budget deficit and a $14 trillion debt, both of which had been dramatically affected by an $819 billion economic stimulus package, a plan that was described at the time as "breathtaking in size and scope."[34] One foreign policy expert predicted that these kinds of economic problems "will fundamentally transform the public life of the United States and therefore the country's foreign policy." A respected author put the matter in more specific terms: "[T]he most unique and important feature of U.S. foreign policy over the last century has been the degree to which America's diplomats and naval, air and ground forces provided global public good—from open seas to open trade and from containment to counterterrorism—that benefited many others besides us. U.S. power has been the key force maintaining global stability and providing global governance, for the last 70 years. That role will not disappear, but it will almost certainly shrink."[35]

Evidence of the kinds of effects that drastically reduced defense budgets have on a nation's ability to protect its national security interests was provided by our closest ally. In a June 2011 letter to a London newspaper, the admiral who led Britain's naval task force in the 1982 conflict over the Falkland Islands declared that if Argentina should invade the Falklands again, Britain could do little or nothing about it. Because of budget reductions since 1982, Britain had no aircraft carriers. "With our land and air forces already over-committed in Afghanistan and Libya, with the defence budget still shrinking, our submarine force more than halved, our destroyer and frigate force halved," the admiral said, "the answer appears to be that we can do precisely nothing."[36]

By the spring and summer of 2011, as the nation's financial problems reached crisis proportions, the need for high-quality, experienced political leadership on defense matters was obvious to all but the most obtuse. On April 13, President Obama proposed to cut $400 billion in projected defense spending by 2023. The proposal was made only months after Gates had directed the chiefs of the military services to make $100 billion in reductions through efficiency savings over the subsequent five years. According to one report, Obama's own Pentagon leadership was startled by the dimensions of the new proposed cuts and weren't even informed of them until the day before the president's announcement.[37] Obama said nothing about how the cuts would be made, what military missions and overseas commitments would have to be terminated, or what strategy should govern decisions about how to pare the defense budget. It was nothing more than an exercise in arithmetic. The $400 billion figure was simply an arbitrary number selected by White House advisors without regard to national security priorities. The White House proposal on defense spending was sufficiently dangerous to become the subject of Gates's final interview as Pentagon chief on June 30. If the DoD budget were cut by 10 percent, "which would be disastrous" for the Armed Forces, he said, that would only be $50 billion of a $1.4 trillion deficit. "We are not the problem," he declared, noting that defense cuts of the magnitude sought by Obama would require strategic tradeoffs and a national willingness to accept greater risks to the nation's security.[38] Worse news was yet to come.

On August 2, only hours before the U.S. Treasury would have been in default of the nation's financial obligations, Congress passed emergency debt-ceiling legislation. The pending DoD base budget request of $553 billion for FY 2012 (not including most spending for the wars in Afghanistan and Iraq) was immediately cut by $28 billion. The new law raised the federal debt ceiling and imposed federal spending cuts of about $917 billion, including the $400 billion in defense cuts that Obama had proposed in April. It further created a special new congressional committee and directed it to recommend, by late November, additional deficit-reduction cuts in the federal budget of $1.5 trillion. In the event that the new committee could not reach agreement on the additional reductions, or if its recommendations were rejected by the full Congress, a drastic new defense cut of an additional $500–600 billion over a decade would automatically be triggered.

The Pentagon's leadership was shaken and predictably very concerned about the potentially cataclysmic development. In his first news conference as the new secretary of defense, Leon Panetta declared that any such "triggered" cut would be "dangerous" and would do "real damage to our security, our troops and their families, and our ability to protect the nation."[39] Army General Martin E. Dempsey warned in his confirmation hearing to be the new chairman of the Joint Chiefs of Staff that cuts of that magnitude would be "extraordinarily difficult and [involve] very high risk."[40] A defense scholar at a liberal Washington, D.C., think tank warned that the nation was in danger of making budget decisions that would cut "real military capability," requiring the acceptance of "real additional risk." Such decisions, he said, would be contrary to what were described as "irreducible requirements in American defense policy—chiefly, winding down current wars responsibly, deterring Iran, hedging against a rising China, protecting global sea lanes, attacking terrorists and checking state sponsors of terror, and ensuring a strong all-volunteer military as well as a flexible and world-class defense scientific and industrial base."[41]

Whatever reductions in the defense budget were ultimately decided upon by Congress, the decisions on where to make the cuts would be very complex and risky. Substantially reduced military capabilities would require changes in the nation's global military strategy, not because of changes in the threats to the nation's security, but purely for budgetary reasons. Even well-grounded decisions on where in the defense budget to make the cuts could lead to what former defense secretary Gates had only recently expressed fear of: a dangerous "U.S. disengagement from the world."[42]

It was exactly these kinds of developments that prompted a member of the DoD Defense Science Board and former chairman of the DoD Defense Business Board[43] to identify a looming and major managerial problem within the Pentagon—a problem that is also present (albeit to a lesser extent) within the Department of Homeland Security and other departments and agencies: "A senior and mid-level leadership that lacks the experience of managing in an environment of ever-diminishing resources. Most successful CEOs ac-knowledge that leading an expanding enterprise is far easier than one in compression, or one that has a political process in which suppliers can make end runs around executive decisions."[44] In the decade following the attacks of 9/11, senior civilian and military leaders had calibrated their "processes and protocols to work best in an up-budget world." An entire generation of military leaders was now accustomed to Congress providing a level of fund-ing for the wars in Iraq and Afghanistan, as well as for other important DoD missions and programs, that was sufficiently great that they were not forced to choose between competing priorities.

Senator John McCain addressed this issue at a September 13, 2011, hear-ing of the Senate Armed Services Committee. Noting that "over the last ten years senior defense management has been inclined to lose sight of afford-ability as a goal and has just reached for more money as the solution to most problems," he called for "an end to the department's systemic tendency to spend the taxpayers' money in a manner that is far too often disconnected from what the warfighter needs." Clearly, military leaders were not equipped "to make the sustained trades and absorb the pain of ever-increasing scar-city."[45]

Nor were the appointees who were their political superiors. In order to make painful budget decisions, senior political appointees in the Pentagon have to work closely with military leaders over several years to evaluate and compare all current and new missions that the Armed Forces have been asked to perform and to decide what force structure, weapons systems, and capabilities are required of each service for those missions as well as what the respective costs are, and also what they will be. Every decision is difficult, complex, and involves risk. Mindless across-the-board cuts only leave the Armed Forces with a hollow and ineffective force structure. The difficult tradeoffs, the matching of resources to specific military capabilities pursuant to a clear strategy, blunt and objective resistance to budget hawks who are as interested in fiscal matters and political security as they are uninformed about national security matters, total reform of an out-of-control acquisition process, and a reshaping of the entire defense workforce is not work for either amateurs or the faint-hearted. The analytical work and the final decisions require the greatest possible competence, experience, and courage in the political appointees who have to engage in that work.

On a smaller scale, I experienced the same problem shortly after I entered the government. In late 1987, and after seven consecutive years of substantial increases in the defense budget, President Reagan and Congress agreed to limit the fiscal year 1989 DoD budget to $299 billion, some $33 billion less than what the president had proposed in his earlier budget request. As a member of the Defense Resources Board (DRB), I had a major role in advising then Secretary of Defense Frank Carlucci on how to make the required cuts. None of the civilian and military leaders then in office had been present the last time the defense budget had to be cut.

I was surprised by the games that were played by the individual military services to minimize their own share of the cuts. I quickly learned that the Pentagon's large and powerful bureaucracy and complex operating environment pose daunting obstacles for even the most experienced, knowledgeable, and determined leaders. A particular problem can be posed by the individual services, who inculcate their members with perspectives based on valid service needs. Those perspectives and the attendant service cultures are beneficial for recruiting and war fighting, but they can be counterproductive at levels of decision-making where integration of military and civilian effort is required to make best use of very limited resources.

Another political challenge for senior appointees is really not new, but history has vividly demonstrated its importance: the totally unexpected national security or other catastrophic events. The idea of the importance of preparation for highly improbable developments is the subject of a recent and popular book. The central idea of *The Black Swan*[46] concerns our blindness with respect to large deviations from the expected. The author asserts that very improbable (improbable according to our current knowledge) events take place "while we spend our time engaged in small talk, focusing on the known, and the repeated."[47] We act, he says, "as though we are able to predict historical events." What is surprising, he continues, "is not the magnitude of our forecast errors, but our absence of awareness of it. This is all the more worrisome when we engage in deadly conflicts: wars are fundamentally unpredictable (and we do not know it)."[48]

One need only look to very recent events to recognize the truth in the argument, as well as the increasing speed and scale of change with which new threats, or at least major new challenges, are presented. The democratic uprisings that arose suddenly and independently across the Arab world in early 2011 caught most international political leaders flat-footed. In what became known as the "Arab Spring," protests against established governments, some of which were longtime allies of the United States, spread to several countries within weeks. By the end of March, American military forces were leading air strikes against Libyan military units loyal to the Libyan president, Muammar Gaddafi. No one in the U.S. government had predicted that development.

Examples of improbable natural disasters are even more common. Despite its reputation for organization and efficiency in business matters, Japan was totally unprepared for the multiple disasters that followed the 9.0 earthquake that struck the country on March 11, 2011. The unprecedented scale of the earthquake, the tsunami, and the subsequent nuclear power crisis at the Fukushima Dai-ichi plant made it very difficult for the government to manage events and to retain public confidence. Government officials admitted that they had not anticipated the disaster. They were heavily criticized for the slowness of the response as well as for failures in coordinating and sharing critically important information with the public. The people who lost loved ones, who were made homeless, and who had no food or water or electricity were left confused and frightened. On a smaller scale, and as we saw in chapter 1, the U.S. government was similarly caught flat-footed when Hurricane Katrina hit the coastlines of Louisiana, Mississippi, and Alabama on August 29, 2005. In the days following the storm, widespread dissatisfaction was repeatedly expressed about the level of preparedness and the response of government officials at all levels.

Related to the need for senior political appointee-leaders to be capable of responding to totally unexpected national security or other catastrophic events is the need for them to have sufficient ability and experience to make wise judgments in very ambiguous and complex circumstances. Our recent history suggests that in the future, the Armed Forces may be asked to perform missions that are not as clear cut as stopping the invasion of one foreign country by another, implementing regime change, or responding to a clear threat to one of our own vital security interests. Our efforts to protect innocent civilians in Libya in 2011 and in response to Serbian atrocities in the Balkans in the 1990s provide examples.

Future missions to stop mass atrocities in foreign countries, to support a political movement that is more sensitive to democratic principles and human rights than an existing government, and to provide various other forms of humanitarian relief may not involve vital American security interests that justify the use of military force at all. Even when American interests are involved, those interests may be limited. When force is used, mission creep follows almost inevitably since there is no established doctrine or rules of engagement for all such missions. In these kinds of circumstances, political leaders must set clear goals. They must anticipate the likely consequences of U.S. military action and be fully prepared to deal with those consequences. They must be capable of generating domestic support, including the support of Congress, through clear articulation of the U.S. interests that are at stake.

They must also have sufficient operational and related experience to know what is possible and what is not and to second-guess the nature and scope of operations proposed by military leaders to achieve stated goals. The total absence of this kind of civilian capability was obvious in April 2011 when civilians in the Obama White House clashed with military leaders over the U.S. response to the uprising against Libyan dictator Gaddafi. The civilians, ever mindful of the 2012 presidential election and opinion polls that reflected public fatigue with the conflicts in Iraq and Afghanistan, pressed the Pentagon for a cheap, essentially risk-free plan to remove Gaddafi from power without the use of U.S. ground forces. Military professionals knew that a forced change in regimes was highly unlikely to succeed if ground forces were barred from participating in the plan of operation. Apparently, the political mechanics in the White House even believed that military leaders were expressing disrespect for the president when they could not devise a politically acceptable operational plan that incorporated the unrealistic idea of no ground troops.[49]

Yet another challenge with which senior appointees must now deal, especially those in DoD and the State Department, is new and unprecedented: the effect of the new era of social media technology and global networking websites on foreign political developments. Since 2009, American business and governmental organizations have been discussing the question of whether and how to use social media as an effective communications tool. The matter has already been settled in many foreign countries. The phenomenal growth of mobile phones and similar devices in recent years has permitted the Internet, computers, and the social media devices to become tools of political revolutions. As developments in the Middle East, North Africa, and the streets of cities in the United Kingdom demonstrated in the spring and summer of 2011, the vast social networking platforms provided by venues like Facebook serve as organizational tools. They permit users to discreetly mobilize in large numbers. They give users access to information, whether it be about government corruption, political protests, stores that are vulnerable to looting, or other developments not reported by the press. As a result, a large "media-gap" has been created between the users, who are primarily young people, and the rulers of autocratic states, whose lack of contemporary media skills have led some to characterize them as archers in the age of gunpowder. As a consequence of this development, American government officials must now be capable of speedily formulating and executing operational plans in areas where we have been accustomed to having long lead times in the emergence of political change that involves an American security interest.

Despite the urgent need to ensure that the right political appointees are placed in the right positions of authority, as we have seen in chapter 3, presidents and those who advise them on personnel matters usually do not think very hard about the process they use to select potential appointees. Many times it is because they simply want to pick people who have strong political credentials or with whom they are comfortable. At many other times, it is because they don't have a precise understanding of what qualifications each position to be filled requires. They haven't defined each job "in terms of its three or four nonnegotiable criteria—things that a person *must* be able to do in order to succeed."[50] As a result, they select people who may have great political credentials and skills for other jobs, but who are doomed to fail in the positions they have been chosen to occupy.

On other occasions, presidential personnel teams, like corporate CEOs and boards of directors, are seduced by qualities of a candidate that are not even relevant to the position for which the candidate is being considered. Perhaps the candidate is articulate, attractive, well educated, and smart. But how good is he at getting things done? Is he a doer, or is he simply glib, someone who is sliding along by talking a good game? Does he get excited about doing things as opposed to simply talking about them? What are his work habits? Does he energize the people around him? Is he decisive on tough issues? Does he follow up to ensure that performance standards are met? Two business leaders have often encountered this failure and have written about it: "We see this problem particularly when highly intellectual staff people or consultants want to move into high-level line jobs. They frequently come from the best business schools, from consulting firms and from internal jobs in finance, accounting, and strategic planning. The trouble is, they have never been tested in mobilizing line people to *execute*."[51]

The failure of presidents to select the right people for the right jobs is more than a cause for great public concern. It is a problem that is growing worse. The April 2011 *Government Executive* survey referred to above and in chapter 4 revealed great skepticism about the ability of political appointees to improve the performance of the departments and agencies in which they serve. One respondent declared, "The role [of senior leadership] has increased, but the effectiveness, skill and knowledge has dramatically decreased."[52] Survey respondents said in particular that Obama appointees lacked functional and agency-specific knowledge and don't understand human resources and procurement rules. The appointees presumed that the "institution is there as an obstruction." As a consequence, they attempt to "break organizations."[53]

A personal attribute that is essential for all successful political appointees, especially those who serve in important positions involving national security or homeland security, is at least as important as leadership, management ability, and intellect: character. On January 23, 1909, less than six weeks before the end of his presidency, Theodore Roosevelt wrote an article for *Outlook*, a magazine of news and commentary of which he would soon become editor. No doubt already aware of his legacy, he vigorously declared that "a nation must be judged in part by the character of its public men, not merely by their ability, but by their ideals and the measure in which they realize these ideals."[54]

He had already written and spoken about the components of character. The first, he said, is clean living. A public official "must be clean of life, so that he can laugh when his public or his private record is searched." This is important, he said, because "no man can lead a public career really worth leading; no man can act with rugged independence in serious crises, nor strike at great abuses, nor afford to make powerful and unscrupulous foes, if he is himself vulnerable in his private character."[55] The second component, he believed, has to do with "resolution, hardihood, courage, a fearlessness in taking the initiative and assuming responsibility."[56]

After World War II ended, the U.S. Army asked Franz Halder, the former German chief of the general staff, to critique the U.S. war effort and offer suggestions for improvement. He advised that this sentence be included in U.S. Army instructions: "In war, the qualities of the *character* are more important than those of the intellect."[57] By that he meant determination, the willingness to assume responsibility, and the ability to handle adversity. He was, of course, referring to a quality required of military leaders, but there is no reason to believe that the quality of character is any less important for senior political leaders.

Character, or integrity, is the quality that helps us, in the words of the Naval Academy's Midshipman's Prayer, "To stand unafraid and unashamed before our shipmates, our loved ones, and [God]." It is the "stuff" of which we are made, the core of who we are as individual human beings. In a commencement address at The Citadel in May 1993, former president Ronald Reagan talked about this quality:

> [T]he character that takes command in moments of crucial choices has already been determined. It has been determined by a thousand other choices made earlier in seemingly unimportant moments. It has been determined by all those "little" choices of years past—by all those times when the voice of conscience was at war with the voice of temptation—whispering a lie that "it doesn't really matter." It has been determined by all the day-to-day decisions made when life seemed easy and crises seemed far away—the decisions that, piece by piece, bit by bit, develop habits of discipline or laziness, habits of self-sacrifice or self-indulgence, habits of duty and honor and integrity—or dishonor and shame.

Churchill said much the same thing in his speech of tribute on the floor of the House of Commons after the death of former prime minister Neville Chamberlain.

> The only guide to a man is his conscience; the only shield to his memory is the rectitude and sincerity of his actions. It is very imprudent to walk through life without this shield, because we are so often mocked by the failure of our hopes and the unsetting of our calculations; but with this shield, however the fates may play, we march always in the ranks of honour.[58]

The importance of character in civilian officials who lead military, law enforcement, and other personnel charged with protecting the nation cannot be overemphasized. Career public servants who engage in dangerous operations or other public activities involving risks cannot afford to overlook character flaws in their political superiors. Their lives may depend upon the character of the civilian leaders. A former chief of the Australian Defence Force has thus noted that colleagues and professional subordinates

> may, over time, forgive a leader an absence of all other qualities—either singly or in combination, because given time and experience most qualities can be acquired or developed to a reasonable standard. The exception to this rule is integrity.[59]

Vice Admiral James B. Stockdale, who was awarded the Congressional Medal of Honor for his own courageous leadership during seven years of imprisonment and torture as a POW in Vietnam, concurred with this view. He also believed that character in a leader is more important than knowledge: "The sine qua non of a leader has lain not in his chesslike grasp of issues and the options they portend, not in his style of management, not in his skill at processing information, but in having the character, the heart, to deal spontaneously, honorably, and candidly with people, perplexities, and principles."[60]

Many times, a political appointee's character is tested in subtle ways. Almost every special interest group in the nation's capital, for example, presents awards each year to a senior government official. The venue is usually elaborate, an evening banquet or perhaps a luncheon in a prestigious hotel. It is seldom a coincidence that a particular awardee is in a position to advance the interests of the presenting group by a policy or administrative decision. This is not to suggest that such awards are always inappropriate. Most are probably well deserved. Even when they are, however, the nation is entitled to have confidence in the fact that the awardee is under no illusion that he or she would have received the award even if not occupying a position of political power.

Another attribute that is related to character, and critical to the real effectiveness of senior political appointees, is moral courage. Paraphrasing Dr. Johnson, Churchill declared, "Courage is rightly esteemed the first of human qualities . . . because it is the quality which guarantees all others." British Prime Minister Benjamin Disraeli advised that one will find as he grows older that "courage is the rarest of all qualities to be found in public life." In today's risk-averse culture, the quality is certainly not common. And yet it is so important in public service, for much more than one's personal career is at stake. An obvious circumstance in which courage as well as character is required is a situation in which a political appointee disagrees with his political superior on a matter of principle. This is not a common occurrence, but it does happen. In this context, people who were adults during the Watergate scandal in the Nixon administration will not soon forget the courageous conduct of Elliot Richardson.

In May 1973, Nixon appointed Richardson, then serving as secretary of defense, to be attorney general. During his confirmation hearing, Richardson pledged that he would not fire any special prosecutor selected to investigate the Watergate matter except for "extraordinary improprieties." In July, the special prosecutor, Harvard law professor Archibald Cox, subpoenaed several tapes of recorded conversations by the president in the White House. Nixon refused to turn over the tapes. Both the U.S. District Court and the U.S. Court of Appeals eventually ordered Nixon to comply with Cox's subpoena. On Saturday, October 20, the White House chief of staff telephoned Richardson at Nixon's direction and instructed him to fire Cox. The dilemma facing Richardson was as simple as it was stark: "Would he, as attorney general, be bound by law and loyalty to obey the president? Or, would he be bound by law and commitment to keep his pledge to the Senate—not to fire Cox except for 'extraordinary improprieties'?"[61]

The domestic crisis could hardly have come at a more difficult time for the president. On October 6, a coalition of Arab states had launched a surprise attack on Israel in what became known as the Yom Kippur War. The Soviet Union, the other nuclear superpower, had immediately begun a large-scale resupply effort in support of its Arab allies. Fearing for their survival, the Israelis had convinced Nixon to provide comparable support. By Friday, October 19, the Soviet government had recognized that its clients were losing the war and had escalated its support, even placing Soviet combat divisions on alert. The risk of a confrontation between the two superpowers was rapidly increasing. This tension had been exacerbated by another development. On October 10, Vice President Spiro Agnew had resigned after pleading no contest to a charge of income tax evasion.

In the midst of this firestorm, Richardson made his decision. But when he went to the White House on the afternoon of the October 20 to resign, the president asserted that a resignation at that time would jeopardize the government's efforts to effect a cease-fire in the Middle East. He asked Richardson to delay his resignation. After a "long strained moment," Richardson declined the president's request, believing that if he delayed his resignation for even a week, "it would be seen as a capitulation to public criticism."[62] Bitterly declaring that Richardson was putting his individual concerns above the nation's interests, Nixon declared, "Let it be on your head."[63] There are few better examples of the kind of character, fearlessness, and assumption of responsibility to which Theodore Roosevelt referred.

A presidential historian has written that Roosevelt believed that great leaders were those who took noble risks and that the politician who cared only for his own success was a curse.[64] He praised his famous "man in the arena" precisely because the man "dared greatly," even if he failed. It has been noted that Roosevelt had the freedom to dare "because there was more to his life than politics."[65] Unfortunately, many political appointees today have no significant life, and certainly no significant occupation, other than politics and closely associated activities like lobbying.

Another experience in which senior political appointees must demonstrate character and courage is in their relationship with Congress. As a veteran of more than fifty congressional hearings, I am well acquainted with the tensions that are routinely generated there. Disagreements and conflict are almost a certainty when an executive branch appointee testifies before a committee of Congress that is controlled by the political party that the president defeated in the most recent presidential election. Since I never had an opportunity to testify before a committee controlled by the party of the presidents who appointed me, I prepared for each hearing as if I were preparing for oral argument before the Supreme Court on a matter of monumental importance. The challenge comes when the appointee-official who is testifying must defend or explain a matter that has political risk—that is, the potential to cause significant embarrassment, to either the administration of which the appointee is a part or to him- or herself. It is in precisely those and other similar circumstances that the nation is entitled to courage and complete candor by the appointee, whatever the political cost.

It has been my experience that while many political leaders in government like to claim that they "speak truth to power," few really do. Truth involves reality, all of the hard facts, not perceived or desired reality. Too often, senior government officials gloss over inconvenient facts in discussions with their political superiors or political opponents, or they strive to convey information they know is in line with the thinking of their superiors, or they remain silent when their political superior has made a decision that is not based on all relevant facts, including embarrassing ones.

Sometimes, political leaders even avoid telling the truth to the American people. In his classic book *The Best and the Brightest*, Pulitzer Prize–winning author and journalist David Halberstam told the story of what happened when the best and the brightest men in the country came to Washington to serve in the Kennedy and Johnson administrations. They came, it was said, to build a Camelot, and when they later left the government, they left behind a country badly divided by the war in Vietnam and torn by dissent. The conclusion of the book provides a sobering reminder of the importance of dealing in truth:

> Lyndon Johnson had lost it all, and so had the rest of them; they had, for all their brilliance and hubris and sense of themselves, been unwilling to look to and learn from the past. . . .
>
> In a way Lyndon Johnson had known better, he had entertained no small amount of doubt about the course he was taking, but he saw, given his own instincts, his own reading of American politics, his own belief in how he had to look to others, no way of getting off. He and the men around him wanted to be defined as being strong and tough; but strength and toughness and courage were exterior qualities which would be demonstrated by going to a clean and hopefully antiseptic war with a small nation, rather than the interior and more lonely kind of strength and courage of telling the truth to America and perhaps incurring a good deal of domestic political risk.[66]

Sooner or later, most political appointees come face-to-face with a moment of truth. My first encounter occurred only a few months after I assumed office as assistant secretary of defense for reserve affairs. Secretary of Defense Carlucci called a senior staff meeting to propose the creation of a new position of undersecretary of defense for personnel and readiness, along with several new positions for the large supporting staff that would be required.

Carlucci further proposed that the assistant secretaries for reserve affairs, health affairs, and force management and personnel would report to the new undersecretary. Creation of the undersecretary position would reduce the secretary's own span of control, something that most managers desire, and it was common knowledge that he had a particular person in mind to fill the position. He went around the room asking for the opinion of each of my colleagues. I could see that, because of the seating arrangement, I would be asked last. Everyone in the room indicated approval of the idea until he turned to me.

When I said that I not only opposed the idea but would also resign if it was adopted, the room was suddenly very quiet. I was now the subject of a collective look of amazement. The other members of the senior staff, all of whom had more experience in Washington than I did, were apparently unaccustomed to such forceful expressions. I was later told by some of my colleagues that they had immediately assumed that I would be fired, or at least that my advice would be rejected. When Carlucci asked why I felt so strongly about the issue, I told him that I would defend to the death his right to organize the Department of Defense any way that the law permitted, since he was responsible for its performance. But, I continued, at a time when we were making substantial cuts in the force structure and weapons systems of the Armed Forces for budgetary reasons, it made no sense to increase the size of the civilian bureaucracy in the Pentagon. I also reminded him that the combat readiness of the reserve components was improving because I had regular, direct access to him to discuss problems and obtain prompt decisions. That would not occur if I first had to go through another level of staff review. To his great credit, Carlucci dropped the idea. I also retained my job.

During the Cold War, citizens of many countries in Eastern Europe risked more than the loss of a job if they told the truth. Slowly, however, the work of a small group of young faculty members at the Catholic University of Lublin (KUL) began to influence political developments in Poland. The group included Father Karol Wojtyla, a specialist in ethics. He would later be known to the world as Pope John Paul II. In their philosophical inquiry into human nature, these teachers adopted the ancient conviction that truth and reality matter, that if human thinking and electoral and other choices lack "a tether to reality . . . raw force takes over the world and truth becomes a function of power, not an expression of things-as-they-are."[67] The biographer of Pope John Paul II later wrote that the political meaning of this realist assumption was ultimately adopted by the Solidarity Independent Trade Union in its confrontation with the Polish Communist government. After the pope's visit to Poland in 1979, a soon-to-be famous Solidarity election poster was created, which read, "For Poland to be Poland, 2 + 2 must always = 4." The biographer went on to observe that human beings can only be free in the truth, and that "the measure of truth is reality."[68]

The problem of poor execution or implementation of strategies, policies, and plans is present in many fields of endeavor. It is self-evident that if a person has no demonstrated skills or experience in baseball, his experience in accounting will not help him win ball games. Even a study of the history of baseball will not teach him how to play the game. It may help him appreciate why a Hall of Fame pitcher was great, and it may give him an understanding of why some pitchers are more effective than others against left-handed hitters. But it will not teach him how to throw a curveball or a slider. That can only be learned through well-structured experience.

The execution of national security strategies, policies, and programs is too important to be left to amateurs, however well intentioned and enthusiastic they may be, and no matter how strong their political connections. The challenges that confront senior political appointees in departments and agencies like Defense and Homeland Security are unique and complex. The stakes are high, too high for the challenges to be left in the hands of anyone other than highly competent and experienced leaders and managers who have a record of getting things done and achieving results. They must be capable of dealing with unexpected crises, for those will certainly occur. They must have character and courage, for they will certainly run into potential conflicts of interest and situations where a statement of the truth is likely to cause embarrassment and perhaps, place their job at risk. For those who give honorable, competent public service, 2 + 2 will always equal 4. The need to get things done and to achieve results became even more important and more complex after the tragic events of September 11, 2001.

Chapter Seven

Professionalism in the Era of Wars of a Different Kind

The Army has embarked on this effort under its own initiative because proactive, continuous examination is what professions do—reflect, review, assess, evolve, and change.
> —Terms of Reference for the Review of the Army Profession in an Era of
> Persistent Conflict, October 27, 2010

[T]he quality of the people [in government] is more important than the quality of the wiring diagrams. . . . Good people can overcome bad structures.
> —Report of the National Commission on Terrorist Attacks upon the United
> States, July 22, 2004

As America entered the first decade of the twenty-first century, a badly flawed president departed the White House amid a firestorm of criticism over a number of inexplicable pardons he had granted in the final hours of his administration and the national trauma that had resulted from his conduct with a twenty-one-year-old White House intern, conduct that had put his entire presidency at risk. He was replaced by a new, untested president who had absolutely no experience, and apparently very little interest, in foreign policy. He had just won an extremely close election in which national security issues had played only a marginal part.

The role of the United States in the post–Cold War world was still being defined. After so many years of clarity during that conflict, the exact nature of the nation's international security interests was a subject of disagreement among those comparatively few who cared about the issue. Not long after the election, one academic wrote that U.S. military forces suffered from several serious, long-term problems. The first, he argued, was strategic in nature: "American strategy still relies on a Cold War–derived understanding of military power and fails to focus on the challenges of the new century."[1] Most Americans simply weren't interested in foreign policy issues, but rather on domestic and more personal matters. "To much of the rest of the world," a distinguished author wrote, "America was immensely powerful, but for a nation that powerful, it was shockingly self-absorbed."[2] All of that changed on September 11, 2001.

Whatever else they accomplished, the attacks on New York and the Pentagon, and the aborted attack that ended in a field in Pennsylvania, ushered in a new era of great complexity for American political and military leaders. Suddenly, the nation's overwhelming superiority in strategic (nuclear) weapons and its capability for fighting conventional conflicts was no longer sufficient for its security. It had major and previously undervalued vulnerabilities. Despite accumulating evidence over several years that we were increasingly at risk from terrorist attacks that might have a catastrophic impact, little had been done about the threat. No strategy was in place; there had been no sense of urgency. Dr. Condoleezza Rice, the new president's national security advisor, summed up the situation with these words: "There was nothing on the shelf for this kind of war."[3]

Three days after the attacks, both houses of Congress approved resolutions authorizing the use of force against those involved. In his address to the nation on September 20, 2001, President Bush declared a very ambitious, long-term, and somewhat open-ended U.S. objective in the new war. "Our war on terror begins with al Qaeda," he said, "but . . . it will not end until every terrorist group of global reach has been found, stopped and defeated." All of the apparent certainties of earlier years were now under review. In the new security environment in which we had been attacked at home, the lines between "foreign" and "domestic" conflicts and between "war" and "crime" were no longer as clear as they had seemed to be prior to September 11, 2001. "War fighting" now had a new meaning. The new form of terrorism did not start or stop at the water's edge or at our land borders with other countries. The American homeland was now part of the battle space.

The distinction between different operational categories of warfare was also now blurred. The nature, location, and military capabilities of the enemy was unclear. Nonstate actors had certainly been involved in the attacks, but how broad was their support, did they have a state sponsor, and what were their aims other than to cause as much death and devastation as possible? Even established societal rules were now being reevaluated. A U.S. Court of Appeals judge was compelled to declare that legality "must sometimes be sacrificed for other values. We are a nation under law," he said, "but first we are a nation."[4]

Not long after the attacks, I revisited a book that I had read when the world seemed more predictable. On April 23, 1987, I was interviewed in the Pentagon by the then secretary of defense, Caspar Weinberger, in connection with my subsequent appointment by President Reagan as assistant secretary of defense. Shortly after the interview, I stopped in the Pentagon bookstore and purchased a copy of the 1986 book *Thinking in Time*.[5] I read it on the plane during the trip back to my home in Colorado. The authors of the book, two professors at Harvard's Kennedy School of Government, urged policy makers to "inspect the history of an issue so that decision objectives can be defined and the likely results of specific actions foreseen," and to think in "time-streams" by viewing present circumstances as part of an unbroken continuum between the past and the future. This new war, however, was of a different kind. It was not at all clear whether it would lend itself to this kind of analysis. In the short term, at least, civilian and military leaders would be groping for the most appropriate actions to take. The only thing certain about the new situation was that it would require the highest order of professionalism from military leaders. It occurred to very few people that the new circumstances also called for a new and much higher level of competence among civilian leaders in the government.

When Operation Enduring Freedom commenced on October 7, 2001, with strikes in Afghanistan by land- and ship-based U.S. aircraft and cruise missiles against Taliban forces, al Qaeda fighters, and certain fixed assets such as terrorist training sites, American civilian and military leaders were scrambling hard to catch up with events. An unconventional campaign soon commenced in which CIA paramilitary teams were deployed with small numbers of Special Operations personnel to aide Afghan forces on the ground and to assist aircraft in designating bombing targets. The longer-term use of U.S. military forces, however, was still under discussion. No one could predict how long it would take to achieve the ambitious and open-ended objective declared by President Bush in his September 20 address, but there was no doubt among military leaders that the war-fighting doctrines of the services would have to change dramatically.

A more immediate concern was manpower, particularly for ground units, which would likely bear the brunt of early combat operations. The manning problem was not one of end strength—that is, the number of soldiers authorized by Congress—but rather how many deployable units were available. Subsequent to the end of the Cold War, Congress had predictably demanded a "peace dividend." By the time of the 2000 election, the number of active army divisions had been effectively reduced from the eighteen that had existed at the time of the 1991 Persian Gulf War to ten. As a consequence, the new circumstances required the immediate support of National Guard and reserve units. Six months after the attacks of 9/11, almost 81,000 reservists from all fifty states, the District of Columbia, and Puerto Rico had been

activated. In September 2003, six months after Operation Iraqi Freedom—
the war in Iraq—began, defense officials found it necessary to extend the
tours of National Guard and reserve forces serving there from six months to
twelve months. By the fall of 2004, over 335,000 reservists had been involuntarily called to active duty. A Government Accountability Office (GAO)
report that year noted that much of the army's reserve component force had
been organized, trained, and resourced as a strategic reserve that would receive personnel, training, and equipment as a later-deploying reserve force,
rather than as an operational force designed for continuous overseas deployments. It went on to say, however, that "the [current] pace of reserve operations is expected to remain high," in what was described as an "indefinite
Global War on terrorism overseas."[6]

Within months, the army's reserve components constituted about 55 percent of the army forces in Iraq. Some 80 percent of the National Guard was
either on active duty or expected to be called to active duty within the next
three years. The chief of the National Guard Bureau declared publicly what
had been obvious to army leaders for some time. Without serious planning,
without any debate in Congress or scrutiny by the public at large, without any
study of the long-term consequences, and with little or no discussion with
state governors about their needs of their guardsmen (in Title 32 or "state"
status) for homeland security or other local emergencies, the raison d'être of
the National Guard and the reserve components was being "shifted." Instead
of serving as a strategic reserve built on a Cold War deterrence construct, all
of the reserve components were becoming an operational reserve that had to
be capable of joint and expeditionary (Title 10 or "federal" status) missions.[7]
By the end of 2010, over 770,000 guardsmen and reservists had been activated since September 11, 2001. In 2011, Pentagon leaders asked Congress for
the authority that would permit the secretaries of the military services to
involuntarily activate members of the Selected Reserve and Individual Ready
Reserve, for any reason. Throughout the nation's history, that authority had
been limited to the president.

The many challenges faced by military leaders since the turn of the new
century have demanded adaptability and a willingness to reassess all aspects
of the wars in Iraq and Afghanistan. Those conflicts have "accelerated
change in ways that DoD theoreticians could not [have imagined]."[8] Army
and Marine Corps leaders have been particularly pressed. Those services
were simply not prepared for the insurgency that began in Iraq after coalition
forces captured Baghdad in 2003.

At his first meeting with the Joint Chiefs of Staff in early 2001, the new
secretary of defense, Donald Rumsfeld, asked what they believed "transfor-

mation" could mean for the Department of Defense. He purportedly had nothing more in mind than the guidance he had received from President George W. Bush to make the Armed Forces "lethal, light and mobile."[9] Nevertheless, while few people could explain the transformation concept, it soon became an umbrella under which various kinds of new activities began. The military services even began to base requests for certain technologies on the argument that the systems were "transformational."

It has been argued that Rumsfeld's focus on transforming the Armed Forces, and the disagreements and tensions with military leaders that flowed from that effort, were a cause of a faulty strategic assessment in 2002–2003—that is, an "inability to generate a strategy that [linked] campaigns and operations within a theater of war to policy."[10] As time passed and it became increasingly recognized that failures in the planning for post-conflict stabilization operations in Iraq had resulted in a full-fledged insurgency, military leaders changed their approach to the conflict. After a well-publicized joint effort led by then Lieutenant General David H. Petraeus, the commander of the army's Combined Arms Center, and Marine Lieutenant General James N. Mattis, a new counterinsurgency doctrine was developed in 2006. On the basis of their combat experience in Iraq, Petraeus and Mattis formalized principles that they would vigorously assert in subsequent years. Their joint objective was to transform military forces from blunt instruments designed to fight force-on-force wars of attrition into learning institutions that give troops the flexibility and creativity to fight the wars of the information age; to change the American tendency to rely on better technology and superior firepower to a search for innovation; and to teach troops adaptability and how to thrive in uncertainty and chaos.

The army reworked its intellectual foundations to reincorporate irregular warfare, including counterinsurgency and stability operations, on a par with traditional combat operations in a comprehensive framework known as "full spectrum operations."[11] New doctrinal publications were produced.[12] The army also made radical changes in its force structure. Large division-size formations trained for conventional combat were no longer a priority. Headquarters staffs that had been an integral part of the divisions were reduced. Brigade-size units were modularized. The idea was to build units that were interchangeable and could be tailored to different types of contingencies. Special Operations forces received significant increases in funding and personnel. Artillery and armored forces were reduced in favor of military police and engineers. New units were created to train and assist foreign forces.

Meanwhile, the Marine Corps was facing a different kind of doctrinal challenge: developing an intellectual rationale for its future beyond Iraq and Afghanistan. After several years of sustained ground operations in those countries and army manpower shortages, and despite the fact that in November 2001 marine helicopters from the USS *Peleliu* (LHA-5) had transported troops some 372 nautical miles inland for the seizure of a desert airfield in Afghanistan, concerns were being raised about the Marine Corps becoming a "second land army" instead of an elite expeditionary force that could assault land positions from the sea. By 2010, Secretary of Defense Gates was challenging the Corps to rethink its post-Afghanistan role.

The problem was exacerbated when Gates recommended in January 2011 that the Corps's Expeditionary Fighting Vehicle, on which it had staked its future amphibious assault capability, be canceled because of budgetary pressures, technical problems, and, perhaps, a desire by the secretary to "rationalize movement of money out of the Marine Corps budget so it [could] be used for other purposes."[13] The Corps had no choice but to start the development of a less expensive landing vehicle. In February 2011, the new Marine Corps commandant, General James Amos, responded to the challenge made by Gates. The Marine Corps of the future, he said, would be a "middleweight force," smaller, with lighter vehicles and lighter protective gear, but ready to move quickly from ships to buy time for senior officials to decide on a long-term response to a crisis.[14]

Two years after the 9/11 attacks, the air force published its updated doctrinal statement. Asserting that air force doctrine is never complete and a continuous work in progress, air force leaders noted that the "American Way of War" had long been described as "warfare based on either a strategy of annihilation or of attrition," and that U.S. air and space power, "if properly focused, offers [the] national leadership alternatives."[15] To that end, the doctrinal publication declared that the air force's capabilities included the ability to deliver air and space superiority—or control of the air ("critical to any military operation")—as well as global attack with a wide range of missiles and munitions, precision engagement, agile combat support, and information superiority that would give American leaders faster command and control than their adversaries. After initial reluctance followed by public pressure from the secretary of defense, the air force began to purchase greater numbers of unmanned aerial vehicles (UAVs) and it established a new career track for specialists in UAV operations.

Twelve years earlier, upon the conclusion of Operation Desert Storm, the first Persian Gulf War, in 1991, naval leaders had recognized that urgent change was needed in the navy's doctrine. A former colleague of mine who subsequently served as vice chairman of the Joint Chiefs of Staff wrote that Desert Storm had been "a doctrinal disaster for the U.S. Navy."[16] Little in that conflict had supported the existing Maritime Strategy's assumptions and implications: "No opposing naval forces challenged us. No waves of enemy aircraft attacked the carriers. No submarines threatened the flow of men and material across the oceans. The fleet was never forced to fight the open ocean battles the navy had been preparing for during the preceding twenty years." Moreover, the "lessons, systems, and techniques that we had honed for open-ocean engagements . . . were all ruled out either by the context of the battle or by the complexity of the sea-land interface in the confined littoral area."[17]

As a result, naval leaders began the difficult tasks of intense self-analysis and the development of a new vision. Consensus soon formed around the ideas that the focus of naval operations should be the littoral, not the open ocean; that naval forces, including marine forces, would maneuver *from* the sea in joint operations with the army and air force, not *on* the sea; and that, in view of the fact that control of the sea was now less important, the primary focus of naval operations in the future would be power projection, which would necessarily require the navy to assume a forward-presence role. These ideas were published collectively in 1994 as a new doctrinal statement titled *From the Sea*.

By 2007, however, the navy was once again operating in virtual obscurity. It had faced no opposition in the wars in Iraq and Afghanistan. Years of budget cuts had reduced the size of the fleet. When I was serving as assistant secretary of defense in 1988, the navy had 569 ships. In the year following the collapse of the Soviet Union, the navy still had 466 ships. By 2001, that number had shrunk to 316. By 2010, the total was only 286 combat and support ships and the chief of naval operations was continuing to plead for 313 ships to meet navy needs. The secretary of defense, however, was publicly observing that the fleet was "still larger than the next thirteen navies combined." He was not observing that the U.S. fleet was the smallest since 1916, that the tempo of its operations and the scope of its responsibilities was greater than any other fleet, or that China was rapidly modernizing its fleet. Budgetary projections indicated that at the current rate of shipbuilding, the total number of U.S. ships would eventually be a quarter less than the number of ships required to perform the navy's assigned missions. Increased costs in shipbuilding and poor management by both naval and civilian leaders in DoD had made matters worse.

In the fall of 2007, the navy joined the other sea services in the development and publication of what was described as a new maritime strategy. *A Cooperative Strategy for Twenty-First-Century Sea Power* was unusual. Declaring that it was raising the prevention of war to a level equal to the conduct of war and that cooperation and integration with the navies of other nations was assuming new importance, the document emphasized operations involving humanitarian assistance, disaster relief, drug trafficking, piracy, terrorism, and "other illicit activities." Unfortunately, the document had the appearance of a strategy tailored to fit neatly within the political and budgetary preferences of the current civilian leaders, rather than one designed by naval professionals to deal with current and emerging security realities. Not a word was said in the document about potential major adversaries such as China.[18]

Two years later, the navy and the air force entered into a new classified agreement to develop a new operational concept called AirSea Battle. The general idea was similar to the AirLand Battle concept that had been developed by the army in the 1980s. Much of the new concept remains classified, but it appeared designed to be a joint effort by which the advanced technologies of the two services could be effectively integrated as part of the navy's effort to strengthen its power projection capabilities in ways which would permit it "to obtain and maintain and exercise sea control or deny it to [an] enemy."[19] It was generally understood that the most likely potential enemy against which the concept would be targeted is China, which, as we will see, is rapidly developing and fielding a wide range of new military capabilities. An important part of AirSea Battle is apparently the idea of making destabilizing deep strikes against targets in mainland China and otherwise overcoming China's anti-access and area-denial measures in order to reclaim control of the maritime commons.

Immediately after the attacks of 9/11, the Armed Forces were mobilized to protect American territory in ways not seen even during World War II. Air National Guard pilots flew combat air patrols over the nation's capital and its largest city. Ships armed with surface-to-air missiles patrolled both coasts. Army National Guardsmen provided security at airports, dams, power plants, border checkpoints, and other critical locations. Coast Guard cutters inspected commercial and recreational vessels. Soldiers stood guard on many street corners. An obvious and major policy question soon captured center stage: What were the most appropriate long-term roles and missions for the Armed Forces in the nation's response to the new terrorist threat? The question was complicated by the fact that the new threat straddled the divide between traditional national security/war fighting matters, law enforcement, and emergency response management. Twenty days after the attacks, part of the answer became clear. On October 1, 2001, the secretary of defense submitted to Congress the Quadrennial Defense Review (QDR) report for 2001. The report rejected the idea that DoD had the sole responsibility for homeland security, but it candidly recognized that "DoD must institutionalize definitions of homeland security, homeland defense, and civil support and address command relationships and responsibilities within the Defense Department" so that it could "identify and assign homeland security roles and missions."[20]

The question of where to place primary operational authority for homeland security took longer to address since the creation of a new Department of Homeland Security lay several months in the future and no other federal department or agency was capable of assuming that responsibility. Over the next several months, the entire unified command plan of the U.S. Armed Forces came under close scrutiny. The matter of the most appropriate military organizational structure for the defense of the country's soil was not merely an issue of management or communications flow. Several complex and unprecedented questions had to be answered: What missions would be assigned to any new command? What kinds of military units would be given homeland security responsibilities? What should be the responsibility of the Army and Air National Guard? Should the Guard be deployed under Title 32 of the U.S. Code, which governs deployments for state missions under the command of individual state governors, or under Title 10, which states that the Guard can be activated for federal missions? How would the cost of a new command be divided between the states and the federal government?

On April 17, 2002, defense officials announced the establishment of a new U.S. Northern Command to be based in Colorado Springs. The new command commenced operations on October 1. It became responsible for the "land, aerospace and sea defenses of the United States."[21] The four-star commander of NORTHCOM also serves as the head of the North American Aerospace Defense Command, a U.S.-Canada command. The responsibilities of all but two of the other unified combatant commands were changed to strengthen the homeland security authority of the new command. The secretary of defense and the chairman of the Joint Chiefs of Staff characterized the changes as the most sweeping since 1946.

While these developments were taking place, a disconnect was growing between U.S. force planning and the evolving global strategic environment. The 2006 DoD Quadrennial Defense Review (QDR) report had acknowledged that "irregular warfare [had] emerged as the dominant form of warfare confronting the United States,"[22] but few Cold War–legacy weapons systems had been eliminated. Even while some military leaders were advocating preparation for low-intensity conflicts—that is, "small asymmetrical conflicts against determined partisans with wicked low-tech weapons like . . . improvised explosive devices"—others were asserting that the Armed Forces must be ready for another kind of potential future conflict, meaning high-tech interstate conventional warfare against Iran, North Korea, or a rising power like China. A weak economy and the lack of time to train for and equipment to fight a major conventional conflict made it unclear whether the United States had "the resources to fight both kinds of war with any assurance of victory."[23]

In speeches and articles subsequent to 2008, then Secretary of Defense Gates made it clear on which side of the debate he fell. Acknowledging that the issue required a balancing of risks, he criticized what he described as "a tendency toward what might be called 'Next-War-itis'—the propensity of much of the defense establishment to be in favor of what might be needed in a future conflict." It makes sense, he said, to "lean toward the most likely and lethal scenarios for our military."[24] He urged the military services to concentrate their preparation for "the dangers posed by insurgencies and failing states."[25]

But here was the rub. Only two years after Gates began making such arguments, it was not at all clear that the risk balance he advocated was a good one. Many military leaders were increasingly speaking of the future likelihood of decades of "persistent conflict," but they were uncertain of the nation's current security priorities. On February 1, 2010, the Obama administration released its first QDR report. It immediately received bipartisan criticism. Two critics described it as a "QDR for all seasons." According to them, the 105-page report directed attention—and defense resources—"to less likely contingencies and the most expensive capabilities to deal with them."[26] For the first time, a QDR linked environmental issues with national security, calling climate change "an accelerant of instability." The Democratic chairman of the House Armed Services Committee (HASC) said that the QDR "seems to . . . advocate for a force that is capable of being all things to all contingencies."[27] The ranking minority member (Republican) was less charitable, declaring that "it's tough to determine what the priority is, what the most likely risk may be, and what may be the most dangerous. It [the QDR] . . . makes no significant changes to major pieces of our current force. . . . The QDR is supposed to shape the Department for 2029, not describe the Pentagon in 2009."[28] In fact, it did not even identify the future roles and missions of the reserve components.

Although the undersecretary of defense for policy, the senior presidential appointee who was responsible for the preparation of the QDR, attempted to defend it in what one long-time observer called "typical diplo-speak,"[29] two former defense leaders, including a former Democratic secretary of defense, gave short shrift to the attempt. The problem, they subsequently wrote, was the "natural tendency of the bureaucracy . . . to plan short-term, operate from the top down, think within existing parameters, and affirm the correctness of existing plans and programs of record." Instead of "unconstrained, long-term analysis by planners who were encouraged to challenge preexisting thinking," the QDR was barely an explanation and justification of established decisions and plans.[30]

Matters proceeded to get worse. In the $553 billion DoD budget proposal that was announced in February 2011, Secretary Gates referred vaguely to a "complex and unpredictable array of security challenges," including pandemic diseases, piracy, human trafficking, rising oceans, national debt, education, cyber warfare, and the wars on terrorism, as well as traditional threats from nation-states.[31] No effort was made to prioritize the many real and potential threats or to connect a strategy with resource decisions, either in the governing "strategy" document (QDR) or in the budget documents. It was not possible to make the case that the proposed budget was driven by what was offered as strategy. Rather, it was clear that the Obama administration had decided to simply use the existing military force structure to respond to whatever national security threat, or threats, might arise first.

The absence of clear strategic or political guidance by civilian leaders was very troubling. The nation had serious economic and budgetary problems. There was no possibility that, in addition to funding the ongoing conflicts in Afghanistan and Iraq, Congress would provide sufficient resources for the Armed Forces to respond to all of the possible threats identified by the secretary of defense. Important questions on priorities were crying out for decisions by civilian leaders.

Meanwhile, and despite Gates's criticism of "Next-War-itis," military leaders necessarily had to keep an eye on future dangers. They could not do so effectively without civilian guidance as to what risks the Armed Forces must be prepared to meet, and what risks were so unlikely that they could be accepted. The problem had been addressed by the chairman of the Joint Chiefs of Staff in a speech in the spring of 2010. "The worst possible world I can imagine," he had said, "is one in which military commanders are inventing or divining their strategies, their own remedies, in the absence of clear political guidance." He added that military leaders "need political leadership constantly immersed in the week-to-week flow" of conflicts.[32]

Even as the ongoing conflicts in the Middle East were continuing, other dark clouds were starting to gather on the horizon. By 2011, military leaders had become persuaded that the threats the nation would face in the future were likely to be hybrid in nature—that is, threats from "combinations of regular, irregular, terrorist, and criminal groups"—and that future military leaders would have to be educated and trained to prevail in the complex new environment against all such threats.[33] Civilian leaders were predicting increases in the frequency and severity of natural disasters that would require the use of regular military forces in support roles, as well as National Guard troops.

It was already apparent that China's rapidly increasing economic strength was permitting it to rapidly expand its military capabilities at a time when the United States was engaged in two wars and very slowly recovering from a severe and prolonged recession. It had commenced sea trials—a prelude to an operational deployment—for its first aircraft carrier, a weapons system designed for offense, for power projection, not defense, and at least two more were planned. It had created the largest force of submarines and amphibious warfare ships in Asia. It had developed a new offensive anti-ship ballistic missile to destroy U.S. aircraft carriers in the event of a conflict over Taiwan or some other matter, and it had unveiled a new J-20 stealth fighter aircraft.

At the same time, it was making aggressive new territorial claims in the international waters of the East China and South China Seas.[34] One could not escape the conclusion that the events were related.

Armed conflict with China or any other nation is certainly not inevitable. Many analysts believe that China is intent on acquiring the means to, in the words of the ancient military theorist Sun Tzu, "win without fighting"—that is, to "establish itself as Asia's dominant power by eroding the credibility of America's security guarantees, hollowing out its alliances and eventually easing it out of the region."[35] But the increasingly complex international security environment and the uncertainties of the future place a high premium on military leaders with the courage to make unwelcome recommendations to their civilian superiors. An equally high premium must necessarily be placed on those senior political appointees who have national security responsibilities. They must be able to make informed, principled judgments with wisdom when options are limited. They must have the competence and character to stay in front of events—that is, to lead!

As the eleventh year of the new century was coming to a close, the American Armed Forces were a much different institution from that which existed on September 11, 2001. The total number of warriors was greater, but growth had been uneven. While the army had expanded from 480,000 to 572,000 and the Marine Corps from 172,000 to 200,000, the navy and air force had lost forces, the former losing about 50,000 and the latter some 20,000. The greatest growth had been in Special Operations Forces, which had increased from 45,600 in 2001 to 61,000.[36] Drone aircraft, like the Predator and MQ-9 Reaper unmanned aerial vehicles and other new technologies, were being routinely used in ways hardly even imagined on 9/11. Public confidence in the institution was at an all-time high. A Gallup poll in June 2011 found that the Armed Forces were the most respected national institution, with 78 percent of those surveyed expressing great confidence in it. That was even eleven points higher than the historical Gallup average dating to the early 1970s.[37]

The quality of individual military leaders was also generally quite high. Most of the officers who led the individual services, who commanded large combat organizations, who occupied important operational billets, and who served in senior positions on joint or service staffs, were a broadly experienced group. Many, if not most, had two or three decades of professional service. That service had taken them all over the world for staff and command positions in a variety of operational assignments. They were practiced in leading and managing large organizations. Almost all had combat experience. Many had served in the Pentagon and were experienced in dealing with civilian leaders and others who influence defense policy, from think tank analysts to congressional staffers.

Although they came almost exclusively from middle-class or working-class families, most military leaders had at least one graduate degree. A small but very influential band of warrior-intellectuals had doctorate degrees. When General David Petraeus, who holds a PhD in international affairs from Princeton University, assumed command of U.S. forces in Iraq, he assembled a team of military officers—who also had doctorates from top-flight universities as well as combat experience in Iraq—to help him make and implement new plans.[38] The development was not part of a new trend. Doctorate degrees had also been held by former chairman of the Joint Chiefs of Staff William J. Crowe (a submariner); then lieutenant general Frederick Franks, the commander of the army's VII Corps, which led the famous left-hook envelopment of Iraqi forces in the 1991 Persian Gulf War; Major General Paul "Butch" Funk, who commanded the army's Third Armored Division in that conflict; and others.

Most senior military leaders were also graduates of the National Defense University and/or service staff and war colleges. Thus, in striking contrast to most senior political appointees, military leaders were "strategically and operationally practiced; organizationally grounded; combat experienced; officially non-partisan; broadly exposed to joint and combined environments; and long tenured."[39] They were also engaged in continuing efforts to improve the profession of arms.

It was October 26, 2010. The setting was the Association of the United States Army Meeting and Exposition in Washington, D.C., an annual event that attracts more than thirty-five thousand participants. The speaker was Army Chief of Staff General George W. Casey Jr. It was a time for reflection. Many in attendance were veterans of multiple tours of combat duty in Iraq and Afghanistan. Over one million soldiers had been deployed there and it was well known that it took two to three years to recover from a one-year tour of combat duty. The army had been in continuous combat now for nine years, the longest war the country had ever fought with an all-volunteer force.

The costs had been high. More than four thousand soldiers had lost their lives in those conflicts to date, leaving more than twenty thousand surviving family members. In addition to the combat deaths, twenty-eight thousand soldiers had been wounded. The wounds of seventy-five hundred of them had been sufficiently serious as to require long-term care. Almost one hundred thousand had been diagnosed with traumatic brain injuries. Another fifty thousand had been diagnosed with posttraumatic stress.[40] The suicide rate within the army was soaring and presented a major problem. In the constant rush to prepare soldiers for the battlefield, less attention had been given by army leaders to drug abuse. Levels of illegal drug and alcohol use were now back to record highs, presenting a significant health problem. Divorce rates among soldiers were also soaring, reflecting the stresses caused by continuous deployment to the combat zones.

The wars had not been the only source of stress for the army. In an era in which one student of the subject has written that "war is fought and re-fought in twenty-four-hour news cycles among diverse genres with their own partic- ular audiences, in which the common denominator is that sensationalism brings in ad revenue or enhances individual careers," and in which the American public is too often more interested in assessing blame than in ensuring that problems are corrected,[41] it had been constantly necessary for army leaders to fight for the emergence of true facts and sober, reasoned analysis of the many mistakes and tragedies that had inevitably occurred in the wars.

As a result of the Base Realignment and Closure Act (BRAC), it had been necessary for the service to undergo the largest closure and restationing of army installations since World War II. The great majority of the brigades in the army had been converted to the new modular formations. Huge numbers of occupational specialty positions had been converted from Cold War skills, such as those in field artillery and armor units, to skills required in civil affairs and military police units, which were more relevant to the ongoing wars. Efforts were also under way to restore what General Casey called "strategic flexibility," the capability to react to unexpected contingencies of unpredictable scope and intensity. This would require the army to maintain its combat edge even as it worked to build its resiliency for what appeared to be a long period of persistent armed conflict.

Then there were the financial pressures. The army's $180 billion Future Combat Systems had been canceled, and nine years of war had badly battered much of the army's equipment. Other equipment was in need of moderniza- tion. A new ground combat vehicle was needed to replace the Abrams tank and the Bradley Fighting Vehicle. Strategies were needed for the replace- ment of aging trucks, the Kiowa Warrior stealth helicopter, and other equip- ment. All of this was occurring at a time when the secretary of defense had ordered major budgetary cuts.

It was in this large public setting that General Casey announced a major new effort at self-scrutiny. It was time, he said, "to examine the impact of 9 years of war on our profession—the Profession of Arms." The American people, he continued, place "special trust and confidence in soldiers as indi- viduals and in the Army as an institution," and they expect the army to perform its duties "with character and competence in the complex cauldron of war." Declaring that the army could never afford to lose that trust, he announced that he had asked General Martin Dempsey, then commanding general of the army's Training and Doctrine Command, to "examine the state of our profession" and to make recommendations for changes to army policies and programs that would strengthen the army as an institution. The overall objective of the new Profession of Arms Campaign would be for army leaders and individual soldiers to refine their understanding of what it means after nine years of protracted armed conflict to be professionals—that is, expert members of the profession of arms—and to recommit to a culture of service consistent with long-established army values, beliefs, ideals, and principles.[42]

The new effort at self-examination was not a dramatic break with the immediate past, or even a break at all. Since 2005, the Center for Army Leadership at Fort Leavenworth, Kansas, had been conducting an annual survey of army leaders serving in a variety of situations. The broad surveys had involved uniformed leaders in the active and reserve components and Department of the Army civilians. The purpose was to assess and track trends in army leader attitudes regarding leader development, the quality of the army's leadership, and the contribution of army leaders to mission accomplishment.

The army to which General Casey was speaking thus bore little resemblance to that which was portrayed in the classic old western movie *She Wore a Yellow Ribbon.* In one of the opening scenes, the hero of that story, Captain Nathan Brittles (John Wayne), declared most emphatically that "the Army is always the same. The sun and the moon change, but the Army knows no seasons." This army was willing to engage in self-inspection and to consider what needed to be changed.

The Profession of Arms Campaign would take place over several months. Individual groupings or cohorts within the army such as noncommissioned officers and career civilians would be surveyed to explore their perceptions and thinking about the current state of the profession. Analyses would be made of trends and indicators of individual and unit behavior and performance. Internal discussion would be encouraged. Scholarly works would be examined for current understanding of what specific attributes are used to define professions and what it means today to be a professional. Debate would be stimulated on such questions as whether the traditional view that, because of their prolonged education, experience, and seniority, only officers are considered to be military professionals is still valid. Should the term professionals now be extended to some enlisted personnel, to career civilians? The reason for the review was made clear in its Terms of Reference: "The Army has embarked on this effort under its own initiative because proactive, continuous examination is what professions do—reflect, review, assess, evolve, and change."[43]

New emphasis would also be placed on leader development since leadership represents what is called the "core function of the army professional's military art, whether leading a patrol in combat or making a major policy or budget decision in the Pentagon."[44] "We have to develop leaders," General Dempsey had said earlier, "who understand that context matters. The complexity of today's challenges and the uncertainties of tomorrow require a much broader approach to leader development and a clear understanding of the operating environment."[45]

In January 2011, three months after the army chief of staff announced his service's Profession of Arms Campaign, another conference on military professionalism was convened at the National Defense University. The chairman of the Joint Chiefs of Staff, who was vaguely described as being concerned "over possible erosion of the professional military ethos,"[46] was the principal speaker. It was not entirely clear what results were expected from the conference, but presumably it was hoped that it would stimulate new thinking and writing about the elements of military professionalism and the incorporation of new findings and updated ethical standards into professional military education and training.

However one might admire this difficult task of professional self-examination, it appeared to many that it might be asking too much. A similar concern had been voiced half a century earlier in different, but in many ways similar, circumstances by a well-known military sociologist. "The military faced a crisis," Morris Janowitz had declared. "How can it organize itself to meet its multiple functions? First, there is continuous technological change. Second, there is the necessity of redefining strategy, doctrine, and professional self-conceptions. Maintaining an effective organization while participating in emerging schemes . . . will require new conceptions and produce new tasks for the military professions."[47]

Few, if any, other professions had ever engaged in an effort at self-examination of such scope and duration, much less as part of a major effort to return to historic values and ideals. I well remembered my own searing experience in watching with helplessness as the profession of law lost its compass in the 1980s and the 1990s. A tectonic shift in the culture of the practice of law had occurred. Profit and individual compensation had replaced talent, wisdom, craftsmanship, character, and high-quality service to the public as the central measures of success. Law firms now regarded themselves as businesses and were dominated by "bottom-line" perspectives, rather than as a group of professionals charged with a public trust. At a convention of the American Bar Association, a senior statesman of the bar had asked rhetorically why the legal profession was no longer considered an honorable calling. He answered his own question with the words "I think the answer is quite simple: Too many lawyers have forgotten who we are and what we're supposed to be."[48]

Actions similar to those being taken by army leaders were also being taken in the other military services. In fact, efforts at self-examination followed by experimentation and concrete action have long been associated with the military services. Whatever conclusions might ultimately be reached, the fact of the self-criticism process was likely to be as important as any recommended changes. Noticeably absent in the media coverage of the steps being taken by the Armed Forces was any call for a similar self-examination and significant improvements in the quality of the senior political appointees to whom the professionals in uniform reported.

As we have seen, the combination of the "American system of transparency and self-criticism"[49] and the rapidly increasing professionalism of our military leaders, especially since the adoption of an all-volunteer force, have permitted the Armed Forces to adapt to the changing threats to our security, if not with rapidity, then at least with informed and honest effort. But the Armed Forces are no longer the sole guardians of the gate. Since September 11, 2001, we have belatedly recognized that our security no longer depends exclusively upon success on battlefields that are "over there," that the battle space now includes our homeland, and that the generals in this theater of operations are primarily civilians. Those civilian leaders face unprecedented challenges.

Prior to 9/11, no national strategy existed for defending the country from terrorist attacks. No senior government officials had experience in defending the homeland. There were no homeland security veterans who might at least offer the wisdom of an earlier conflict. No literature on the subject could be found within professional libraries. The task of organizing the nation for the battle against terrorism at home was consequently enormously difficult from the start. "Most of what the United States brings to the fight," wrote one critic, are federal agencies that are "stovepipe" or top-down hierarchies "designed 50 years [earlier] to harness a massive industrial and military power to struggle against the Soviet Union."[50] The contrast with loosely organized "floating networks of temporary cells" of terrorists acting "independently, stealthily and unpredictably"[51] was, and remains, stark.

The dangers remain great and real. In December 2008, the national Commission on the Prevention of Weapons of Mass Destruction Proliferation and Terrorism reported that "unless the world community acts decisively and with great urgency, it is more likely than not that a weapon of mass destruction will be used in a terrorist attack somewhere in the world by the end of 2013."[52] In February 2011, the FBI's assistant director in charge of its Weapons of Mass Destruction Directorate declared that the probability that the

United States would be hit with a weapon of mass destruction attack at some point is 100 percent.

The challenge of protecting the nation has been almost overwhelming to political leaders in the years following the 9/11 attacks. The threat of terrorist attacks on the many sectors of the nation's critical infrastructure is particularly troubling since approximately 90 percent of the infrastructure is in private hands and beyond the control of the government. Attacks might involve physical components on the electronic and computer networks that link the sectors and their constituted parts. The former include such things as endless numbers of electrical power lines, treatment plants, reservoirs, 152,000 miles of rail, and 361 ports with more than 3,700 terminals through which cargo and passengers must pass. The vulnerabilities are endless. One small example is illustrated by the facts that twenty-one U.S. nuclear reactors are located within five miles of an airport and that 96 percent of all U.S. reactors were designed without any consideration of the effects of a crash by even a small aircraft.[53] A similarly complex problem involves cargo containers. A decade ago, some eighteen million containers were entering the country and thousands of trucks were crossing our borders with Mexico and Canada each day. A weapon of mass destruction could easily be hidden in a single container and fewer than 5 percent of the containers were being inspected.[54]

In their rush to establish a new Department of Homeland Security (DHS) to deal with these matters, President George W. Bush and Congress brought about what has been characterized as "the most significant transformation of the U.S. Government" since passage of the National Security Act of 1947 created the Department of Defense and the Central Intelligence Agency.[55] The new department, the third-largest cabinet department, was formally established in early 2003. As we saw in chapter 1, it was a consolidation of twenty-two separate federal agencies from nine departments. It then had almost 170,000 employees and a budget of almost $38 billion. The creation of such a large and complex new organization immediately became the subject of much critical comment. The associate dean of the Yale School of Management had declared that while the attempt had to be made, it only had about a 20 percent chance of working.[56] An expert on large corporate mergers asserted that no company would attempt a change on the scale of the new department and that it would be five years before it would have even modest efficiency.[57] The difficulty of creating a single departmental culture out of so many disparate organizational cultures was also the subject of much commentary.

Under those circumstances, one of the most difficult tasks the nation faced in creating new protections is one that will never end: finding qualified leaders for the effort. Only half in jest, one journalist who wrote on governmental matters had declared that the head of the new Department of Homeland Security would always have to be a larger-than-life figure. She even suggested a job notice:

> Wanted: drill sergeant, manager, cheerleader, politician, guerrilla fighter, tent preacher, juggler, comedian, school principal, arm-twister, and multitasker for thankless job. Expertise necessary in: national defense, management of a large government agency, state, or company, law enforcement, intelligence analysis, and domestic threat assessment. Familiarity with corporate or government mergers, large computer systems, natural disasters, immigration law, industry lobbying, environmental protection, maritime safety, drug interdiction, and animal diseases a plus. Candidates under retirement age preferred.[58]

One additional attribute would be necessary: patience. The executive responsibilities of the head of the new department are constantly interrupted by the need to testify before an endless number of congressional committees. Eighty-seven separate committees and sub-committees of the Senate and House of Representatives have some sort of homeland security oversight authority.[59]

Four and a half years after DHS began operations, its leadership was still dealing with major problems. In a 2007 report, the Government Accountability Office said that DHS had "not yet addressed key elements . . . such as developing a comprehensive strategy for agency transformation and ensuring that management systems and functions are integrated. This lack of a comprehensive strategy and integrated management systems and functions," the report went on to say, "limits DHS's ability to carry out its homeland security responsibilities in an effective, risk-based way."[60]

In February 2010, DHS issued its first congressionally mandated Quadrennial Homeland Security Review (QHSR). The QHSR failed to include anything about budget plans for executing the QHSR missions.[61] In October 2010, the GAO reported that DHS was still falling short on the management and integration of various systems and functions. It was also reported that DHS had not received an unqualified audit opinion on its financial statements and that it ranked twenty-eighth out of thirty-two federal organizations in employee satisfaction and commitment.[62]

Seven years after DHS was established, there was not even agreement about what homeland security means. The 2006 *National Strategy for Homeland Security* had defined it as "a concerted national effort to prevent terrorist attacks within the United States, reduce America's vulnerability to terrorism, and minimize the damage and recover from attacks that do occur." Others believed that DHS's responsibilities should be even broader and not limited to countering terrorism. By 2010, the new department had undergone a major internal reorganization, two externally driven reorganizations, and several smaller, agency-driven reorganizations. It was implementing a risk assessment process to prioritize the many (man-made and natural) threats facing the nation, but the process relied on intuition far more than hard data.[63] Leaders of the department remained too focused on interagency rivalries and turf battles, especially those with the Departments of Defense and Justice.

In September 2011, the Government Accountability Office reported to Congress on the overall performance of DHS in the ten years since the 9/11 attacks. By now, the department was the third-largest in the federal government, with more than two hundred thousand employees and an annual budget of more than $50 billion. The report cited several "gaps and weaknesses in its operational and implementation efforts." The management problems included "schedule delays, cost increases, and performance problems in major programs aimed at delivering important mission capabilities." The department still lacked sufficient "skilled personnel to carry out activities in various areas, such as acquisition management," and it had not yet "developed an integrated financial management system." In a conclusion aimed directly at DHS's political leadership, the GAO said that "limited strategic and program planning by DHS and limited assessment to inform approaches and investment decisions have contributed to programs not meeting strategic needs in an efficient manner."[64]

In the real world, of course, no single political appointee, or even the entire group of appointees that are authorized for DHS, can possibly have all of the expertise and experience that is required. It still is not apparent what personal qualities are most important for the political leadership of DHS. Is experience in emergency response and recovery more important than experience in leading and managing large organizations? How does operational experience in the Armed Forces or law enforcement compare to political experience? How important is interagency experience within the federal government compared to experience in risk management, which has been described as at the heart of all that DHS does?[65] How about the ability to communicate effectively and to provide badly needed leadership and reassurance to a frightened public during a major crisis, versus experience in managing a bewildering number of programmatic and budgetary issues?

As in other large organizations, it will continue to be necessary to seek to fill the experience gaps of the secretary of homeland security by the appointment of other senior leaders within the department who have experience in areas where he or she has none. But the scope of the responsibilities of the new department is so large that no potential political appointees can have experience in more than a few of the operational or other areas that are placed under their control. They will necessarily continue to be dependent upon career civil servants. This fact, said an expert in organizational behavior at Princeton University, was a recipe for "a holding company, not a department."[66]

However difficult the search for high-quality and properly experienced political appointee leaders might be, it is critically important. No matter what organizational scheme may be established, it is still people that matter. Or, as the National Commission on Terrorist Attacks upon the United States reported in July 2004, "the quality of the people [in the government] is more important than the quality of the wiring diagrams. . . . Good people can overcome bad structures."

Chapter Eight

Trust and Clashes of Culture and Competence

This is what I'm willing to take on, politically. . . . I can't lose all the Democratic Party.

—President Barack Obama, November, December 2009

I've heard it said that the Government had no mandate for rearmament until the General Election. Such a doctrine is wholly inadmissible. The responsibility of Ministers for the public safety is absolute and requires no mandate.

—Winston S. Churchill, November 12, 1936

Any serious discussion of the comparative quality of the nation's civilian and military leadership must necessarily take into account the stark differences between the culture of American society at large—the source of political appointees who are selected for temporary, often far too temporary, public service—and the unique culture of the permanent military establishment from which career military leaders emerge. Since the nation adopted an all-volunteer *professional* military force, this subject has become increasingly important.

The word "culture" (Latin: *cultura*) is a term that has several meanings. Probably the most commonly understood meaning is one listed by Merriam-Webster: the set of shared attitudes, values, goals, and practices that characterize an organization. A definition that is perhaps more relevant here is "what a group learns over a period of time as that group solves its problems of survival in an external environment and its problems of internal integration."[1] War, it is said, reflects culture: "Weapons, tactics, notions of discipline, command, logistics—all such elements of battle arise not just from the constraints of terrain, climate, and geography, but also from the nature of society's economy, politics, and sociology."[2] Organizations within society have their own unique cultures as many American business leaders have discovered to their great regret after the formalities of a merger of their companies with another have been completed. The popular roots of interest in the concept of organizational culture—in contrast to academic research, which began earlier—can probably be dated to the 1980s.[3] One of the earliest books to address the subject of an organization's shared values, or culture, was the best-selling *In Search of Excellence: Lessons from America's Best-Run Companies*.[4] Business journalists and senior business leaders paid attention when the authors declared that their research indicated that within excellent companies, the dominance and coherence of culture was "an essential quality."[5]

Since an organization's culture is an intangible asset, it is often difficult to define and measure. Generally speaking, an organization's culture is a peculiar blend of its values, traditions, beliefs, and priorities. It is "a sociological dimension that shapes [leadership and] management style as well as operating philosophies and practices." It helps establish the "normal and unwritten rules" that guide employee actions.[6] Even though the characteristics that contribute to a particular culture are organization specific, it is usually difficult to value them independently. What is clear is that, taken together, they have great capacity for adding to (or diminishing) the overall value of the organization.

For this reason, most successful senior business executives work hard to both establish and maintain a values-driven organizational culture, whether the important attributes of the organization are accountability, integrity, efficiency, intense focus on customer needs, lowest product price, happy employees, or something else entirely. One executive put the matter this way: "I have spoken to any number of people who I would deem brilliant and provocative. These are people I'd like to have dinner with who I wouldn't necessarily bring into [my company] because of my sense that they wouldn't thrive within our culture."[7]

Increasing numbers of executives in industry recognize that a good organizational culture permits employees to do their best work. It can also strengthen employee loyalty and reduce costs. In the late 1980s, for example, the turnover rate of employees at Starbucks was creating an attrition rate of 150–175 percent a year. The company decided to establish a new culture. It became the first company in America to provide equity, in the form of stock options and comprehensive health care, to part-time employees. "We concluded very quickly," chairman and CEO Howard Schultz said, "that the costs of those benefits were dramatically lower than the cost of hiring and training new people. And most importantly, the performance in terms of the passion and the commitment was so much greater." The attrition rate soon became four to five times lower than the national average for retailers and restaurants.[8] The chairman and CEO of the world's largest pharmaceutical company made allegiance to the company's culture a primary criteria in selecting the company's senior leaders. One of the two most important criteria, he said, "obviously was ability and a track record of accomplishment. But also very important," he continued, "was the fact that I wanted to be sure to name people to key positions who would be seen by others within [the company] as being absolutely the right person for the right job. They needed to be people who demonstrated the core values of the company, people who would inspire our employees."[9]

One of the personal attributes valued by the chiefs of successful organizations in the selection of leaders who will maintain the organization's culture is attitude. The head of a major airline company described his approach this way: "You know," he said, "we really focus on attitude." He went on to say that otherwise excellent credentials in education, experience, and expertise were not sufficient because "if [applicants] have a lousy attitude, we don't want them." He rejected the opinions of people who warned that he could not maintain the company's culture as the number of employees grew. "Well, of course," he said, "if you think that way you're doomed. You can't do it. But if the culture is your number one priority, you can."[10]

Culture is even more important to the fighting spirit of military organizations. The military commander has concerns far beyond those of corporate CEOs. By any standard, war is a harrowing experience. Military personnel who serve in combat units, or in support units that must necessarily work within a battle zone, must be prepared to endure hardship not imaginable by company employees. In addition to the physical risks of death or crippling injury, the soldier is subjected to "the intense psychological pressures generated by exhaustion, privation, noise, worries about families and friends, and the sight of comrades being killed and wounded."[11] It is thus no accident that British Field Marshal Viscount Montgomery of Alamein believed that the morale of the soldier is the greatest single factor in war.

It is also no accident that military leaders do all that is possible to strengthen the intangibles that contribute to morale and fighting spirit. Discipline will help the subordination of self-interest to the protection and success of a military unit, but any commander worth his salt knows that more is required. Training produces a certain level of technical or tactical expertise and it is also important because of the way in which it inculcates unit cohesion and solidarity. Cultural norms, "reflecting habits and values which are far more deep-seated than those springing from short-term political ideology,"[12] also play an important part in the morale, fighting spirit, and behavior of men and women in uniform. A highly respected military historian has thus noted that "professional standards and soldierly honour were key motivating factors, especially as far as officers and NCOs were concerned," in the performance of German soldiers in both World Wars. Those factors "helped them not only to maintain the Second World War German Army at what was, man for man, and division for division, a remarkably high level of combat effectiveness, but also to fight on when all hope was gone and defeat seemed imminent and inevitable."[13]

A year after I left the government in early 1993, a public debate on the state of civilian-military relations arose within academic and journalistic circles. A serious rift was perceived in the relations. Initially, the debate focused on the official relationships between senior political appointees who served in policy-making positions, and senior military leaders. Allegations were made that the Armed Forces were "more alienated from [their] civilian leadership than at any time in American history"[14] and that civilian control of the nation's military was dangerously thin. It was even asserted that civil-military relations were in a state of "crisis."[15] Because I had just completed more than five years of service as a senior political appointee in the Pentagon, I thought then, as I do now, that most of the rhetoric of those who were making the allegations was uninformed and overblown, and that many of the asserted facts upon which the allegations were based were just plain wrong.[16]

Eventually, the focus of the debate broadened. Journalists began to tell their readers that sociologists had "warned of a day when the Nation's military and civilian leaders would stare at one another across a nearly unbridgeable cultural divide."[17] There was general agreement that American society had changed significantly over the previous few decades, but it was usually assumed that the "correct" cultural standards were those of contemporary society, not those of the Armed Forces. Seldom, except in very summary fashion, was attention paid to the nature and extent of the changes that had taken place in the popular culture, or what effects those changes were having upon the kinds of people who step forward to serve in the all-volunteer force. This is not the place to engage in extended discussion of the current standards of popular American culture. But because the cultural setting from which the leaders of any organization are selected is important, it is necessary to consider, if only briefly, the immense shift in cultural norms that has taken place within the United States during the past half century and the implications of that shift for civilian and military leaders.

Whatever else it did, the cultural revolution that began in the 1960s ushered in a period in which traditional American culture was increasingly rejected. Young radicals in the baby boom generation rebelled against religion, authority, and almost every restraint on personal behavior. Disrespect for the law, government, and other institutions became acceptable. Historically prized values like duty, commitment, sacrifice, accountability, courage, loyalty, and patriotism were ridiculed, or at least ignored. The voice of the adolescent sixties radicalism was "impatient, destructive, nihilistic."[18] Stories about massive demonstrations and students burning buildings on college campuses in protest against the war in Vietnam may have grabbed the headlines, but they masked something more important. Stephen Ambrose, the late and popular historian, asserted, "The permanent influence of the antiwar movement was not to shorten the war, but to pave the way for and extend the boundaries of the counterculture."[19] A distinguished former federal judge and member of the U.S. Senate concurs, recently observing that those activities "were just the most visible manifestations of a deeper, seismic shift from age-old standards. . . . [M]ost Americans once shared the same understanding of right and wrong, of acceptable and unacceptable behavior. Now, just about anything goes; and if anyone raises an eyebrow, he is condemned for being judgemental."[20] If he criticizes the collapse of traditional standards, he is also likely to be attacked by someone in the media as a purveyor of "right-wing . . . rhetoric."[21]

The characteristics of the counterculture could not be missed in the 1960s and many are still present today. Since the baby boom generation first assumed positions of political power in the 1990s, cultural trends that began in the decades of the 1960s and 1970s have continued. A coarsening debasement of social behavior has now taken place over five decades. Depravity is no longer automatically rejected. Like many countries in Europe, America is increasingly characterized by extreme consumerism and sexual hedonism. The age of moral relativism has arrived. A new moral code of self-fulfillment has been used to justify efforts to expand or break the boundaries of traditional morality. One of the most important consequences has been the collapse of the traditional American family.[22] Radical egalitarianism (the equality of outcomes rather than of opportunities) is in open warfare with the historical American concept of meritocracy. Alleged victimization, or the argument that "everyone does it," is too often used to justify failures to meet reasonable standards of performance and behavior. The late Senator Daniel Patrick Moynihan, a liberal Democrat, referred to this development a quarter of a century ago with the phrase "defining deviancy down." By that, he meant that we were lowering the bar for what was previously considered to be deviant, repugnant, illegal, or otherwise unacceptable behavior through the practice of labeling it as legitimate and legal.

Changes in American values and evidence of a national cultural war are now apparent to even the most uninformed. "The manifestations of American cultural decline," another distinguished jurist has written, range "across virtually the entire society from the violent underclass of the inner cities to our cultural and political elites, from rap music to literary studies, from pornography to law, from journalism to scholarship. Wherever one looks, the traditional virtues of this culture are being lost, its vices multiplied, its values degraded—in short, the culture itself is unraveling."[23]

It has now been several years since a former cabinet official spoke of the many ways in which the culture has been unraveling. "America is the greatest nation in the history of the world," he said then, "the richest, most powerful, most envied, most consequential. And yet, America is the same nation that leads the industrialized world in rates of murder, violent crime, juvenile violent crime, imprisonment, divorce, abortion, sexually transmitted diseases, single-parent households, teen suicide, cocaine consumption, per capita consumption of all drugs, and pornography production and consumption."[24]

After noting that America is a place of heroes, honor, achievement, and respect, he continued: "[I]t is as well a place where far too often heroism is confused with celebrity; honor with fame; true achievement with popularity; individual respect with political correctness." He characterized American culture as one "that celebrates self-gratification; the crossing of all moral boundaries; and now even the breaking of all social taboos." Despite our greatness, he concluded, "we are a society that has experienced so much social regression, so much decadence, in so short a period of time, that in many parts of America we have become the kind of place to which civilized countries used to send missionaries."[25]

It has also been several years since the senior judge referred to previously spoke of the consequences of the cultural war. "We are now two nations," he said. "These are not, as [British prime minister Benjamin] Disraeli had it, the rich and the poor, or, as presidential commissions regularly proclaim, whites and blacks. Instead, we are two cultural nations. One embodies the counterculture of the 1960s, which is today the dominant culture. Their values are propagated from the commanding heights of the culture: university faculties, journalists, television and movie producers, the ACLU, and major segments of the Democratic Party. The other nation, of those who adhere to traditional norms and morality, is now a dissident culture. Its spokesmen cannot hope to match the influence of the dominant nation. The dissident culture may survive by withdrawing, so far as possible, into enclaves of its own."[26] This view was generally endorsed by religious leaders. One of the most eloquent wrote, "One of the most profound truths about America . . . is that we are no longer one nation under God. We really are two separate nations with two . . . basic competing visions for America. . . . The two views can best be characterized as either support for or opposition to Judeo-Christian morality playing a role in American public life."[27]

In 2008, the editor of the highly regarded journal of the Churchill Centre wrote an essay about the changes that had taken place in America over the previous forty years. "[T]he world has changed beyond the imagination of those alive and sentient in 1968," he said. "Unprecedented events—assassinations, undeclared wars, impeachments, scandals, natural catastrophes and those of our own making—have accompanied the end of empires evil and benign, the liberation of some but not all peoples, the replacement of state terror with a stateless variety, the growth of the collective, the diminishment of the individual." He sensed "a torpor . . . a reluctance to focus on the essentials, a preference for inconsequentia. We indulge a film and broadcast media, that brothel of the western dream, as Mark Weingarden put it: 'morally uncomplicated, comic-book depictions of heroes and villains, simple stories for uncurious people.' We strain those views through Politically Correct lenses so that moral lessons are homogenized, no one offended, no 'insensitivity' expressed. Problems and threats are now 'issues' and 'challenges,' lest they be of our own making. Poll-driven politicians demonstrate, in the words of the historian Paul Johnson, 'how far a meretricious personal charm will get you in the media age.'"[28] More recently, another observer of the cultural changes has summarized one of their consequences. "The passing of the Christian West signifies the end not only of a worldview, but of a character type—one based on honor, family, self-help, blood-and-soil patriotism, personal responsibility and a God-centered moral order. Self-indulgence, self-expression, and an increasingly secular worldview have filled the vacuum. Life is no longer about sacrifice and duty; it's about maximizing pleasure and self-fulfillment."[29]

These developments have been reflected in the halls of government. Most objective observers of the crimes committed during the Watergate scandal in the 1970s believe that they were the almost inevitable result of a standardless political culture fostered and continuously reinforced by the Nixon administration. Many also believe that a similar claim can be made about the Lewinsky scandal in the Clinton administration, which was characterized by "skullduggery, half-truths, stonewalling, breeches of ethics, and even contempt for the law."[30]

To some extent, military leaders have avoided the daily impact of much of the current popular culture. From the time of the establishment of the all-volunteer force in 1972 to the attacks of 9/11, many of them made regular peacetime deployments at sea or to foreign countries, or else served in armed conflicts in the Persian Gulf or the Balkans. Since 9/11, a high percentage has served in Iraq or Afghanistan. All have served within a self-selecting volunteer organization that constantly teaches, and reinforces, conservative military values.

As a practical matter, military leaders, like all other soldiers, have long been thought to be significantly different from civilians. The distinguished British military historian John Keegan has observed that, in general, soldiers are not as other men. Rather, they belong to a "world apart, a very ancient world, which exists in parallel with the everyday world but does not belong to it."[31] Even U.S. Supreme Court Justice Oliver Wendell Holmes Jr., who was thrice wounded in the Civil War, reportedly said that the fact that he had been in combat forever separated him in small but vital ways from those who had not. Broad generalizations are dangerous, but it may at least be said that service in uniform in the last two decades of the twentieth century and the first decade of the twenty-first has attracted a special breed of American citizen and that it influences its adherents in unique ways.

Research over the last two decades has helped us better understand the personal characteristics and values of military leaders and enlisted personnel. Many of those characteristics, such as comfort in working in a regimented environment, in dealing with uncertainty and chaos, and rejection of self-centeredness and situational ethics, are obvious. Perhaps less apparent, but still one of the most important characteristics, has been referred to as a "worldview."[32] According to a recent report, a clear majority of the Armed Forces adhere to "a decidedly Judeo-Christian worldview, which holds a belief in a higher power, absolute truth, the real presence of good and evil in the world, and the ultimate triumph of good over evil."[33] The author of the report further asserts that their "clear moral compass leads many in the military to look at American society as degenerate and lacking in those qualities that once made the Nation great."[34] In short, in contrast to much of American society, the Armed Forces have not moved away from traditional moral values.

It is not surprising, therefore, that on these grounds alone, a major disconnect exists between military leaders who tend to have a clear sense of what is right and wrong, and search for absolute truth, and many of the political and social elite who prefer a world of moral relativism in which they can seek only "personal truth." The kind of "moral ambiguity that is so important to many elite [civilian] decision makers" is simply "antithetical to the nature of the military profession."[35] In his memoirs, written several decades ago, former French president and general Charles de Gaulle described these and some of the other cultural differences between political and military leaders in blunt terms: "The soldier often regards the man of politics as unreliable, inconstant, and greedy for the limelight. Bred on imperatives, the military temperament is astonished by the number of pretenses in which the statesman has to indulge. . . . The terrible simplicities of war contrast strongly to the devious methods demanded by the art of government. The impassioned twists and turns, the dominant concern with the effect to be produced, the appearance of weighing others in terms not of their merit but of their influence—all inevitable characteristics in the civilian whose authority rests upon the popular will—cannot but worry the professional soldier, habituated as he is to a life of hard duties, self-effacement, and respect shown for services rendered."[36]

Members of the Armed Forces also tend to value, and often display, courage and hardiness (or resiliency) in the face of great stress. Effective leaders (and those most likely to be promoted to senior ranks) "tend to be less emotional than ineffective leaders . . . [and] to defer to others and cooperate rather than compete."[37] This characteristic can be very helpful during contentious, joint or interagency discussions in which turf-related, bureaucratic antagonisms are in play. Military leaders have risen to the top of a profession that "functions more as a . . . meritocracy, where wealth and breeding, or tribal affiliations and favoritism, do not necessarily guarantee rank, privilege, and promotion."[38] They tend to be very positive in outlook, if not openly enthusiastic about their work. Thus, a "principal challenge [they face] today is not only to hone [the Armed Forces] in the face of constantly evolving challenges, but also to convince an affluent, leisured, and often cynical American public that we should even try to do so."[39]

One of the cultural factors that is most important to military leaders was discussed in chapter 4. It is not often associated with political appointees: accountability. This is not an abstract concept within the Armed Forces. As soon as they are admitted, for example, first-year midshipmen at the Naval Academy are taught the only five verbal responses that are acceptable to their seniors: "Yes, Sir"; "No, Sir"; "Aye, aye, Sir"; "I'll find out, Sir"; and "*No excuse, Sir.*" As in other services, the ethic of individual responsibility is applied at every step of an officer's career. The first page of *The Armed Forces Officer*, a handbook that has been published at varying intervals since the 1950s, declares unequivocally, "A leader of character, you accept unmitigated personal responsibility and accountability to duty, for your actions and those of your subordinates."

It is not necessary to subscribe to an idealized concept of military culture to note that accountability in the Armed Forces means something very different from what it does among the political class. While it is not difficult to find an instance where strict standards of accountability have not been enforced in circumstances involving the Armed Forces, such instances tend to be rare exceptions to the general rule. The navy, for example, has long prided itself on the leadership qualities of its operational commanders and is quick to dismiss officers who don't meet its standards of professional and personal conduct. In January 2011, the commanding officer of the aircraft carrier USS *Enterprise* (CVN–65) was suddenly relieved of his duties just weeks before the ship was scheduled to get under way on a seven-month deployment to support the war in Afghanistan. His offense? None as commanding officer, but he purportedly permitted profane videos to be shown over the ship's closed-circuit television station four to five years earlier when he was serving as the vessel's executive officer. The intended purpose of the videos was purportedly to improve and maintain the morale of the ship's company during a long and stressful deployment to the war zone.

By the end of the day on which he was relieved, thousands of current and former members of the crew were coming to his defense within Facebook groups.[40] Nevertheless, despite the fact that the relieved officer was a decorated former top gun pilot, the admiral who relieved him was unequivocal. In a statement issued the same day, the admiral declared, "The responsibility of the Commanding Officer for his or her command is absolute. While [the discharged officer's] performance as Commanding Officer . . . has been without incident, his profound lack of good judgment and professionalism while previously serving as Executive Officer . . . calls into question his character."[41] It was widely recognized that the officer's naval career (including his probable future promotion to rear admiral), as well as the careers of several other officers, might soon be at an end.[42] The incident was not unusual. In 2010, some seventeen commanding officers were relieved, the highest number since 2003, when twenty-six were relieved.[43] The reasons ranged from "inappropriate conduct" and fraternization with junior naval personnel to collision with a buoy. Between 2000 and August 2010, 145 navy commanding officers were relieved for such causes.[44]

High standards of accountability are also the objective of the other military services. In December 2010, for example, it was reported that, since the summer of 2008, some thirteen air force general officers "from four-star commanders to brigadiers in staff assignments" had been given letters of admonishment. Letters of admonishment are potential career killers. In addition, a lieutenant general had been given a more serious letter of reprimand.[45] It is not uncommon for senior officers to be admonished or reprimanded for the mistakes of subordinates of which they were unaware or for actions that they personally took without knowledge that the actions were wrong. This standard is harsh, but it is reasonable, especially in the case of senior officers, because they have "direct influence on levels of supervision two or three positions down the chain of command."[46]

The fog of combat sometimes complicates the process of holding leaders accountable. The July 2008 Battle of Wanat, which took place in a remote mountain village in Afghanistan near the Pakistan border, is illustrative. Nine U.S. soldiers were killed when Taliban forces attacked a platoon-sized unit at a small U.S. patrol base. The number of casualties triggered several investigations into the events leading up to the battle. There was disagreement about the degree of culpability, if any, of the brigade, battalion, and company commanders, who were not present at the battle. One of the senior officials involved in an early investigation stated that none of the three officers, all of whom were recommended for disciplinary action, were incompetent, but rather "were all truly professional officers." Nevertheless, he added that "officers have to be held accountable for their actions. They can't be given a free ride when lives are involved. If you screw up, you have to pay a price."[47] The army ultimately concluded that the three officers had been neither negligent nor derelict. In the first six months of 2011, the army relieved or disciplined three brigade commanders, all of whom were en route to, or returning from, war zones in Iraq and Afghanistan.[48] The results of the individual cases are less significant than the fact that so much effort was expended on self-criticism and a thorough analysis of the actions and omissions of everyone involved.

It must be said that such rigid accountability is not endorsed in all quarters. Only recently, a former secretary of the navy blasted the U.S. Navy and Marine Corps for their policies on alcohol abuse by naval aviators. He asserted that because the best aviators are calculated but intelligent risk takers, "they have always been vulnerable to the system. But now," he continued, "in the age of political correctness and zero-tolerance, they are becoming an endangered species."[49] Nevertheless, while there is obvious merit in Kipling's reminder that "single men in barracks don't grow into plaster saints," experience has long proven that accountability works.

Even though the individual military services have very distinct cultures, their leaders have much in common. The author of one well-received recent study, which has been described as the "definitive commentary on the moral imperatives of naval command," asserts that there are, in fact, clear "requisite qualities for successful American military leadership." They include, he says, "(1) willingness to put service before self; (2) the desire and strength of character to achieve positions that require making tough decisions; (3) a 'sixth sense' that enhances the judgment required for most sound decisions; (4) an aversion to 'yes' men; (5) maturity in perception and judgment attained through lifelong professional reading; (6) mentorship, which reflects an understanding of the need to develop successors from among the most promising men and women under one's command; (7) delegation of authority and leadership responsibility among one's most responsible subordinates; and (8) true character, the cardinal requisite of leadership, as illustrated by a leader who fixes problems and does not blame others or look for a scapegoat when things go wrong. Acceptance of personal accountability," he says, is the "prerequisite for character."[50]

One of the military services not only has a culture much different from that of society at large, but it also believes that it represents "a different breed from the vast majority of men and women who make up the [other] Armed Forces of the United States."[51] Its leaders unapologetically proclaim that during times of peace this service has "often found itself crossways and alone in its resistance to fall in step with some new political expedient or social trend."[52] I refer, of course, to the Marine Corps. One of its former leaders, Major General O. K. Steele, USMC (Ret.), a Stanford University graduate, decorated combat veteran, former commanding general of the Second Marine Division, and the best trainer of combat troops I have ever met, believes that "being a Marine . . . means to share an ethos once imbued in the minds of ancient Greek warriors when going off to battle: Either return carrying your shield with honor, or be carried on it."[53]

There are obvious and strong reasons why a distinct military ethos exists and is necessary. "A military organization cannot govern itself on the basis of the same liberal principles that characterize the very society it defends."[54] The values that matter to the Armed Forces are "the hard values of the battlefield."[55] In his study of the unpreparedness of American forces for the conflict in Korea, T. R. Fehrenbach, a historian and combat veteran of that war, wrote, "By the very nature of its missions, the military must maintain a hard and illiberal view of life and the world. Society's purpose is to live; the military's is to stand ready, if need be, to die."[56] In short, "the military is the way it is because of what it does and where and under what circumstances it does it."[57]

Leading civilians share this view. "We are told all the time," one such civilian, a Pulitzer Prize–winning journalist, said several years ago, "that there is a large and growing problem and that there is a need to close the gap between the military and society. I think that the gap is healthy and . . . is necessary, that the gap must exist in any society and, in a sense, especially in a democratic society. That is because the military must be an exemplar of certain virtues that will, at any given time, seem anachronistic and it is a function of the military to be exemplars."[58] He continued: "[A]s American society becomes more individualistic, more self-absorbed, more whiney, in a sense, more of a crybaby nation . . . it becomes doubly important that the gap between the military and society remain substantial."[59] In addressing a military audience, another civilian leader put the matter this way. "[Y]ou are supposed to be different," he said, "and in some important ways, you are supposed to be better. It was a wise man who said that when a man enters military life, he enters a higher form of civilization. . . . So yes, the military is—and ought to be—different in some important ways from the world outside its walls. It operates with a different code of conduct; a different set of activities; a different way of life."[60] None of this discussion is intended to suggest that all political appointees or other civilian leaders inevitably have personal value systems that are significantly different from those of military leaders who have spent their professional lives within a much different organizational culture. Some public officials are, of course, military veterans. Most try to do the right thing. One former senior political appointee has stated the obvious: "Most Presidents do not commit illegal acts, or lie under oath, or thumb their noses at the law. Most Presidents do not chronically deceive, delay, obfuscate, and stonewall Federal investigations. This does not mean they are perfect or near perfect; it means merely that most live up to their oath to execute faithfully the laws of the land, and behave in at least a reasonably responsible way. The same is true of most political figures in the nation's capital. Washington, D.C., is not, in fact, a den of thieves, or a house of knaves."[61]

What the discussion here is intended to suggest is that, in addition to a lack of absolutely essential ability and relevant experience, many political appointees who have responsibility for national security matters have personal value systems that predictably and inevitably clash with the culture of the Armed Forces. One unimportant example from my personal experience is illustrative. I remember talking to an assistant secretary of the army just prior to a panel discussion at a military conference in which we both participated. She was complaining about her unhappiness with West Point cadets, because, she said, "they are elitists." While no successful leader can condone pure arrogance, she had absolutely no understanding of how important the ethic of undisputed excellence is to those who must be ready to deploy, fight, and risk their lives whenever the nation calls. It is no more undemocratic for the nation's warriors to believe that they are the best in the world than it is for an Olympic athlete to believe that no competitor can beat her. Fortunately, this political appointee was forced to resign after publicly declaring that "Marines are extremists," a statement that was promptly condemned in a concurrent resolution passed by the U.S. House of Representatives.

For the reasons already set forth, it should surprise no one that relations between career professionals in the Armed Forces and political appointees who temporarily serve as their constitutional masters can vary widely and are often strained. One incisive student of the issue has written that in the last sixty or so years, two recurrent sources of friction stand out: "One is about strategy and operations: the tendency for military professionals to oppose undertaking combat actions without a commitment to application of 'overwhelming force,' in frequent contrast to politicians' interest in waging low-profile war, intervention on the cheap, or economically efficient operations. Another is about management and control: the question of where to draw the line between military expertise and political authority, and whether military leaders have too much influence or not enough."[62] It must be said that, for some, there is also a third source of friction—the recurring ability of political leaders to escape accountability for actions or conduct that would be career-enders for military leaders.

When a new president is elected and the senior political appointees he has selected to serve in the Pentagon merge with the existing military establishment, several difficulties may occur. Initially, they are likely to relate primarily to unimportant matters such as process and work style. As the only assistant secretary of defense in the Reagan administration to be asked to continue in the new administration of President George H. W. Bush in 1989, I was in a unique position to view that "merger." The first noticeable changes were in the personal office of the new secretary of defense, Dick Cheney. Unlike his immediate two predecessors, Cap Weinberger and Frank Carlucci, Cheney made it clear that he did not like meetings and preferred to work alone. The number and length of senior staff meetings was immediately reduced. A perception quickly gained currency on the Joint Staff that Dick Cheney was like a super staff action officer who gave little or no guidance, was very reluctant to delegate authority, and liked to do things himself. Neither Weinberger nor Carlucci had relied upon a political special assistant, each being content with the military flag or general officer who served as their senior military assistant. Cheney promptly installed a bearded thirty-two-year-old lawyer with no military experience as his bureaucratic enforcer. Eyebrows were also raised by Bush's abrupt replacement of so many of the senior political appointees in the Pentagon who had served in the Reagan administration while he was vice president. Reagan appointees were requested to submit their resignations and, except for a few senior officials, most were gone by the day of the inauguration.

Far more extensive replacements of senior political appointees take place, of course, when one of the major political parties replaces the other in the White House. The new civilian leaders in the Pentagon and the other departments and agencies are usually accompanied by strategic objectives and policy preferences that differ greatly from those of the departing leaders. The new civilian leaders also bring to their work widely varying degrees of ability, experience, motives for entering government service, integrity, political courage, and other important qualities. The senior political appointees of any new administration usually benefit from a honeymoon period that starts when they assume power, but eventually hard decisions on complex issues have to be made and implemented. Eventually, they must integrate the culture that develops within their new administration with that of the military establishment that has long been in place. That process can only succeed if an important element is present: *trust*.

One of the most important reasons why there were so many shrill allegations by academics and journalists of a crisis in civilian-military relations during the administration of President Clinton was the absence of trust. It would have been very difficult at that time to think of any commander in chief less likely to attract the trust and respect of military personnel. Part of the problem was due to initial policy decisions by the new administration.

The end of the Cold War had raised new concerns among military leaders about what the Armed Forces would be asked to do in the future and whether they would be given sufficient resources to do it. Several officials in the new administration and members of Congress were calling for a "peace dividend" that would move major defense appropriations to domestic priorities. The Bush administration, in which I had served, had attempted to minimize the kind of unthinking demobilization that had followed World War II and other American wars by developing a new rationale for the kind and size of post–Cold War Armed Forces we believed was necessary. Before we left office after the 1992 presidential election, we knew that the new Clinton administration was likely to use a much larger and perhaps duller knife. By 1996, the military services had every reason to feel off balance: Clinton had cut the military force structure by a third more than we had, even though the tempo of peacetime operations had increased dramatically.[63] The defense budget had been cut by 35 percent since the end of the Cold War and the budget for FY 1997 was $239 billion less than the amount Americans had bet in legal gambling three years earlier.

Budget issues were not, however, the primary source of friction between civilian and military leaders. Clinton's antimilitary activities while he was a college student and his well-known efforts to dodge the draft remained offensive to many Americans, not just officers who had lost friends and risked their own lives during the war in Vietnam. Clintonites were cowed "because the men in uniform were a constant reproach to their own strategic amateurism and privileged absence from service in their generation's war."[64] Clinton's total lack of experience and interest in national security matters was obvious.[65] Military personnel also resented what was later euphemistically called "the administration's ham-handedness in the later phase of the Somalia mission," a peacekeeping operation in which eighteen American soldiers were killed, seventy-three were wounded, and one was captured.[66] As we have seen, Clinton's selection of Congressman Les Aspin as secretary of defense was not well received and several of the new senior political appointees that Aspin brought to the Pentagon were perceived to be both incompetent and insufferably arrogant.

To make matters worse, in his first meeting with the Joint Chiefs of Staff after his inauguration, Clinton had not said a word about emerging terrorist or other threats to U.S. security, the difficulties of dealing with Saddam Hussein since the end of the 1990–1991 Persian Gulf War, the conflict in Bosnia, or even his plans for the post–Cold War relationship with Russia and China. Rather, he talked domestic politics, reminding the chiefs of his election campaign promise to remove the prohibition against military service by homosexuals. Less than four weeks later, a terrorist bomb detonated in the parking garage of New York's World Trade Center, killing six people, injuring more than one thousand, and causing great destruction.

By the middle of his second term, debate about the current state of the relationship between Clinton and the Armed Forces was still going strong. By then, however, a new but related subject was capturing daily headlines and causing dismay among not only military leaders but all Americans: the Lewinsky scandal and allegations of suborning perjury, making false statements under oath, and obstruction of justice, all involving the president of the United States. Clinton's reckless and irresponsible behavior in the White House with a young intern was not perceived by very many military leaders as purely a private matter. Aside from the nature of the conduct, which was reprehensible in and of itself, it had taken place in the People's House, the residence from which Lincoln had governed during the Civil War, where FDR and Churchill had discussed strategy during World War II, and where young American warriors had received the Medal of Honor. By almost any standard, Clinton had defiled the office of the commander in chief.

Those who fretted so much at the time about the lack of respect shown to Clinton by some members of the Armed Forces failed to understand what any new military officer learns soon after he is commissioned: Neither leaders nor those they lead are automatons. Whatever authority may be conferred by law upon a leader, whatever theory of leadership or civil-military relations may be espoused by academics, trust and respect from the people whom a leader is charged to lead are not necessarily automatic or permanent. Usually, those feelings have to be earned. It should, of course, be presumed that a political leader is entitled to trust and respect by virtue of his lawful authority. In human relations, however, such a presumption can be silently rebutted by the leader's actions or failures to act. Despite all of the challenges to the civil-military relationship during his administration, however, Clinton had no major difficulties with the Armed Forces.

Since the commencement of the war in Iraq, a new focus has been established regarding civilian-military relations in the country. Civilian control of the Armed Forces narrowly defined is not the issue, for, as one scholar has noted, "Civilian control is constitutionally, structurally and historically well grounded in America."[67] Rather, the issue continues to be *trust*: "The mutual respect and understanding between civilian and military leaders and the exchange of candid views and perspectives between the two parties as part of the decision-making process."[68] One student of the relationship of the two groups of leaders asserted in 2008 that it is "strained by acrimonious accusations of professional incompetence" in the planning and execution of the war in Iraq.[69] It was further asserted that a decade of war had "exacerbated tensions and dysfunctional elements inherent in American civil-military relations," and that the situation was "appreciably worse after Iraq than before when 'erosion' and 'crises' were common adjectives used to describe the state of U.S. civil-military relations."[70]

Others are much less concerned. One scholar has written, "Struggles for influence and control among political and bureaucratic constituencies pervade our national life. But contrary to the fears of many . . . civil-military relations are not an out-sized problem as conflicts in a democracy go. . . . Conflict between technical specialists and political generalists is natural in democratic government."[71] There is certainly a history of such conflict. While writing about the dispute between British political and naval leaders in World War I over the use of convoys as a method of defense against Germany's U-boats, Churchill referred to the "long, intense, violent struggle between the amateur politicians, thrown by democratic Parliamentary institutions to the head of affairs, on the one hand, and the competent, trained, experienced experts of the Admiralty and their great sea officers on the other."[72] It has been suggested that the perceived reemergence of a "gap" between the U.S. military and society in recent years reflects, at least in part, "egalitarian resentment at the vanishing involvement of social elites in responsibility for national defense."[73]

Nor should the conservative social and political views of military leaders be considered any cause for concern. "Professional officers," it has been said by an academic who is a Democrat and was involved in the Mondale presidential campaign in 1984, "have always been conservative in ideology. . . . They became overtly Republican after the 1960s because [political] realignments concentrated conservatism unambiguously in that party." In any event, to the extent that military leaders identified with the principles of the Republican Party in the 1990s, that "affinity did not compromise civilian control when Democrats took power."[74]

The potential for problems in the civilian-military relationship does exist, however, whenever civilian or military leaders exercise their respective powers *incompetently*. A strong case can be made that the performance of *both* sets of leaders in planning for operations in Iraq after the capture of Baghdad in April 2003 was flawed. "Most of the problems," it has been said, "resulted from inaccurate judgments about how the Iraq War would unfold."[75] Nevertheless, for several years a significant disparity has existed between the competence of too many senior political appointees serving in positions involving the nation's security and senior military leaders. The reasons are obvious from the previous chapters of this book. First, many civilian leaders are nominated for political reasons unrelated to competence. Many are "technocrats rather than innovative thinkers . . . [or part of] a Pentagon bureaucracy that is increasingly resigned to 'look like America.'"[76] Many others have no experience whatsoever running a large organization, *implementing* complex policies, or otherwise "getting things done." Even when appointees have certain undeniable credentials, they are too often nominated and confirmed for a position for which they have no credentials. Second, military leaders are the beneficiaries of improvements in professional military education, which "emphasize the relationship of policy, strategy, and resources" and which foster "a military perspective with a coherence that is often absent among the civilian officials who make defense policy."[77]

The question of competence is particularly relevant to what has been called "a canonical question for civil-military relations theory: What is the proper division of labor for strategic supreme command decisions during war?"[78] Generally speaking, two broad groups of thought exist on the issue. One group, recently referred to by one scholar as "professional suprema-cists," argues that civilian leaders should assign political objectives and end states for a conflict, ensure that military leaders have an adequate voice in the policy-making and planning processes, and avoid micromanagement of oper-ational, tactical, and perhaps, even military strategy matters.[79] The second group, referred to as "civilian supremacists," asserts that civilian leaders should be forcefully and directly involved in the business of war making, "even to the extent of pressing military officers on matters that the military might consider as being squarely in their zone of professional autonomy"—that is, to probe deeply and critically the grounds of military advice.[80]

Upon the basis of his study of four great political figures (Abraham Lin-coln, Georges Clemenceau, Winston Churchill, and David Ben-Gurion), an-other scholar asserts that great statesmen do not turn their wars over to their generals and then stay out of the way. He recommends that political leaders "must immerse themselves in the conduct of their wars no less than their great projects of domestic legislation; that they must master their military briefs as thoroughly as they do their civilian ones; that they must demand and expect from their military subordinates a candor as bruising as it is neces-sary; that both groups must expect a running conversation in which, although civilian opinion will not usually dictate, it must dominate; and that that conversation will cover not only ends and policies, but ways and means."[81]

Most people who have served in senior policy-making positions in war-time would agree with this general formulation. But most presidents are not Abraham Lincolns. Very few senior political appointees can be called great statesmen. Almost none today have the military experience and insight of Churchill or the toughness and determination of Clemenceau. Indeed, with each succeeding administration, fewer and fewer senior political appointees have any significant national security experience at all. This does not detract from the obvious wisdom of the "running conversation" ideal since it may be presumed that appointees will have political competence. But it does place a high premium upon the nomination by presidents of senior civilian defense officials who have demonstrable skill and experience in national security matters in general and proven competence for the specific office to which they are being nominated. When civilian leaders exercise their authority *incompetently*, there is more at stake than simply the trust of their military subordinates.

An even greater problem arises when civilian control is exerted *irresponsibly*. Civil-military relations theory may postulate that civilian political leaders have the legal "right to be wrong," but that principle assumes good faith effort to be right. Legal authority exercised irresponsibly cannot be justified in any part of government, but most certainly not on matters involving the nation's security. Appropriate sanctions should immediately follow an irresponsible exercise of power, either through the termination of the responsible political appointee or by ballot. When a senior political official acts irresponsibly, political subordinates, like Elliot Richardson in the Watergate crisis, must be prepared to resign. In this context, the standard of behavior of then secretary of state George Marshall on the afternoon of May 12, 1948, is one that every political appointee should be required to study.

The setting was the Oval Office. President Truman was meeting with his top advisors on the question of Palestine and the possible creation of a Jewish state. The General Assembly of the new United Nations was debating the matter and official Washington was sharply divided. The Pentagon, the State Department, the foreign policy establishment in general, and the new Central Intelligence Agency all believed that American strategic interests in the Near and Middle East would be adversely affected by U.S. support for a Jewish state. There was great concern that war between such a state and the Arab nations was inevitable, that the United States would have to use military force even to maintain influence in the area, and that a real danger existed that the Soviet Union would support the Arab states and thus the Middle East, with its vast oil reserves, would fall under Russian influence.

Marshall and his deputy, Robert Lovett, laid out the national security concerns and recommended that any decision on recognition of the new state be deferred. Truman then asked Clark Clifford to respond. Clifford, a former trial lawyer in St. Louis who would serve very briefly as secretary of defense twenty years later in the administration of President Lyndon Johnson, was then serving as counsel to the president for domestic political affairs and as manager of Truman's election campaign.[82] It was believed that the Jewish vote would be decisive in New York, Illinois, and California in November's presidential election campaign.[83] Therefore, Clifford argued that, in order to establish his position among Jews, the president should immediately announce that he intended to formally recognize the new State of Israel as soon as it was proclaimed by Israeli leaders. At the time, the borders of the Jewish state had not even been defined, nor had its name been adopted.[84]

In his memoirs, Clifford later described Marshall as being red "with suppressed anger as I talked." When Clifford finished, Marshall exploded, saying, "Mr. President, I thought this meeting was called to consider an important, complicated problem in foreign policy. I don't even know why Clifford is here." He continued, saying, "I fear that the only reason Clifford is here is that he is pressing a political consideration with regard to this issue. I don't think politics should play any part in this."[85]

Marshall then made a remarkable statement, saying to the president, "If you follow Clifford's advice and if I were to vote in the election, I would vote against you."[86] After the meeting concluded and Marshall returned to his office, he inserted his own account of the meeting into the State Department's official record as follows:

> I remarked to the President that, speaking objectively, I could not help but think that suggestions made by Mr. Clifford were wrong. I thought that to adopt these suggestions would have precisely the opposite effect from that intended by him. The transparent dodge to win a few votes would not, in fact, achieve this purpose. The great dignity of the Office of the President would be seriously damaged. The counsel offered by Mr. Clifford's advice was based on domestic political considerations, while the problem confronting us was international. I stated bluntly that if the President were to follow Mr. Clifford's advice, and if I were to vote in the next election, I would vote against the President.[87]

Despite the confrontation, the Truman administration recognized the new State of Israel eleven minutes after it was established at 12:01 Israeli time on May 15. Although several of Marshall's friends urged him to resign, he remained a man of the strictest rectitude. He supposedly replied that he did not resign "because the President, who had a constitutional right to make a decision, had made one."[88] The question of whether the president's decision was an irresponsible one was left to the voters.

Few periods in American history have demonstrated more vividly the need for high-quality political appointee leaders in the Pentagon who have leadership and management capabilities and relevant experience than the years following the election of 2008. The need for high-quality leaders in the executive branch was particularly apparent because of the absence of military or other relevant experience in both houses of Congress.

In the 91st Congress (1969–1971), there were 398 military veterans (69 senators and 329 members of the House of Representatives). Ten years later, in the 96th Congress (1979–1981), only 58 senators and 240 representatives were veterans.[89] But the Senate veterans included such highly decorated former soldiers as Senator Daniel Inouye (D-HI), a recipient of the Medal of Honor; Senator Strom Thurmond, who participated in the June 1944 Normandy invasion; and Senator Ted Stevens, who flew unescorted cargo planes over the "hump" in the China-Burma-India Theater in World War II. Between 1987 and 1993, I had many occasions to testify before the Armed Services and Appropriations committees of each house. When I made my first appearances on the Hill, I was impressed by the experience that was evident in most of the questions asked of me. By my last year of government service, however, some 50 percent of the membership of the House of Representatives had changed. The reduced level of knowledge about military matters was apparent from the moment the gavel sounded. By 1994, the Senate had only 45 veterans and the House fewer than 130. Two years later, the number of veterans who had served in a war zone included only 15 senators and 27 members of the House. Fewer still had been involved in combat.[90] By 2010, the number of senators who had worn a military uniform had dropped to 25, and the number of representatives to 94.[91]

The implications of this trend are important. Representative Tim Griffin (R-AR), one of the new members of the House elected in the 2010 midterm elections, stated the obvious. "If you've been in the military," he told *Stars and Stripes*, "you can take policy proposals and think about how that change is going to play out, not from an academic standpoint. It helps to understand what troops go through, what families go through on deployment."[92] Another newly elected member concurred, asserting that it is very important to "have people there who have been on the ground and can bring that technical knowledge back to Congress."[93] Yet another member has put the matter in more stark terms. "Few members of Congress," he has written, "understand very much about the use of military force."[94]

Unfortunately, and despite the inescapable facts that the nation was involved in intense armed conflicts in Iraq and Afghanistan and that when he was elected Barack Obama had merely four years of experience in the federal government, no executive experience, and no experience whatsoever in military or other national security matters, the new political leadership team in the Pentagon in 2009 was noticeably weak in experience. This development was the latest in a trend that had started in the Clinton administration. If George Washington is counted as a military professional, it may be said that, by 1957, one-fifth of all U.S. presidents had been professional generals. In the Clinton administration four decades later, and for the first time, neither the president, the secretary of defense, the national security advisor, the secretary of state, nor any of their deputies had ever served in uniform.

Obama made highly symbolic political appointments in 2009 when he asked Robert Gates, President George W. Bush's secretary of defense, to continue in office; when he appointed Jim Jones, a retired marine general, as his national security advisor; and when he appointed retired army general Eric Shinseki as secretary of veterans affairs and retired admiral Dennis Blair as director of national intelligence. Gates and Jones were undoubtedly selected in part because they could help insulate Obama from the traditional criticism that Democrat presidents are "weak" on national security matters.

Politics affected intelligence matters as the Obama administration got under way. Only four months after the inauguration, Director of National Intelligence Blair reportedly concluded that on national security issues, current military leaders and former military leaders then serving in the administration "were outsiders."[95] Obama preferred to rely upon his team of domestic political advisers in the White House, people whose primary purpose often had little or nothing to do with national security or foreign policy, but everything to do with his anticipated 2012 campaign for reelection. Air Force General Michael Hayden, a career intelligence professional, was replaced as director of the CIA by Leon Panetta, a former Democratic congressman from California and Clinton White House chief of staff who had no experience on intelligence matters. That appointment, and the fact that it would require on-the-job training for Panetta, even drew criticism from leaders of Obama's own party. Democrat Dianne Feinstein of California (Panetta's home state), the chair of the Senate Select Committee on Intelligence, released a statement saying, "I believe the Agency is best-served by having an intelligence professional in charge." An aide to Democratic senator Jay Rockefeller said that his boss had "always believed that the director of the CIA needs to be someone with significant operational intelligence experience, and someone outside the political realm."[96]

The element of *trust*, so crucial to the relationship between any administration and military leaders, was soon tested in a much more serious way. In May 2009, Army Lieutenant General Stanley M. McChrystal was announced as the new commander of U.S. and NATO forces in Afghanistan. He soon commenced a thorough assessment of the situation there with an eye to making a subsequent recommendation of the troop levels required to execute the new strategy for that country. An unusually lengthy Afghan policy review was subsequently commenced in the White House. Obama's ambivalence on the policy options presented was apparent from the beginning. The review process was disorganized and highly politicized. On December 1, he finally announced that he had authorized thirty thousand additional troops. At the same time, he announced that a withdrawal of troops would begin at a fixed date only eighteen months later, a decision that the Marine Corps commandant would later say was "probably giving our enemy sustenance" since it transmitted a clear signal that the administration was unwilling to complete the mission that Obama himself had championed during the presidential campaign.

Even more damaging was Obama's split-the-difference rationale for authorizing only thirty thousand of the forty thousand troops requested by McChrystal and demanding an "exit strategy" for all of the troops. Drawing on classified memoranda and many interviews with Obama and his national security advisors, a well-known author of books on political leadership reported that the compromise decisions were only loosely related at best to military need or sound strategic analysis. Instead, they were based almost exclusively on political grounds. "This is what I'm willing to take on, politically," Obama reportedly said to his advisors regarding the troop request. The decision on troop withdrawal was necessary, he said, because "I can't lose the whole Democratic Party."[97] It can only be imagined what George Marshall or any of a number of other successful secretaries of state would say about that rationale.

The decision was immediately attacked by independent observers, less for the obvious lack of leadership qualities in its content, than for the politicized process used to reach it. "It is the most basic duty of a commander in chief," wrote one commentator "to pursue the national interest above any other interest. The introduction of partisan considerations into strategic decisions merits a special contempt."[98] The strength and tone of the criticism evoked memory of a lonely but courageous speech by Winston Churchill in similar circumstances. During a debate on the floor of the House of Commons on November 12, 1936, Churchill responded to the excuses made by Stanley Baldwin's government for the delays in embarking upon a rearmament program between 1933 and 1935. "I have heard it said," he declared, "that the Government had no mandate for rearmament until the General Election. Such a doctrine is wholly inadmissible. The responsibility of Ministers for the public safety is absolute and requires no mandate. It is in fact the prime object for which Governments come into existence."[99]

In a speech to the House of Commons on the war situation almost five years later, Churchill again spoke words of which several presidents have apparently been ignorant, but which provide good counsel to future commanders in chief. At the time, German troops were less than two hundred miles from Moscow and Germany's U-boat warfare was being conducted by larger numbers of U-boats than ever before. The United States had not yet entered the war and domestic opponents were criticizing the British government's conduct of the war. Speaking of "the fate which awaits nations and individuals who take an easy and popular course or who are guided in defense matters by the shifting winds of well-meaning public opinion," the prime minister declared, "Nothing is more dangerous in wartime than to live in the temperamental atmosphere of a Gallup poll, always feeling one's pulse and taking one's temperature. . . . There is only one duty, only one safe course, and that is to try to be right and not to fear to do or say what you believe to be right."[100]

If a president is willing to risk a break in the bonds of trust between his administration and military leaders, little can be done about the matter until the next election. The U.S. Senate, however, has tools at its disposal that can be used to lessen the danger that political appointees will risk such a breach. It is only necessary to ensure that during the confirmation process for each individual nominated by the president to serve in a position related to national security, the nominee clearly demonstrates two things: first, high competence to serve in the particular position to which he has been nominated; and second, an understanding of military culture and an ability and willingness to manage his relationship with military leaders in a way that will minimize the possibility of a clash between the culture of the broader society of which he is a part and that of the men and women in uniform whom he is about to lead.

Chapter Nine

Politics in the Middle of War

The wise General seeks . . . to make his men obey not because he makes them but because they so wish. And the most effective means of attaining that state of consent is by fostering among them bonds of loyalty and regard for each other too strong for the strains of battle to break.

—John Keegan

Soldiers fix the problem, not the blame.

—General George C. Marshall

King George V of Britain was once asked which was the worst time he had encountered during his reign. Was it the shattering catastrophe of World War I, in which more than seven hundred thousand British soldiers had been killed, or the constitutional crisis of 1910, in which a House of Lords with a large Conservative majority had used its unlimited veto power to reject a budget passed by a great Liberal majority in the House of Commons? "For me," he reportedly replied, "the most difficult was the Constitutional crisis. In the War we were all united, we should sink or swim together. But then, in my first year, half the nation was one way and half the other." [1]

In December 2010, half of America was one way and half the other. Only two years after President Obama and large Democratic majorities in the Senate and House of Representatives had been elected, voters had just returned control of the House to the Republicans (242 Republicans, 193 Democrats) and increased GOP representation in the Senate (51 Democrats, 47 Republicans, 2 Independents). The nation was in its ninth consecutive year of war, but it was certainly not united regarding either the justification of the armed conflicts in Iraq and Afghanistan or the conduct of and future plans for those conflicts. Fewer than 1 percent of Americans had participated in them and the overwhelming majority had not been personally touched by war at all. Military leaders were focused not only on unpredictable daily developments in the combat but also on the growing number of suicides, broken families, and the many other war-related stresses among the nation's fighting forces. They were also attempting to come to grips with the implication of very serious national economic problems and the election results for future defense budgets and the future use of the Armed Forces.

The commander in chief and his senior political lieutenants in the White House and Pentagon were focused on politics. Whatever they might say about democracy in Iraq, Afghanistan, Egypt, Libya, or other countries in the Middle East, they were not interested in acting in accordance with the expression of the will of the people at home in the recent election. No, they had only a short period of time to satisfy the president's liberal political base. If they waited for only a few more days until the new 112th Congress convened, they might not succeed on one of the most contentious issues ever to confront the Armed Forces. But if they acted with sleight of hand, perhaps they could use what was left of the exhausted power of the current lame-duck Congress to ram through the legislation that they desired: repeal of the 1993 "Don't ask, don't tell" statute that barred avowed homosexuals from serving in the Armed Forces. They knew that Democrats who had just lost their bids for reelection in Congress could now ignore the will of the people in their states with impunity. Ironically, they were counting on the professionalism of the Armed Forces to implement the new legislation. Now it was only necessary to ignore the election results and aggressively push for passage of a new law while the rest of America was diverted by the celebrations of the holiday season.

Almost ten years earlier, a Pulitzer Prize–winning journalist had declared in a speech to a military audience that "there are aspects of democracy, systemic problems with a society organized around the premises of democracy, that tend to make it soft." He had quoted a French officer's proposition: "Democracy is the best system of government yet devised, but it suffers from one grave defect. It does not encourage those military virtues on which, in an envious world, it must frequently depend for survival." The journalist had then reflected on democracy as practiced in America in January 2001. "Think of what the democratic ethos has become," he said. "It is materialist. It is individualistic. Its language is 'rights' talk, the constant minting of new rights and the casting of every conflict as a collision of absolute rights, which means it is a litigious society governed by lawyers."[2]

President Obama and his political lieutenants in the White House and Pentagon were experienced practitioners of the new form of democracy. And the path to this point in their efforts to repeal the "Don't ask, don't tell" statute had been surprisingly easy. All the Obama political team had to do was claim that homosexuals have some "right" to serve in the Armed Forces despite the previously expressed finding of Congress to the contrary and the absence of any Supreme Court opinion in support of the claim; dispute detailed factual findings previously made by both Houses of Congress;[3] close their ears to the almost unanimous advice of military leaders who were combat veterans on the importance in combat of unit cohesion, high morale, and good order and discipline; avoid discussions of military needs; act like the Armed Forces were not involved in two wars; ignore the signs that repeated combat deployments were already creating huge stresses among large numbers of individual soldiers and their families; announce the fig-leaf results of a faulty survey that purportedly reflected the opinions of military personnel; count on military discipline to prevent public declarations against the legislation by even its most vehement opponents within the Armed Forces; rely upon a predictably liberal media to spin the issue in a favorable way; join academics in expressing concern about civilian control of the military, an issue upon which Obama had based his firing of General Stanley McChrystal; encourage Secretary of Defense Gates to keep talking about the fact that those who step forward to serve in uniform are part of a culture that does not mirror American society at large (as if that was, somehow, the "fault" of the volunteers in the Armed Forces); and, most importantly, forget about the importance of *trust* in the relationship between civilian and military leaders.

President Obama's campaign promises to push the political agenda of homosexuals were no secret. They had given him substantial support during the 2008 campaign. The situation was exactly that discussed thirteen years earlier by Jim Webb, a former secretary of the navy now serving as a Democratic member of the U.S. Senate. He had written then that some of the greatest challenges to military culture come from small groups of politically motivated activists, aided and abetted by national leaders who are far less interested in matters like military capability than in avoiding any appearance of being "out-of-step" with liberal thinking regarding issues of gender and sexuality.[4]

When Bill Clinton had made a similar pledge to homosexuals seventeen years earlier, General Colin Powell, then chairman of the Joint Chiefs of Staff, had bristled when a left-wing member of Congress suggested that homosexuals were merely trying to establish the same kind of rights that had been achieved by blacks during the civil rights turmoil of the 1960s. "Skin color is a benign, non-behavioral characteristic," he had declared. "Sexual orientation is perhaps the most profound of human behavioral characteristics." He subsequently told Clinton that the heart of the problem was privacy: "How [could a change in the law] be made to work given the intimate living conditions of barracks and shipboard life?"[5] Even Clinton had conceded that he didn't want to see "soldiers holding hands or dancing together at military posts."[6] Powell subsequently told midshipmen at the Naval Academy that if they found Clinton's proposed plan on homosexuals in the Armed Forces to be "completely unacceptable and it strikes the heart of [your] moral beliefs, then [you] have to resign."[7]

Senate members of Clinton's party had shared a related concern with the Joint Chiefs of Staff. Democratic senator Dave Boren, a close friend of Democratic senator Sam Nunn, then chairman of the Armed Services Committee, had been quoted as saying, "It's not [just] about allowing gays in the military—not to Sam and Powell and some others. It's about assuming gays will next push for non-regulation of behavior and fearing that Clinton won't resist. A lot of people think that if they get in they'll want to act out the gay culture—kissing, holding hands, dancing on the dance floor. So their worry is that Clinton will allow the gay *culture* in addition to the status, and they think gays are going to push for that. They're worried whether Clinton will be strong enough to let the Chiefs write rules that the gays don't like."[8]

These kinds of concerns did not prove justified in the Clinton administration since Congress refused to go along with Clinton's plan. They became the center of attention of many people, however, when Obama assumed office and called for the repeal of the 1996 Defense of Marriage Act. That statute prohibits the federal government from recognizing same-sex marriages for purposes of taxes, social security, and other federal programs. The concerns would reach fever pitch on February 23, 2011. Obama, however, was apparently not the least bit disturbed by those concerns. He was also undisturbed by the fact that in conducting twelve hearings, debating, and passing the "Don't ask, don't tell" legislation in 1993, Congress had made an express finding of fact that "[t]he presence in the armed forces of persons who demonstrate a propensity or intent to engage in homosexual acts would create an unacceptable risk to the high standards of morale, good order and discipline, and unit cohesion that are the essence of military capability."[9] Nor was he bothered by the fact that, if his efforts succeeded, only military personnel would have to pay the price of his political commitments. After all, they were *volunteers* and were prevented by law from complaining.

By March 2010, the question of whether to permit avowed homosexuals to serve in the Armed Forces was becoming the subject of a new debate after a bill to repeal the existing ban was introduced by Senator Joe Lieberman (I-CT). At the same time, and acting as if a repeal of existing law was merely an administrative matter that did not require the vote of both Houses of Congress, Secretary Gates took a highly unusual step. Many already believed that he engaged in excessive risk avoidance on hard political decisions. He tended "to hang back, figure out which way decisions were going, where everyone else, including the president, was leaning and then jump that way."[10] The president's position on the issue was clear, so Gates declared that the Pentagon was already preparing for a change in the law. He directed the Armed Forces to ease enforcement of the "Don't ask, don't tell" statute. A week later, the secretary of the army, a former congressman who had never served in uniform, announced that he had no plans to initiate action against any soldier who "technically" violated the law by disclosing to him his or her sexual orientation, even though existing law required their discharge.

In an early appearance before the Senate Armed Services Committee, Gates had acknowledged that Obama's aggressive push to repeal the existing law presented "a very difficult and, in the minds of some, controversial policy question." Consistent with his reputation for being exceptionally opaque on contentious issues, he told the committee that the Pentagon would conduct "a final detailed assessment of [the] proposal before proceeding." But it soon became clear that the "assessment" would not be an objective analysis of whether repeal of the law would improve military capabilities and effectiveness. Since Gates had agreed to continue to serve as secretary of defense for a president who had campaigned on a promise to convince Congress to repeal the "Don't ask, don't tell" statute, and because he had already personally endorsed a repeal, it was clear that the "assessment" would merely be used as part of an effort to justify a repeal. He made no effort to explain why consideration of the highly controversial repeal legislation could not wait until the conflicts in Iraq and Afghanistan were concluded, or at least until the intensity of the combat operations was reduced. He also said nothing about a survey conducted two months earlier by the *Military Times* newspapers, which found that 51 percent of all troops remained opposed to military service by homosexuals whose sexual orientation was known and that as many as 25 percent would likely leave the service if the existing law was repealed.

The debate in Congress was taking place at a time of epic national discontent with its members. In surveys taken by the Pew Research Center in March and April 2010, only 22 percent of Americans said that they could trust the government in Washington almost always or most of the time, one of the lowest measures in half a century. Opinions about elected officials were particularly poor. Just 25 percent expressed a favorable opinion, the lowest rating in all Pew Research Center surveys. Even though Democrats controlled the White House, the Senate, and the House of Representatives, only 40 percent of the Democrats surveyed had a favorable view of Congress, the lowest positive rating ever among members of the majority party. Large majorities (no fewer than 76 percent) of those surveyed agreed with the statements that elected officials in Washington "care only about their careers, are influenced by special interests . . . and are . . . out of touch."

Meanwhile, military leaders continued to express great concern about the homosexual issue. Less than a year earlier, over 1,060 retired senior military officers, including two former chairmen of the Joint Chiefs of Staff, several former service chiefs, and a large number of former combatant and other major commanders, had written to Obama to warn of the dangers of his efforts to repeal the law. In an open letter, the senior officer leaders had declared, "Our past experience as military leaders leads us to be greatly concerned about the impact of repeal [of the 'Don't ask, don't tell' statute] on morale, discipline, unit cohesion, and overall military readiness. We believe that imposing this burden on our men and women in uniform would undermine recruiting and retention, impact leadership at all echelons, have adverse effects on the willingness of parents who lend their sons and daughters to military service, and eventually break the All Volunteer Force." Within months, an army study of the mental health of U.S. troops in Afghanistan would announce, "Reports of acute stress symptoms among soldiers surveyed in 2010 have significantly increased and reports of individual morale have significantly decreased relative to 2009."[11]

In June, the current chiefs of all of the military services wrote letters to Congress urging the lawmakers to take no action on the issue until at least such time as the "assessment" announced by Gates was completed in December. "What I worry about," Army Chief of Staff George W. Casey Jr. told an interviewer, "is you've got a force that's already been stretched and been at war for eight-and-a-half years. The young company commanders and mid-level non-commissioned officers—the ones who would have to implement [such a] policy—when I talk to them, they're kind of in the mode of 'my God, what else do you want us to do right now?'"[12] Still, neither Obama nor Gates made any effort to explain why it was necessary to raise the issue in the middle of two wars. Clearly, Obama was gambling with military morale and related factors when personnel in uniform were already under great stress. His desire to satisfy one of his core political constituencies was being given precedence over the professional judgment of senior military leaders on a matter involving the best interests of the Armed Forces as a whole.

Military chaplains also pleaded for no change in the law, expressing concern that its repeal would threaten the religious freedom of both chaplains and service members.[13] They had great reason to be concerned. In addition to the understanding of most Christians for more than two thousand years, for over three thousand years "Jewish tradition and Jewish law have been unambiguous about homosexuality: it is a sin."[14] The proposed new legislation would use the power of public law to impose upon the less than 1 percent of the population who had volunteered for potentially dangerous military service a requirement to accept—at least to some extent—conduct that is totally contrary to the long-held religious or other personal beliefs of many of them.

Marine Commandant General James T. Conway forcefully informed Congress that the law should not be changed, and that even if it was, he would not force straight marines to share military quarters with homosexual ones, citing what he called "overwhelming" opposition in the Corps to such an arrangement. After Conway retired and General James F. Amos assumed the leadership of the Corps, the new commandant expressed the same opposition to the ban. "There is nothing more intimate than young men and young women—and when you talk of infantry, we're talking our young men—laying out, sleeping alongside of one another and sharing death, fear, and loss of brothers," he said. "I don't know what the effect of that will be on cohesion, I mean, that's what we're looking at. It's unit cohesion, it's combat effectiveness."[15]

Inside the Obama White House, concepts like "unit cohesion" meant nothing to civilian advisors who had never served in close quarters aboard ship or in ground combat units in the Armed Forces, especially in comparison to the perceived "rights" of the vocal minority of political activists who were aggressively pushing for the change. Military commanders, however, know that a man defies human instincts in order to engage in the terrible experience of combat, not because he is ordered to do so, but for "fear of losing 'what he holds more dear than life itself, his reputation as a man among other men.'"[16] Military cohesion thus refers to "the feelings of identity and comradeship that soldiers hold for those in their immediate military unit, the outgrowth of face-to-face . . . group relations."[17] Studies over several decades have convincingly shown that, on the whole, "soldiers do not fight cohesively because of ideology or patriotism. Rather . . . the key factor is loyalty to other members of the unit."[18] John Keegan, the distinguished military historian, has written that the most effective means of convincing soldiers to engage in what is basically irrational conduct, in order to achieve success on the battlefield, is to foster among them "bonds of loyalty and regard for each other too strong for the strains of battle to break."[19] The bonds of loyalty are developed in many ways, including ceremonies of induction, the salute, emphasis on the unit's martial history, good leadership, and the use of unit flags, battle streamers, special uniform insignia, and other visible symbols. Together, these factors work to instill in the current custodians of the unit's reputation and traditions an almost sacred responsibility never to let the "family" down.

While the concept is currently referred to as "unit cohesion," it has existed in good military units for time immemorial. "The hoplites of the Greek city-state militias took their place in the phalanx at the side of neighbors whose good opinion counted more strongly with them than fear of the enemy. The Roman legions made their smallest tactical unit the tent full of men who messed together throughout their service. In the medieval 'lance,' neither knight, squire nor servant could flinch before the enemy without being damned for good in the eyes of others. Regular armies made the platoon or company the unit of both comradeship and firepower."[20] In his book *Fighting Power*, an Israeli military analyst attributes Germany's "frighteningly effective performance during World War II" to its fighting power, which he defines as "the sum total of mental qualities that makes armies fight." He cites a French nineteenth-century military theorist who argued that four brave men who are not close to each other are less likely to take on a lion than four less brave men who know each other well.[21] In a book on the German army general staff, a respected American military historian wrote that the fighting power of Germany permitted German ground soldiers, on a man-to-man basis, to inflict casualties "at about a 50 percent higher rate than they incurred from the opposing British and American troops," and, in words similar to those used by another historian and referred to in chapter 8, to fight on "long after any hope of victory had evaporated."[22]

Military leaders understand that senior political appointees in the Pentagon are part of a political administration, and that each administration usually pursues whatever agenda it campaigned on. The political team in the Obama Pentagon, however, was going too far. Shortly after Obama pledged in his January 2010 State of the Union Address to end the ban on open homosexuals, Gates and all three service secretaries promptly fell in line and publicly endorsed the idea before Congress even had time to seek the views of the chiefs of the military services, combatant commanders, and other military leaders. At minimum, those actions eliminated any belief that political leaders in the Pentagon were truly interested in the impact that a change in the law would have on combat capabilities. The actions also removed any hope that those leaders would serve as honest bridge builders and mediators between the White House and the military establishment on the highly contentious political issue. "Command influence" was also involved. Any effort by a senior military commander to influence the outcome of a court-martial proceeding may be prohibited by the Uniform Code of Military Justice, but the Pentagon political team was clearly trying to raise the risks associated with any attempt by a military leader to publicly express a view contrary to the ones they had just expressed. Because the political appointees had little idea what impact a removal of the ban would have on morale, much less upon combat readiness and capability, their early public endorsement of a removal of the ban removed their credibility on the issue.

The next breach of trust came in the late spring. As Democrats in Congress began to recognize that a very unhappy voting public was likely to send a much different Congress to Washington after the November election, they began to work frantically for an early vote on the issue. As recently as April 30, Gates had at least sounded like a wartime defense secretary when he said in a letter to the House Armed Services Committee that "I believe in the strongest possible terms" that the Armed Forces "must be afforded the opportunity to inform us of their concerns, insights and suggestions. . . . Therefore," he continued, "I strongly oppose any legislation that seeks to change [the statutory ban] prior to the completion of [the] vital assessment process."[23] Within days, Gates's spokesman in the Pentagon announced that the secretary had suddenly changed his mind and no longer opposed a congressional vote before completion of the assessment, which was not expected to reach Congress until December 1.

Even after Senate Republicans blocked the administration's aggressive push for an early vote, Gates continued to urge Congress to act quickly. After the November 2010 election, in which Democrats lost both control of the House of Representatives and their commanding control of the Senate, he tried a new and disingenuous, if not outright misleading, argument. Calling the issue again "a matter of some urgency," he warned in ominous tones that it was only a matter of time before a change in the law would "be imposed immediately by judicial fiat," a scenario he described as "one of the most hazardous to military morale, readiness and battlefield performance."[24]

Surely, he didn't believe that. If he did, then he was very poorly informed. Any action by a single federal judge or even by a U.S. Court of Appeals would not be dispositive of the issue. Over the years, other federal courts had upheld the constitutionality of the "Don't ask, don't tell" statute on several occasions. Clearly, any final adjudication of the issue would be made by the United States Supreme Court. That Court had long ago held that "matters intimately related to foreign policy and national security are rarely proper subjects for judicial intervention. . . . It is 'obvious and unarguable' that no government interest is more compelling than the security of the Nation."[25] Moreover, it is self-evident that Article I, Section 8 of the U.S. Constitution expressly vests Congress, not the president and not the Supreme Court, with power to *raise and support Armies*, to *provide and maintain a Navy*, and to *make Rules for the . . . Regulation of the land and naval Forces*. Nor would a temporary ruling by a lower court cause the sky to fall in. An expedited appeal of any such ruling would be almost certain, and the effect and enforcement of the ruling stayed until the matter could be heard by a more senior court. Gates's argument about battlefield performance was particularly absurd, since his own commanders had already expressed their fears about the impact of a *change* in the current law upon morale and combat performance.

In July, the Defense Department sent the survey on the issue to four hundred thousand service members. It was announced that the results of the survey would be one of the tools by which the "assessment" referred to by Gates would be made. Defense officials worked hard to keep the survey questions a secret. Their reasons were clear. Not a single question asked *whether* military personnel thought the ban of avowed homosexuals should be removed. Rather, it assumed that Congress was going to pass the Obama-proposed legislation.

Two further obstacles to any credibility the survey might otherwise have had were the co-chair of the Pentagon task force assigned overall responsibility for it, and the public affairs official who would determine how the matter was presented to the media. Jeh C. Johnson, Obama's appointee as the Department of Defense general counsel, was co-chair of what was called the Comprehensive Review Working Group (CRWG). He had never served in the Armed Forces, but he had been an early political fundraiser for Obama in New York and he was an outspoken opponent of the existing law. Doug Wilson, the assistant secretary of defense for public affairs, was DoD's highest-ranking openly homosexual official. He had purportedly been picked for the position in December 2009, at least in part to be a point man within the Pentagon on the homosexual issue.[26] Both would soon have a great deal to do with the way the results of the survey were reported.

The conduct of the civilian leadership in the Defense Department throughout the debate thus far had been troubling at best. Gates and the three secretaries of the military services had unnecessarily added to the polarization of the issue. They had permitted their own inexperienced judgment on something as important as military unit cohesion, especially for ground combat units, submarines, and small ships, and political pressure from the White House, to predominate over the professional judgment of military service chiefs and other senior military professionals who were combat veterans. They had ignored the risks to morale and combat capability in order to march lockstep in the direction of political correctness. They had placed the demands of a militant minority ahead of the needs and concerns of a respectfully silent majority of military leaders. In so doing, they had significantly damaged the trust that is essential to a smooth functioning of the complex civilian-military decision-making machinery in the Pentagon. Nothing can more quickly cause the loss of confidence in civilian leaders by uniformed service members than the perception that, for reasons of self-interest, the civilians have abandoned their role as spokesmen for the services and as mediators between the political leadership of the incumbent administration and the military leadership. Gates had already solidified his reputation as a capable government technocrat who was adept at working for a president of any political persuasion, so long as the effort did not interfere with his own career legacy. It was now becoming increasingly clear how he could hold the same position under two presidents with such starkly different ideological views as George W. Bush and Barack Obama.

However harmful to the element of trust the conduct of senior Obama administration officials in the Pentagon might be, it could at least be said that such conduct by self-interested political appointees was not entirely surprising. The conduct of another person involved in the intense political debate, however, was also disturbing, and it was not expected at all.

There is strong anecdotal evidence, often repeated within the Armed Forces, that the most senior general and flag officers do not reach senior rank by taking risks. One student of the evidence has noted that "portraits of a number of past service chiefs and Joint Chiefs of Staff are consistent with this conception, while portraits of the nation's great warrior-commanders look very different."[27] Unlike combatant and other field commanders, whose performance is usually measured by their success on the battlefield or by other strategic and operational mission standards, the performance of flag and general officers serving in the Pentagon is often measured by their political superiors according to the degree of their support of the policies of the incumbent administration and their ability to navigate the strong political currents that flow in Washington, D.C.

There is also considerable evidence to suggest that many senior military leaders are unthinkingly willing to sacrifice, or at least to compromise, elements of classic military culture that have proven to be essential to effectiveness in combat in order to make the Armed Forces more closely mirror contemporary society. One experienced observer of the matter asserts that "military leaders will continue to conform the military to the values of contemporary society so long as no one in uniform or leaders on Capitol Hill put up too much of a fight. The Pentagon appears trapped in an historical pattern of making sure that if American society is going to culturally backslide, the military [must] make sure it is right alongside."[28] Another experienced observer has written that "the danger to the Republic does not arise from any military threat to liberal American society, but from the reverse: the civilization of the U.S. military ethos."[29]

The role of the chairman of the Joint Chiefs of Staff is thus particularly important since the media usually assume—incorrectly—that any statement made by the most senior officer in the Armed Forces represents the opinion of all military officers, or at least the strong majority. There is obvious merit in Churchill's observation that in war it is often difficult to draw precise lines between military and nonmilitary problems, but on many (perhaps most) issues, it is possible. Some issues are overwhelmingly political in nature even though their resolution may impact the Armed Forces. Others are clearly military in nature. If a chairman of the Joint Chiefs abuses his authority in the way he manages a matter that affects the Armed Forces, whatever the respective political and military elements of the issue may be, he does great disservice to all of the men and women in uniform.

Statutory authority and political power are different things, but when he served as chairman of the Joint Chiefs of Staff, General Colin Powell took a very expansive view of his power, often injecting himself into matters that were more political in nature than military. He tended to shape his advice to the political views of his civilian superiors and he would later say that he "was not the pipeline for the composite opinions of [the other Joint] Chiefs. I was speaking for myself."[30] Powell's predecessor, Admiral William J. Crowe Jr., exercised the power of the chairman with less bravado and arrogance. "No matter what legislation Congress passes, and no matter how much authority he has," Crowe wrote in his autobiography, "the Chairman needs the chiefs' expertise and support."[31] In this context, the actions of Admiral Mike Mullen, chairman of the Joint Chiefs of Staff, on several issues (many of which were primarily political in nature, and about which in some cases there was strong disagreement among senior military professionals) were particularly disturbing.

Even though they are nominated by the president and must be confirmed by the Senate, the chairman and members of the Joint Chiefs of Staff are not, of course, political appointees in the legal and conventionally understood sense of that term. Nevertheless, because the Joint Chiefs must routinely deal with matters that have a high political content, political considerations are inevitably involved in the appointment of a person selected to fill the position of chairman. Mullen had been appointed by President Bush to his first two-year term of office, President Obama appointed him to a second term in September 2009.

Senior military officers are usually clumsy at best and often totally inept when they work to be seen as politically correct. In those circumstances they may talk about "speaking truth to power," but they don't act accordingly. Even in the absence of an intention to be politically correct, some senior officers act like a deer in the proverbial headlights when they find themselves the subject of criticism in politically charged circumstances. They seldom remember the observation made by British Field Marshal Montgomery in his 1958 *Memoirs*: "War is a pretty rough and dirty game. But politics!"[32] Naval leaders may comfortably handle strong ocean winds and sea currents, but the winds that blow over the political landscape in the Pentagon are strange, unpredictable, unfair, and (usually) unforgiving.

Such winds were also blowing strongly at the annual Tailhook Association[33] symposium in 1991, and the scandal that took place at that symposium provides a good prism through which we may view the developments relating to the "Don't ask, don't tell" statute in 2010. That improper and indecent behavior by several U.S. Navy and Marine Corps officers who had attended the symposium occurred was never really in doubt. The investigation of the incidents was badly conducted,[34] however, and while several officers received administrative or nonjudicial punishment, no convictions were ever obtained by courts-martial. The secretary of the navy was forced to resign, and after the chief of naval operations (CNO) was accused by a navy judge of lying about his personal involvement at the symposium,[35] he retired early.

Strong criticism of the CNO was later made by a former secretary of the navy[36] for the former's failure to object when the political appointee serving as the new acting secretary of the navy asserted that the Tailhook activities were symptomatic of a broader "cultural problem" within the navy relating to the role of women in the naval service. The CNO was further criticized for a remarkable change of navy policy. Shortly before the symposium, he had testified on Capitol Hill that it would be a mistake to let women serve on combat ships or fly warplanes in squadrons assigned to aircraft carriers.[37] That position was based upon his decades of personal experience. He would later describe his opposition to the idea, saying that a change in the historical policy would be "adding [an undesirable] load to the unit commanders . . . ship commanders, the issue that [had] always been there with males and females . . . commander running a submarine," he continued. "I felt I was about up to here with the load on my back."[38] In November 1992, the Presidential Commission on the Assignment of Women in the Armed Forces had endorsed the CNO's view and, for several reasons, recommended that women not be assigned to combat aviation duties.

Enter Pat Schroeder, a left-wing Democrat, radical feminist, and member of the House Armed Services Committee. Rushing to characterize the Tailhook incidents as much more than unacceptable conduct by a group of drunken naval aviators, she declared that her mission was to "break the culture" of naval aviation and that the situation could only be remedied by removing the prohibition against women serving in combat. Not long thereafter, without the benefit of any new supporting study or data regarding the needs of the navy, and without discussing the matter with the several admirals who were in command of the navy's worldwide operating forces, the CNO reversed his position. Some suggested that his about-face in policy was part of an ultimately unsuccessful effort to retain his job for the full term.[39] His only declared explanation was a new personal belief, which, he said in a *Navy Times* interview,[40] he began to develop after the confirmation hearing for Supreme Court Justice Clarence Thomas caused him to conclude that "there really is a jungle in the workplace." His thinking was apparently further influenced by his civilian daughter, who told him that she had "felt discriminated against in her (non-Navy) job."[41] He did not explain what that had to do with the combat readiness and capability of the navy. The point is not that the change in policy was obviously incorrect. Rather, the evidence strongly suggests that the CNO was making a political judgment that was properly the prerogative of political leaders.

By 2010, Admiral Mike Mullen had made his own share of major policy decisions and recommendations based on nothing or little more than his purported personal beliefs, some of which had at least the appearance of having been designed to please political leaders. He had also not hesitated to express his unsolicited views, even on subjects outside of his jurisdiction. In 2009, for example, and after he had been nominated by President Obama for a second two-year term as chairman of the Joint Chiefs, the Senate Armed Services Committee asked him to answer several written questions in preparation for his confirmation hearing. Without being asked, he had volunteered the following comment: "One policy I would like to see changed is the one barring [the service of women] aboard submarines."[42] He cited no navy need requiring a change in current policy, he made no argument that putting women on submarines would improve combat capabilities or reduce costs, nor did he attempt to rebut the several reasons advanced over the years by other naval leaders who believed that a change in policy would be unwise. One of the objections previously advanced had to do with the inescapable fact of very limited space on submarines. To accommodate the privacy needs of females, including separate berthing and "heads" (toilet/shower facilities), would be "prohibitively expensive," it was argued. A study for the navy conducted in 1994 also found that watch duties, the management of sleeping quarters, the need for extra supplies, and likely incidents of fraternization and harassment would unnecessarily complicate life aboard a submarine and adversely affect discipline.[43] Mullen didn't even explain why he had raised an issue over which he had no authority and that was completely within the responsibility of the CNO. It is difficult to avoid the conclusion that his effort was designed to curry favor with the new president, the confirmation committee, and the full Senate, and to limit the discretion of the current CNO to make a contrary judgment.

When the policy change advocated by Mullen took effect, the navy did not have to wait long to find out if the predictions of the 1994 study were valid. Only a month after the first female submariners began reporting to ballistic-missile submarines, a master chief petty officer who served as chief of the boat aboard the USS *Nebraska* (SSBN-739), and who was a twenty-one-year veteran, was fired after allegations were made that he had had an inappropriate relationship with a female Naval Academy midshipman aboard the submarine.[44]

More controversial was the navy's effort to implement Mullen's order for greater racial diversity in the officer ranks. In an August 2005 speech when he was serving as CNO, he had told an audience in New Orleans that diversity is critical to the navy's success because it "strengthens the very fabric of who we are."[45] He did not say how diversity relates to an officer's capability. In 2009, after the election of the first black president, he continued to voice an earlier assertion that having Armed Forces that reflect the demographics of the country is "a *strategic imperative* for the security of our country." He even ventured the hyperbolic opinion that it was "dangerous" for the social representativeness of the Armed Forces to vary from that of the country at large.[46] While the achievement of greater diversity in the navy's leadership was a reasonable policy objective, Mullen did not explain the military importance or relevance of demographic profiles, or how or why the matter was "strategic" in nature, much less why it had dangerous implications. At the same time that he was making his assertions, a respected defense scholar was writing, "Whatever the desirability of social representativeness of military personnel might be, there is scant evidence that it matters much for civilian control. If purchased at the price of long-service professionalism, it also limits military effectiveness."[47]

As the navy attempted to translate Mullen's vague "guidance" into tangible policy, a storm of criticism arose. In July 2010, his successor as CNO asked navy flag officers to identify minority (diverse) officers with high potential and to describe the plan for their career progression to ensure that they were considered for key follow-on billets. A newspaper editorial in the nation's capitol immediately accused the navy of "creating a list of privileged diverse officers who will enjoy special benefits and career mentoring not available to people of the wrong race." This type of "backward, 20th-century, overtly racial thinking," the editorial continued, "has no place in 21st-century post-racial America." The piece concluded with this observation: "In the contemporary naval bureaucracy, this type of politically correct nonsense has run out of control like a loose cannon on deck."[48]

Meanwhile, the leadership of the U.S. Naval Academy was encountering a different kind of storm due to the methods employed to satisfy Mullen's pressure for diversity. Critics of the Academy's admissions policies alleged that the school was admitting far too many marginal students, most of them minority students and recruited athletes. Academy records indicated that while the normal cut-off for the SAT scores of applicants was about 600 out of a possible 800 points, selected students were being admitted with math scores as low as 410 and verbal scores of 370.[49] A tenured civilian professor at the Academy asserted that 75 percent of black midshipmen had (either math or verbal) SAT scores below 600, while only 25 percent of whites did.[50] He subsequently argued that the admission policies "guarantee [marginally qualified students] a seat that . . . is denied to much more highly qualified applicants."[51] By January 2012, minorities made up nearly a third of the class of 2016.[52]

No argument was made by the Academy's Admissions Office that the marginal students being admitted had leadership potential that was greater than all other applicants who received higher entrance exam scores, or that marginal students elect to remain in the navy for careers at rates much higher than graduates who enter with higher scores. No explanation was given as to why the admission of minority applicants with lower test scores could not be delayed until they had received sufficient academic preparation to compete fairly with all other applicants. One would think it self-evident that sailors and marines going into harm's way want to be led by the best officers the nation can produce, irrespective of their ethnic heritage, and that a dilution of the quality of the officer corps is likely to have negative consequences, but after the professor wrote an opinion-page article in June 2009 asserting that the Academy operates a two-tiered admission system that makes it substantially easier for minority applicants to be admitted, he was denied a routine merit pay increase.[53] A former member of the Admissions Board was quoted as saying, "We say we are striving for excellence, and this is not excellence."[54]

Critics of the admissions policy claimed that it violated the U.S. Constitution. In fact, arguments could be made on both sides of the issue, given the state of existing law. But the admissions policy was risky business. In a 2003 decision in the case of *Gratz v. Bollinger*,[55] the U.S. Supreme Court ruled 6–3 that a university's undergraduate admissions policy was unconstitutionally discriminatory because it effectively awarded a bonus in admissions criteria to applicants who were underrepresented minorities. At the same time, in the case of *Grutte v. Bollinger*,[56] the Court ruled 5–4 that the use of a race-conscious admissions program was lawful, but it declared that such programs must be reviewed with "strict scrutiny" to ensure that they are necessary to "further a compelling government interest," that they are "narrowly tailored" to further that interest,[57] that each applicant is evaluated as an individual, that the program is flexible and free of quotas, and that it is "limited in time."

Significantly, Justice Sandra Day O'Connor, who wrote both opinions for the Court in 2003, has now been replaced by Justice Samuel A. Alito Jr., who is perceived to be far more skeptical of racial remedies. Perhaps more significantly, the Supreme Court announced in February 2012 that it would reconsider the issue in the fall. The point here is not that the diversity sought is not a desirable policy. The point is rather that in lowering admissions standards, instead of applying whatever effort and resources may be necessary to help all minority applicants meet the existing standards, navy leaders were unnecessarily injecting themselves into a political and constitutional thicket properly left to elected and appointed civilian leaders.

Whatever the constitutionality of the Academy's admissions process,[58] it appeared to stand in stark contrast to the approach taken by the Marine Corps. Concerned that there were too few black officers in the Corps, in the summer of 2011 the new commandant announced a plan of new outreach and recruiting efforts that would double that number. In making the announcement, he said, "And you might ask, 'Are you going to change your standards?' The answer is 'hell no.'" An aide to the commandant reiterated that standards of performance, test scores, and qualifications to be an officer would remain unchanged. "It's not about dropping any standards," he said.

"Those things are set in stone, and it would be an insult to our institution to do so."[59]

In addition to the injection of his personal views on controversial personnel issues, Admiral Mullen had also appeared at times to be trimming his sails on more important national security and foreign policy matters. According to one report, he took an unusual position during the Obama administration's 2009 Afghanistan-Pakistan strategy review. For some time, he had agreed with the opinion of General McChrystal that forty thousand additional troops would be needed in Afghanistan in order to successfully implement a counterinsurgency strategy there. Aware that for political reasons Obama was almost desperate to begin a withdrawal of troops from Afghanistan, and concerned that the president was not persuaded of the need for that many troops for even short-term objectives, Mullen reportedly told Obama, "We won't ask for more troops again."[60] Less than thirty days later, he apparently repeated the promise.[61] How could such a promise be made? What if it unexpectedly became clear that additional troops were necessary to protect gains in the Afghanistan conflict for which so many sacrifices had already been made? Mullen's concession and less-than-courageous promise may have impressed the president, but it could hardly have encouraged the battlefield commanders who were having to deal with the operational and tactical realities on the ground in the combat zones in which they were operating.

Because of his history of injecting himself into debates of contentious political issues that were often more appropriate for civilian than military decision, Mullen's scheduled testimony before Congress in early 2010 attracted considerable attention. On February 2, only days after Obama called for repeal of the existing law regarding homosexuals and military service, Mullen appeared before the Senate Armed Services Committee, where he declared that it was his "personal belief" that changing the law to permit military service by open homosexuals was "the right thing to do." He admitted that prior to his headline-making testimony he had not discussed the issue with combat commanders. He cited no evidence that the current law was impairing the combat effectiveness of the Armed Forces or that changing the law would improve combat capabilities. His acknowledgment that he had no idea how a lifting of the ban would affect the combat performance of U.S. units currently engaged in two wars was little short of astounding. Even though he had never been awarded the Navy Combat Action Ribbon, which is given to those who have actively participated in ground or surface combat,[62] he made no effort to explain why anyone should care about his uninformed personal opinion. Perhaps it was because of the fact that, less than three years earlier, his predecessor as chairman of the Joint Chiefs, a ground combat veteran, had expressed, in the strongest possible terms, a totally contrary view.[63]

It was clear to even the most uninformed that there were two distinct bodies of opinion on the question within the Armed Forces: homosexuals and certain others who wished to have the "Don't ask, don't tell" statute repealed, and a second group who believed that the practice of homosexuality is immoral or that a change in the law would impair combat effectiveness. To a great extent, the views of many in the latter group were based upon the teachings of their religion, which is not surprising since all four major faith groups in the country have always had a traditional understanding that homosexuality is immoral. It is not appropriate, of course, for either political appointees in the Department of Defense or the chairman of the Joint Chiefs of Staff to take a position in favor of, or against, a particular theological position. That is "the prerogative of those who profess that particular faith."[64] The Establishment Clause of the First Amendment to the Constitution is unequivocal on this point. But in expressing his personal view on the repeal of an existing law so early, Mullen abandoned even an appearance of objectivity and neutrality on the issue. Skeptics could be forgiven for suspecting that his testimony had been a political condition of his reappointment as chairman by Obama.

The absence of a public reaction by Secretary of Defense Gates to Mullen's statement to the Senate was also noteworthy. Three years earlier, he had publicly chastised Mullen's predecessor for expressing a personal opinion on the controversial issue that was *consistent* with existing law as well as the policy of the then incumbent Bush administration.[65] Gates had also denied the then chairman of the Joint Chiefs the customary two-year reappointment, making him the first chairman in over forty years not to be reappointed. Gates was conspicuously quiet when Mullen expressed a personal opinion that was *contrary* to existing law.

By failing to cite compelling *military* reasons for changing the law, by expressing his "personal belief" on the heavily politicized and religion-related issue without the presence of the other members of the Joint Chiefs of Staff or any combatant or other field commanders, and by expressing his opinion months before the completion of the Pentagon study that would assess the potentially disruptive impact of any change in the law upon members of the Armed Forces, Mullen appeared to be attempting to preempt other military leaders on this issue by making it extremely difficult for them to express a contrary opinion. He appeared to many to be acting as nothing more than a political functionary executing the president's political agenda, rather than the nation's senior military officer expressing an informed, considered, and objective judgment on a military matter of such great consequence to the Armed Forces.

In March, a lieutenant general who was serving as the army's Pacific commander encouraged troops who opposed the repeal to express their opinions through their chain of command. Mullen, who had just expressed his own personal views on the question, publicly suggested that the general should "vote with his feet" and resign.[66] Whatever criticism may be made of the method used by the general, Mullen's comment was widely perceived to be an effort to muzzle any military leader who did not support the administration's political position on the issue. He was obviously ignorant of the principle that military subservience to civilian control applies to existing law, not to debates about changes in the law.

In late May, Mullen took another controversial action. When Obama asked the Democratic leaders of Congress to move toward an immediate vote on the homosexuality issue, a political matter totally outside the scope of his authority, he endorsed the effort. No military reason was given for his endorsement. Indeed, he made it without even informing the other members of the Joint Chiefs of Staff. When asked why the Chiefs had been shut out of the discussion and had been prevented from seeing the language that appeared in a White House announcement of the planned early vote, Mullen's spokesman claimed scheduling conflicts, an excuse that was blatantly absurd.[67]

By December 10, 2010, administration leaders and Democratic leaders in Congress were on the verge of panic. After their attempt to attach a bill repealing the "Don't ask, don't tell" statute to the Defense Appropriation Act failed on a procedural vote in the Senate, they again resorted to misleading political hyperbole. Obama declared, "A minority of senators are standing in the way of the funding upon which our troops, veterans and military families depend."[68] Gates told reporters again that if the law wasn't changed within the next week, the Armed Forces would "be at the mercy of the courts."[69] Senate Majority Leader Harry Reid (D-NV) threatened to reconvene the Senate after the Christmas holiday to vote again on the issue. It was obvious to most observers, however, that no real urgency existed. The only thing that was "urgent" was the desire of Democratic leaders to vote again on the repeal issue before the new and recently elected representatives of the American people could assume office, and express the most current public opinion on the issue.

Even though they controlled both the Senate and the House until the new Congress convened the following month, at least some Republican votes would be required in the Senate to secure passage of the repeal initiative in the current congressional term. In order to obtain the necessary Republican support, the swing Republican senators would have to be given "political cover on a key question: How would the military respond to such a dramatic change in its traditions, culture and code of conduct?"[70] It was thus with intense interest that the results of the Pentagon survey were anticipated.

When the results were released in early December, the Comprehensive Review Working Group in the Pentagon said that the negative impact on the Armed Forces if the existing law was changed would be "low." It would be alleged later, however, that that conclusion was false and that "deliberate efforts [had been made] by senior executive branch officials to mislead Congress into taking a step that the administration's own surveys had established would be deeply injurious to the U.S. military."[71] Citing a report of an investigation by the Department of Defense inspector general, a Washington think tank reported that "a skewed response [to the survey] was manufactured and leaked to friendly journalists by top Pentagon and White House officials. Specifically, an executive summary of [the survey] was written by the department's general counsel, Jeh C. Johnson, before the survey was even begun on July 7, 2010."[72] The inspector general purportedly concluded further, "We consider it likely that the primary source [of the leaked information from the survey] disclosed content from the draft [CRWG] Report with the intent to shape a pro-repeal perception of the draft Report prior to its release to gain momentum in support of a legislative change during the 'lame duck' session of Congress following the November 2, 2010 elections."[73]

Despite the absence of any question in the survey that asked service members directly *whether* they believed the law should be changed, the CRWG Report contained the conclusion that "[o]ur sense is that the majority of views expressed were against repeal."[74] The report further noted, "Nearly 60 percent of respondents in the Marine Corps and in Army combat arms said they believed there would be a negative impact on their unit's effectiveness . . . among Marine combat arms the number was 67 percent."[75] The responses further indicated that if the existing law were repealed, more than a third of experienced close-combat troops would decline reenlistment or consider leaving the Armed Forces.[76] For marines, the percentage was reportedly as high as 48 percent.[77]

Any doubts that may have existed at the time about the authenticity of the description of the survey results by public affairs officials were soon overcome by rapidly moving events. On December 15, 2010, Gallup announced its latest poll on the assessment by Americans of the way the Congress was doing its job. Only 13 percent of Americans said that they approved of the work of the Congress. The "83 percent disapproval rating" was described as "the worst Gallup has measured in more than 30 years of tracking congressional job performance."[78] In a lame-duck session on Saturday, December 18, in the middle of two wars, the Senate, 75 percent of whose members had never served in the Armed Forces even in peacetime, voted to permit avowed homosexuals to serve in the Armed Forces. The legislation was signed into law by President Obama three days before Christmas. Only twelve days later, the new 112th Congress convened and the newly elected members of the Senate and House of Representatives began their work.

Speaking to a Duke University audience on September 29, 2010, less than sixty days before the Senate vote on repeal of the "Don't ask, don't tell" statute, then Secretary of Defense Gates expressed concern about what he described as a growing "disconnect" between American society at large and the less than 1 percent of the population who serve in uniform and fight America's wars. He spoke of the nine years of continuous combat, the almost five thousand deaths, the growing suicide figures, the long separations from families, the rapidly increasing divorce rate, and the other heavy burdens on the nation's warriors. He failed to mention the burden of having to unnecessarily deal with a social experiment as complex as the integration of open homosexuals into military units in the middle of two wars. There is no evidence that Gates had previously made his perceived "disconnect" issue a matter of high priority, or that he had ever offered any suggestions about what, if anything, he thought should be done about the matter. Within days, he had once again joined Democratic leaders in the Senate in characterizing the homosexual issue as urgent and in lending his support to calls for a vote on the proposed repeal legislation before a newly elected Congress could assume office.

Not to be outdone on political correctness, even by his political boss, the chairman of the Joint Chiefs of Staff addressed a conference on military professionalism at the National Defense University in early January 2011. In his speech to military officers, Admiral Mullen acknowledged that the "American people are extraordinarily supportive of our men and women" in the Armed Forces. He then proceeded to declare that military leaders cannot afford to be out of touch with the American people and that "to the degree we are out of touch, I think it's a very dangerous course." He made no effort to explain *how* the Armed Forces were out of touch with a very supportive American public or what was "dangerous" about the situation. Having failed to identify the perceived problem with any specificity, he also failed to offer any solutions, saying, "I don't have any answers."[79]

Mullen touched upon the same theme in May 2011 when he told the graduating class at West Point that the Armed Forces are "fairly insular, speaking our own language of sorts, living within our own unique culture, isolating ourselves out of fear or from perhaps even our own pride." In addition to leading the army's warriors, he said that it was the duty of each new young officer "to be a statesman as well as a soldier," to communicate "often and much with the American people to the degree you can."[80] A few days later, he erased any doubt about whose "fault" he believed it was for the existence of the "gap" between society and the Armed Forces. In an interview, he declared, "Long term, if the military drifts away from its people in this country, that is a catastrophic outcome we as a country can't tolerate, can't afford, in no way."[81] He reportedly even lamented the proud tradition within many military families—such as that of the person only recently named as his successor—of the children of a military leader also choosing a career of service to the nation in uniform.

Like Gates, Mullen conspicuously avoided any explanation of exactly how he thought the Armed Forces were "drifting away" or why he characterized the development as potentially "catastrophic." He did, however, leave the remarkable implication that it was because the values and opinions of many military personnel differ from those of a large segment of society. It apparently never occurred to him that it is not the military community that has "drifted away" from the nation's historic and traditional values, but rather contemporary society. The accusatory tone of his theme was especially troubling. Did he mean to say that the Armed Forces should mirror all contemporary cultural values? Did he, for example, believe that the Armed Forces should undo the hard work of more than three decades and permit soldiers and sailors to abuse drugs and alcohol, as many in civil society do? Should the Armed Forces forget about the principles of duty, sacrifice, accountability, service before self, and other historically prized values and instead embrace situational ethics, self-centeredness, and other postmodern values? Was he arguing that those in uniform should throw away their moral compass and enroll in a college of moral relativism? Did he not understand that some of the very factors that attract men and women to military service are factors that separate them from the values of much of the popular culture? Was he saying that the 1 percent of society who volunteer to accept the hazards and hardships of military service—rather than the remaining 99 percent—must be prepared not only to risk their lives and deal with stresses most Americans cannot imagine but also to bear the burden of stopping the drift he described? If not, then what *was* he saying?

It was not clear why Gates and Mullen had decided to rehash the "gap in civil-military relations" debate of the 1990s, a favorite of some of the nation's leading journalists and academics. It is undisputed that over four decades various factors have worked to reduce the number of contacts that the average American has with the Armed Forces. The most significant, of course, was the national decision to abolish the draft and establish an all-*volunteer* military force structure. As a result of that decision, a disproportionate number of those who do volunteer to serve come from the Southern states and a few other areas. Frequent and lengthy deployments remove military personnel from civilian communities. The Base Realignment and Closure (BRAC) process has also had a major impact. Hundreds of military bases across the country, some very large, have been closed. The remaining bases tend to be concentrated in a handful of areas. Major naval facilities are of necessity located on the coasts. As we have seen, it is also clear that a substantial percentage of those individuals who volunteer for military service do not share many of the prevailing values of contemporary American society, especially the lingering values of the counterculture movement of the 1960s and 1970s.

To any extent to which they believed that the military-society gap to which they were referring is due to cultural differences, neither Gates nor Mullen made an effort to explain *why* a military culture that is different from that of society at large should be considered unacceptable, or even unhealthy. Were they merely expressing frustration with the fact that so many military leaders had rejected their leadership on the "Don't ask, don't tell" issue? Were they adopting the discredited theory of some writers during the Clinton administration that a military that does not share the values of the society it protects might "cease to behave as its servant"?[82] That theory has no more historical support or current factual foundation now than it did then.

Having broadly described the "gap" problem, which most fair-minded observers can agree does exist, at least with respect to the general level of comparative competence between political appointees and senior military leaders, certain cultural differences between the military and some American elites, and the lack of shared experience and understanding; having now explicitly fixed the blame on the serving members of the Armed Forces, Gates and Mullen studiously avoided any recommendation of possible remedies. Perhaps they were unaware of Eisenhower's comment that "[l]eadership consists of nothing but taking responsibility for everything that goes wrong and giving . . . subordinates credit for everything that goes well." Perhaps they had never heard of General George Marshall's admonition to leaders to "[f]ix the problem, not the blame."[83] Perhaps in the rarefied atmosphere of Washington, D.C., they had forgotten what every sergeant major and chief petty officer knows instinctively—that leaders must lead! It was recognized more than a decade ago that the gap, to the extent that it is a problem, is a public policy problem that can be managed effectively through good leadership and hard policy work.[84] It does not have to be, and should not be, closed if the price of "pleasing the social mores of contemporary society" is the abolition of the military ethos that is essential to success in war.

Since the idea of volunteering for military service appeals in disproportionate measure to individuals who do not share the values of the popular culture, did Gates and Mullen recommend a return to a military draft or some other system of national service? If so, why did they not say so? Did they have any ideas about how to bring the sons and daughters of the intellectual, social, financial, and political elite of the country into military service so that they could share the same risks as other members of the Armed Forces, engage in the same necessary dirty work, and become exposed to the cultural values of others who serve?[85] Did they believe that the BRAC process should be immediately terminated? Did they have a program in mind that would increase the number of military recruits who come from New England and other areas from which comparatively few volunteers now step forward? Did they have any other ideas about how Americans not in uniform could more effectively share the sacrifices and burdens of the nation's armed conflicts? Did they believe that the president should use his "bully pulpit" to encourage young men and women to join the Armed Forces or to rally popular support for the values of those in uniform? Gates and Mullen didn't even approach the question of how the military ranks would be filled with the kind of *quality* people who have served in the Armed Forces for the last two decades if the volunteers who serve today should "vote with their feet" and leave the Armed Forces because of a lack of trust and confidence in the nation's political and most senior military leadership.

Mullen had concluded his remarks at the January conference by urging military leaders to be an "apolitical" instrument of the state. That principle has indisputable and obvious merit, but he cited no evidence—almost certainly because none existed—that currently serving military leaders were engaging in political party activities or publicly supporting particular political candidates. In the absence of such evidence, and because even seemingly technical military issues often have political implications, military leaders could be pardoned for interpreting Mullen's remarks to mean that they should not express—much less vigorously oppose, even privately—informed professional opinions on any policy, program, or course of action proposed by the political appointees of an incumbent administration, no matter how unwise or contrary to the national interest the policy or action might be. Mullen's memory was also astonishingly short. For the past several months, he had forcefully injected himself into the middle of some of the most contentious political issues in decades.

The conduct of Barack Obama's political appointees in the White House and the Pentagon and of the leaders of the Democratic-controlled Senate on the repeal of the "Don't ask, don't tell" statute involved a high-risk gamble with the critical element of *trust* between civilian and military leaders. It would not be the only politicization of a sensitive issue by the secretary of the navy.[86] Irrespective of the wisdom or lack of wisdom of the repeal legislation and of the arguments that were made both for and against it, the actions taken by the secretary of defense, the three service secretaries, and the chairman of the Joint Chiefs of Staff in concert with the congressional proponents of the repeal legislation were very troubling. Domestic politics were permitted to trump the well-being of military personnel who had endured the stresses of war for more than nine consecutive years. The civilian leadership in the Pentagon had acted as self-interested politicians in failing to properly supervise the administration of the survey of military personnel and the release of the survey findings, and to ensure that the process had transparency. They had ignored the opinions of the senior combat and other military leaders and a clear majority of the soldiers and marines engaged in ground combat regarding the effect of a change in the law on the effectiveness of their units. Perhaps their most indefensible conduct was their efforts to assist in the rush to evade the most recent measure of the national will—as expressed in the results of the 2010 election—including the effort to conduct a last-minute vote by a lame-duck Congress on highly controversial social legislation for which the potential consequences to the Armed Forces were so great.

The public breach on the legislation between the Obama administration's political appointees in the Pentagon and the chairman of the Joint Chiefs, on the one hand, and the military service chiefs, most other military leaders, and a majority of troops in the combat arms, on the other, was unprecedented.[87] The consequences for a president who was so sensitive to public opinion polls should have been very disturbing. An analysis of more than 238,000 interviews of active-duty military personnel and veterans conducted by Gallup over the fifteen months between January 2010 and April 2011 determined that barely more than a third of all of those surveyed approved of the commander in chief's job performance.[88]

It remains to be seen what history's final verdict on the conduct and performance of the political appointees in the Obama White House and the Pentagon will be. In the short term, military leaders, as well as many others, will be anxious to see if any civilian leaders are held accountable for the actions described by the DoD inspector general in connection with the survey of military personnel, actions that have been characterized as "misconduct at the highest levels of government."[89] But, whatever else may be said about their performance (which, in the case of Gates, had generally been previously perceived as good), the failure of the Pentagon's civilian leadership to prevent the public breach on the repeal legislation in the middle of two long wars will not be forgotten soon.

Chapter Ten

The "Professionalization" of Amateur Appointees

It is always important in matters of high politics to know what you do not know. Those who think they know, but are mistaken, and act upon their mistakes, are the most dangerous people to have in charge.
—Former British prime minister Margaret Thatcher, *Statecraft* (2002)

[Winston Churchill] hated yes men—he had no use for them. What he wanted was people who would stand up to him.
—Earl Alexander of Tunis, British Minister of Defence, 1952

Political leaders at the national level are loath to modify long-established practices and the ways of accommodating the political needs of all concerned in both parties, until the needs of the nation and the demands of the voting public can no longer be ignored. To that end, in this chapter I will summarize the thesis of this book and propose solutions to the problems I have discussed.

I have attempted to describe in broad strokes what I believe to be generally accepted facts, facts that I now assert. Since the founding of the nation, and especially in the decades since the close of World War I, American military leaders have adapted to armed conflicts, constantly changing circumstances, changes in national policy, and unpredicted security challenges by working consistently, if at varying paces and sometimes with uneven success, to improve their own capabilities and those of all American men and women under arms. I further assert that military leaders have been increasingly sensitive to their relations with their civilian superiors, a relationship for which political scientists, military sociologists, and others worked for decades to establish governing principles under the broad term *professionalism*. Finally, I assert that presidents and members of the Senate have *not* worked with similar diligence to ensure that senior political appointees in those departments and agencies that are responsible for our security meet comparable professional standards. The central argument of my case is that because of the nature of the threats to the nation's security since 9/11, we can no longer afford the kinds of mediocre to poor (and sometimes clearly incompetent) senior political appointees who, in far too many presidential administrations in recent decades, have been given authority far in excess of their levels of experience and competence. Much of what follows in this chapter focuses on examples of such appointments in the Obama administration, not because that administration is necessarily unique in the number of unqualified appointed officials, but because it provides the most recent examples.

Two and a half years into the Obama presidency, evidence in support of my argument was apparent on the front pages of the nation's newspapers, in professional journals, and even in national surveys. In the April 2011 *Government Executive* survey of senior career federal executives and managers to which I referred in chapters 4 and 6, more than 30 percent of the respondents gave Obama's political appointees a "D" or an "F" for overall job performance, evaluations lower even than those in previous administrations. One respondent spoke for many in saying, "The role of [senior leadership] has increased, but the effectiveness, skill and knowledge has dramatically decreased."[1] Data was not available from all military leaders, but in a separate survey of more than twenty-two thousand army personnel, less than 32 percent of the respondents agreed with the statement "I trust elected and appointed civilian officials to do what is best for the army."[2] That finding was consistent with the result of the 2010 Pew Research Center survey of all Americans, as noted in chapter 9.

In announcing his candidacy for the presidency on February 10, 2007, Obama had blasted "the cynics, the lobbyists, the special interests," who he said have "turned our government into a game only they can afford to play. They write the checks," he had asserted, "and you get stuck with the bill, they get the access while you get to write a letter, they think they own this government, but we're here today to take it back." In June 2011, however, more than two years after Obama's inauguration, it was reported that "nearly 200 of his biggest donors [had] landed plum government jobs and advisory posts, won federal contracts worth millions of dollars for their business interests, or attended numerous elite White House meetings and social events."[3]

Most of the large donors were "bundlers," people who, in addition to their personal contributions, had circumvented the individual contribution limits of $2,500 imposed by law in federal elections by pooling donations from fundraising networks. The bundlers had raised at least $50,000, and sometimes more than $500,000, in donations for Obama's campaign. Nearly 80 percent of those who collected at least $500,000 for Obama had been appointed to "key administration posts," as defined by the White House.[4] Obama was not the first president to appoint bundlers to important positions, but in little more than two years, he had appointed more bundlers than George W. Bush had during two full terms of office.[5]

Of particular concern were Obama's appointments of bundlers to positions in departments and agencies responsible for the nation's safety. Eric Holder, for example, was a $50,000 bundler. During his service as deputy attorney general during the Clinton administration, his judgment had been seriously questioned and he had been accused of politicizing the Justice Department in connection with Clinton's pardon of fugitive financiers Marc Rich and Pincus Green and the clemency given to Puerto Rican members of the terrorist FALN. That did not bother Obama, who nominated Holder as the new U.S. attorney general in early 2009. Since then, Holder's judgment has repeatedly been called into question by such actions as his decision to open a criminal investigation of CIA officers who had interrogated leaders of al Qaeda, his refusal to enforce the Defense of Marriage Act, and his decision to try 9/11 mastermind Khalid Sheik Mohammed in New York.

Another bundler of at least $500,000 for Obama had been appointed principal deputy assistant attorney general in the Department of Justice's Office of Legal Policy.[6] That office assists the attorney general in recommending candidates for all federal judgeships, including seats on the U.S. Supreme Court. Interestingly, only six years prior to his appointment, this bundler, a former George Washington University law professor, had written about the disproportionate influence that wealthy donors have with these words: "The most pressing problem posed by money in politics is that an overwhelming majority of citizens are effectively excluded from an important stage of the political process."[7] Nevertheless, the bundler's expressed concern for average Americans did not prevent the Obama administration from offering, or him from accepting, the senior Justice Department position.

Only ten months had passed since Obama had abruptly fired General Stanley McChrystal, the commander of all U.S. and International Security Assistance Forces in Afghanistan following unflattering remarks that had allegedly been made by McChrystal's aides to a young reporter for a frivolous and controversial magazine. The purported remarks had immediately been published. McChrystal had been handpicked for the job by the chairman of the Joint Chiefs of Staff because of his expertise and experience in counterinsurgency warfare and special operations. At the time of the firing, the war in Afghanistan was at a critical stage. The secretary of defense recommended against the firing. Nevertheless, a president who, to put it kindly, had entered office unschooled and untrained in the management of national security matters and international affairs fired his top field commander in the middle of a war for reasons unrelated to the commander's performance in the field.

The president's White House political aides were reportedly thrilled with the humiliating downfall of General McChrystal.[8] Informed observers saw the action for what it was: an effort by a very inexperienced president to create a public image of an undisputed fact—that is, that he was in charge. A foreign journalist put the matter in clear terms: "Obama didn't want to be seen as a wimp."[9] Regrettably, a distinguished military career was sacrificed unnecessarily for a self-serving political end. After a lengthy investigation, the Pentagon's inspector general subsequently cleared McChrystal of any wrongdoing and pointedly noted that his office had been unable to verify that any of the remarks alleged in the magazine article had ever been made to anyone.

Having had no difficulty removing an admittedly blunt-spoken military leader, Obama soon made a political appointment that highlighted his strong tendency to give domestic politics priority over national security and to place advisors in senior jobs inappropriate to their experience and competence. In the fall of 2010, General James Jones, a former commandant of the Marine Corps and NATO commander, announced his intention to resign in October as Obama's national security advisor. Tom Donilon, who was Obama's immediate choice as successor to Jones, was an unknown Democratic Party operative and former lobbyist who had never served in the Armed Forces or had any other significant experience in national security strategies. His real experience was in politics and he had an established reputation as a political junkie.[10] His only serious work in government had been as a sidekick and an advisor on press relations and other matters to Warren Christopher, President Clinton's secretary of state and Donilon's former law partner. Donilon had been known then as "a street fighter, constantly on the prowl for ways to show his boss to advantage—sometimes by implication derogating his boss's competitors, and even [President Clinton]."[11] He was now perceived to be Obama's toady as he had been Christopher's.

Donilon's main claim to fame was his service to Fannie Mae, the federally chartered mortgage giant, as executive vice president for law and policy during the financial crisis and what the *Wall Street Journal* called "the company's accounting scandals."[12] According to the *Los Angeles Times*, Donilon had earned "millions in salary, bonuses and stock" between 1999 and 2005, and "got out as Fannie Mae was faltering."[13] In 2008, the company was taken over by the federal government.[14] Donilon's connection with Fannie Mae was described as so toxic that he might have had serious problems if the law had required Senate confirmation of a new national security advisor.[15]

Informed observers knew that Donilon was "no one's idea of a serious strategic thinker"[16]—hardly a good qualification for someone who is responsible for the formulation of strategies to deal with the complex post-9/11 world. He was also thought to be "hugely skeptical of the entire uniformed chain of command."[17] Even his friends conceded that the appointee knew little about national security. Within months, one of Obama's inner circle expressed concern that Donilon was too focused on "message management"—that is, public relations—rather than on substance. A longtime friend agreed and was quoted as saying that Donilon's interest was more on how it plays than on what to do. "Tom is not a strategist," he said. "He's a pol. That's the heart of what he is and does."[18] He would later be euphemistically described as a "process guy" and a "political guy."[19]

This was too much for even prominent Democrats. Zbigniew Brzezinski, who served as Jimmy Carter's national security advisor, had already declared that he did not believe that the "central role of the national security advisor is to make the trains run on time. It's much more a matter of deciding what the schedule ought to be, and where the trains should be heading. The advisor's job," he continued, "is to 'flesh out' ideas into a strategy."[20] Despite his obvious lack of qualifications for the position of national security advisor, Donilon had one important quality: the president felt "comfortable with him." That was the sole reason given when an inquiry was made for an explanation of the appointment.[21]

An early consequence of the appointment of Donilon was particularly surprising since, to a large extent, it involved his presumed area of expertise—public relations. After Navy Seals conducted a model operation in Pakistan on May 1, 2011, that resulted in the death of Osama bin Laden, White House officials devalued the success by creating unnecessary controversy over the next several days regarding the details of the raid. The shifting versions by White House aides of what actually happened caused one observer to write, "The White House converted a picture-perfect military operation into a public-relations disaster."[22]

What were the implications of the firing of General McChrystal and the appointment of an unqualified national security advisor? One implication, certainly, was that Obama wanted predictable national security advice with which he was certain to agree rather than objective and informed advice with which he was likely to disagree. Another implication, one journalist opined, was future conflicts between the political objectives in the Obama White House, and military leaders. "We may," he said, "be headed for one of the greatest showdowns in decades."[23]

By April 2011, Obama's leadership in national security matters was under strong attack. His foreign policy was being described as one of "hesitation, delay and indecision."[24] One of his own aides described his actions in Libya as "leading from behind."[25] Even Brzezinski, formerly a strong supporter of the president, had apparently become disillusioned, saying of Obama, "He doesn't strategize. He sermonizes."[26] It was thus with considerable attention that the nation awaited the announcement of the other members of Obama's new national security team. Disappointment soon followed.

To replace Bob Gates as secretary of defense, Obama selected CIA Director Leon Panetta. This appointment was predictably met with unquestioning acceptance by the incestuous political class in the nation's capital. In fact, it was another example of a failure to match an appointee with a position for which he is qualified. Panetta was the oldest man ever nominated to be secretary of defense. He had been a Washington fixture since the 1960s. But, it was pointed out, he had "more experience in walnut farming than in military matters."[27] He had been at the CIA—a job for which he had had no credentials whatsoever prior to his appointment—for only two years.

While one journalist defended the appointment by asserting that what the Defense Department needed was the skills and "charms of a politician,"[28] others were quick to point out that Panetta had no experience in leading a large, complex organization. People familiar with the government were quick to note that the number of workers in the Pentagon building alone is almost equal to the total number of CIA officers and analysts, and that the secretary of defense must "oversee 2.2 million uniformed active and Reserve troops and a complex, multibillion-dollar acquisition system."[29] Panetta had never served on either the Armed Services Committee or the Foreign Relations Committee during his years in Congress. Only the day before Panetta's confirmation hearing, Obama's deputy secretary of defense had declared that the wars of the future will be longer, deadlier, and waged against a more diverse variety of enemies than ever before.[30] At a time when major decisions would soon have to be made about the wars in Iraq and Afghanistan, the U.S. involvement in Libya, and smoldering problems relating to the attempts by Iran and North Korea to produce nuclear weapons, Panetta had no experience in formulating defense strategy.

Even Panetta's service as the director of the Office of Management and Budget during the Clinton administration, the only apparent reason for his nomination other than his personal relationship with political movers and shakers as a Washington insider, was unlikely to be particularly helpful. In order to make drastic cuts in the defense budget in the middle of three armed conflicts, as proposed by Obama, a defense secretary would need to have sufficient familiarity with costly and complex weapons systems and other defense programs, and sufficient experience with military roles, missions, and capabilities, to make hard decisions and trade-offs without doing harm to the nation's security. There was no reason to believe that the nominee could accomplish that critical task.

Indeed, there was reason to believe that he could not. The *Economist* reacted to the nomination with these words: "[It is not] clear just how suited

Mr. Panetta's particular political pedigree is for the immediate job in hand. . . . Although both parties claim to accept in a general way that defense spending must be squeezed, it may be harder for a Democrat numbers-man like Mr. Panetta than it was for the well-liked Mr. Gates to win over touchy service chiefs and suspicious Republican hawks in Congress."[31] A former Democratic leader in Congress wistfully observed that "there's no on-the-job training to become Secretary of the Department of Defense."[32] Nevertheless, in a Senate confirmation hearing controlled by his own party, the nominee was not even made to give specifics or to answer difficult questions. The questions asked were described in the press as "gentle."[33]

In a town where personality and personal relations mean much more than capability, where domestic politics routinely takes precedence in attention and understanding to matters affecting the nation's security, and where the nominee's party controlled the Senate, the outcome of the nomination was never in doubt. On June 22, 2011, the Senate unanimously confirmed Panetta as the new secretary of defense. The director of a Washington think tank spoke for many when he said, "The Pentagon is a much bigger place [than the CIA] and nobody expects him to stick around long enough to figure it out. I think the priority mission for Panetta is to get the president re-elected."[34] Although no one in the Senate noticed, the need for the skills and experience of the other senior political appointees in the Pentagon to be exceptionally high had just reached a critical level.

Even more surprising and disappointing than the appointment of Panetta was the appointment of his successor at the CIA—General David Petraeus, the former commander of U.S. Central Command and now McChrystal's replacement in Afghanistan. It was undisputed that Petraeus was the most experienced and most capable commander of forces in Afghanistan and Iraq in the U.S. Armed Forces. He had deep and wide knowledge of the U.S. security challenges in the Middle East, and was uniquely qualified to serve as the chairman of the Joint Chiefs of Staff, a position that would soon become open because of the retirement of Admiral Mike Mullen. Petraeus would have "no learning curve and could oversee the strategy he helped to devise for Afghanistan."[35] Petraeus told friends that he wanted the chairman position[36] and he had certainly earned the job, having agreed to take a demotion and assume leadership in Afghanistan after McChrystal was fired.

But Petraeus had two disqualifying characteristics. First, like McChrystal, he was not a "yes" man. He also believed it to be his duty to give civilian leaders objective, unvarnished advice based upon hard facts, advice "with the bark off." Second, Petraeus had relentlessly cultivated lawmakers in Washington and was popular with the public. His job performance was widely perceived to be higher than Obama's. In a burst of fantasy, Rahm Emanuel, the highly partisan White House chief of staff, was even reported to see Petraeus as "a potential man on horseback" who might help Republicans win back the White House in 2012.[37] This would not do. Despite his own total lack of experience and competence in national security and foreign policy matters, Obama wanted to maintain personal control over those areas. He did not want to rely on experts who had opinions based upon years of study and personal experience.[38]

Moreover, it was well understood within the White House that Obama did not want to hear disruptive opinions. If he found it necessary to overrule the U.S. commander in Afghanistan, he would prefer that the commander be someone who was relatively unknown. According to one longtime observer of White House politics, Obama's "high self-esteem [which] often slides over the thin line to arrogance, trickles down . . . to much of his staff."[39] As recently as the end of 2010, Obama appeared to be interested in no opinions except those offered by his chief of staff and three other White House aides who had no previous experience in governing.[40] Indeed, "a common complaint about the Obama White House in the first two years [had] been that there were no 'grown ups' around, people who knew more about governing and who would tell Obama that he was wrong."[41] Whenever it was suggested that someone with experience should be brought in, "that person was rejected as 'not one of ours.'"[42] A former senior official in the White House had described Obama's team as one "where we don't have a lot of bad antibodies. . . . When we bring anybody new into this organization we really have to be sure we're not bringing in someone who's going to disrupt the *team*."[43] What the Obama team failed to recognize, of course, is the political truism that in those moments when the military voice overwhelms that of the civilian, military leaders are usually only filling a vacuum of indecisiveness that is created by incompetent, divided, and/or weak political leadership.

In February 2011, and after months of disagreement between political leaders in the administration and military leaders, the administration had announced a new development in the policy for Afghanistan. Efforts to negotiate with the Taliban would be accelerated. The Taliban would no longer have to break with al Qaeda, renounce violence, or embrace the Afghan constitution as preconditions for negotiations. Sensitive to the fact that this idea might be difficult to sell to the American public, particularly in light of the opinion of some military leaders that such negotiations were premature and could jeopardize hard-fought, recent gains on the battlefield,[44] Obama and his White House staff were hardly anxious to hear more hard-nosed advice based on military, political, and economic realities in the country from Petraeus. The general had declared publicly on several occasions that the pace of withdrawal of U.S. troops from Afghanistan would depend upon conditions on the ground—that is, on assessments of the pace at which Afghan troops and police were being prepared to relieve American troops, the strength of the Taliban, and the extent of progress in the economic and political reconstruction of the country. No, someone else would be preferable as the new chairman of the Joint Chiefs, someone other than the general who symbolized American will in Afghanistan, someone who would not strenuously object if Obama changed course and adopted the counterterrorism strategy long advocated by Vice President Biden and Obama's political advisors, someone who would perhaps be less skeptical than Petraeus of political pressure to pursue an early exit strategy. What better way to isolate Petraeus and keep him quiet than to sideline him to the CIA, where he would no longer be offering unwelcome military advice?

There was almost certainly another factor at play in Obama's failure to appoint the most qualified military leader as the next chairman of the Joint Chiefs. He already had a candidate, an officer who was purportedly his favorite general.[45] General James Cartwright was virtually unknown in comparison to the highly popular Petraeus, but he had already demonstrated that he was prepared to offer military advice much more in line with the views of White House political operatives than that offered by field commanders.[46] But problems soon developed. Cartwright had no combat experience. He was serving as vice chairman of the Joint Chiefs of Staff and was intelligent, but he had never commanded troops in either Iraq or Afghanistan, or even served in a war zone.[47] Because more than 90 percent of the approximately six thousand troops killed in those two countries were either soldiers or marines, that lack of combat experience was very conspicuous. It was also reported that Cartwright was viewed with suspicion by many of his general officer colleagues in the Pentagon for not doing enough to inform them of his recommendations before he made them to the White House staff—not a good characteristic of a chairman who would have to build a consensus among the service chiefs on difficult and contentious decisions if Obama's drastic budget plan for the Pentagon was to be realized.[48] Gates denied that this was a factor in his own recommendation to Obama for a replacement for Mullen, but he did not deny that he had recommended someone other than Cartwright.

In late May, Cartwright was informed that he would not be selected as the next chairman. On May 30, Obama announced that General Martin Dempsey, a respected veteran of Iraq, who had only weeks before assumed office as the new army chief of staff, would be the new chairman. Unlike Petraeus, who, despite his vigorous denials, was often mentioned as a potential Republican opponent of Obama in the 2012 presidential election, Dempsey was perceived to be among the least self-aggrandizing of the senior commanders to emerge from the conflicts in Iraq and Afghanistan. Conspicuous among those standing next to the president during the announcement was Tom Donilon. News accounts of the selection process noted that it had exposed lingering tensions and fault lines "between civilian aides in the White House and military leaders."[49]

In June, a clash between civilian and military leaders was once more on the front pages. On this occasion, the issue was the pace of the planned withdrawal of American and coalition troops from Afghanistan. On June 22, President Obama announced his decision on the matter. Yet again he rejected the advice of senior military commanders on an important strategic issue in the middle of a war in which the country had already invested billions of dollars and fifteen hundred American lives. Yet again he failed to provide leadership. Rather, he demonstrated what was called his "propensity to split the difference among his inner circle of national security advisors,"[50] to compromise on national security issues rather than make bold decisions, and to permit political considerations (especially those relating to his reelection bid in 2012) to take precedence over sound military logic. White House aides sought to depict the president's decision as one well within the range of options developed by military leaders, but that view was disputed by one in a position to know.[51]

That a "fierce internal debate" had taken place on the withdrawal issue was well known.[52] It was also widely reported that General Petraeus had recommended that one brigade combat team of about five thousand troops be withdrawn by the end of 2011, that an additional five thousand be withdrawn over the winter months, and that any remaining withdrawals be delayed until the end of 2012. He and battlefield commanders argued that the ten months since the surge in troops (which Obama had approved in 2009, an arbitrary increase of ten thousand fewer troops than had been requested) had reached full strength and the remaining time before the start of the 2012 fighting season did not permit sufficient time to consolidate the recent fragile gains that had been made in Helmand and other provinces.

The military campaign plan for 2012 "envisioned building on security gains earned by troops who had already flowed into Afghanistan's south and southwest, with plans to turn some of those areas over to local forces. This would [free] American troops to pivot toward the porous eastern border with Pakistan,"[53] where major strongholds of the Taliban and the al Qaeda–linked Haqqani network were located. Military commanders also argued that maintaining pressure on the battlefield would be supportive of American diplomatic efforts to negotiate a reconciliation between the government of Afghanistan and the Taliban, efforts that had met with no significant success up to that point.

Secretary Gates, who had recently traveled to Afghanistan, had long warned against risking the success of the surge in troops over the last several months with a speedy withdrawal. He had consistently argued that the number of troops to be withdrawn immediately was much less important than the slope or speed of the overall drawdown. "Frankly, there is too much talk about leaving and not enough talk about getting the job done right," he had declared in March. "Too much discussion of exit and not enough discussion about continuing the fight. Too much concern about when and how many troops might redeploy, and not enough about what needs to be done before they leave."[54] Commanders in the field were also adamant about delaying any further drawdowns until the end of 2012 in order to retain sufficient strength through the summer months, which are the peak fighting season, to carry out the campaign plan.

Obama and his White House advisors, however, were less interested in the Taliban's fighting season than in the U.S. presidential election in November 2012. National Security Advisor Tom Donilon and other senior White House aides argued that all of the surge forces should be withdrawn by the end of 2011. It was even reported that they welcomed a dispute between Obama and his military commanders because it "might help the president rebut a criticism he has faced within his party."[55] It was probably not coincidental that recent polls had indicated a drop in the president's approval rating to 46 percent and that 40 percent of the most likely voters strongly disapproved of his job performance.[56]

With his public support on the economy at an all-time low, Obama was sensitive to a restive and war-weary public, whatever the national security implications. Declaring publicly, prematurely, and with an optimism unjustified by the facts that the United States had largely achieved its goals in Afghanistan, he announced that ten thousand troops would be withdrawn by December 2011, double what military commanders desired, and that an additional twenty-three thousand troops would leave by the end of the summer of 2012—two months before the election.

The implications of the decision were clear. In order to meet the president's deadline, the twenty-three thousand troops scheduled to leave in 2012 would have to "spend most of the summer on the downsizing effort when they arguably should spend most of the summer fighting and taking away safe havens from extremists."[57] The military campaign would have to be modified significantly. No explanation was given by the president as to why the nation, having already paid so high a price in blood and treasure in Afghanistan over ten years, could not afford to delay the completion of the withdrawal of the twenty-three thousand troops in 2012 for only sixty to ninety days in order to achieve important military objectives. Perhaps the real reason for Obama's decision was too obvious even for any effort by White House political advisors to spin it.

Criticism of the president's decision among informed observers was immediate, primarily because the withdrawal date selected was completely arbitrary, it lacked any semblance of a strategic rationale, and it was unrelated to conditions on the ground in Afghanistan. Two particularly experienced observers said that it was very difficult to fathom the military logic of setting a withdrawal deadline right in the middle of the fighting season. "This is a rushed ending," one said, "to what has been a fairly effective surge."[58] The chairman of the House Intelligence Committee said, "The President is trying to find a political solution with a military component, when it needs to be the other way around."[59]

One person's response to Obama's arbitrary decision was a study in tightrope walking. Admitting that the president had rejected his military recommendations and that the troop withdrawal decision that was made increased the risk that American military objectives in Afghanistan would not be achieved, the nation's senior military commander in Afghanistan informed the Senate Intelligence Committee at his confirmation hearing to be CIA director—the day after the withdrawal decision was announced—that "the commander in chief has decided, and it is then the responsibility . . . of those in uniform to salute smartly and to do everything humanly possible to execute it."[60] When he was asked by a member of the committee whether it would now be more difficult for his successor as military commander to accomplish the American mission in Afghanistan, "a clearly uncomfortable [General David] Petraeus answered that he could not provide 'a direct answer.'"[61] If Petraeus suspected that he had not been appointed chairman of the Joint Chiefs for political reasons unrelated to the nation's national security interests, evidence for the suspicion would soon emerge. At the August 31 ceremony marking his retirement from the Armed Forces, the outgoing chairman showered Petraeus with superlatives, at one point declaring that Petraeus stood "among the giants not just in our time but of all time, joining the likes of Grant and Pershing and Marshall and Eisenhower."[62] Neither the president nor the vice president, or even the new secretary of defense, attended the ceremony.

It is the common belief in Washington, D.C., that presidents are entitled to surround themselves with advisors with whom they feel "comfortable." President Obama is only the most recent proponent of that view. "Once they got to the White House," a respected author and commentator has written, "Obama and his campaign team (virtually all of his top assistants) seemed to live in a hermetically sealed box—cut off from and not interested in . . . what experienced people who tried to help them had to say."[63] Whatever merit the idea may have elsewhere, it has none inside the arena in which national security strategies and policies are fought, developed, and implemented. No president is "entitled" to receive only that advice that is consistent with his known policy preferences. To paraphrase Justice Holmes, the best policies are made where there is a "free trade in ideas." That is, the best test of a proposed policy, as well as of truth, is the power of the policy or the thought "to get itself accepted in the competition of the market,"[64] for it is only there that 2 plus 2 will most likely equal 4.

Good leaders are not threatened by unwelcome advice from informed subordinates. Indeed, Churchill was fond of saying that it was the role of a political leader to organize "creative tension" for the purpose of obtaining the best results.[65] He exercised command by encouraging free debate between colleagues who shared full access to the widest sources of information. By the time he became prime minister in World War II, Churchill had already served as minister for all three military services (including service as First Lord of the Admiralty in two world wars), had been a member of Lloyd George's and Neville Chamberlain's war cabinets, and had fought as a soldier in the Sudan, on the North-West Frontier, in South Africa, and on the Western Front. Despite his substantial military experience, however, he did not hesitate to pick military commanders and civilian subordinates "who disagreed with him—and did so violently."[66]

When he was serving as Churchill's minister of defense in 1952, former field marshal Harold Alexander declared that Churchill "hated yes men—he had no use for them." General "Pug" Ismay, who served as Churchill's chief military assistant during the Second World War, recalled that "the one thing that was necessary, and indeed that Winston preferred, was someone to stand up to him."[67] Lord Halifax, who served as Churchill's minister for foreign affairs and later as the British ambassador to Washington, responded to a question from a colleague about how to handle Churchill in this way: "Always stand up to him. He hates doormats. If you begin to give way he will simply wipe his feet upon you."[68]

Churchill understood that people of strong character ("live wires") often possessed "an independence of judgment and action that was the one thing most needful in time of war."[69] A respected student of Churchill has written that he exercised "one of his most important functions as war leader by holding the calculations and assertions of his subordinates up to the standards of massive common sense, informed by wide reading and experience at war. When his military advisors could not come up with plausible answers to [his] harassing and inconvenient questions, they usually revised their views; when they could, Churchill revised his. In both cases, British strategy benefited."[70] It is significant, however, that "not once during the whole war did [Churchill] overrule his military advisers on a purely military question."[71]

It is safe to assume that future American presidents are very unlikely to have either Churchill's military experience or his willingness to pick senior advisors who are prepared to violently disagree with the president's view on any given national security matter. Even if the appointee-advisors are prepared to argue with the president, they may be unwilling to accept the limitations of their own competence and experience. It has been said, "Economists suffer from what one of them calls 'the pretense-of-knowledge syndrome.' They act as if they understand more than they do and presume that their policies, whether of the left or right, have benefits more predictable than they actually are."[72] Advisors and officials who are responsible for national security are not immune to this lethal weakness. The risk to the nation is obvious. If the president and the political appointees who serve as his key national security advisors think they have all of the answers but are mistaken, and act upon their mistakes, they will be, in the words of former British prime minister Margaret Thatcher, "the most dangerous people to have in charge."[73]

It has been almost four decades since a former senior political appointee and aide to Secretary of Defense Robert McNamara wrote of the tensions between civilian and military leaders. "[M]ilitary men," he said, "are anxious to receive policy guidance from their civilian 'masters,' at the same time they seek to protect their professional autonomy." "The problem is not the overweening military," he added, "but the inadequate civilians, who, lacking the means, cannot even test their determination to exercise effective control."[74]

Twenty years later, a respected scholar on civil-military relations noted that nothing had changed: "Our system of government frequently puts civilians into positions of great responsibility without proper preparation or experience. They stay a few years and move on."[75] He acknowledged the critical need for knowledgeable and experienced civilian leadership. "But," he asked, "where are we to get such leadership when our best colleges and universities so neglect the study of war and the military, and abhor ROTC, and when our political leadership will increasingly lack personal or professional experience in military affairs?"[76]

This question certainly resonated with me. In 1967–1969, I served as an assistant professor of naval science in the Naval ROTC unit at Dartmouth College. Having arrived at Dartmouth after two back-to-back tours of combat duty in the war in Vietnam, I watched with dismay as the majority of faculty members of the historic Ivy League institution worked feverishly to have all ROTC programs removed from the campus as a form of protest against the war. Were they unaware of the admonition of Thucydides: "A nation that makes a great distinction between its scholars and its warriors will have its laws made by cowards and its wars fought by fools"? Apparently so. By the early 1970s, all traces of the army, navy, and air force ROTC programs had been removed.

Thirty-five years later, the lingering impact of the college's antimilitary attitude could be seen in disturbing ways. In 2005, Pulitzer Prize–winning historian David McCullough, a Presidential Medal of Freedom recipient, addressed a leadership conference. He reflected upon his experience a few years earlier when he taught a course at Dartmouth. "I taught a seminar at Dartmouth of seniors majoring in history," he said, "honor students, 25 of them. The first morning we sat down and I said, 'How many of you know who George Marshall was?' Not one."[77] Not one of twenty-five honor students was familiar with the five-star army general whom Winston Churchill hailed as the "true organizer of victory" in World War II, the only army general to be awarded the Nobel Peace Prize, the only person in the nation's history to serve as both secretary of defense and secretary of state!

The relative absence of sound educational opportunities on national security subjects, the contemporary lack of interest in them, the fact that even the nation's own wars receive comparatively little news coverage,[78] and the fact that only about 1 percent of the population volunteers for military service could easily lead anyone to agree with the conclusion of one student of the problem. In a journalistic debate on civil-military relations, Professor Richard H. Kohn was candid. "[T]he reason I did not emphasize the civilian side (and that was purposeful)," he said, "is that I have little confidence, given past practice, that a remedy will be forthcoming. Civilians come and go in Congress and the executive branch; some will be wise, understanding, brave, decisive, and perhaps even disinterested. Many, if history is any guide, will not."[79]

Perhaps he is right. On the basis of our experience to date, he is certainly right. Perhaps the most able Americans will continue to be deterred from serving in the government because of the highly partisan atmosphere in the nation's capital, because of a reluctance to make public their family's financial condition, or for other reasons. Perhaps there is no obvious way to stimulate more young Americans of all ages to volunteer for public service. Perhaps there is no way to convince self-centered academics to create exciting and balanced new courses on national security-related subjects for young Americans. But do those facts close the discussion? I think not. Solutions do exist. It is only a matter of will.

If a president who is unschooled and inexperienced in national security matters proves to be inadequate to the demands of his work and consistently closes his mind to informed but unwelcome advice, little can be done about the matter until the next election. Much can be done, however, to ensure that highly competent, informed advice is at least available and that current policies and programs are being successfully executed and implemented. It only requires two things. First, honest, energetic effort by new administrations is needed to ensure that nominations of people to serve as presidential appointees in positions relating to the nation's security are only given to those who have already demonstrated great competence and performance in the field of policy and activity for which they would be responsible, or at least in a related field; second, there must be much greater effort by the U.S. Senate to look past paper qualifications, to thoroughly examine all presidential nominees, and to refuse to confirm those who do not meet the high standards to which the American people are entitled. Rocket science is not involved—

only hard work, integrity, and the use of road maps that have long been available. A good place to start for the Senate would be the mandatory use by all committees that conduct confirmation hearings of those questions for nominees which were recommended by the Government Accountability Office in August 2000 (see chapter 4) and that relate to leadership and management issues.

One of the best-known and influential consultants on the theory and practice of management argued that business executives spend more time on managing people and making people decisions than on anything else. Despite the fact that "[n]o other decisions are so long lasting in their consequences or so difficult to unmake," he believed that no more than a third of the decisions turn out right.[80] One certain way to ensure that the selection of people for presidential appointments is no more successful, and almost inevitably less so, is for presidents to abdicate their personal responsibility to choose senior officials who are unquestionably qualified to successfully meet the heavy duties that will be expected of them. If a president is not personally committed to the people process and deeply engaged in it, if he doesn't have the courage to discriminate between strong and weak candidates for appointment, and between strong and weak performers who have already been appointed, large failures in policy formulation and execution are inevitable.

America now faces a period of time—perhaps a decade, perhaps a half century—of global disorder. No one can predict with any degree of certainty what the eventual geopolitical fallout from the Arab Spring will be. Despite the Obama administration's rush to withdraw American troops from Afghanistan, the actual conditions on the ground may preclude such a precipitous move. China is likely to continue its efforts to rapidly build a navy that can project force and threaten U.S. interests in the Pacific. It will almost certainly continue its aggressive move to stake out new territorial claims in the international waters of the South China Sea. Iran and North Korea will continue to build, and perhaps even attempt to export, nuclear weapons. Syria and Iran will continue their support of the Hezbollah in Lebanon in order to undermine the elected government there. Meanwhile, and notwithstanding the death of Osama bin Laden, the threat of terrorism will go on.

The weak U.S. economy and large cuts in the defense budget as part of a national effort to address the deficit crisis will make defense planning immeasurably more difficult. Smaller defense budgets will mean smaller Armed Forces and fewer military options to protect U.S. security interests and to maintain America's long-standing role and influence in the world. The political polarization of the Congress will continue, at least for some period, thereby placing a premium on the need for very high-quality executive branch officials who can both exercise great wisdom in making tradeoffs between our worldwide commitments and available resources, and persuade Congress to approve the tradeoffs.

In these circumstances, we can no longer afford presidential indifference to important decisions. If a position in one of the departments and agencies responsible for the nation's safety has been deemed by the Congress of the United States to be sufficiently important as to require confirmation by the Senate of a president's nominee for the position, a much greater effort must be made to select the best available person for that position. President-elect Reagan's order to his aides to recommend only "the best people" should obviously be the model of choice.

If a president-elect should desire to instruct his aides in the manner of President George H. W. Bush to "go beyond white males" or to set some other objective in making recommendations of people for senior positions, or if he should feel compelled for other political reasons to consider the recommendation of a political party leader, a campaign supporter, or a member of Congress—that is, if there is a compelling political reason to consider a particular candidate—then, before selecting the candidate as the nominee, the president-elect should at least ensure that the candidate's qualifications for the position in question are equal to those of the best two or three other candidates for the same position. If the candidates from the president-elect's own political party are not the best available, they should be rejected. So long as a nominee can give a president his unqualified support on matters that will be within the nominee's scope of responsibility and he is unquestionably the best qualified of available candidates, it should not even matter that he is registered as a member of an opposing political party. The performance of Bob Gates as secretary of defense for presidents George W. Bush and Barack Obama and that of Secretary of War Henry L. Stimson for presidents William Howard Taft and Franklin D. Roosevelt demonstrate the merit of this principle.

In order to tightly control the quality of their nominees, future presidents should not delegate the selection of people for presidential appointments to individual members of their cabinet. Rather, the selection process should be managed entirely by the White House Office of Presidential Personnel. That office should be headed by a seasoned executive search professional. Cabinet members should be encouraged to suggest the names of individuals for particular positions within their departments, but the people suggested should undergo the same strict level of scrutiny by the White House as all other candidates.

A most useful first step for candidates for the presidency, at least for those who are serious contenders, could and should be taken months before the election. Following the model employed by key supporters of President Reagan, a staff of volunteers should be established under the leadership of an experienced executive search professional. A detailed job description should be prepared or otherwise obtained for every national security-related position to be filled by a presidential appointee. Existing job descriptions should be reviewed closely and updated as necessary to meet current realities and needs.

Upon the basis of recommendations from members of previous administrations and any guidance received from the presidential candidate, key criteria for the future selection of potential nominees for each position should be established. Vague and meaningless descriptions by advocates of particular candidates for appointment, such as "Bob's a great leader," or "Joe gets along with people and he's smart as hell," or "Shirley did a great job in raising money and getting out the vote in Michigan," must be rejected. Similarly, the educational and intellectual qualities of a potential nominee ("Ken is a visionary") must be discounted. There is usually "very little correlation between those who talk a good game and those who get things done come hell or high water."[81] Rather, each position should be defined in terms of its three or four nonnegotiable criteria—things a person *must* be able to do well in order to succeed.[82] For each of the nonnegotiable criteria, it will be necessary to ask a fundamental question about each candidate for appointment: How good is this person at getting things done?

The nature of the work which is likely to be a priority for each position during the next two to four years should be determined and a preliminary list of potential cabinet, subcabinet, and White House appointees developed. If, for example, budgetary problems and the analysis of the comparative value of various weapons or other complex systems or programs will be the focus of attention in the near term, one kind of leader will be required. If, on the other hand, advocacy before Congress of controversial new personnel policies is likely to be the priority, then another kind of nominee should be considered.

Shortly after becoming the army chief of staff during World War II, General George C. Marshall moved quickly to replace general officers who were unfit for the pressures of war by reason of age or other factors. Over the years, Marshall had maintained a virtual "black book" of promising younger officers. He recorded the strengths and weaknesses of each. When selecting officers for particular positions of responsibility during the war, he "always looked first at the nature of the assignment" over the near term. In selecting a division commander, for example, he knew that "to raise a division and train it is one assignment. To lead it in combat is quite another. To take command of a division that has been badly mauled and restore its morale and fighting strength is another still."[83]

Ideally, the work I have described thus far should be performed prior to a presidential election. Immediately after the election, the president-elect should form teams of volunteer advisors who have expertise and long experience in areas that are relevant to the work that will be required of nominees who are confirmed for particular positions. For positions that require decisions on major acquisitions, for example, the relevant volunteer team should include people who are experienced in at least some part of the DoD or DHS acquisition process. Hopefully, the leader and at least some of the members of the teams will have served as active advisors to the president-elect during the campaign and will provide continuity by serving in the Office of White House Personnel in the first years of the new administration.

A number of qualified people should be considered for each presidential appointment, but formal qualifications should be a minimum standard of consideration. As tempting as it is for every new administration to reward its campaign supporters with senior positions, the temptation must be resisted if it skews the selection process in favor of supporters over people who are demonstrably better qualified to serve. A president-elect must serve as president of all of the people, not just those who contributed to his election. The standard described by John F. Kennedy in chapter 3 is a good place to start. He did not want politicians, he said, but rather "people to run a government, serious men."

The most important question to be asked is not "What are the strengths of this candidate?" but rather "Are the strengths of this candidate the right strengths for this particular position?" After other volunteers, perhaps former campaign workers, have weeded out all but the three to six most competitive of the candidates who have applied for a particular DoD or other national security position, the volunteer team of specialists and/or senior executives, which would include people with the same kind of expertise as that required of the eventual nominee, should be asked to evaluate the remaining candidates. Once again, the work of General Marshall is instructive: "If . . . a division needed an officer for a training assignment, Marshall looked for people who could turn recruits into soldiers. Every man that was good at this task usually had serious weaknesses in other areas. One was not particularly effective as a tactical commander and was positively hopeless when it came to strategy. Another had foot-in-mouth disease and got into trouble with the press. A third was vain, arrogant, egotistical, and fought constantly with his commanding officer. Never mind, could he train recruits? If the answer was yes—and especially if the answer was 'he's the best'—he got the job."[84]

One of the most challenging tasks in selecting the right person for the right presidential appointment, is that of discussing the professional performance of a candidate with several people who have actually worked with him. Most candidates for senior political appointments have strong political support from some quarter. Perhaps they have been strongly recommended by someone who played a major role in the president-elect's successful campaign, or by a member of the Senate or House whose support will be critical to the new administration's legislative agenda. The fact is that political credentials are usually of little use in predicting how a person will perform in a particular position in the government. Of much greater value are discussions with the candidate's former supervisors, bosses, or colleagues.

Two or three candidates should be presented to the person likely to be key to a final decision. If, for example, the president-elect should ask the secretary of defense to recommend someone to fill the position of assistant secretary of defense, the best two or three candidates who have already been vetted and approved by the White House Office of Presidential Personnel should be brought to the secretary for consideration. During these interviews, the secretary should seek to determine which of the candidates has the best skills, experience, personality, and even intangible qualities to get things done and accomplish the new administration's priorities for the office to be filled.

An answer to an important question should also be required of each of the final candidates. Are they willing to serve for all four years of the president-elect's term of office or until their resignation is requested? The questions may be unwelcome and even offensive to some potential candidates who are more interested in getting their professional tickets punched and serving only briefly in a prestigious government position before moving on, but it must be asked. Very little of significance can be accomplished in any department or agency in only a couple of years. When a senior official resigns, it may take more time than is desirable to find a fully qualified successor. During the interim, career civil servants are reluctant to make decisions that may be overruled by the new political appointee. It will also take some time for the new appointee to come up to speed on the requirements of the job and to get a handle on the levers of power. If the department or agency is in the middle of an ongoing crisis, the early departure of the first appointee will make matters much worse. A recent example is illustrative.

In June 2011, it was reported that Secretary of the Treasury Timothy Geithner had informed President Obama of his likely resignation within a few weeks. Geithner, who was described as "an architect of the administration's economic strategy,"[85] was the only remaining member of Obama's original economic team. While his twenty-nine months of service were not unusually short by contemporary standards, his professed intent to resign could hardly have come at a worse time for Obama. The nation's economic recovery had slowed, the unemployment rate remained at a record level, seniors were seeing their retirement investments disappear as stock values plummeted, and the U.S. credit rating would soon be downgraded for the first time ever. Geithner and the president were engaged in negotiations with congressional leaders—in a highly charged political environment—as part of an effort to resolve the nation's huge deficit and debt problems. Critical matters had yet to be decided, such as the design of a regulatory scheme to govern financial institutions, the nation's housing policy, and the future of mortgage financiers Fannie Mae and Freddie Mac.[86] Geithner was finally persuaded to remain until the 2012 presidential election, but given that his financial policies had received strong criticism, many were left wondering whether the request for him to remain was really a function of the president's inability to attract a high-quality replacement for what could be a very unpleasant term of only one year.

Even if the selection process used by a new administration for the selection of presidential appointees is good, great need will remain for a system of orientation and training—that is, a system of transition into government service that will give the appointees the tools that are necessary to successfully master their new jobs. No one is born a successful Defense Department, State Department, or Department of Homeland Security official any more than one is born a concert violinist. Talent and substantial relevant experience are, of course, essential. But they are seldom sufficient. Even the most talented appointee is an amateur when he commences his first government service. In the context of Ralph Waldo Emerson's observation ("Every artist was first an amateur"), most capable new appointees hope to make significant contributions during their public service. A few may achieve artistry. But before they can perform in tuxedo or gown in Carnegie Hall, they must first study music theory and composition and immerse themselves in a variety of musical genres.

New presidential appointees in the departments and agencies responsible for the nation's security have particular needs. It is obviously important that they have a uniform understanding of and familiarity with the president-elect's national security priorities, the new secretary's policy and process guidance, the governing law, the missions, the budgeting and programming system, available resources, the organization and organizational culture, personnel and administrative processes, and so on of their department or agency. In addition, they need to have a sound grasp of particular policies relating to their new area of responsibility, the general demands of their new position, and the most serious problems or challenges they are likely to face upon entering office. Finally, they are likely to need information and even instruction on a range of other subjects, such as how to present testimony to Congress and how to manage the media.

A study conducted in 2001 concluded that the White House is unlikely to play a significant role in the orientation and training of political appointees. "By necessity," the author of the study noted, new presidents must spend their limited time, energy, and political capital pushing legislation and *selecting* their appointees, not orienting their appointees.[87] Moreover, by the time an administration realizes that political appointee orientation is desirable, it is usually too late. Some administrations have, of course, used orientation programs of one form or another. The Reagan administration, for example, engaged in an effective use of orientation programs to make appointees aware of ethics rules and to promote unity among its appointees in all departments and agencies. But White House programs make little or no effort to prepare appointees for the demands of their individual jobs.

I submit, therefore, that the primary tool that should be given to all new political appointees in departments and agencies responsible for our security is a structured, mandatory—yes, I said *mandatory*—program of professional education and training. Even newly elected members of Congress undergo an official six-day crash orientation course. In the House of Representatives, new members receive basic and practical nuts-and-bolts information on such subjects as how to set up their office, congressional ethics, parliamentary procedure and floor operations, how Congress works, and so forth. Since there are 435 members of the House, no individual new member will incur major responsibilities in the short term other than responding to constituent needs. In contrast, most presidential appointees in the executive branch do not have the luxury of on-the-job training. Policy and program decisions usually do not await the convenience of the new official.

Currently, new presidential appointees receive from their respective departments, agencies, and offices whatever introductory briefings those departments, agencies, and offices believe to be appropriate. The result is that a new assistant secretary of the air force may be able to get a handle on the most immediate issues facing the air force, but he or she is likely to have little understanding of the way the same issues are seen from the office of the secretary of defense, much less any understanding of the main issues confronting the other military services and how the resolution of those issues may affect his or her own work.

A brief period of common professional education for each new appointee could thus pay large dividends. It would permit them to assume office with fundamentals in hand. It would permit them an opportunity to make a strong first impression upon their new colleagues and certain senior career civil servants upon whom they will depend for support. It would increase the likelihood that the one hundred or so presidential appointees within the Department of Defense would be able to operate, even if somewhat loosely, as a *team*. These are not inconsequential factors in any workplace, especially in the Pentagon.

Such an education and acculturation process would also benefit senior appointees who assume office in the middle of an administration. Instead of receiving briefings only within the Department of the Navy, a designated new assistant secretary of the navy would have exposure to the challenges facing the army and air force as well. New appointees within the departments of the army and air force would begin to understand the unique challenges of the navy. When they assumed office, it would be much more likely that they would be able to contribute to policy decisions that are sound for the Armed Forces as a whole, rather than serving merely as special interest pleaders for their respective services.

The idea expressed here is not new. In November 2002, more than two hundred former presidential appointees—Democrats and Republicans—including sixteen former cabinet members, signed what was characterized as an "open letter" to President Bush and the 108th Congress, requesting immediate bipartisan action to solve the problems with the current presidential appointments process. Among the specific improvements requested was one that would provide "all nominees with both a formal orientation to the Federal Government and an additional orientation to their respective agency or department."[88] There may be better locations at which such a formal orientation program could be conducted, but one obvious place is the National Defense University at Fort McNair in Washington, D.C., the nation's premier joint professional military educational institution. Its proximity to federal officials from all relevant departments and agencies has obvious advantages.

Despite the obvious benefits of providing all new presidential appointees with sufficient tools to at least begin their new jobs, it can be expected that there will be opposition to the idea. There is always some pressing matter which deserves attention. New cabinet members always want their senior lieutenants to be onboard as soon as possible. In order to have any hope of success two things are essential. First, presidents-elect must have a personnel selection process in place *prior to* the election that will identify tentative nominees, especially the most critical ones, sufficiently early to permit all FBI and other background investigations to be completed as soon as possible, preferably no later than inauguration day.

The second essential is for the formal orientation program to be made *mandatory* by the U.S. Senate. At each confirmation hearing before the appropriate committee of the Senate, an additional "final question" should be asked of each nominee. At my own confirmation hearing, I well remember being asked, "Mr. Duncan, do you promise to appear for testimony before all committees of Congress which request your testimony?" I had no idea that my answer would eventually result in my testimony in significant hearings on more than fifty occasions, but I had no doubt of the likely vote on my nomination if I answered in the negative. One additional question should now be asked: "Mr. Nominee, do you agree to complete the (formal orientation program) at the earliest possible date?"

Soon after a nominee has been confirmed and has been sworn into office, the new political appointee should meet one-on-one with his or her political superior to discuss specific policy, program, and/or operational objectives for the office. These should be committed to writing and form a major part of the standards by which the appointee's performance will be evaluated. Additional standards and metrics should likewise be identified. In the case of cabinet officials, the meetings should be with the president or at least his chief of staff. Subcabinet appointees should normally meet with the department or agency head to whom they will report. Ultimately, hiring and firing authority should be retained by the president acting through the White House Office of Presidential Personnel, of course, but authority to evaluate the performance of senior appointees should be delegated to department and agency heads. Cabinet and subcabinet officials are very busy people, but it is critically important that all presidential appointees below cabinet rank be held to clear standards of performance and evaluated regularly. No matter how busy people are, it is not asking too much for them to be evaluated in some ongoing fashion. A candid dialogue between each appointee and his political superior is essential. Continuous improvement in performance should be required of each appointee.

The dangers of failing to regularly evaluate political appointees were vividly demonstrated in 2011 and 2012. In February 2010, a new undersecretary of defense for personnel and readiness assumed office as the third-ranking Pentagon official. In May 2011, staff members in the undersecretary's office sent a letter to members of Congress that expressed grave concerns about his conduct. On July 11, six senior staff members, including senior civilian executives, other civilian employees, and uniformed officers, filed a complaint with the Department of Defense inspector general accusing the undersecretary of fraud, incompetence, waste and abuse, and creating a command climate marked by fear and mistrust.[89] In October, while an investigation of the charges was being conducted by the IG, the undersecretary abruptly resigned. His departure could hardly have come at a worse time. Budget battles were threatening to eliminate or reshape pay, benefits, retirement, and family programs that had defined military life for decades. The departure of the undersecretary left the entire organization without a permanent leader during two armed conflicts. It was necessary to fill the position at least temporarily with the former undersecretary's deputy, a tax attorney and former university administrator who had no previous experience with the Armed Forces prior to assuming office only five months earlier.[90]

On April 2, 2012, the administrator of the General Services Administration and two other senior GSA executives were fired or asked to resign because of spending abuses. Four civil servants were placed on administrative leave pending further disciplinary action and congressional hearings were scheduled to consider the abuses. An investigation by the agency's inspector general found that a devil-may-care culture among the agency's leadership had resulted in the spending of almost $823,000 for a conference at a resort spa casino in Las Vegas in October 2010. The chairman of the House Transportation and Infrastructure Committee declared that the agency "has lost control."[91] The scandal was a great embarrassment for the president in the middle of a reelection campaign. Similar incidents had, of course, occurred in other administrations, but if the performance of the leadership of the agency had been evaluated regularly, the incident might not have happened at all. At the very least, it would not have taken seventeen months for the abuses to be discovered and the agency's leaders dismissed.

People who have been appointed to positions beyond their competence, who aren't meeting the established goals, should be removed, or at least moved to another position. Such actions should be taken quickly and fairly, but they must be taken. Too much is at stake to do otherwise. Presidents and supervisory appointees must remember the words of the famous British prime minister William Gladstone. "The first requirement for a prime minister," he purportedly remarked, "is to be a good butcher . . . his head must always rule his heart."[92]

The recommendations I have proposed here are not entirely original. Many similar recommendations have been made over the years by the Partnership for Public Service, the National Commission on Public Service, current and former government officials, and others. Even if all of the recommendations were accepted and implemented, we could not be certain that all future political appointees would have the competence for their particular positions that is now necessary. No vetting process can detect all of the idiosyncrasies, personality characteristics, or secret past conduct of individual candidates. The measures I have proposed will not prevent the nomination, confirmation, and retention of all inept nominees, nor will they make a national security professional of any nominee. But perhaps they will, in some measure, however small, especially if they are somehow institutionalized, increase the chances that our future military leaders and other national security professionals are led by political appointees who are highly competent for the specific positions for which they have been nominated; who have agreed to serve, if not for a full presidential term, then at least for the minimum period required to get important things done; and who understand fully the importance of the element of trust with those whom they will lead.

Conclusion

In the eighty years since Churchill wrote the essay mentioned in the introduction to this book, Americans have lived through a world war; the Cold War; and hot wars in Korea, Vietnam, the Persian Gulf, the Balkans, Iraq, and Afghanistan. We have watched the continued march of science in a world in which we must be concerned now not only with rogue nations that have the capability to attack our homeland with nuclear-tipped intercontinental ballistic missiles, but also with the real possibility of an attack by a single deranged human being carrying a weapon of mass destruction. Writing about the July 2011 incident in Norway in which a single individual triggered a bomb blast outside a government building and then went on a shooting rampage at a youth camp, one observer reminded us of how much the world has changed just since 9/11: "[T]he next time," he said, "the weapons of choice may not be a bomb and a semiautomatic rifle, as in the case of the Oslo attacker who killed 76 people. Lunatics and sane plotters alike may have access to chemical and biological weapons that could kill thousands."[1]

In some ways, our defenses against threats to our security have also improved, though not at the pace of scientific discoveries. No military force in the history of the world has been as effective as the American Armed Forces in the application of force and violence in support of national policy. American technological advances in weapons and related systems are not matched by any nation. The professionalism of American military leaders today is substantially greater than that of those who were our military leaders at the time of Churchill's article. And yet, in many ways, we are less secure than we were then.

The year before the tragic events of September 11, 2001, three military sociologists argued that the "postmodern military" is characterized by five major organizational changes. The two changes that are relevant here include "the change in the military purpose from fighting wars to missions that would not be considered military in the traditional sense" and "the increasing interpenetrability of civilian and military spheres both structurally and culturally."[2] The blurring of the lines—that is, the "permeability between military and civilian structures"—was characterized as "a major new historical phenomenon."[3] It remains to be seen how much of a blurring of cultural lines will take place, but at least two developments are likely to keep the Armed Forces linked with society. The first is the greatly increased reliance in recent years upon the part-time "citizen warriors" of the National Guard and other reserve components. The second is the continuing expansion of modern communications that "make the day-to-day connections of military personnel with people and institutions elsewhere easy."[4]

Since the events of 9/11, the question of the appropriate use of the Armed Forces has become much less clear. In a Memorial Day article written ten years, two wars, and almost six thousand U.S. combat fatalities later, the benefit of hindsight led one military veteran to speak for many when he categorically rejected the idea of routinely using military forces for nonmilitary missions. "Our military isn't an all-purpose Band Aid," he said, "it's an instrument for radical surgery. Too often, our political leaders send in the troops because they're out of other ideas. Military leaders receive vague, impractical, or downright senseless missions. And the chain of command, from the Oval Office on down, tinkers with tactics in the absence of a strategy."[5]

Debate about the proper use of the Armed Forces is, of course, likely to be endless. Certainly, there will be no shortage of opportunities. A president may be elected at a moment in history when there appear to be no threats to our security and the nation is focused on economic and domestic issues, but threats are likely to arise, however unexpectedly. During the 1990s alone, and before the age of terrorism initiated by the attacks of 9/11 began, there were fifty-seven major armed conflicts in the world in forty-five locations.[6]

It is not necessary to enter the academic debate on civilian-military relations to understand and accept that the nation benefits when civilian and military leaders engage in some form of give and take on strategic and operational decisions in wartime, and on some policy decisions even in peacetime. Most leaders, both civilian and military, would also agree with one scholar's characterization of the lessons American leaders have learned over the last century—namely, that "political leaders must immerse themselves in the conduct of their wars no less than in their great projects of domestic legislation; that they must master their military briefs as thoroughly as they do their civilian ones; that they must demand and expect from their military subordinates a candor as bruising as it is necessary; that both groups must expect a *running* conversation in which, although civilian opinion will not usually dictate, it must dominate; and that that conversation will cover not only ends and policies, but ways and means."[7]

When, however, the political appointees who must decide (or at least recommend) what risks the nation should or should not incur, and who must provide the political leadership, management experience, and resources to ensure the success of missions assigned to the Armed Forces, are not competent for the official positions they occupy, success will always be elusive. If the appointees are motivated by short-term personal or political considerations rather than the long-term security interests of the nation, failure is almost inevitable. If the appointees are limited by their own irresponsibility, the nation will not be prepared for the unpredictable but certain threats of the future.

It matters not if we have sufficient numbers of quality military leaders, sufficient kinds of weapons systems, sufficient quotas of other essential resources, and good policy-making processes if we have failed to obtain and retain the resources of *competence* and *character* in our appointed political leadership. We are reminded, "Surgeons achieve eminence by what they do 'in office'—in operating rooms, performing surgery. Politicians achieve eminence simply by securing office . . . a skill often related loosely, if at all, to their performance in office."[8] In the world in which we now live, high-quality performance in leadership and management by political appointees in departments and agencies responsible for our security is no longer a luxury—it is a critically important necessity. No longer can we be content with incompetent or poorly qualified nominees by our presidents; with casual, unfairly partisan, or even negligent scrutiny of nominees by the Senate; or with appointees who are satisfied with merely securing office. High-quality *performance* in office must be demanded and made a condition of obtaining and retaining office.

This means, of course, that presidents who are inexperienced in the selection of senior executives must rely upon the expertise of those who are, not just upon their political supporters. It means that if a president wants to rely primarily upon political factors in the selection of some candidates for positions in the government, those candidates should only be placed in positions that do not involve the nation's security. It means that capable people will only be nominated for positions in which their skills and experience are well matched with the requirements of the particular national security position to which they have been nominated. It means that the Senate will act with diligence, rigorous objectivity, and dispatch when deciding whether to confirm a nominee. It means that the performance of every appointee will be regularly evaluated and that nonperformers will be terminated. We have learned many hard lessons during the two-and-one-quarter centuries of our democratic experience. One of the most important is that the character, skill, and competence of a single leader at a crucial point can change history.

In the summer of 1787, eighty-one-year-old Benjamin Franklin was by far the oldest of the fifty-five delegates to the Constitutional Convention in Philadelphia. Working from May to September 17, the delegates produced a Constitution that John Adams described in a letter to Rufus King as "if not the greatest exertion of human understanding, the greatest single effort of national deliberation that the world has ever seen."

On the last day of the Convention, and after brief speeches by Franklin and a handful of other delegates, the moment came to sign the new Constitution. The delegates ranged themselves in accordance with the geography of the states, starting with New Hampshire and working southward. With the last signature, the Convention dissolved itself by an adjournment *sine die* and the injunction of secrecy that had long governed the proceedings was removed.

There is a story, which has become legend, that, upon exiting the Pennsylvania State House, now Independence Hall, Dr. Franklin was approached by a woman who asked what sort of government the delegates had created. With no hesitation, Franklin responded, "A republic, if you can keep it." Scholars have long reminded us of the meaning of his response—that is, that our republic was not founded only upon the consent of the delegates or the states that subsequently ratified the Constitution. It also depends upon continuous, active, and informed involvement by all of us, not just our elected or appointed political leaders. If we are to "keep it," we must exercise the same diligence in evaluating the performance of our presidents and members of the Senate that we expect them to exercise in nominating and confirming the political officials who will hold many of the reins of power in their hands. Only then will our great nation be led by our most able men and women.

Notes

INTRODUCTION

1. Winston Churchill, "Fifty Years Hence" (originally published in *Strand*, London, December 1931), in *Thoughts and Adventures* (New York: W.W. Norton, 1991), 201.

2. Ibid., 202.

3. Jon Cohen, Dan Balz, "Confidence in Government Is Crushed after Debt Crisis," *Washington Post*, August 11, 2011, A1.

4. Charles S. Clark, "Low Morale at DHS Linked to Heavy Turnover, Weak Training," *GovExec.com*, March 22, 2012.

5. Carlo D'Este, *Warlord: A Life of Winston Churchill at War, 1874–1945* (New York: HarperCollins, 2008), 390.

6. Michael Useem, "Four Lessons in Adaptive Leadership," *Harvard Business Review*, November 2010, 18.

7. D'Este, *Warlord*, 379.

8. Defense Science Board 2003 Summer Study, *DoD Roles and Missions in Homeland Security*, Vol. II, Part B: *Supporting Reports*, September 2004, 4.

9. Ibid.

10. "Presidents and Their Generals: A Conversation with Eliot Cohen," *American Interest* 6, no. 1 (September/October 2010), 7.

11. See, e.g., Richard H. Kohn, "An Exchange on Civil-Military Relations," *National Interest* 36 (Summer 1994), 30.

12. Frank Ninkovich, introduction to *The Influence of Sea Power upon History* by Alfred Thayer Mahan (Norwalk: Easton Press, 1989), xxxiv.

13. Bruce S. Allardice, *Confederate Colonels* (Columbia: University of Missouri Press, 2008), 1.

1. THE POWER TO APPOINT CIVILIAN LEADERS

1. James Schlesinger, "The Office of Secretary of Defense," in *Reorganizing America's Defense: Leadership in War and Peace*, ed. Robert J. Art, Vincent Davis, and Samuel P. Huntington (Washington, DC: Pergamon-Brassey's, 1985), 262.

2. Colin Powell with Joseph E. Persico, *My American Journey* (New York: Random House, 1995), 578; Charles A. Stevenson, *SECDEF* (Washington, DC: Potomac Books, 2006), 96.

3. Powell, *My American Journey*, 578.

4. Fred Barnes, "You're Fired," *New Republic*, January 10 and 17, 1994, 13.

5. Eric Schmitt, "Aspin Resigns from Cabinet; President Lost Confidence in Defense Chief, Aides Say," *New York Times*, December 16, 1993.

6. Stevenson, *SECDEF*, 96.

7. Powell, *My American Journey*, 578.

8. Ibid., 586.

9. David Halberstam, *War in a Time of Peace: Bush, Clinton, and the Generals* (New York: Scribner, 2001), 191.

10. "Aspin Came Under Fire from Brass," *Los Angeles Times*, December 16, 1993.

11. Exec. Order 12, 148, 44 Fed. Reg. 43239, 3 C.F.R. at 412 (1979 Comp.).

12. Daniel Franklin, "The FEMA Phoenix," *Washington Monthly*, July/August 1995.

13. Daren Fouda and Rita Healy, "How Reliable Is Brown's Resume?" *Time.com*, September 8, 2005.

14. In asking the president to withdraw his nomination, Kerik, a former New York City police commissioner, explained that he had employed an illegal immigrant as a nanny. Reportedly, several other matters soon surfaced that would have made his confirmation difficult. On November 8, 2007, he was the subject of a 370-count criminal indictment. On November 5, 2009, he was convicted on several charges, including tax fraud and seven other felonies. He was sentenced to four years in prison on February 18, 2010.

15. Ann Gerhart, "Tom Ridge, on High Alert," *Washington Post*, November 12, 2001, C1.

16. Elizabeth Becker and Elaine Sciolino, "A New Federal Office Opens," *New York Times*, October 9, 2001.

17. *House Report 109-377 A Failure of Initiative: The Final Report of the Select Bipartisan Committee to Investigate the Preparation for and Response to Hurricane Katrina*, February 15, 2006, 155.

18. Ibid., 153.

19. Ibid., 133.

20. Ibid., 135.

21. Ibid., 137.

22. Ibid., 131.

23. Ibid., 158.

24. Ibid., 320.

25. Ibid., 311.

26. Ibid., xi.

27. Washington's secretary of war, Henry Knox, was an incompetent administrator. After certain questionable activities designed to resolve his personal debts led to lawsuits, he purportedly "turned to recommending friends for public office who in turn 'helped' with his legal difficulties." See Stuart C. Gilman, "Contemporary Institutional Arrangements for Managing Political Appointments and the Historical Processes of Depoliticization: The Experience of the United States at the Federal Level and in Some States" (paper prepared for the World Bank for presentation at the International Anticorruption Conference, Seoul, South Korea, May 2003).

28. Encyclopedia Britannica, eb.com, "Facts about William L. Marcy."

29. Allan Nevins, *The War for the Union: The Improvised War, 1861–1862* (New York: Scribner, 1960), 34.

30. Rufus Rockwell Wilson, ed., "Intimate Memories of Lincoln," *Century Magazine*, November 1890, 33–34.

31. Charles M. Segal, ed., "Conversations with Lincoln," *New York Tribune*, November 20, 1860, 42.

32. Harry J. Carman and Reinhard H. Luthin, *Lincoln and the Patronage* (New York: Columbia University Press, 1943).

33. Carl Sandburg, *Abraham Lincoln: The War Years*, Vol. 4 (New York: Harcourt, Brace & World, 1939), 105.

34. Thomas B. Buell, *The Warrior Generals: Combat Leadership in the Civil War* (New York: Three Rivers Press, 1997), 31.

35. James M. McPherson, *Tried by War: Abraham Lincoln as Commander in Chief* (New York: Penguin Press, 2008), 43.

36. James M. McPherson, *Battle Cry of Freedom: The Civil War Era* (New York: Ballantine Books, 1988), 328.

37. See, for example, David Work, *Lincoln's Political Generals* (Urbana: University of Illinois Press, 2009), 3–5, 234.

38. McPherson, *Tried by War*, 42–43.

39. Ibid.

40. McPherson, *Battle Cry of Freedom*, 328.

41. William S. McFeely, *Grant* (New York: W.W. Norton, 1982), 385.

42. In 1875, a group of whiskey distillers operating mainly in St. Louis, Chicago, Milwaukee, New Orleans, and Cincinnati, retained funds that should have been paid in taxes by bribing Internal Revenue officials in Washington, D.C. After an investigation by the U.S. Treasury Department, 238 criminal indictments were returned and 110 convictions obtained. President Grant was not involved, but his reputation was tarnished by the scandal. His private secretary, Brigadier General Orville E. Babcock, was indicted as a co-conspirator, but acquitted on Grant's testimony.

43. See Ari Hoogenboom, "Outlawing the Spoils: A History of the Civil Service Reform Movement, 1865–1883" (PhD thesis, Columbia University, 1958), 372.

44. Theodore Roosevelt, "Six Years of Civil Service Reform," *Scribner's Magazine*, August 1895.

45. Theodore Roosevelt, Letter to Sir George Otto Trevelyan, May 13, 1905.

46. Alexander Hamilton, Federalist No. 76.

47. Ibid.

48. Ibid.

49. Ibid.

50. James Kent, *Commentaries on American Law, Volume I* (New York: Halsted, 1826), 269.

51. Ron Chernow, *Washington: A Life* (New York: Penguin Press, 2010), 591.

52. David E. Lewis, "Patronage, Policy and Politics in Presidential Appointments," Woodrow Wilson School, Princeton University (paper prepared for presentation at the 2007 annual meeting of the Midwest Political Science Association, Chicago, Illinois), 38.

53. Paul C. Light, "Creating High Performance Government: A Once-in-a-Generation Opportunity," *The Campaign for High Performance Government*, New York University, June 21, 2011, 3.

54. Paul Light and Russ Feingold, "Slimming Our Federal Leadership," *Washingtonpost.com*, April 15, 2010.

55. Karen Rutzick, "Fight to the Finish," *GovExec.com*, May 15, 2007.

56. Fareed Zakaria, "The Lonely Conservative," *Washington Post*, August 16, 2010, A13.

57. Light, "Creating High Performance Government," 12.

58. Data provided by the Aspen Institute Commission to Reform the Federal Appointments Process, www.crfap.org.

59. Donald Rumsfeld, *Known and Unknown* (New York: Sentinel, 2011), 292–93.

60. Partnership for Public Service, "Ready to Govern: Improving the Presidential Transition," January 13, 2010, iii.

61. Anne Joseph O'Connell (Center for American Progress), "Waiting for Leadership," Executive Summary, April 21, 2010; Partnership for Public Service Statement on President Obama Signing the Pre-Election Presidential Transition Act, October 16, 2010.

62. Ibid.

63. Bill Frist, Charles S. Robb, Thomas F. "Mack" McLarty, and Clay Johnson, "Our Vacant Government," *Washington Post*, April 13, 2011, A15.

64. Partnership for Public Service, "Ready to Govern."

65. Ibid.

66. Ibid.

67. Albert Bushnell Hart and Herbert Ronald Ferleger, eds., *Theodore Roosevelt Cyclopedia* (New York: Roosevelt Memorial Association, 1941), 21.

68. James MacGregor Burns, *Roosevelt: The Lion and the Fox* (New York: Harcourt, Brace, 1956), 188.

69. Sherman Adams, *First-Hand Report: The Story of the Eisenhower Administration* (New York: Harper & Brothers, 1961), 59.

70. Ibid.

71. Richardson (1920–1999), was one of the most distinguished people ever to serve in the government. A hero of the Watergate scandal, during which time he was serving as attorney general, he was a recipient of the Presidential Medal of Freedom, the nation's highest civilian award. A Prize for Excellence in Public Service is awarded in his name by the National Academy of Public Administration. I was honored that he personally moved my admission to the bar of the Supreme Court of the United States.

72. Congressional Record—Senate, January 19, 1999, S555–S556.

73. Jonathan Alter, *The Promise: President Obama, Year One* (New York: Simon & Schuster, 2010).

74. Cheryl Y. Marcum, Lauren R. Sager Weinstein, Susan D. Hosek, and Harry J. Thie, *Department of Defense Political Appointments* (Santa Monica, CA: RAND), 2001, xv.

75. Ibid., 6.

76. Stuart C. Gilman, "Contemporary Institutional Arrangements for Managing Political Appointments and the Historical Processes of Depoliticization: The Experience of the United States at the Federal Level and in Some States" (paper prepared for the World Bank, May 2003).

77. Frist et al., "Our Vacant Government."

78. Alter, *The Promise*, 54.

79. Partnership for Public Service, "Ready to Govern," 18.

80. In 2005, Gordon England was nominated to be the deputy secretary of defense. He soon ran into a twenty-five-year-old rule of the Senate Armed Services Committee, which conducted his confirmation hearing. The rule required senior Pentagon officials with pensions from private companies to purchase an insurance policy, or surety, that locked the value of their benefits. The purpose of the rule was to ensure that senior DoD leaders did not make decisions on multibillion defense contracts that favorably affected their personal financial condition. The only company that insured pensions had recently stopped doing so. The obstacle was removed when another company was persuaded to provide the insurance.

81. "A Tyrannous Minority," *Economist*, January 10, 1998, 20–21.

2. THE PROFESSIONALISM OF MILITARY LEADERS PRIOR TO 1972

1. Victor Hugo's *Les Miserables* (1862) put the matter this way: "Nothing will mix and amalgamate more easily than an old priest and an old soldier. In reality, they are the same kind of man. One has devoted himself to his country upon earth, the other to his country in heaven; there is no other difference."

2. Richard Goldhurst, *Pipe Clay and Drill: John J. Pershing, the Classic American Soldier* (New York: Readers Digest Press, 1977), 3.

3. Department of Defense, *The Armed Forces Officer* (Washington, DC: U.S. Department of Defense, January 2006), 12.

4. Ibid.

5. Ibid., 17.

6. David Chandler, *Sandhurst, the Royal Military Academy: 250 Years* (London: Harmony House, 1991), 19.

7. When Washington assumed command of the Regiment in 1755, it consisted of sixteen companies of approximately 1,200 men. He had to handle almost everything himself, from

supervising the construction of barracks, overseeing training, appointing officers, resolving rank disputes, and designing uniforms to planning for actual conflicts. Edward G. Lengel, *General George Washington: A Military Life* (New York: Random House, 2005), 63–64.

8. Emily L. Schulz and Laura B. Simo, *George Washington and His Generals* (Mount Vernon, VA: Mount Vernon Ladies Association of the Union, 2009), 171–80.

9. Lengel, *General George Washington*, 164.

10. Martin van Creveld, *The Training of Officers* (New York: The Free Press, 1990), 14.

11. Theodore J. Crackel, *The Illustrated History of West Point* (New York: Harry N. Abrams, 1991), 65.

12. William P. Leerman, "The School of the Ship," *Shipmate*, September–October 2010, 10–11.

13. Jack Sweetman, *The U.S. Naval Academy: An Illustrated History* (Annapolis, MD: Naval Institute Press, 1979), 10.

14. Allan R. Millett and Peter Maslowski, *For the Common Defense: A Military History of the United States of America* (New York: The Free Press, 1984, 1994), 135.

15. While it was not abolished, it was much different. The army in subsequent decades consisted mainly of volunteers and/or militia units that were under the command of regular officers.

16. William B. Skelton, *An American Profession of Arms: The Army Officer Corps, 1784–1861* (Lawrence: University Press of Kansas, 1992), 34.

17. Samuel P. Huntington, *The Soldier and the State: The Theory and Politics of Civil-Military Relations* (Cambridge, MA: The Belknap Press of Harvard University Press, 1985), 193.

18. Ibid., 195.

19. He apparently digested a tome known as *Practical Considerations on the Errors Committed by Generals and Field-Officers, Commanding Armies and Detachments from the Year 1748 to the Present Time*, by William Armstrong, Esq., a former adjutant-general in Britain's army.

20. His point of departure for research included manuals that he had used himself, the French *Legislation Militaire* and Britain's *General Regulations*.

21. John S. D. Eisenhower, *Agent of Destiny: The Life and Times of General Winfield Scott* (New York: The Free Press, 1997), xiii.

22. Matthew Moten, "Who Is a Member of the Military Profession?" *Joint Forces Quarterly*, Issue No. 62, 3rd Quarter 2011, 16.

23. General Sir John Hackett, *The Profession of Arms* (New York: Macmillan, 1983), 99.

24. Huntington, *The Soldier and the State*.

25. Ibid., 7–8.

26. Ibid., 8–9.

27. Williamson Murray, "Thoughts on Military History and the Profession of Arms," in *The Past as Prologue*, ed. Williamson Murray and Richard Hart Sinnreich (Cambridge: Cambridge University Press, 2006), 87.

28. Ibid.

29. Huntington, *The Soldier and the State*, 10, 16–18.

30. Matthew Moten, "Who Is a Member of the Military Profession?" 15.

31. Lieutenant General (USMC Ret.) Paul K. Van Riper, "The Relevance of History to the Military Profession: An American Marine's View," in Murray and Sinnreich, *The Past as Prologue*, 35.

32. "[Wood had] such extraordinary physical strength and endurance that he grew to be recognized as one of the two or three white men who could stand fatigue and hardship as well as an Apache; and such judgment that . . . he was given, though a surgeon, the actual command of more than one expedition against the bands of renegade Indians. . . . [H]e combined, in a very high degree, the qualities of entire manliness with entire uprightness and cleanliness of character." Theodore Roosevelt, *The Rough Riders* (New York: P.F. Collier & Sons, 1899), 7–8.

33. Ibid., 5–40.

34. Byron Farwell, *Mr. Kipling's Army* (New York: W. W. Norton, 1981), 20.

35. The practice of purchasing commissions started in 1683 during the reign of Charles II. It was abolished as part of a series of reforms undertaken by Edward Cardwell, the secretary of state for war, between 1868 and 1874.

36. Farwell, *Mr. Kipling's Army*, 104.

37. Ibid., 72.

38. Ibid., 13.

39. William Manchester, *The Last Lion, Winston Spencer Churchill, Visions of Glory, 1874–1932* (Boston: Little, Brown, 1983), 222.

40. Anthony Clayton, *The British Officer* (Edinburgh Gate, UK: Pearson Education, 2006), 119.

41. Andrew Gordon, "Military Transformation in Long Periods of Peace: The Victorian Royal Navy," in Murray and Sinnreich, *The Past as Prologue*, 151.

42. Ibid.

43. Matthew Moten, *The Army Officers' Professional Ethic: Past, Present, and Future* (Carlisle, PA: Strategic Studies Institute, U.S. Army War College, 2010), 7.

44. Edward M. Coffman, *The Regulars: The American Army 1898–1941* (Cambridge, MA: The Belknap Press, 2004), 142.

45. Ibid., 184.

46. Ibid., 190.

47. Moten, *The Army Officers' Professional Ethic*, 8.

48. John Keegan, *The First World War* (New York: Alfred A. Knopf, 1999), 372.

49. General John J. Pershing, *My Experiences in the World War* (New York: Frederick A. Stokes, 1931), 1:18.

50. Goldhurst, *Pipe Clay and Drill*, 259.

51. Russell F. Weigley, *History of the United States Army* (New York: Macmillan, 1967), 400.

52. Coffman, *The Regulars*, 233.

53. Quoted in C. Joseph Bernardo and Eugene H. Bacon, *American Military Policy: Its Development Since 1775* (Harrisonburg, VA: Stackpole, 1955), 388.

54. Coffman, *The Regulars*, 281.

55. Ibid.

56. Ibid., 280.

57. Secretary of the Navy Donald C. Winter, Address to the Current Strategy Forum, Naval War College, June 13, 2006.

58. Phyllis I. McClellan, *Silent Sentinel on the Potomac* (Bowie, MD: Heritage Books, 1993), 159.

59. Harry S. Truman, *Years of Trial and Hope, 1946–1952* (Garden City, NY: Doubleday, 1956), 46.

60. Ibid.

61. Ibid., 49.

62. The act also established the Central Intelligence Agency and a National Security Council to coordinate foreign and defense policy.

63. Truman, *Years of Trial and Hope*, 47.

64. Robert A. Pollard, *Economic Security and the Origins of the Cold War, 1945–1950* (New York: Columbia University Press, 1985), 20–23.

65. David Halberstam, *The Coldest Winter* (New York: Hyperion, 2007), 3.

66. Lieutenant General Gordon Sullivan, "Doctrine: An Army Update," in *The United States Army: Challenges and Missions for the 1990s*, ed. Robert L. Pfaltzgraff Jr. and Richard H. Shultz Jr. (Lexington, MA: Lexington Books, 1991), 77.

67. Dwight D. Eisenhower, *Mandate for Change, 1953–1956* (Garden City, NY: Doubleday, 1963), 453.

68. Ibid., 452.

69. Ibid., 454.

70. Theodore C. Sorensen, who served as special counsel to the president in the John F. Kennedy administration that followed Eisenhower's asserted that the doctrine "could deter a nuclear attack. It could probably deter a massive conventional attack on a strategic area such as

Europe. But it was not clear that it could deter anything else [since] for at least a decade the most active and constant Communist threat to free world security was not a nuclear attack at the center, but a nonnuclear nibble on the periphery—intimidation against West Berlin, a conventional attack in the Straits of Formosa, an invasion in South Korea, an insurrection in Laos, rebellion in the Congo, infiltration in Latin America and guerillas in Vietnam." Theodore C. Sorensen, *Kennedy* (New York: Harper & Row, 1965), 625.

71. Kennedy's other campaign tactic involving national security was much less successful. He continually attacked his opponent, Vice President Richard Nixon, for being part of an administration that had permitted a "missile gap" to arise between the Soviet Union and the United States. In fact, the United States was not lagging behind the Soviets in the number of deployed ballistic missiles, but was actually significantly ahead. It is not clear whether Kennedy was aware of this fact.

72. McNamara introduced systems analysis to public policy. The tool was a new Planning, Programming and Budgeting System (PPBS). A cyclical process required each military service to produce a master plan, called the Program Objective Memorandum (POM), that allocated projected future budgets in order to change current forces into those required to meet future threats. Explicit measures of need versus cost were established and ultimately a Five Year Defense Plan (FYDP) was established.

73. Harold Brown, who served under McNamara as secretary of the air force, and who subsequently served as secretary of defense in the Jimmy Carter administration, has declared that McNamara "became skeptical about the Vietnam War well before he stopped talking about how great it was going," all because he was "extremely loyal" to President Lyndon Johnson. Steve Vogel, "McNamara Long Skeptical of Vietnam War, Book Reveals," *Washington Post,* April 11, 2012, A17. The author of a well-known book on the war in Vietnam would later refer to McNamara as "the most corrupt civilian head of the American military in the nation's history." See Harry Summers, "Clinton and the Joint Chiefs," *Washington Times,* February 10, 1993, E-1.

74. Lewis Sorley, *Honorable Warrior: Harold K. Johnson and the Ethics of Command* (Lawrence: University Press of Kansas, 1998), 139.

75. H. R. McMaster, *Dereliction of Duty: Lyndon Johnson, Robert McNamara, The Joint Chiefs of Staff, and the Lies That Led to Vietnam* (New York: HarperCollins, 1997), 3–4, 328.

76. Oral history interview of General Andrew Goodpaster, reported in Sorley, *Honorable Warrior,* 290.

77. McMaster, *Dereliction of Duty,* 41.

78. Rowland Evans and Robert Novak, *Lyndon B. Johnson: The Exercise of Power* (New York: New American Library, 1966), 539.

79. Sorley, *Honorable Warrior,* 146.

80. Henry Kissinger, *White House Years* (Boston: Little, Brown, 1979), 34.

81. Ibid., 34–35.

82. Interview of General Alfred Gray, USMC, in Al Santoli, *Leading the Way: How Vietnam Veterans Rebuilt the U.S. Military* (New York: Ballantine Books, 1993), 76.

83. Mark Perry, *Four Stars* (Boston: Houghton Mifflin, 1989), 152.

84. Ibid., 163–66.

85. Sorely, *Honorable Warrior,* 304.

86. Ibid.

87. Powell, *My American Journey,* 149.

88. McMaster, *Dereliction of Duty,* 333–34.

3. PERSONNEL IS POLICY

1. Norman Augustine and Kenneth Adelman, *Shakespeare in Charge* (New York: Hyperion, 1999), 1.

2. Jack Welch and Suzy Welch, *Winning* (New York: HarperCollins, 2005).

3. W. Edwards Deming, *Out of the Crisis* (Cambridge, MA: MIT Press, 2000), x.

4. Ibid., 248–49.

5. Larry Bossidy and Ram Charan, *Execution: The Discipline of Getting Things Done* (New York: Crown Business, 2002).

6. Warren Bennis, Gretchen M. Spreitzer, and Thomas G. Cummings, *The Future of Leadership* (San Francisco: Jossey-Bass, 2001), 3.

7. Ibid., 14.

8. Thomas J. Neff and James M. Citrin, *Lessons from the Top: The Search for America's Best Business Leaders* (New York: Doubleday, 1999), 7.

9. Rudolph W. Giuliani, *Leadership* (New York: Hyperion, 2002), 69.

10. Interview of Robert J. Brudno, May 9, 2011.

11. Ibid.

12. Caspar Weinberger, *Fighting for Peace* (New York: Warner Books, 1990), 41.

13. David Halberstam, *The Best and the Brightest* (New York: Random House, 1972), 4.

14. Ibid., 10.

15. Ibid., 31.

16. Ibid., 36.

17. Peter W. Rodman, *Presidential Command* (New York: Alfred A. Knopf, 2009), 287.

18. George F. Will, "JFK's Berlin Blunder," *Washington Post*, August 14, 2011, 17.

19. Rowland Evans Jr. and Robert D. Novak, *Nixon in the White House* (New York: Random House, 1971), 9.

20. Alvin S. Felzenberg, ed., *The Keys to a Successful Presidency* (Washington, DC: Heritage Foundation, 2000), 49.

21. Evans and Novak, *Nixon in the White House*, 66.

22. Ibid.

23. Ibid., 68.

24. Ibid., 70.

25. Jules Witcover, *Marathon: The Pursuit of the Presidency, 1971–1976* (New York: Viking Press, 1977), 655.

26. James Wooten, *Dasher: The Roots and Rising of Jimmy Carter* (New York: Summit Books, 1978), 373.

27. Pat Caddell, Carter's pollster, was quoted as saying to Carter, "Too many good people have been defeated because they tried to substitute substance for style; they forgot to give the public the kind of visible signals that it needs to understand what is happening." Victor Lasky, *Jimmy Carter: The Man and the Myth* (New York: Richard Marek Publishers, 1979), 319.

28. "Jimmy Carter: Person of the Year," *Time*, January 3, 1977.

29. Vincent Davis, "Carter Tries on the World for Size," in *The Post-Imperial Presidency*, ed. Vincent Davis (New York: Praeger, 1980), 176.

30. Ibid., 178.

31. Lawrence J. Korb, "The Evolving Relationship between the White House and the Department of Defense in the Post-Imperial Presidency," in *The Post-Imperial Presidency*, 109.

32. Peter G. Bourne, *Jimmy Carter* (New York: Scribner, 1997), 367.

33. Ibid., 363, 366.

34. Ibid., 367.

35. Ibid.

36. Ibid., 364.

37. Adriana Bosch, writer, producer, director, *Jimmy Carter* (film), *The American Experience* (Washington, DC: Public Broadcasting Service, 2002).

38. Ibid.

39. Allan R. Millet and Peter Maslowski, *For the Common Defense* (New York: The Free Press, 1994), 609.

40. Quoted in Michael R. Beschloss and Strobe Talbott, *At the Highest Levels: The Inside Story of the End of the Cold War* (Boston: Little, Brown, 1993), 26.

41. Interview with Frank Carlucci, final edited transcript, Ronald Reagan Oral History Project, Miller Center of Public Affairs, University of Virginia, August 28, 2001.

42. Stephen F. Hayes, *Cheney: The Untold Story of America's Most Powerful and Controversial Vice President* (New York: HarperCollins, 2007), 43.

43. Bob Woodward, *The Commanders* (New York: Touchstone, Simon & Schuster, 1991), 62.

44. The formal title of the new position was Coordinator of Drug Enforcement Policy and Support.

45. Herbert S. Parmet, *George Bush: The Life of a Lone Star Yankee* (New York: Scribner, 1997), 358.

46. Ibid., 360.

47. Ibid., 358.

48. Sally Bedell Smith, *For Love of Politics: Bill and Hillary Clinton: The White House Years* (New York: Random House, 2007), 30.

49. John F. Harris, *The Survivor: Bill Clinton in the White House* (New York: Random House, 2005), xxvii.

50. Richard K. Betts, "Are Civil-Military Relations Still a Problem?" in *American Civil-Military Relations: The Soldier and the State in a New Era*, ed. Suzanne C. Nielsen and Don M. Snyder (Baltimore: Johns Hopkins University Press, 2009), 30.

51. Elizabeth Drew, *On the Edge: The Clinton Presidency* (New York: Simon & Schuster, 1994), 28, 359.

52. Spencer Ackerman, "The Making of Michelle Flournoy," *Washingtonian*, February 2011, 36.

53. Smith, *For Love of Politics*, 27–28.

54. George Stephanopoulos, *All Too Human* (Boston: Little, Brown, 1999), 118.

55. Ibid., 119.

56. Smith, *For Love of Politics*, 30; Drew, *On the Edge*, 39.

57. Smith, *For Love of Politics*, 31.

58. Partnership for Public Service, "Ready to Govern: Improving the Presidential Transition," January 13, 2010, 111.

59. Drew, *On the Edge*, 37.

60. Steve R. Weisman and Daniel Patrick Moynihan, *A Portrait in Letters of an American Visionary* (New York: Public Affairs, 2010), 612.

61. G. Calvin Mackenzie, "The Real Invisible Hand: Presidential Appointees in the Administration of George W. Bush," *PS: Political Science and Politics*, 2002, 27.

62. Ibid., 28

63. See transcript of *Meet the Press*, November 21, 1999.

64. James Mann, *Rise of the Vulcans: The History of Bush's War Cabinet* (New York: Viking Press, 2004), 261.

65. According to Bush's memoir, one of the major factors in his selection of Rumsfeld was the perception that "he had the strength and experience to bring major changes to the Pentagon" and that "[h]e would run the bureaucracy, and not let it run him." George W. Bush, *Decision Points* (New York: Crown, 2010), 84.

66. Bob Woodward, *Bush at War* (New York: Simon & Schuster, 2002), 74.

67. After Bush assumed office, Rove told reporters that increasing the GOP share of the Latino vote was the administration's "mission and our goal," one that would "require all of us in every way and every day working to get that done." Paul Waldman, "GOP Candidates Alienate Latino Voters," *American Prospect*, August 15, 2007 (web only). See also Karl Rove, *Courage and Consequence* (New York: Threshold Editions, 2010), 364.

68. Jim Hoagland, "For Bush, Personnel as Policy," *Washington Post*, March 20, 2005, B7; David S. Broder, "Tight Little Cabinet," *Washington Post*, December 15, 2004, A33.

69. Thomas L. Friedman, "Saying No to Bush's Yes Men," *New York Times*, May 17, 2006.

70. "Bush Cronyism Weakens Government Agencies," *Bloomberg News*, September 30, 2005.

71. Recess appointments are made by a president while the Senate is in recess, pursuant to Article II, Section 2 of the U.S. Constitution. To remain in effect, a recess appointment must be approved by the Senate by the end of the next session of Congress.

72. ICE has more than fifteen thousand employees in four hundred domestic and fifty international offices. It investigates a wide range of security matters, such as weapons traffick-

ing, smuggling (including weapons of mass destruction), financial crimes, and threats to the nation's critical infrastructure.

73. Bush's top candidate had been FedEx founder and chief executive officer Fred Smith, a decorated combat veteran of Vietnam. Just as Bush was preparing to offer the position to him, Smith learned that he had a heart condition and found it necessary to withdraw from consideration. Bush, *Decision Points*, 83, 91.

74. Rumsfeld's reason apparently related to his unhappiness with Thomas E. White, a retired army brigadier general, who was fired as secretary of the army after purportedly lobbying Congress to block Rumsfeld's cancellation of an $11 billion weapon system and supporting the army chief of staff's estimate of the number of troops that would be needed to occupy Iraq.

75. Bush, *Decision Points*, 91–93.

76. In his memoir, Bush declared that "there was no way I was going to let a group of retired officers bully me into pushing out the civilian secretary of defense. It would have looked like a military coup and would have set a disastrous precedent." Bush, *Decision Points*, 93.

77. Partnership for Public Service, "Ready to Govern," 7.

78. Jonathan Alter, *The Promise: President Obama, Year One* (New York: Simon & Schuster, 2010), 45–46.

79. Ibid., 64.

80. Ibid., 46.

81. Michelle Malkin, *Culture of Corruption* (Washington, DC: Regnery, 2009), 39.

82. Fred Schulte, John Aloysius Farrell, and Jeremy Borden, "Obama Rewards Big Bundlers with Jobs, Commissions, Stimulus Money, Government Contracts, and More," *iWatch News* (The Center for Public Integrity), June 15, 2011.

83. Alter, *The Promise*, 54.

84. Schulte et al., "Obama Rewards Big Bundlers."

85. Michelle Levi, "Obama Says Sorry. A Lot," CBS News *Political Hotsheet*, February 4, 2009.

86. Malkin, *Culture of Corruption*, 18–39.

87. Alina Selyukh, "Obama Challenges Clinton for Most Nominee Dropouts," *National Journal*, February 17, 2009.

88. Nicholas Kralev, "Career Diplomats Protest Obama Appointments," *Washington Times*, July 10, 2009.

89. Schulte et al., "Obama Rewards Big Bundlers."

90. The undersecretaries included one for policy and a second for acquisition.

91. *Defense '92 Almanac*, September/October 1992, 24.

92. Cong. Rec. H21381 (October 6, 2000).

93. Vanderbilt University, "Obama's Appointees: Some Strong, Some Not, Vanderbilt Expert Finds," August 25, 2009.

94. Bob Woodward, *Obama's Wars* (New York: Simon & Schuster, 2010), 27.

95. Ibid., 28.

96. Ibid., 28–31.

97. Ibid., 30.

98. "At critical junctures of her life," one journalist wrote, "Hillary makes the same mistake. She comes on strong, showing an arrogant, abrasive side, gets brushed back, and then repackages herself in a more appealing way." Maureen Dowd, "Watch Out, Meryl Streep! She's a Master Thespian," *New York Times*, June 8, 2008.

99. See Woodward, *Obama's Wars*, 23, 138, 189. Gates had served as an analyst and career professional in the Central Intelligence Agency for twenty-six years and nearly nine years at the National Security Council before being appointed as director of the CIA by President George H. W. Bush. He had subsequently served as president of Texas A&M University. From March to December 2006, he had served as a member of the ten-person Iraq Study Group, a bipartisan panel appointed by Congress.

100. Anne E. Kornblut, "Daley Aims to Mend Rifts within Obama Team," *Washington Post*, March 9, 2011, A4.

101. Michelle Malkin, "Stuck on Stupid: Obama's Czar Fetish," *Creators Syndicate*, June 15, 2010.

102. Lori Montgomery, "Republicans Agree to Fiscal Panel," *Washington Post*, February 19, 2010, A14.

103. Dana Milbank, "Keep Passing the Buck on Budget Reform? Yes, We Can," *Washington Post*, February 15, 2011, A2.

104. Ibid.

105. Edwin Meese III, *With Reagan: The Inside Story* (Washington, DC: Regnery Gateway, 1992), 63.

106. Lou Cannon, *President Reagan: The Role of a Lifetime* (New York: Simon & Schuster, 199), 65.

107. Felzenberg, *The Keys to a Successful Presidency*, 50.

108. Ibid., 51; Meese, *With Reagan*, 63.

109. Kiron K. Skinner, Annelise Anderson, and Martin Anderson, *Reagan: A Life in Letters* (New York: Free Press, 2003), 710–11.

110. Rodman, *Presidential Command*, 283–84.

111. Felzenberg, *The Keys to a Successful Presidency*, 55.

112. Drew, *On the Edge*, 361.

4. POLITICS AND UNQUALIFIED CIVILIAN LEADERS

1. Kevin Rozzoli, *Gavel to Gavel: An Insider's View of Parliament* (Sydney: University of New South Wales Press, 2006), 273.

2. Gerald Gunther, *Learned Hand: The Man and the Judge* (New York: Alfred A. Knopf, 1994), 61.

3. Winston S. Churchill, *Lord Randolph Churchill* (London: Macmillan, 1907), 243.

4. The comment was made by Chuck Hagel, a former U.S. senator from Nebraska. See "Noble Calling, Rich Rewards," *U.S. News & World Report*, November 2010, 50.

5. See Paul C. Light, "Recommendations Forestalled or Forgotten? The National Commission on the Public Service and Presidential Appointments," *Public Administration Review*, June 11, 2007.

6. David E. Lewis, "Patronage, Policy, and Politics in Presidential Appointments," Woodrow Wilson School, Princeton University (paper prepared for presentation at the 2007 annual meeting of the Midwest Political Science Association, Chicago, Illinois), 9n11.

7. Peter W. Rodman, *Presidential Command* (New York: Alfred A. Knopf, 2009), 11.

8. Nationwide cries of nepotism arose when President-elect John F. Kennedy appointed his brother Robert, who had managed the 1960 campaign, to the cabinet position, but they were ignored.

9. See chapter 1, note 14.

10. Peter Baker, "Obama's Pledge to Reform Ethics Faces an Early Test," *New York Times*, February 3, 2009.

11. Drew Griffin and Scott Bronstein, "Defense Official Example of Revolving Door between Governing, Lobbying," *CNN.com*, February 23, 2010.

12. Frank James, "Gates: Ethics Rules May Be Doing Harm," *Swamp*, www.swamppolitics.com, January 27, 2009.

13. Greg Jaffe, "Pentagon's No. 2 Civilian Plans to Resign," *Washington Post*, July 8, 2011, A3.

14. Lewis, "Patronage, Policy, and Politics," 8.

15. Ibid.

16. Ibid., 38.

17. Henry Kissinger, *White House Years* (Boston: Little, Brown, 1979), 39.

18. David M. Cohen, "Amateur Government: When Political Appointees Manage the Federal Bureaucracy," The Brookings Institution, 1996, 1–2.

19. Bob Kerrey, Mark L. Alderman, and Howard Schweitzer, "The First U.S. Chief Operating Officer?" *Washington Post*, November 5, 2010, A10.

20. Cohen, "Amateur Government," 3. Emphasis added.

21. Brookings Institution, "A Survivor's Guide for Presidential Nominees," Council for Excellence in Government, Presidential Appointee Initiative, November 2000, 19.

22. U.S. General Accounting Office, *Confirmation of Political Appointees*, GAO/GGD-174, August 2000, 1.

23. Ibid., 2.

24. National Commission on the Public Service, *Urgent Business for America: Revitalizing the Federal Government for the 21st Century* (Washington, DC, January 2003), iii.

25. Ibid., iv.

26. Ibid., 6

27. Ibid., 16–17.

28. John B. Gilmour and David E. Lewis, "Political Appointees and the Competence of Federal Program Management," *American Politics Research* 34, no. 1 (January 2006): 22–50.

29. Ibid., 25.

30. William D. Eggers and John O'Leary, *If We Can Put a Man on the Moon: Getting Big Things Done in Government* (Boston: Harvard Business Press, 2009), 249.

31. Ibid., 253.

32. General Gordon R. Sullivan and Michael V. Harper, *Hope Is Not a Method* (New York: Random House, 1996), 43.

33. Carlo D'Este, *Warlord: A Life of Winston Churchill at War, 1874–1945* (New York: HarperCollins, 2008), 381.

34. Brian O'Keefe, "Battle-Tested: How a Decade of War Has Created A New Generation of Elite Business Leaders," *Fortune*, March 22, 2010, 114.

35. Interview of Admiral Thad Allen, USCG (Ret.), in *Harvard Business Review*, November 2010, 78.

36. Boris Groysberg, Andrew Hill, and Toby Johnson, "Which of These People Is Your Future CEO?" *Harvard Business Review*, November 2010, 82.

37. Adi Ignatius, "From the Battlefield to the Boardroom," *Harvard Business Review*, November 2010, 18.

38. O'Keefe, "Battle-Tested," 111–12.

39. Ibid., 110.

40. Michael Useem, "Four Lessons in Adaptive Leadership," *Harvard Business Review*, November 2010, 87.

41. Ibid., 89.

42. Andrew Cockburn, *Rumsfeld: His Rise, Fall, and Catastrophic Legacy* (New York: Scribner, 2007), 153–54.

43. General (Ret.) Hugh Shelton, Ronald Levinson, and Malcolm McConnell, *Without Hesitation* (New York: St. Martin's Press, 2010), 402–3.

44. Ibid., 169–70.

45. Thomas E. Ricks, *Fiasco: The Military Adventure in Iraq* (New York: Penguin Press, 2006), 156. Rumsfeld would later say that he was not invited to the ceremony and that, in any event, he was in Europe at the time. "An Interview with Donald Rumsfeld," U.S. Naval Institute *Proceedings*, March, 2011, 24. That response ignores the reasons for which he was not invited.

46. Even though McChrystal was forced to resign after he and some of his aides were accused of using flippant and disrespectful language in reference to the vice president, the national security advisor, and the president's special representative to Afghanistan and Pakistan, Secretary of Defense Robert Gates attended the ceremony and praised McChrystal as "one of America's greatest warriors."

47. Bush has written that even if Rumsfeld was not invited to the retirement ceremony, "he should have gone anyway." George W. Bush, *Decision Points* (New York: Crown, 2010), 92.

48. Steve Vogel, "Obama Appointee at Labor Resigns after Ethics Probe," *Washingtonpost.com*, July 28, 2011; Sam Hananel, "Labor Official Resigns Amid Corruption Probe," *Ctpost.com*, July 29, 2011.

49. According to at least one view, the term "neoconservative" originally referred to "former liberals and leftists who were dismayed by the countercultural movements of the 1960s and the Great Society, and adopted conservative views, for example, against government welfare

programs, and in favor of interventionist foreign policies." See Elizabeth Drew, "The Neocons in Power," *New York Review of Books*, June 12, 2003.

50. The term "chickenhawk" is a political epithet that has been used by both liberals and conservatives to criticize politicians who are zealous in their support of military action in particular circumstances, but who actively avoided military service when they were of the age to serve.

51. Todd S. Purdum and Patrick E. Tyler, "Top Republicans Break with Bush on Iraq Strategy," *New York Times*, August 16, 2002.

52. James Bamford, "Untested Administration Hawks Clamor for War," *USA Today*, September 17, 2002.

53. Eliot A. Cohen, "Hunting 'Chicken Hawks,'" *Washington Post*, September 5, 2002, A31.

54. Sir Fitzroy Maclean (1911–1996) was a legendary and highly decorated Scottish soldier who rose from private to brigadier general in World War II. He served as a professional diplomat with the British Diplomatic Service prior to the war. In addition to considerable combat action in North Africa and the Balkans during the war, Maclean served as Prime Minister Churchill's diplomatic/military emissary to Marshal (Josip Broz) Tito, the leader of the Partisans in Yugoslavia, who subsequently became that country's president. After the war, and after thirteen years of service as an elected member of Parliament (he eventually served for thirty-three years), Churchill appointed Maclean undersecretary of state for war.

55. Ricks, *Fiasco*, 76.

56. Ricks, *Fiasco*, 76; General Tommy Franks and Malcolm McConnell, *American Soldier* (New York: HarperCollins, 2004), 330.

57. Bob Woodward, *Plan of Attack* (New York: Simon & Schuster, 2004), 281.

58. Franks and McConnell, *American Soldier*, 362; Ricks, *Fiasco*, 78.

59. Ibid.

60. Shelton et al., *Without Hesitation*, 411.

61. Douglas J. Feith, *War and Decision* (New York: HarperCollins, 2008), 275–76.

62. Bill Clinton, *My Life* (New York: Alfred A. Knopf, 2004), 811.

63. Senator Robert Byrd (D-WV), Cong. Rec. (February 12, 1999).

64. E. J. Dionne, "Biden Admits Plagiarism in School but Says It Was Not 'Malevolent,'" *New York Times*, September 18, 1987.

65. Jules Witcover, *Joe Biden* (New York: HarperCollins, 2010), 190.

66. Ibid.

67. David Greenberg, "The Write Stuff: Why Biden's Plagiarism Shouldn't Be Forgotten," *Slate*, August 25, 2008.

68. Witcover, *Joe Biden*, 409.

69. Wil Haygood, "Censure and Consternation," *Washington Post*, January 31, 2011, C1, C5.

70. Sam Stein, "Pentagon Problems: Obama Runs into Delays Staffing Defense Team," *Huffpost Reporting*, December 23, 2008.

71. Admiral William J. Crowe Jr., *The Line of Fire* (New York: Simon & Schuster, 1993), 206.

72. Peter, Sixth Lord Carrington, *Reflect on Things Past* (London: Collins, 1988), 368–70.

73. In 2008, six nuclear cruise missiles were mistakenly attached to the pylons of a B-52, which was then flown from Minot Air Force Base in North Dakota to Barksdale Air Force Base in Louisiana. The missiles subsequently sat unguarded on the tarmac for several hours before the mistake was discovered.

74. Associated Press, "Poll Shows Public Has Little Confidence in Government," *New York Post*, April 19, 2010.

75. Linda J. Bilmes and W. Scott Gould, *The People Factor* (Washington, DC: Brookings Institution Press, 2009), 4.

76. Erin Dian Dumbacher, "Senior Executives Give Low Marks to Obama Appointees," *GovernmentExecutive.com*, May 27, 2011.

77. Bilmes and Gould, *The People Factor*, 10–11.

78. Cheryl Y. Marcum, Lauren R. Sager Weinstein, Susan D. Hosek, and Harry J. Thie, *Department of Defense Political Appointments* (Santa Monica, CA: RAND, 2001), 5–6.

79. Gilmour and Lewis, "Political Appointees," 23.

80. Paul Light and Russ Feingold, "Slimming Our Federal Leadership," *Washingtonpost.com*, April 15, 2010.

81. Mark Shields, "America Needs More Marine Corps Values," *Creators.com*, July 24, 2010.

5. THE PROFESSIONALISM OF MILITARY LEADERS FROM 1972 TO SEPTEMBER 11, 2001

1. Andrew J. Goodpaster, Lloyd H. Elliot, and J. Allan Hovey Jr., *Toward a Consensus on Military Service* (New York: Pergamon Press, 1982), 43.

2. Bernard Rostker, *I Want You: The Evolution of the All-Volunteer Force* (Santa Monica, CA: RAND, 2006), 3.

3. Ibid.

4. Goodpaster et al., *Toward a Consensus on Military Service*, 42.

5. Ibid.

6. Mark Perry, *Four Stars* (Boston: Houghton Mifflin, 1989), 152.

7. Thomas Barn, "Fragging: A Study," *Army*, April 1977, 46; Eugene Linden, "Fragging and Other Withdrawal Symptoms," *Saturday Review*, January 8, 1972, 12.

8. U.S. House of Representatives Report No. 96–1462, 6350.

9. Secretary of Defense Melvin Laird, Memorandum to the Secretaries of the Military Departments, August 21, 1970. This memorandum is reprinted in the Congressional Record, Cong. Rec. 30968 (September 9, 1970).

10. Department of Defense, *Annual Report to the Congress, Fiscal Year 1972*, 36.

11. Secretary of Defense James R. Schlesinger, Memorandum, "Readiness of the Selected Reserve," August 23, 1973, 1–2.

12. *America's Volunteers: A Report on the All-Volunteer Armed Forces* (Washington, DC, December 1978), 366.

13. Admiral Elmo R. Zumevalt Jr., *On Watch* (New York: Quadrangle/New York Times Book Company, 1976), 279.

14. See Stephen M. Duncan, *Citizen Warriors: America's National Guard and Reserve Forces and the Politics of National Security* (Novato, CA: Presidio Press, 1997), 147.

15. Ibid., 148–49.

16. The Selected Reserve consists of those units and individuals in the National Guard (when in a federal status) and federal reserve components that have been designated by their respective military services and approved by the Joint Chiefs of Staff as so essential to initial wartime missions that they have priority over all other reserve forces. Title 10, U.S. Code, Section 268(c).

17. Stephen M. Duncan, Hearing before the Subcommittee of Military Manpower and Personnel, Armed Services Committee, United States Senate, June 9, 1989.

18. James Kitfield, *Prodigal Soldiers: How the Generation of Officers Born of Vietnam Revolutionized the American Style of War* (New York: Simon & Schuster, 1995), 230.

19. I was serving simultaneously as assistant secretary of defense for reserve affairs and as the DoD coordinator for drug enforcement policy and support, responsible for all international and domestic strategies, policies, and actions involving the use of the U.S. Armed Forces to carry out statutory counterdrug missions assigned by Congress and the additional initiatives necessary for implementation of the president's National Drug Control Strategy. See also chapter 6.

20. Stephen M. Duncan, Testimony to the Defense Subcommittee, House Appropriations Committee, April 1, 1990.

21. Samuel P. Huntington, "Inter-service Competition and the Political Roles of the Armed Services," *American Political Science Review* 55, no. 1 (March 1961), 48.

22. Ibid.

23. Lieutenant General Gordon Sullivan, "Doctrine: An Army Update," in *The United States Army: Challenges and Missions for the 1990s*, ed. Robert L. Pfaltzgraff Jr. and Richard H. Shultz Jr. (Lexington, MA: Lexington Books, 1991), 79–80.

24. Kitfield, *Prodigal Soldiers*, 192.

25. DePuy's effort to "reorganize, re-equip, retrain, refocus, and professionalize the post-Vietnam, post-draft Army" has been widely acknowledged as "highly successful." See, for example, Thomas E. Ricks, "A Great but Forgotten General," *Washington Monthly*, July 17, 2009.

26. Message (291305Z) from Commander TRADOC to distribution list, Subject: "The Air-Land Battle," January 1981.

27. Admiral James D. Watkins, "The Maritime Strategy," *U.S. Naval Institute*, January 1986, 4.

28. Frederick H. Hartmann, *Naval Renaissance: The U.S. Navy in the 1980s* (Annapolis, MD: Naval Institute Press, 1990), 150.

29. Secretary of the Navy/CNO Report, FY 1983, 4.

30. Admiral James D. Watkins, "The Maritime Strategy," 11.

31. Ibid., 13.

32. Frank G. Hoffman, "235 Years of Individual Valor and Institutional Adaptation," *Foreign Policy Research Institute (fpri.org)*, November 10, 2010.

33. U.S. Marine Corps, *Concepts & Programs 2010*, 22.

34. General P. X. Kelley and Major Hugh K. O'Donnell, "The Amphibious Warfare Strategy," *U.S. Naval Institute*, January 1986, 26.

35. Ibid.

36. These concepts and terms were developed by then Marine Corps Commandant General Charles C. Krulak in the late 1990s. The "Three Block War" concept conveyed the idea that, in the future, military operations would be more complex and rapidly evolving, possibly requiring everything from peacekeeping and humanitarian aid to full combat, all within the space of three contiguous city blocks. Such circumstances would place huge responsibility on the corporal, the lowest-ranking noncommissioned officer of a ground unit, who would typically be in charge of as many as thirteen individuals organized into fire teams. To prepare corporals so that they would be equipped to exploit time-critical information into their decision-making process and minimize the risk of damage to noncombatants and infrastructure, leadership training at even low levels of the chain of command would have to be very high.

37. Kitfield, *Prodigal Soldiers*, 287.

38. Colin L. Powell with Joseph E. Persico, *My American Journey* (New York: Random House, 1995), 472.

39. William J. Taylor Jr. and James Blackwell, "The Ground War in the Gulf," *Survival* 33, no. 3 (May/June 1991), 245.

40. Powell, *My American Journey*, 528.

41. Rick Atkinson, "U.S. Victory Is Absolute," *Washington Post*, March 1, 1991, 1.

42. Letter from General William E. DePuy to General Colin Powell, September 26, 1991.

43. Michael R. Gordon and Bernard E. Trainor, *The General's War* (Boston: Little, Brown, 1995), 470–71.

44. Al Santoli, *Leading the Way: How Vietnam Veterans Rebuilt the U.S. Military* (New York: Ballantine Books, 1993), xvii.

45. Title XI, Section 1102, National Defense Authorization Act for FY 1989.

46. When in state active duty or Title 32 (of the U.S. Code) status, National Guard forces remain under the operational, tactical, and administrative control of the governor of the state. When service is performed under Title 10 of the U.S. Code, command and control of the National Guard rests solely with the president and the federal government.

47. Secretary of Defense Dick Cheney, Memorandum, Department of Defense Guidance for Implementation of the President's National Drug Control Strategy, September 18, 1989, 1.

48. Report of the Armed Services Committee, United States House of Representatives, 102nd Congress, First Session, May 1991.

49. Francis Fukuyama, "The End of History," *National Interest* 16 (Summer 1989), 3–18; John Keegan, *War and Our World* (New York: Vintage Books, 2001), 1, 64.

50. Robert D. Kaplan, *Warrior Politics* (New York: Random House, 2002), 14–15.

51. General Jack N. Merritt, "Foreword," in *Landpower in the Information Age* by Lieutenant General Frederic J. Brown (Washington, DC: Brassey's, 1993), x.

52. Ibid.

53. Eliot A. Cohen, "Defending America in the Twenty-First Century," *Foreign Affairs* (November/December 2000), 41.

54. General Gordon R. Sullivan and Michael V. Harper, *Hope Is Not a Method* (New York: Random House, 1996), xvii.

55. Ibid., 5.

56. Louis E. Lataif, "Foreword," in Sullivan and Harper, *Hope Is Not a Method*, vii–viii.

57. Admiral Hal Gehman, "JFCOM's Mission Is Far from Complete," *(Norfolk) Virginian-Pilot*, September 26, B10.

58. Report of the U.S. House of Representatives, Committee on Armed Services, Subcommittee on Oversight and Investigations, *Another Crossroads? Professional Military Education Two Decades after the Goldwater-Nichols Act and the Skelton Panel*, April 2010, 9.

59. 10 U.S.C. Sec. 668(a)(2).

60. The title "commander in chief" for the senior U.S. military commander in each region was changed to "combatant commander." There are currently ten unified combatant commands, including U.S. Central Command, U.S. European Command, U.S. Africa Command, U.S. Pacific Command, U.S. Northern Command, U.S. Southern Command, U.S. Strategic Command, U.S. Transportation Command, U.S. Special Operations Command, and U.S. Joint Forces Command.

61. Wesley K. Clark, *Waging Modern War* (New York: Public Affairs, 2001), 452.

62. H. R. McMaster, *Dereliction of Duty: Lyndon Johnson, Robert McNamara, the Joint Chiefs of Staff, and the Lies That Led to Vietnam* (New York: HarperCollins, 1997).

63. Carl von Clausewitz, as quoted in Peter Paret, *Clausewitz and the State: The Man, His Theories, and His Times* (Princeton, NJ: Princeton University Press, 1985), 369.

64. Weinberger had been very concerned about the attitude of the State Department and National Security Council on the use of American military force. "Their feeling seemed to be," he wrote, that when an American troop presence in some foreign locale would add "a desirable bit of pressure and leverage to diplomatic efforts . . . we should be willing to do that freely and virtually without hesitation." Caspar Weinberger, *Fighting for Peace: Seven Critical Years in the Pentagon* (New York: Warner Books, 1990), 159. In a speech to the National Press Club on November 28, 1984—thirteen months after the tragic terrorist attack in Lebanon that had killed 241 American servicemen—Weinberger set forth several principles that he believed should govern the use of military power. "First," he said, "the United States should not commit forces to *combat* overseas unless the particular engagement or occasion is deemed vital to our national interest or that of our allies. Second," and only if we decide that it *is* necessary to put *combat* troops into a given situation, "we should do so wholeheartedly, and with the clear intention of winning. Third, if we *do* decide to commit forces to combat overseas, we should have clearly defined political and military objectives. Fourth, the relationship between our objectives and the forces we have committed—their size, composition and disposition—must be continually reassessed and adjusted if necessary." The fifth principle required that before the U.S. committed forces abroad, "there must be some reasonable assurance we will have the support of the American people and their elected representatives in Congress." Finally, Weinberger believed that the commitment of U.S. forces to combat "should be a last resort." Powell expanded upon the doctrine by asserting that when a nation is engaging in war, every resource and tool should be used to achieve decisive force against the enemy, minimizing U.S. casualties and ending the conflict quickly.

65. Department of Defense, *Final Report to Congress: Conduct of the Persian Gulf War*, April 1992, 295.

66. Frederick W. Kagan, "Strategy and Force Structure in an Interwar Period," *Joint Forces Quarterly* (Spring/Summer 2001), 94.

67. John Keegan, *War and Our World* (New York: Vintage Books, 2001), 1, 64.

68. Winston S. Churchill, *The World Crisis, Vol. I* (London: Odhams Press Limited, 1938), 33.

69. David Halberstam, *War in a Time of Peace: Bush, Clinton, and the Generals* (New York: Scribner, 2001), 482.

70. Condoleezza Rice, "Promoting the National Interest," *Foreign Affairs* (January/February 2000), 51.

6. CIVILIAN LEADERS WHO CAN GET THINGS DONE

1. Anne E. Kornblut, "Daley Aims to Mend Rifts within Obama Team," *Washington Post*, March 9, 2011, A1.

2. Ibid., A4.

3. Lolita C. Baldor, "Gates: Air Force Must Find Balance for Future Wars," Associated Press, *WashingtonExaminer.com*, March 4, 2011.

4. Eliot A. Cohen, "Churchill and His Generals," in *No End Save Victory*, ed. Robert Cowley (New York: G.P. Putnam's Sons, 2001), 283.

5. Ibid.

6. Ibid., 289. Emphasis added.

7. Immediately upon becoming prime minister in May 1940, Churchill appointed Lord Beaverbrook to be minister of aircraft production. At the time, Germany had an almost three-to-one superiority in numbers of aircraft and Britain's deficiencies in aircraft presented great dangers. During the Dunkirk evacuation in June, 436 aircraft were lost in a single week. Beaverbrook's energetic efforts soon produced significant increases in production, all of which were vital to the country's later success in the Battle of Britain. See Martin Gilbert, *Churchill: A Life* (New York: Henry Holt, 1991), 645, 655.

8. Army Lieutenant General James F. Hollingsworth was recognized by General George Patton as one of the two best armored battalion commanders in World War II. He later served as the commander of all combined forces in South Korea.

9. Larry Bossidy and Ram Charan, *Execution: The Discipline of Getting Things Done* (New York: Crown Business, 2002), 22. Emphasis added.

10. Ibid.

11. Jack Welch and Suzy Welch, *Winning* (New York: HarperCollins, 2005), 87. Emphasis added.

12. Larry Bossidy and Ram Charan, *Confronting Reality: Doing What Matters to Get Things Right* (New York: Crown Business, 2004), 1.

13. John C. Whitehead, *A Life in Leadership* (New York: Basic Books, 2005), 243.

14. Paul C. Light, "Creating High Performance Government: A Once-in-a-Generation Opportunity," *The Campaign for High Performance Government*, New York University, June 21, 2011, 2–3.

15. Ibid., 4.

16. Ibid.

17. John B. Gilmour and David E. Lewis, "Political Appointees and the Competence of Federal Program Management," *American Politics Research* 34, no. 1 (January 2006), 22.

18. Ibid.

19. Norman Augustine and Kenneth Adelman, *Shakespeare in Charge* (New York: Hyperion, 1999), 29.

20. Victor Davis Hanson, "A Tottering Technocracy," *National Review Online*, August 9, 2011. Emphasis added.

21. Augustine and Adelman, *Shakespeare in Charge*, 32.

22. Eliot A. Cohen, *Supreme Command* (New York: The Free Press, 2002), 1.

23. DoD Instruction 5125.1, January 12, 1984.

24. See Stephen M. Duncan, *Citizen Warriors: America's National Guard and Reserve Forces and the Politics of National Security* (Novato, CA: Presidio Press, 1997).

25. Linda J. Bilmes and W. Scott Gould, *The People Factor* (Washington, DC: Brookings Institution Press, 2010), 102–5.

26. Sheila C. Bair, "Stop Selling the Long Term Short," *Washington Post*, July 10, 2011, B1. Ms. Bair served as chairwoman of the FDIC from June 23, 2006, through July 8, 2011.

27. Bilmes and Gould, *The People Factor*, 104.

28. Ibid., 104–5.

29. Erin Dian Dumbacher, "Senior Executives Give Low Marks to Obama Appointees," *GovernmentExecutive.com*, May 27, 2011.

30. "The Gates Farewell Warning," *Wall Street Journal*, May 28, 2011, 14; Tom Vanden Brook and Calum MacLeod, "China's Military Flexes Its Muscle," *USA Today*, July 28, 2011, 1.

31. Shaun Waterman, "Future Wars Seen as Longer, Deadlier," *Washington Times*, June 9, 2011, 9; Otto Kreisher, "Pentagon's No. 2 Argues for Broad Portfolio of Capabilities," *National Journal Daily AM*, June 9, 2011.

32. Waterman, "Future Wars Seen as Longer, Deadlier."

33. Ibid.

34. Paul Kane, "House Passes Obama Stimulus Package," *Washington Post*, January 29, 2009.

35. Thomas L. Friedman, "Superbroke, Superfrugal, Superpower?" *New York Times*, September 5, 2010.

36. Thomas Harding, "Britain Unable to Defend Falklands, Says Admiral," *London Daily Telegraph*, June 13, 2011, 15.

37. Nathan Hodge, "Gates Cautions of Military Rollback," *Wall Street Journal*, April 15, 2011, 5.

38. David Alexander, Phil Stewart, and Missy Ryan, "Defense Not the Cause of Budget Deficit: Gates," *Reuters.com*, June 30, 2011.

39. Megan Scully, "Better Than They Expected," *National Journal*, August 6, 2011.

40. Elisabeth Bumiller, "Pentagon Faces Possibility of Hundreds of Billions in Spending Cuts over 10 Years," *New York Times*, August 2, 2011, 1.

41. Michael O'Hanlon "Warning on Defense Budget Cuts," *Washington Times*, August 3, 2011, B3.

42. Gregg Jaffe, "Debt 'Trigger' Has Pentagon Budget in Its Crosshairs," *Washington Post*, August 2, 2011, 4.

43. The Defense Science Board is a committee of not more than forty-five civilians who have expertise in various fields and who are appointed to advise the secretary of defense on scientific, technical, manufacturing, acquisition process, and other matters. It was established in 1956. The Defense Business Board is a federal advisory board of civilians that conducts studies and advises the secretary of defense on best business practices. It was established in 2002.

44. Michael Bayer, "The Looming Challenge," *Defense News*, March 14, 2011, 29.

45. Ibid.

46. Nassim Nicholas Taleb, *The Black Swan: The Impact of the Highly Improbable* (New York: Random House, 2007).

47. Ibid., xxvii–xxviii.

48. Ibid., xx.

49. See, for example, David Wood, "Obama White House, Pentagon at Odds over Libya Policy," *HuffingtonPost.com*, April 20, 2011.

50. Bossidy and Charan, *Confronting Reality*, 113.

51. Ibid., 120.

52. Dumbacher, "Senior Executives Give Low Marks."

53. Ibid.

54. Albert Bushnell Hart and Herbert Ronald Ferleger, eds., *Theodore Roosevelt Cyclopedia* (New York: Roosevelt Memorial Association, 1941), 493.

55. Ibid., 70

56. Ibid., 69.

57. Henrik Bering, "The Perfect Officer," *Policy Review* 168 (August–September 2011): 59–61.

58. Winston Churchill, House of Commons, 12 November 1940.

59. Patrick Lindsay, *Cosgrove: Portrait of a Leader* (Sydney: Random House Australia, 2006), 233–34.

60. Jim Stockdale, *Thoughts of a Philosophical Fighter Pilot* (Stanford, CA: Hoover Institution Press, 1995), 31–32.

61. Theodore H. White, *Breach of Faith: The Fall of Richard Nixon* (New York: Atheneum, 1975), 264.

62. Ibid., 267

63. Ibid.

64. Michael Beschloss, *Presidential Courage* (New York: Simon & Schuster, 2007), 153.

65. Ibid.

66. David Halberstam, *The Best and the Brightest* (New York: Random House, 1972), 655.

67. George Weigel, *Witness to Hope* (New York: HarperCollins, 1999), 133.

68. Ibid.

7. PROFESSIONALISM IN THE ERA OF WARS OF A DIFFERENT KIND

1. Eliot A. Cohen, "Defending America in the Twenty-First Century," *Foreign Affairs* (November/December 2000), 41.

2. David Halberstam, *War in a Time of Peace: Bush, Clinton, and the Generals* (New York: Scribner, 2001), 490.

3. James Carney and John F. Dickerson, "Inside the War Room," *Time*, December 24, 2001.

4. Richard A. Posner, "Security versus Civil Liberties," *Atlantic Monthly*, December 2001.

5. Richard E. Neustadt and Ernest R. May, *Thinking in Time: The Uses of History for Decision Makers* (New York: The Free Press, 1986).

6. GAO-04-1031, "DoD Needs to Address Long-Term Reserve Force Availability and Related Mobilization and Demobilization Issues," September 2004, 1–2.

7. George Cahlink, "Changing of the Guard," *Government Executive*, April 15, 2004, 44.

8. Robert B. Killebrew, "It Is a Daunting Time to Be a Soldier," U.S. Naval Institute, *Proceedings*, June 2004, 75.

9. Donald Rumsfeld, *Known and Unknown* (New York: Sentinel, 2011), 293–94.

10. See Risa Brooks, *Shaping Strategy: The Civil-Military Politics of Strategic Assessment* (Princeton, NJ: Princeton University Press, 2008); Macubin Thomas Owens, *U.S. Civil-Military Relations After 9/11* (London: Continuum, 2011), 14–15, 120.

11. Richard A. Lacquement Jr., "In the Army Now," *American Interest*, September/October 2010, 27.

12. The most prominent publications were the Field Manual 3-24 *Counterinsurgency* (2006), Field Manual 3-0 *Operations* (2008), Field Manual 3-7 *Stability Operations* (2008), and a U.S. Army Training and Doctrine Command pamphlet on "Operational Adaptability: Operations Under Conditions of Uncertainty and Complexity in an Era of Persistent Conflict" (2009).

13. Loren Thompson, "Gates Challenges Marine Corps' Mission," *Forbes.com* (*Forbes* blog), January 17, 2011.

14. "Marine Corps Will Be Smaller, Lighter but Just as Deadly, Commandant Promises," *LATimes.com*, February 8, 2011.

15. *Air Force Basic Doctrine*, November 17, 2003, ix.

16. Admiral William A. Owens, *High Seas* (Annapolis, MD: Naval Institute Press, 1995), 4.

17. Ibid.

18. A former deputy undersecretary of the navy in the Reagan and George H. W. Bush administrations has written that Obama administration policy "clearly limits the extent to which the navy can candidly discuss Chinese naval modernization." Seth Cropsey, "Ebb Tide," *American Interest*, September/October 2010, 20.

19. Milan Vego, "AirSea Battle Must Not Work Alone," U.S. Naval Institute *Proceedings*, July 2011, 64.

20. Donald H. Rumsfeld, Secretary of Defense, *Report of the Quadrennial Defense Review* (Washington, DC: U.S. Department of Defense, September 30, 2001), 19.

21. Jim Garamone, "U.S. Northern Command to Debut in October," *Armed Forces Information Service*, April 17, 2002.

22. U.S. Department of Defense, *Quadrennial Defense Review* (Washington, DC: U.S. Department of Defense, February 6, 2006), 36.

23. Evan Thomas and John Barry, "The Fight Over How to Fight," *Newsweek*, March 24, 2008.

24. Secretary of Defense Robert Gates, Address in Colorado Springs, May 13, 2008.

25. Robert M. Gates, "A Balanced Strategy," *Foreign Affairs*, January/February 2009, 30.

26. Roy Godson and Richard H. Schultz Jr., "A QDR for All Seasons?" *Joint Forces Quarterly* 59 (4th Quarter 2010): 53.

27. George C. Wilson, "Forward Observer: QDR Is a Quite Disappointing Report," *GovernmentExecutive.com*, March 8, 2010.

28. Ibid.

29. Ibid.

30. The comments appeared in *The QDR in Perspective: Meeting America's National Security Needs in the Twenty-First Century*, a report of the Quadrennial Defense Review Independent Panel, chaired by former secretary of defense William J. Perry (Clinton administration) and former assistant secretary of defense (George H. W. Bush administration) and national security advisor (George W. Bush administration) Stephen J. Hadley.

31. Nancy A. Youssef, "Pentagon Budget Multiplies as Security Threat List Grows," *McClatchy Newspapers* (mcclatchydc.com), February 10, 2011.

32. Admiral Michael Mullen, Address in the Landon Lecture Series, Kansas State University, Manhattan, Kansas, March 3, 2010.

33. Walter Pincus, "Changes Coming to the Army under Odierno," *Washington Post*, July 26, 2011, A15. At the confirmation hearing on his nomination to be the new army chief of staff, General Ray Odierno focused his testimony on the new hybrid threats, noting that while future leaders will have to be able to execute with lethality, "they also must understand the environment they're going to operate in is going to be very different, and they have to be able to adapt and adjust." Ibid.

34. A December 31, 2010, article in *Asahi Shimbun*, the most respected daily newspaper in Japan, stated that the PLA has developed an internal tactical plan to forcibly seize control of islands in the South China Sea that are under the effective control of other nations. The plan purportedly would employ units of the North China Sea Fleet and the East China Sea Fleet to block any approach of U.S. aircraft carriers.

35. Aaron L. Friedberg, "China's Challenge at Sea," *New York Times*, September 5, 2011, 19.

36. Robert Burns (AP), "Pentagon, Scarred by 9/11, Adapts to New Fight," *Yahoo.com*, August 21, 2011.

37. Jeffrey M. Jones, "Americans Most Confident in Military, Least in Congress," *Gallup*, June 23, 2011.

38. Thomas E. Ricks, "Officers with Ph.Ds Advising War Effort," *Washington Post*, February 5, 2007.

39. Richard D. Hooker, "Soldiers of the State: An Alternative View of the Civil-Military Relations in America Today" (research paper), National War College, 2003.

40. General George W. Casey Jr., Address to the Association of the U.S. Army, October 26, 2010.

41. Victor Davis Hanson, *The Father of Us All: War and History, Ancient and Modern* (New York: Bloomsbury Press, 2010), 184–85.

42. See the pamphlet *Army: Profession of Arms 2011*, i, iv.

43. *Terms of Reference for the Review of the Army Profession in an Era of Persistent Conflict*, October 27, 2010.

44. Information Paper on the Army Profession Campaign, July 27, 2010, 4.

45. Remarks by General Martin E. Dempsey at the Association of the United States Army's Chapter Presidents' Dinner, Washington, DC, October 4, 2009.

46. Albert C. Pierce, "Chairman's Conference on Military Professionalism: An Overview," *Joint Forces Quarterly* 62 (3rd Quarter 2011): 8.

47. Morris Janowitz, *The Professional Soldier* (Glencoe, IL: Free Press, 1960), vii.

48. See Karen Dillon, "Can the Profession Save Itself?" *American Lawyer*, November 1994, 5.

49. Hanson, *The Father of Us All*, 177.

50. David Wood, "War on Terror Pits Networks of Cells against Bureaucracies," *Newhouse.com*, October 4, 2001.

51. Ibid.

52. *World at Risk: The Report of the Commission on the Prevention of WMD Proliferation and Terrorism* (New York: Vintage Books, 2008), xv.

53. Josh Meyer, "Nuclear Plants Said to Face Big Attack Risk," *Los Angeles Times*, March 26, 2002, 1.

54. "Poor Tom," *Economist*, April 20, 2002, 33.

55. Dana Milbank, "Plan Formed in Extraordinary Secrecy," *Washington Post*, June 7, 2002, 1A.

56. Del Jones, "Homeland Security: a Tough Merger," *USA Today*, June 11, 2002, 3B.

57. Ibid.

58. Siobhan Gorman, "Homeland Security Job May Require Larger-Than-Life Figure," *GovExec.com*, June 14, 2002.

59. Karen Tumulty and Ed O'Keefe, "The Government Tends to Resist Reorganization," *Washington Post*, January 28, 2010, A1.

60. GAO Report (GAO-07-454), "Department of Homeland Security: Progress Report on Implementation of Mission and Management Functions," August 2007, ii.

61. GAO Report (GAO–11-153R), "Quadrennial Homeland Security Review," December 16, 2010.

62. Alice Lipowicz, "DHS Still Falls Short on Management and Integration, GAO Official Says," *FederalComputerWeek.com*, October 1, 2010.

63. Charles B. King, III, "The Department of Homeland Security: An Organization in Transition," *Joint Forces Quarterly* 55 (4th Quarter 2009): 153–54.

64. Gene L. Dodaro, "Progress Made and Work Remaining in Implementing Homeland Security Missions 10 Years After 9/11," GAO-11-919T, September 7, 2011.

65. Ibid.

66. Louis Jacobson, "Merging Cultures of Homeland Security Agencies Will Be Big Challenge," *GovExec.com*, June 13, 2002.

8. TRUST AND CLASHES OF CULTURE AND COMPETENCE

1. Edgar H. Schein, "Organizational Culture," *American Psychologist*, February 1990, 111.

2. Victor Davis Hanson, *The Father of Us All: War and History* (New York: Bloomsbury Press, 2010), 137.

3. Naomi Stanford, *Corporate Culture* (Hoboken, NJ: John Wiley & Sons, 2011), 2.

4. Thomas J. Peters and Robert H. Waterman Jr., *In Search of Excellence: Lessons from America's Best-Run Companies* (New York: Harper & Row, 1982).

5. Ibid., 75.

6. Price Pritchett, Donald Robinson, and Russell Clarkson, *After the Merger* (New York: McGraw-Hill, 1997), 10.

7. Thomas J. Neff and James M. Citrin, *Lessons from the Top* (New York: Doubleday, 1999), 224–25.

8. Ibid., 262–63.

9. The comments were made by Ray Gilmartin, chairman, president, and CEO of Merck & Company, Inc. The 1998 revenues of this company were $26.9 billion. See Neff and Citrin, *Lessons from the Top*, 145.

10. Ibid., 190–91.

11. John Keegan and Richard Holmes, *Soldiers* (New York: Konecky & Konecky, 1985), 39.

12. Ibid., 49.

13. Ibid.

14. See, for example, Richard H. Kohn, "Out of Control: The Crisis in Civil-Military Relations," *National Interest*, Spring 1994, 3–17.

15. Ibid.

16. One example of an incorrect fact, and of the author's lack of understanding of how senior Pentagon officials actually worked, was the allegation that during the administration of President George H. W. Bush, General Colin Powell, then chairman of the Joint Chiefs of Staff, "circumvented the established programming budgeting procedures in place in the Defense Department since the early 1960s" by developing a proposed new post–Cold War military force structure "without any guidance from the . . . Secretary of Defense." Kohn, "Out of Control," 9–10. In fact, a vigorous and continuing debate on force structure and (active/reserve) force mix options took place during May–July 1990, with Powell and the undersecretary of defense for policy presenting one recommendation to Secretary of Defense Dick Cheney and the Defense Planning and Resources Board (the "Base Force" proposal), and the assistant secretary of defense for force management and personnel and I presenting a separate, alternative recommendation. See Stephen M. Duncan, *Citizen Warriors: America's National Guard and Reserve Forces and the Politics of National Security* (Novato, CA: Presidio Press, 1997), 167–75.

17. James Kitfield, "Standing Apart," *National Journal*, June 13, 1998, 1352.

18. Robert H. Bork, *Slouching Towards Gomorrah* (New York: HarperCollins, 1996), 34.

19. James L. Buckley, *Freedom at Risk* (New York: Encounter Books, 2010), 200.

20. Ibid., 195.

21. See, for example, Thomas E. Ricks, "The Widening Gap between the Military and Society," *Atlantic Monthly*, July 1997, 66, 77.

22. Writing in 2007, one scholar described the cultural collapse in these terms: "As late as 1960, the traditional family was the unquestioned norm and the predominate reality in America. The divorce rate was 5 percent. Illegitimacy was rare. Virtually all children lived in two-parent households. The vast majority of mothers stayed home to look after their children." He continued: "The divorce rate in America is [now] 50 percent. One in three American children is born out of wedlock. One-third of American children are living apart from their biological father. Even in two-parent families, two-thirds of women with young children have full-time jobs, so most children under school age are cared for in day-care centers. There have been more than 30 million abortions in America in the past three decades. The very concept of family no longer seems to refer to a married couple with children—it is now an umbrella term covering cohabiting couples, 'blended families' resulting from divorce and remarriage, single-parent households, lesbian couples with adopted children, and so on." Dinesh D'Souza, *The Enemy at Home* (New York: Doubleday, 2007), 153–54, 165.

23. Robert H. Bork, "Hard Truths about the Cultural War," in *A Time to Speak* (Wilmington, DE: ISI Books, 2008), 574.

24. Dr. William J. Bennett, Forrestal Lecture, U.S. Naval Academy, November 24, 1997.

25. Ibid.

26. Robert H. Bork, "Conservatism and the Culture," in Bork, *A Time to Speak*, 669.

27. Rabbi Daniel Lapin, *America's Real War* (Sisters, OR: Multnomah, 1999), 46.

28. Richard M. Langworth, "Forty Years On, Growing Older and Older," *Finest Hour*, Autumn 2008, 5.

29. Jeffrey T. Kuhner, "America Going the Way of Greece, Persia, Rome," *Washington Times*, January 10, 2011, 31.

30. Dr. William J. Bennett, *The Death of Outrage* (New York: The Free Press, 1998), 5.

31. John Keegan, *A History of Warfare* (New York: Alfred A. Knopf, 1993), xvi.

32. One author has used an individual's answer to three questions to determine his worldview. The questions include the following: (1) Who are we and where did we come from? (2) What is wrong with the world? (3) How can it be fixed? See Charles Colson and Nancy Pearcey, *How Now Shall We Live?* (Carol Stream, IL: Tyndale, 1993).

33. Dr. Adam B. Lowther, "The Post–9/11 American Serviceman," *Joint Forces Quarterly* 58 (3rd Quarter 2010): 79.

34. Ibid.

35. Ibid.

36. Charles de Gaulle, *The Edge of the Sword* (New York: Criterion Books, 1960), 98–99.

37. Ibid.

38. Hanson, *The Father of Us All*, 140.

39. Ibid., 136.

40. Sara Sorcher, "Sailors Support Capt. Honors over Videos," *Government-Executive.com*, January 4, 2011.

41. Anna Mulrine, "USS *Enterprise*: Do Lewd Videos Point to Deeper Problem for Military?" *csmonitor.com*, January 4, 2011.

42. The commander of U.S. Fleet Forces Command, who conducted an investigation of the activities aboard *Enterprise*, recommended that the secretary of the navy issue letters of censure to two rear admirals who had previously served as commanding officers of the ship and a captain who had also previously served as executive officer. Nonpunitive letters of caution were recommended for a vice admiral and rear admiral who had previously served as (aircraft) strike group commanders aboard the ship. Letters of caution were also recommended for thirty-two additional officers and sailors.

43. Norman Polmar, "A Crisis in Leadership," U.S. Naval Institute, *Proceedings*, January 2011, 84.

44. Gidget Fuentes, "Roughead: Standards for Fleet Will Remain High," *NavyTimes.com*, August 28, 2010.

45. See Bruce Rolfsen, "Not Above Reproach," *Air Force Times*, December 20, 2010, 20.

46. Ibid.

47. Greg Jaffe, "Army Edits Its History of Deadly Battle of Wanat," *Washington Post*, December 29, 2010, A1, A5.

48. Craig Whitlock, "Navy's Top Ranks Seeing Turmoil," *Washington Post*, June 18, 2011, 1.

49. John Lehman, "Is Naval Aviation Culture Dead?" U.S. Naval Institute, *Proceedings*, September 2011, 40.

50. Edgar F. Puryear Jr., *American Admiralship: The Moral Imperatives of Naval Command* (Annapolis, MD: Naval Institute Press, 2005), x.

51. Major General (Ret.) O. K. Steele, USMC, "Foreword," in *One of Us: Officers of Marines—Their Training, Traditions, and Values*, ed. Jack Rupport (Westport, CT: Praeger, 2003), xiii.

52. Ibid., xiv.

53. Ibid.

54. Mackubin Thomas Owens, *U.S. Civil-Military Relations after 9/11: Renegotiating the Civil-Military Bargain* (New York: Continuum International Publishing Group, 2011), 138.

55. This observation was made by General Walter T. "Dutch" Kerwin Jr., a distinguished combat veteran of Korea and Vietnam. See Mark Thompson, "Walter Kerwin," *Time.com*, July 24, 2008.

56. T. R. Fehrenbach, *This Kind of War: A Study in Unpreparedness* (New York: Pocket Books, 1964), 457.

57. John Hillen, "Must U.S. Military Culture Reform?" *Orbis* 43, no. 1 (Winter 1999): 46.

58. George F. Will, Forrestal Lecture, U.S. Naval Academy, January 24, 2001.

59. Ibid.

60. Bennett, Forrestal Lecture.

61. Bennett, *The Death of Outrage*, 68.

62. Richard K. Betts, "Are Civil-Military Relations Still a Problem?" in *American Civil-Military Relations: The Soldier and the State in a New Era*, ed. Suzanne C. Nielsen and Don M. Snyder (Baltimore: Johns Hopkins University Press, 2009), 14.

63. The administration's tendency to use military personnel for purposes other than armed conflict ("operations other than war") and in circumstances where no important American security interest was at stake, extended to reservists, as well as to active forces. One senior political appointee even called for reservists to be actively involved in "defending America at home" by attacking "low literacy levels, high unemployment rates, increasing numbers of high school dropouts, unavailability of health care, rising crime, and drug abuse." See Deborah R. Lee, Remarks to the National Guard Association of the United States, Boston, Massachusetts, September 2, 1994.

64. Betts, "Are Civil-Military Relations Still a Problem?" 30.

65. Even the director of the CIA was unable to meet personally with Clinton and that lack of access had become the subject of White House jokes. For a description of Clinton's failures of leadership on foreign policy matters, see Stephen M. Duncan, *Citizen Warriors*, 187–91.

66. See Ricks, "The Widening Gap," 69. In the October 1993 Battle of Mogadishu, a task force of army soldiers attempted to capture two warlords.

67. Frank G. Hoffman, "Post-Iraq American Civil-Military Relations," *Orbis* 52, no. 2 (Spring 2008): 218. In this context, the opinion of U.S. Supreme Court Justice Hugo Black in the 1957 case of *Reid v. Covert* is relevant. "Perhaps no group in the nation has been truer [to the tradition of civilian control of military power] than the military men themselves," the jurist said. "Unlike the soldiers of many other nations, they have been content to perform their military duties in defense of the nation in every period of need and to perform those duties well without attempting to usurp power which is not theirs under our system of constitutional government." *Reid v. Covert*, 354 U.S. 40, 77 S.Ct. 1222, 1243 (1957).

68. Owens, *U.S. Civil-Military Relations after 9/11*, 8, 62.

69. Frank G. Hoffman, "Post-Iraq American Civil-Military Relations," 221.

70. Ibid., 231.

71. Betts, "Are Civil-Military Relations Still a Problem?" 11.

72. Winston Churchill, *Thoughts and Adventures* (New York: W.W. Norton, 1990), 89.

73. Betts, "Are Civil-Military Relations Still a Problem?" 25.

74. Ibid., 24–25.

75. Peter D. Feaver, "The Right to Be Right: Civil-Military Relations and the Iraq Surge Decision," *International Security* 35, no. 4 (Spring 2011): 123.

76. Owens, "Civilian Control: A National Crisis?" *Joint Forces Quarterly* (Autumn/Winter 1994–1995): 83.

77. Ibid.

78. Peter D. Feaver, "The Right to Be Right," 89.

79. Ibid., 89–96.

80. Ibid., 89–90, 96.

81. Eliot A. Cohen, *Supreme Command: Soldiers, Statesmen, and Leadership in Wartime* (New York: The Free Press, 2002), 206.

82. Forrest C. Pogue, *George C. Marshall: Statesman, 1945–1959* (New York: Viking Penguin, 1987), 337.

83. Ed Cray, *General of the Army: George C. Marshall, Soldier and Statesman* (New York: W.W. Norton, 1990), 659.

84. Dr. Alfred M. Lilienthal, "Remembering General George Marshall's Clash with Clark Clifford over Premature Recognition of Israel," *Washington Report on Middle East Affairs*, June 1999, 49–50.

85. Clark Clifford, *Counsel to the President: A Memoir* (New York: Random House, 1991), 12.

86. Ibid., 13.

87. United States Department of State, *Foreign Relations of the United States: The Near East, South Asia and Africa*, vol. 5, part 2 (Washington, DC: Government Printing Office, 1948), 972–78.

88. Forrest C. Pogue, *George C. Marshall*, 373.

89. Jennifer E. Manning, "Membership of the 111th Congress: A Profile," *Congressional Research Service*, November 19, 2010.

90. John Hillen, "The Gap Between American Society and Its Military: Keep It, Defend It, Manage It" (paper presented to the American Bar Association's Standing Committee on Law and National Security, November 1998, Washington, DC), 13; *VFW* magazine, February 1997, 15.

91. Data on the 111th Congress was provided by the Military Officers Association of America.

92. Leo Shane III, "Groups Have High Hopes for Vets Joining Congress," *Stars and Stripes* (European edition), January 2, 2011, 6.

93. Ibid.

94. Jim Marshall, "Foreword," in *American Civil-Military Relations: The Soldier and the State in a New Era*, ed. Suzanne C. Nielsen and Don M. Snider (Baltimore: Johns Hopkins University Press, 2009), xi.

95. Bob Woodward, *Obama's Wars* (New York: Simon & Schuster, 2010), 122.

96. Greg Miller and Christi Parsons, "Leon Panetta Is Obama's Pick for CIA Director," *Los Angeles Times*, January 6, 2009.

97. Woodward, *Obama's Wars*, 308, 336.

98. Michael Gerson, "Our Reluctant Commander," *Washington Post*, September 24, 2010, 19.

99. Martin Gilbert, *Churchill: A Life* (New York: Henry Holt, 1991), 565.

100. Winston Churchill, House of Commons, September 30, 1941.

9. POLITICS IN THE MIDDLE OF WAR

1. Winston Churchill, *Great Contemporaries* (New York: W.W. Norton, 1990 (1932), 204.

2. George F. Will, Forrestal Lecture, U.S. Naval Academy, January 24, 2001.

3. Fifteen legislative findings were made, including the following:

(2) There is no constitutional right to serve in the armed forces;

(4) The primary purpose of the armed forces is to prepare for and prevail in combat should the need arise;

(6) Success in combat requires military units that are characterized by high morale, good order and discipline, and unit cohesion;

(8) Military life is fundamentally different from civilian life in that . . . ; and

(13) The prohibition against homosexual conduct is a longstanding element of military law that continues to be necessary in the unique circumstances of military service.

4. James Webb, "The War on the Military Culture," *Weekly Standard*, January 20, 1997.

5. General Colin Powell with Joseph E. Persico, *My American Journey* (New York: Random House, 1995), 547.

6. Ibid., 572.

7. Elizabeth Drew, *On the Edge: The Clinton Presidency* (New York: Simon & Schuster, 1994), 45.

8. Ibid.

9. Title 10, U.S. Code, Section 654 (1993).

10. Bob Woodward, *Obama's Wars* (New York: Simon & Schuster, 2010), 138.

11. See Mark Thompson, "U.S. Troops' Mental Health Continues to Erode," *Time.com*, May 19, 2011.

12. John M. Donnelly, "Casey: Majority of U.S. Soldiers Opposes Repeal of 'Don't Ask, Don't Tell,'" *CQ Today Online News*, March 30, 2010.

13. The chaplains were particularly concerned about the recent revocation of an invitation to a religious leader who had been invited to speak at Andrews Air Force Base. The leader's organization opposed a change in the law.

14. Rabbi Daniel Lapin, *America's Real War* (Sisters, OR: Multnomah, 1999), 40.

15. Rowan Scarborough, "New Top Marine Backs Homosexual Ban," *Washington Times*, November 15, 2010, 24.

16. John Keegan and Richard Holmes, *Soldiers* (New York: Konecky & Konecky, 1985), 18.

17. Don M. Snider, "An Uninformed Debate on Military Culture," *Orbis* 43, no. 1 (Winter 1999): 18.

18. Ibid., 18–19.

19. Keegan and Holmes, *Soldiers*, 18.

20. Ibid.

21. Henrik Bering, "The Perfect Officer," *Policy Review* 168 (August–September, 2011): 51, 59.

22. Bering, "The Perfect Officer," 51, 59; Colonel Trevor Dupuy, *A Genius for War: The German Army General Staff, 1807–1945* (Englewood Cliffs, NJ: Prentice-Hall, 1977).

23. Bill Gertz, "Inside the Ring," *Washington Times*, May 27, 2010, 9.

24. Jonathan Capehart, "Gates's Message on Don't Ask," *Washington Post*, December 1, 2010, 17.

25. *Haig v. Agee*, 453 U.S. 280, 292, 307 (1981).

26. Austin Wright, "Wilson Had Role in 'Don't Ask' Repeal," *Politico.com*, March 21, 2012.

27. Adam B. Lowther, "The Post-9/11 American Serviceman," *Joint Forces Quarterly* 58 (3rd Quarter 2010): 79.

28. John Hillen, "The Gap between American Society and Its Military: Keep It, Defend It, Manage It" (paper presented to the American Bar Association's Standing Committee on Law and National Security, November 1998, Washington, DC), 19–20.

29. Mackubin Thomas Owens, "'American Society and the Military': Is There a Gap?" *Providence Journal*, March 27, 1998.

30. Powell, *My American Journey*, 447.

31. Admiral William J. Crowe Jr., *The Line of Fire* (New York: Simon & Schuster, 1993), 160.

32. Field Marshal the Viscount Montgomery of Alamein, *Memoirs* (London: Collins, 1958), 533.

33. The Tailhook Association is a fraternal, nonprofit organization that was formed in 1956 for the purpose of supporting the interests of naval aviation. Its members are primarily active-duty and retired navy and marine aviators.

34. The U.S. Court of Military Appeals later said that the investigation reflected "a most curiously careless and amateurish approach to a very high-profile case. . . . At worst, it raises the possibility of a shadiness in respecting the rights of military members caught up in a criminal investigation that cannot be condoned." Eric Schmitt, "Military Court Assails Navy in Ruling on Tailhook," *New York Times*, January 12, 1994.

35. Rowan Scarborough, "Navy Judge Says Kelso Lied in Tailhook Probe: Rebukes Admiral, Dismisses Last 3 Cases," *Washington Times*, February 9, 1994, A1.

36. See James Webb, Address at the U.S. Naval Institute's 122nd Annual Meeting and Sixth Annapolis Seminar, April 25, 1996.

37. Gregory L. Vistica, *Fall from Glory: The Men Who Sank the U.S. Navy* (New York: Simon & Schuster, 1995), 373.

38. PBS *Frontline*, "The Navy Blues," Interview with Admiral Frank Kelso, aired on October 15, 1996.

39. PBS *Frontline*, "The Navy Blues"; Editorial, "Frightened Chiefs, Abandoned Troops," *Washington Times*, April 30, 1993, A4 (suggesting that the CNO had "become a pathetic caricature, so eager to retain his brass buttons and silk stripes that he would buy his uniforms at Victoria's Secret if Patsy Schroeder suggested it").

40. Elaine Donnelly, "The Tailhook Scandals," *National Review*, March 7, 1994, 76.

41. PBS *Frontline*, "The Navy Blues."

42. Tom Philpott, "Mullen: It's Time for Women on Subs," *Stars and Stripes*, September 26, 2009.

43. Ibid.

44. Sam Fellman, "Top Enlisted Man Fired from Submarine Nebraska," *Military Times*, February 10, 2012.

45. John J. Kruzel, "Mullen Reveals Lessons That Shaped His Stance on Diversity," *American Forces Press Service*, September 17, 2009.

46. Kruzel, "Mullen Reveals Lessons," emphasis added; Admiral Mike Mullen, Address to the Military Leadership Diversity Commission, September 17, 2009.

47. Richard K. Betts, "Are Civil-Military Relations Still a Problem?" in *American Civil-Military Relations*, ed. Suzanne C. Nielsen and Don M. Snider (Baltimore: Johns Hopkins University Press, 2009), 26.

48. Editorial, "High Seas Segregation: The Navy Is Listing Dangerously in Politically Correct Water," *Washington Times*, July 30, 2010.

49. "Naval Academy Admissions under Scrutiny," *The Capital* (Annapolis, MD), January 31, 2011.

50. Ibid. The class of 2014 entered the Academy with 438 minority students, approximately 35 percent of the class.

51. Dr. Bruce Fleming, *Bridging the Military-Civilian Divide* (Washington, DC: Potomac Books, 2010), 11.

52. MC2 Alexia Rivercorrea, "USNA Dean of Admissions Receives MLK Award," *Navy.mil* (Story Number NNS120119-26), January 19, 2012.

53. After the pay increase was denied, the professor filed a complaint with the U.S. Office of Special Counsel. An investigation determined that the Academy had "illegally denied the employee a merit pay increase because of his public statements." Ibid. A settlement of the matter was reached without further litigation.

54. "Naval Academy Admissions under Scrutiny."

55. 539 U.S. 244 (2003).

56. 539 U.S. 306 (2003).

57. To be "narrowly tailored," a race-conscious admissions program cannot "insulat[e] a category of applicants with certain desired qualifications from competition with all other applicants. Instead, it may consider race or ethnicity only as a 'plus' in a part of an applicant's file." 539 U.S. at 309.

58. Assuming that there is a compelling government interest in achieving greater diversity in the navy's officer ranks, the constitutional issue is whether, and to what extent, the Fourteenth Amendment's guarantee of "equal rights under the laws" permits race to be used as a factor in efforts to achieve it.

59. Mark Walker, "Increasing Number of Black Officers in Marine Corps Called Overdue," *North County (CA) Times*, August 7, 2011.

60. Bob Woodward, *Obama's Wars* (New York: Simon & Schuster, 2010), 260.

61. Ibid., 293.

62. Woodward, *Obama's Wars*, 237. The principal eligibility criterion for the Combat Action Ribbon is that the individual must have participated in a "bona fide ground or surface combat fire-fight or action during which he/she was under enemy fire and his/her performance while under fire was satisfactory." SECNAVNOTE 1650 of 17 February 1969.

63. In March 2007, General Peter Pace, then chairman of the Joint Chiefs of Staff, expressed his personal view that homosexual acts are immoral and that defense policies should not condone immoral conduct in any way.

64. Al Shine and Don Snider, "The Right to Be Wrong," *Armed Forces Journal*, May 2011, 28.

65. Tom Vanden Brook and David Jackson, "Pace, Gates: Personal Views on Gays in Service Out of Line," *USA Today*, March 13, 2007.

66. Elaine Donnelly, "Homosexual Left Flubs Military Culture War," *Washington Times*, October 8, 2010, B1; Shaun Waterman, "Retired General Warns of 'Rush' to End 'Don't Ask,'" *Washington Times*, May 10, 2011, 1.

67. Rowan Scarborough, "Military Chiefs Split with Mullen on Gays," *Washington Times*, June 2, 2010, 1.

68. Ed O'Keefe and Paul Kane, "Major Setback for 'Don't Ask' Repeal," *Washington Post*, December 10, 2010, 1.

69. Lolita C. Baldor, "Gates Frustrated as Senate Delays Gay Ban Repeal," *Washingtonpost.com*, December 10, 2010.

70. Frank J. Gaffney Jr., "A Smoking Gun," *Washington Times*, June 29, 2011, B4.

71. Ibid.

72. Ibid.

73. Ibid.

74. Ibid.

75. Elaine Donnelly, "Don't Spin 'Don't Ask' Repeal," *Washington Times*, January 21, 2011, B2.

76. Ibid.

77. Bill Gertz, "Inside the Ring," *Washington Times*, December 2, 2010; Gaffney, "A Smoking Gun."

78. Jeffrey M. Jones, "Congress' Job Approval Rating Worst in Gallup History," *Gallup*, December 15, 2010.

79. Admiral Michael Mullen, Speech at NDU Conference on Military Professionalism, National Defense University, Washington, DC, January 10, 2011; Charley Keyes, "Joint Chiefs Chair Warns of Disconnect between Military and Civilians," *CNN.com*, January 10, 2011.

80. Thom Shanker, "At West Point, A Focus on Trust," *New York Times*, May 22, 2011, 21; "Worrying Gap between U.S. Military, Civilians: Mullen," *Yahoo News*, May 21, 2011; Admiral Michael G. Mullen, "From the Chairman," *Joint Forces Quarterly* 62 (3rd Quarter 2011): 4–5.

81. Mark Thompson, "Top Officer Warns of 'Catastrophic Outcome' If Military and Nation Continue to Drift Apart," *Time.com*, June 2, 2011.

82. See John Hillen, "Must U.S. Military Culture Reform?" *Orbis* 43, no. 1 (Winter 1999): 54.

83. Cited in Edgar F. Puryear Jr., *American Generalship* (Novato, CA: Presidio Press, 2000), 285.

84. John Hillen, "The Civilian-Military Gap: Keep It, Defend It, Manage It," U.S. Naval Institute *Proceedings*, October 1998, 2; Hillen, "Must U.S. Military Culture Reform?"

85. In the four years of World War II, Harvard University lost 691 of its students. In 1956, while the nation was at peace, 400 of Princeton's 750 graduates served in uniform. During the twelve years of the Vietnam War, Harvard lost only twelve students. By 2004, only nine members of Princeton's graduating class entered the Armed Forces. George F. Will, Forrestal Lecture; Fleming, *Bridging the Military-Civilian Divide*, 6.

86. Secretary of the Navy Edwin Mabus would soon come under fire from members of Congress, veterans associations, and others for what would be called "a spate of ship names . . . described as stupid and insensitive." In May 2011, Mabus named a replenishment ship not for a naval hero, but for the late Cesar Chavez, a labor activist who had described his limited naval service as "the two worst years of my life." The thirteen previous ships of the class had been named for famous American explorers and other heroes. Mabus had already named an amphibious transport dock ship for a Democratic congressman who had heavily criticized marines in Iraq. All previous twenty-five ships of the class, going back to 1962, had been named for geographic locations. In February 2012, another similar naming was made. See Norman Polmar, "There's a Lot in a Name," U.S. Naval Institute, *Proceedings*, April 2012, 88.

87. Scarborough, "Military Chiefs Split"; Sara Sorcher, "Don't Ask, Don't Tell Divides Secretaries, Commanders," *govexec.com*, October 22, 2010.

88. Frank Newport, "U.S. Military Personnel, Veterans Give Obama Lower Marks," *Gallup*, May 30, 2011.

89. Gaffney, "A Smoking Gun."

10. THE "PROFESSIONALIZATION" OF AMATEUR APPOINTEES

1. Erin Dian Dumbacher, "Senior Executives Give Low Marks to Obama Appointees," *GovernmentExecutive.com*, May 27, 2011; Erin Dian Dumbacher, "'C' Is for Change," *Government Executive.com*, June 15, 2011, 14–15.

2. The survey was taken as part of the "Profession of Arms Campaign" directed by the secretary of the army and army chief of staff (see the *Terms of Reference for the Review of the Army Profession in an Era of Persistent Conflict*, dated October 27, 2010, and HQDA EXORD 139–11).

3. Fred Schulte, John Aloysius Farrell, and Jeremy Borden, "Obama Rewards Big Bundlers with Jobs, Commissions, Stimulus Money, Government Contracts, and More," *iWatch News* (part of the Center for Public Integrity), June 15, 2011.

4. Ibid.

5. Ibid.

6. Ibid.

7. Spencer Overton, "Campaign Reform's Next Step," *Boston Globe*, December 12, 2003.

8. Charles Hurt, "O Aide's Squeals of Delight for Gen. Firing," *New York Post*, September 24, 2010.

9. Toby Harnden, "What Does Firing General Stanley McChrystal Say about Barack Obama?" *Telegraph (UK)*, June 24, 2010.

10. Bob Woodward, *Obama's Wars* (New York: Simon & Schuster, 2010), 40.

11. Elizabeth Drew, *On the Edge: The Clinton Presidency* (New York: Simon & Schuster, 1994), 142–43.

12. "Donilon of National Security," *Wall Street Journal*, October 9, 2010.

13. Peter Nicholas and Christi Parsons, "National Security Chief Keeps a Low Profile," *Los Angeles Times*, April 30, 2011.

14. Thomas E. Donilon was never accused of accounting irregularities, but he reportedly worked as a registered lobbyist for Fannie Mae and was paid more than $1.8 million in bonuses before the government took over the company in the wake of the scandal. A 2006 report by the Office of Federal Housing Oversight (OFHEO) concluded that Fannie Mae lobbyists tried to discredit federal regulators who were looking into the finances of the company. Jim McElhatton, "Obama Choice Helped Fannie Block Oversight," *Washington Times*, October 18, 2010, 14.

15. Woodward, *Obama's Wars*.

16. Elizabeth Drew, "In the Bitter New Washington," *New York Review of Books*, December 23, 2010.

17. Woodward, *Obama's Wars*, 323.

18. David Ignatius, "The Pol and the Policy," *Washington Post*, April 27, 2011, 17.

19. Ibid.

20. David Ignatius, "Obama's Foreign Policy: Big Ideas, Little Implementation," *Washington Post*, October 17, 2010.

21. Drew, "In the Bitter New Washington."

22. Wesley Pruden, "The Insult to the American Soldier," *Washington Times*, May 9, 2011, 4.

23. Peter Beinart, "Obama's War with the Pentagon," *DailyBeast.com*, October 10, 2010.

24. Charles Krauthammer, "Leading from Behind," *Washington Post*, April 29, 2011, A21.

25. Ryan Lizza, "The Consequentialist: How the Arab Spring Remade Obama's Foreign Policy," *New Yorker*, May 2, 2011, 10.

26. Ibid.

27. Craig Whitlock, "Another Bureaucratic Challenge," *Washington Post*, April 28, 2011, 1.

28. Yochi J. Dreazen, "The Politician," *National Journal*, March 24, 2012.

29. Rowan Scarborough, "Panetta to Carry Political Baggage to the Pentagon," *Washington Times*, June 23, 2011, 1.

30. Shaun Waterman, "Future Wars Seen as Longer, Deadlier," *Washington Times*, June 9, 2011, 9.

31. "Bob Gates Leaves the Pentagon," *Economist*, April 30, 2011.

32. Whitlock, "Another Bureaucratic Challenge."

33. Craig Whitlock, "Panetta's Confirmation Appears Safe," *Washington Post*, June 10, 2011, A2.

34. Scarborough, "Panetta to Carry Political Baggage."

35. "Obama's Security Reshuffle," *Wall Street Journal*, April 29, 2011.

36. Elisabeth Bumiller, "In His Military Farewell, Petraeus Issues a Warning on Looming Budget Cuts," *New York Times*, September 1, 2011.

37. John Berry, "Petraeus's Next Battle," *Newsweek*, July 25, 2011. The Merriam-Webster Dictionary defines a "man on horseback" as a "military figure whose ambitions and popularity mark him as a potential dictator."

38. Nicholas and Parsons, "National Security Chief Keeps a Low Profile."

39. Drew, "In the Bitter New Washington."

40. Ibid.

41. Ibid.

42. Ibid.

43. Ibid. Emphasis added.

44. Rajiv Chandrasekaran, "U.S. Sees Chance to Accelerate Negotiations with Taliban," *Washington Post*, May 4, 2011, A1, A12.

45. Woodward, *Obama's War*, 235–38; Craig Whitlock, "Military Advisor Undone by Critics," *Washington Post*, May 29, 2011, A1.

46. Cartwright reportedly "won plaudits from many senior White House aides" in 2010 when he circumvented the military chain of command by working independently and behind the scenes with Vice President Biden to develop a policy option for additional troops in Afghanistan that was opposed by Admiral Mullen, Cartwright's nominal superior as chairman of the Joint Chiefs. See Woodward, *Obama's War*, 234–38; Yochi J. Dreazen, "Man Most Likely to Take Top Military Job Has Never Seen War," *NationalJournal.com*, May 2, 2011.

47. Dreazen, "Man Most Likely."

48. Greg Jaffe, "Marine Not in Running to Head Joint Chiefs," *Washington Post*, May 25, 2011, 2.

49. "Gates Denies U.S. General Punished for Dissent," *Yahoo.com*, June 2, 2011; Thom Shanker, "Obama Expected to Name Army's Leader to Head Joint Chiefs," *New York Times*, May 29, 2011, 19.

50. "Obama's Afghan Gamble," *DailyBeast.com*, June 21, 2011.

51. According to Petraeus's successor, Lieutenant General John Allen, the option Obama picked was "not on the menu." Peter Feaver, "The Right to Be Wrong, but Not the Right to Lie," *ForeignPolicy.com*, June 29, 2011.

52. Mark Landler and Helene Cooper, "Obama Will Speed Pullout from War in Afghanistan," *New York Times*, June 23, 2011, 1.

53. Thom Shanker, "2012 Troop Pullback Worries Military Experts," *New York Times*, June 23, 2011.

54. Howard P. "Buck" McKeon, "Obama Drawdown Is Cause for Concern," *Washington Times*, July 6, 2011, B3.

55. David S. Cloud and Christi Parson, "A Gamble amid Dual Pressures," *Los Angeles Times*, June 24, 2011, 1.

56. Gallup, "Presidential Job Approval," June 15, 2011; Rasmussen Reports, "Daily Presidential Tracking Poll," June 25, 2011.

57. Shanker, "2012 Troop Pullback Worries Military Experts."

58. Ibid.

59. Landler and Cooper, "Obama Will Speed Pullout."

60. Mark Mazzetti and Scott Shane, "Mullen Backs Afghan Pullout Plan but Calls It Riskier," *New York Times*, June 24, 2011, 9.

61. Cloud and Parsons, "A Gamble amid Dual Pressures."

62. "Did The White House Snub Petraeus?" *DailyBeast.com*, September 4, 2011.

63. Drew, "In the Bitter New Washington."

64. See Justice Oliver Wendell Holmes, Dissenting Opinion in *Abrams v. United States*, 250 U.S. 616 (1919).

65. John Keegan, ed., *Churchill's Generals* (New York: Grove Weidenfeld, 1991), 13.

66. Eliot A. Cohen, "Churchill and His Generals," in Robert Cowley, ed., *No End Save Victory* (New York: G.P. Putnam's Sons, 2001), 287.

67. Ibid.

68. Carlo D'Este, *Warlord: A Life of Winston Churchill at War, 1874–1945* (New York: HarperCollins, 2008), 386.

69. Steven F. Hayward, *Churchill on Leadership: Executive Success in the Face of Adversity* (Rocklin, CA: Prima Publishing, 1998), 63.

70. Eliot A. Cohen, "Churchill and His Generals," 286.

71. Hastings L. Ismay, *The Memoirs of General Lord Ismay* (New York: Viking, 1960), 166.

72. Robert J. Samuelson, "Hunkered-Down America," *Washington Post*, June 12, 2011.

73. Margaret Thatcher, *Statecraft: Strategies for a Changing World* (New York: HarperCollins, 2002), 104.

74. Adam Yarmolinsky, "Civilian Control: New Perspectives for New Problems," *Indiana Law Journal* 49 (1974), 654–55.

75. Richard H. Kohn, "Out of Control: The Crisis in Civil-Military Relations," *National Interest*, Summer 1994, 14.

76. Richard H. Kohn in "An Exchange on Civil-Military Relations," *National Interest*, Summer 1994, 29–30.

77. David McCullough, "Knowing History and Knowing Who We Are," Remarks delivered at a Hillsdale College National Leadership Seminar on the topic "American History and America's Future," February 15, 2005.

78. In December 2010, the *New York Times* reported on the low coverage of the war in Afghanistan: "The grueling war there, where a day rarely goes by without an allied casualty, is like a faint heartbeat, accounting for just 4 percent of the nation's news coverage in major outlets." Brian Stelter, "Afghan War Just a Slice of U.S. Coverage," *New York Times*, December 19, 2010.

79. Kohn in "An Exchange on Civil-Military Relations."

80. Peter Drucker, *On the Profession of Management* (Boston: Harvard Business School Press, 1998), 33.

81. Larry Bossidy and Ram Charan, *Execution: The Discipline of Getting Things Done* (New York: Crown Business, 2002), 119.

82. Ibid., 113.

83. Peter Drucker, *On the Profession of Management*, 36.

84. Ibid., 37.

85. Zachary A. Goldfarb, "Geithner Weighs Exit after Debt Talks," *Washington Post*, July 1, 2011, A1.

86. Ibid.

87. Robert Maranto, "Political Appointees, Career Executives, and Presidential Transitions" (paper prepared for delivery at the 2001 Annual Meeting of the American Political Science Association, August 30–September 2, 2001), 40.

88. News Release: "Former Presidential Appointees Issue Open Letter to President Bush and the 108th Congress," Brookings Institution, November 20, 2002.

89. Karen Jowers, "DoD Personnel Chief Slammed in IG Complaint," *marinecorps-times.com*, July 18, 2011.

90. Andrew Tilghman and Karen Jowers, "Stanley Leaves Personnel Office 'Without a Pilot,'" *Army Times*, November 14, 2011, 10.

91. Charles S. Clark, "GSA Turmoil Will Live on in Congressional Hearings," *GovExec.com*, April 3, 2012; Lisa Rein and Joe Davidson, "GSA Rocked by Spending Scandal," *Washington Post*, April 3, A1.

92. Former president Richard Nixon referred to Gladstone's remark during an interview with British journalist David Frost, May 1977.

CONCLUSION

1. David Ignatius, "Why the Surprise on Norway," *Washington Post*, July 27, 2011, A17.

2. Charles C. Moskos, John Allen Williams, and David R. Segal, eds., *The Postmodern Military* (New York: Oxford University Press, 2000), 2.

3. Ibid., 11.

4. Richard K. Betts, "Are Civil-Military Relations Still a Problem?" in *American Civil-Military Relations: The Soldier and the State in a New Era*, ed. Suzanne C. Nielsen and Don M. Snider (Baltimore: Johns Hopkins University Press, 2009), 26.

5. Ralph Peters, "What We Owe Our Troops," *New York Post*, May 31, 2010, 24.

6. *Sipri Year Book* (New York: Oxford University Press, 2002), 63.

7. Eliot A. Cohen, *Supreme Command: Soldiers, Statesmen, and Leadership in Wartime* (New York: The Free Press, 2002), 206.

8. George F. Will, "Self-Esteem Problem," *Washington Post*, September 20, 2011.

Index